THE FAMILY IN LATE ANTIQUITY

THE FAMILY IN LATE ANTIQUITY

The rise of Christianity and the endurance of tradition

Geoffrey S. Nathan

London and New York

First published 2000
by Routledge
11 New Fetter Lane, London EC4P 4EE

Simultaneously published in the USA and Canada
by Routledge
29 West 35th Street, New York, NY 10001

Routledge is an imprint of the Taylor & Francis Group

©2000 Geoffrey Nathan

The right of Geoffrey Nathan to be identified as the Author of this
Work has been asserted by him in accordance with the Copyright,
Designs and Patents Act 1988

Typeset in Garamond 3 by
Keystroke, Jacaranda Lodge, Wolverhampton
Printed and bound in Great Britain by
St Edmundsbury Press, Bury St Edmunds, Suffolk

British Library Cataloguing in Publication Data
A catalogue record for this book is available from the British Library

Library of Congress Cataloging in Publication Data
has been applied for

ISBN 0–415–16665–9

To Nobuko, Emily and Lucas, my own family

CONTENTS

Acknowledgements   ix
Abbreviations   x

1   Introduction   1

2   Two traditions   15

3   Constantine and The Confluence of Two Traditions   55

4   Marriage   74

5   Alternatives to marriage   107

6   Children   133

7   The extended family   160

8   Household slaves   169

9   Final thoughts   185

    Appendix   190

    Notes   192
    Bibliography   246
    Index   262

ACKNOWLEDGMENTS

There are a number of people I should like to thank for their help in the production of this book. Ronald Mellor first suggested the topic to me when I was still a graduate student, and Claudia Rapp helped to make that topic a reality when I worked on my dissertation. It is from my doctoral work that this book was largely taken.

Over the years, many people have given me valuable advice and input about various aspects of this work. Michele Salzman and Brent Shaw offered useful advice early on. Two experts were also particularly helpful on the matter of law: Judith Evans Grubbs and Antti Arjava pointed me in useful directions. Scott Bartchy has also been helpful, offering essential information on early Christianity, particularly in the area of slavery.

Several institutions also deserve thanks. UCLA's history department has helped to defray the costs of travel when presenting parts of my book at conferences. The Center for Medieval and Renaissance Studies, the Association for Ancient Historians, and the Byzantine Studies Conference have also permitted me to present some of my findings.

Finally, I wish to thank an important layperson: my wife, Nobuko. Over the years, she has given me consistent and unqualified support, both emotional and financial. Without her, I would not have had the strength to finish my work. To her, I owe a heavy debt of gratitude.

GSN
Los Angeles
February 1999

ABBREVIATIONS

AM	Anno Mundi (in the year of the world)
cos.	consul
fr.	fragment
L.l.	Libertus/Liberta (freedman or woman)
NRSV	New Revised Standard Version
or.	oratio
pr.	praefatio
s.c.	senatusconsultum

Sources

Note: numbers in parentheses after legal or canon citations indicate the date.

AE	*L'Année Epigraphique* (1888–)
Amb., *Comm. in Iac.*	Ambrose, *Commentarium in Iacobum*
de ob. Theo.	*de obitu Theodosii*
de off.	*de officiis*
de vid.	*de viduis*
de virg.	*de virginitate*
de myster.	*de mysteriis*
Ep.	*Epistulae*
Ambr., *Quaest. vet. et nov. Testam*	Ambrosiaster, *Quaestiones veteris et novi Testamenti*
Amm. Mar.	Ammianus Marcellinus, *Res Gestae*
Anon. Val.	Anonymous Valesianus
App., *Bell. Civ.*	Appian, *Bella Civilia*
Apul., *Apol.*	Apuleius, *Apologia*
Met.	*Metamorphoses*
Aug., *Conf.*	Augustine, *Confessiones*
de bono coniug.	*de bono coniugali*
de cat. rud.	*de catechizandis rudibus*
de civ. Dei	*de civitate Dei*

de cur. pro mort. ger.	*de cura pro mostis gerenda*
de doc. Christ.	*de doctrina Christiana*
de fide et oper.	*de fide et operibus*
de Gen. ad litt.	*de Genesi ad litteram*
de incomp. nupt.	*de incomptentibus nuptiis*
de nat. et gratia	*de natura et gratia*
de quant. anim.	*de quantitate animae*
de sanct. vir.	*de sancta virginitate*
de serm. Dom. in mon.	*de sermone Domini in monte*
Enarr. in psalmos	*Enarrationes in psalmos*
Ep.	*Epistulae*. Note: an * after the number indicates it is one of Augustine's new letters.
Serm.	*Sermones*
Aul. Gel., *Att. Noct.*	Aulus Gellius, *Atticae Noctes*
Aur. Vict., *Caes.*	Aurelius Victor, *Liber de Caesaribus*
Epit.	*de Caesaribus Libri Epitome*
Aus., *Ep.*	Ausonius, *Epistulae*
Ep. in patrem	*Epicidion in patrem*
Epi.	*Epigrammata*
Epita.	*Epitaphia*
Par.	*Parentalia*
Prof.	*Commemoratio Professorum Burdigalensium*
Av. Vienn., *Ep.*	Avitus of Vienne, *Epistulae*
Basil, *Ep.*	Basil, *Epistulae*
Bede, *Comm. in I Thess.*	Bede, *Commentarium in I Thessalonicensem*
Ben., *Reg.*	Benedict, *Regula*
Boethius, *Cons. Phil.*	Boethius. *Consolatio Philosophiae*
Caes., *ad virg.*	Caesarius, *ad virgines*
Ep.	*Epistulae*
Serm.	*Sermones*
Caesar, *Bell. Gall.*	Caesar, *de Bello Gallico*
Cass., *Div. Inst.*	Cassiodorus. *Institutiones Divinae*
Var.	*Variae*
Cato, *De Ag.*	Cato the Elder, *de Agricultura*
Chron. Min.	*Chronica Minora (MGH AA 9:660)*
Chron. Pasch.	*Chronicon Paschale*
Cic., *Att.*	Cicero, *Epistulae ad Atticum*
de leg.	*de legibus*
de Nat. Deor.	*de Natura Deorum*
de off.	*de officiis*
de repub.	*de republica*
Fam.	*Epistulae ad Familiares*
Phil.	*Orationes Philippicae*

pro Cael.	*pro Caelio*
pro Clu.	*pro Cluentio*
pro Flac.	*pro Flacco*
pro Marc.	*pro Marco*
CIL	*Corpus Inscriptionum Latinarum* (1863–)
CJ	*Codex Iustinianus*
Claud., *Epith. de nup.*	Claudian, *Epithalamium de nuptiis*
Hon. Aug.	*Honorii Augustii*
Clem. Al. *Paed.*	Clement of Alexandria. *Paedagogus*
Col., *de Re Rust.*	Columella, *de Re Rustica*
Comm., *Inst.*	Commodianus, *Instructiones*
CTh	*Codex Theodosianus*
Curt.	Quintus Curtius Rufus
D.	*Digesta*
Dio	Dio Cassius
Don., *Comm. Terenti*	Donatus, *Commentarium Terentii*
En., *Trag.*	Ennius, *Tragedies*
Enn., *Ep.*	Ennodius, *Epistulae*
Ep. ad cast.	*Epistula ad castitatem* (PL: *Supplementum* i, coll. 1482–3)
Epi., *adv. Haer.*	Epiphanius, *adversus Haereses*
Euch., *de laud. her.*	Eucherius, *de laudibus heremi*
Eug., *V. S. Sev.*	Eugippius, *Vita Sancti Severini*
Eus., *HE*	Eusebius, *Historia Ecclesiastica*
Mart. Pal.	*Liber de martyribus Palaestinae*
V. Cons.	*Vita Constantini*
Eutrop., *Brev.*	Eutropius, *Breviarium*
FIRA	*Fontes Iuris Romani AnteIustiniani* (1941)
FIRA²	*Fontes Iuris Romani AnteIustiniani* (1954)
Frag. Vat.	*Fragmenta quae dicuntur Vaticana* (FIRA² ii, 464–540)
Fronto, *Ep.*	Marcus Fronto, *Epistulae*
G.	Gaius, *Institutiones*
Galen, *de Hyg.*	Galen, *de Hygenia*
Gaud., *Serm.*	Gaudentius of Brescia, *Sermones*
Tract.	*Tractates*
Gel., *Ep.*	Gelasius, *Epistulae*
fr.	*fragmenta*
Greg. Mag., *Dial.*	Gregory the Great, *Dialogi*
Ep.	*Epistulae*
Greg. Nyssa, *V. Mac.*	Gregory of Nyssa, *Vita Macrinae*
Greg. Tuor., *Hist. Franc.*.	Gregory of Tours, *Historia Francorum*
Herm., *Shep.*	Hermas, *Shepherd*
Hipp., *Ref. Haer.*	Hippolytus, *Refutatio omnium Haeresium*

Hor., *Sat.*	Horace, *Satires*
Ign. *ad Polycarp*	
Ign. *Ep. ad Phil.*	Ignatius of Antioch.
ILS	*Inscriptiones Latinae Selectae* (1892–1916)
Inn., *Ep.*	Innocentius, *Epistulae*
Jer., *Adv. Helv.*	Jerome, *Adversus Helvidium (de virginitate Mariae)*
Adv. Jov.	*Adversus Jovinianum*
Chron.	*Chronicon*
Ep.	*Epistulae*
Hom. in Psalm.	*Homiliae in Psalmos*
Joh. Cass., *Conl.*	John Cassian, *Conlationes*
Jos. *Bel. Jud.*	Flavius Josephus, *Bellum Judaeicum*
Just. Mart., *Apol.*	Justin Martyr, *Apologia*
Juv., *Sat.*	Juvenal, *Satires*
Lact., *Div. Inst.*	Lactantius, *Divinae Institutiones*
Mort. Pers.	*de Mortibus Persecutorum*
Laud. Tur.	*Laudatio Turiae* (*ILS* 8393)
Leo, *Ep.*	Leo, *Epistulae*
Lib., *Ep.*	Libanius, *Epistulae*
Or.	*Orationes*
Lib. Pont.	*Liber Pontificalis*
Lux., *Ana. in med.*	Luxorius, *Anacreontium in medicum*
Mar., *Epi.*	Martial, *Epigrams*
Marc. comes	Marcellinus comes
Min. Fel., *Oct.*	Minucius Felix, *Octavius*
Mus. Ruf., *fr.*	Musonius Rufus, *fragmenta*
N. Anth.	*Novella Anthemii*
N. Jus.	*Novella Iustiniani*
N. Maj.	*Novella Maioriani*
N. Marc.	*Novella Marciani*
N. Sev.	*Novella Severi*
N. Th.	*Novella Theodosii II*
N. Val.	*Novella Valentiniani III*
Nepos, *Att.*	Nepos, *Attica*
Nic. Call., *HE*	Nicephorus Callistus, *Historia Ecclesiastica*
Olymp., *fr.*	Olympiodorus, *fragmenta*
Opt., *contra Par. Don.*	Optatus, *contra Parmenianum Donatistum*
Oros., *Hist. adv. pag.*	Orosius, *Historia adversus paganos*
Ovid, *Met.*	Ovid, *Metamorphoses*
Oxy. Pap.	*Oxyrhynchi Papyri* (1898–)
Pach., *Praec.*	Pachomius, *Praecepta*
Pall., *Hist. Laus.*	Palladius, *Historia Lausiaca*
Pan. Lat.	*Panegyrici Latini*

xiii

Pass., Ss. Perp. et Fel.	*Passio Sanctis Perpetuae et Felictae*
Paul. Mil., *V. Amb.*	Paulinus of Milan, *Vita Ambrosii*
Paul. Nol., *carmen*	Paulinus of Nola, *carmina*
Ep.	*Epistulae*
Paul. Pella, *Euch.*	Paulinus of Pella, *Eucharisticus*
Paul., *Sent.*	Paulus, *Sententiae*
Pet., *Sat.*	Petronius, *Satyricon*
Plaut., *Men.*	Plautus, *Menippus*
Merc.	*Mercator*
Most.	*Mostellaria*
Pliny, *Ep.*	Pliny the Younger, *Epistulae*
Pan.	*Panegyricus (ad Traianum)*
Pliny, *Nat. Hist.*	Pliny the Elder, *Naturalis Historia*
PLRE	*Prosopography of the Later Roman Empire* (1970–92)
Plut., *Brut.*	Plutarch, *Brutus*
Caes.	*Caesar*
Cat. min.	*Cato the Younger*
de Am. Prol.	*de Amore Prolis*
Mor.	*Moralia*
Quaest. Rom.	*Quaestiones Romanae*
Poss., *V. Aug.*	Possidius, *Vita Augustini*
Proc. *Anec.*	Procopious. *Anecdota*
Prop.	Propertius
Prosp. Tiro, *Chron.*	Prosper Tiro, *Chronicon*
Prud., *lib. cath.*	Prudentius, *liber cathemarinon*
praef.	*praefatio*
Ps-Aug., *Serm.*	Pseudo-Augustine, *Sermones*
Ps.-Clem., *Recogn.*	Pseudo-Clement, *Recognitiones*
Ps.-Plut., *de lib. educ.*	Pseudo-Plutarch, *de liberalis educandis*
Ps.-Quin., *Decl.*	Pseudo-Quintillian, *Declarationes*
Pub. Syr., *Max.*	Publilius Syrus, *Maxims (Sententiae)*
Quer.	*Querolus*
Quint., *Inst.*	Quintillian, *Institutio oratoria*
Reg. Mag.	*Regula Magistri*
Ruf., *HE*	Rufinus, *Historia Ecclesiastica*
Rut. Nam., *de red. suo*	Rutilius Namatianus, *de reditu suo*
Salv., *de gub. Dei*	Salvian, *de gubernatione Dei*
Ep.	*Epistulae*
Sen., *ad Luc. ep.*	Seneca, *ad Lucam epistulae*
de ben.	*de beneficiis*
de clem.	*de clementia*
de cons. sap.	*de constantia sapientis*
de prov.	*de providentia*

Ep.	*Epistulae*
Ep. Mor.	*Epistulae Moralia*
Sen. Maior, *Cont.*	Seneca the Elder, *Controversiae*
Serv., *Comm. in Verg.*	Servius, *Commentarium in Vergilium*
Sext. *Sent.*	Sextus, *Sententiae*
SHA	*Scriptores Historiae Augustae*
Sid. Ap., *Ep.*	Sidonius Apollinaris, *Epistulae*
Sirm. Cons.	*Constitutiones Sirmondianae*
Soc., *HE*	Socrates, *Historia Ecclesiastica*
Sor., *Gyn.*	Soranus, *Gynaikeia*
Soz., *HE*	Sozomen, *Historia Ecclesiastica*
Suet., *Aug.*	Suetonius, *Augustus*
Caes.	*Caesar*
Claud.	*Claudius*
de gramm.	*de grammaticis*
Tib.	*Tiberius*
Vesp.	*Vespasianus*
Sulp. Sev., *Chron.*	Sulpicius Severus, *Chronicon*
V. S. Mar.	*Vita Sancti Martini*
Symm., *Ep.*	Symmachus, *Epistulae*
Tab. Herc.	*Tabula Herculaneum*
Tac., *Agr.*	Tacitus, *Agricola*
Ann.	*Annales*
Ger.	*Germania*
Hist.	*Historiae*
Tert., *ad Ux.*	Tertullian, *ad Uxorem*
de Mod.	*de Modestia*
de Mon.	*de Monogamia*
de Pud.	*de Pudicitia*
de test. ani.	*de testimonia animae*
de Virg. Vel.	*de Virginis Velandis*
Ex. ad cast.	*Exhortatio ad castitatem*
Theo., *Ad Auto.*	Theophilus, *Ad Autolycum*
Theo., *Chron.*	Theophanes, *Chronicon*
Theod., *Ep.*	Theoderet, *Epistulae*
HE	*Historia Ecclesiastica*
Ulp., *Reg.*	Ulpian, *Regulae*
Val. Max.	Valerius Maximus
Varro, *de Agr.*	Varro, *de Agricultura*
Vig. Tri., *Ep.*	Vigilius Tridentinus, *Epistulae*
V. Mel.	*Vita Melaniae*
Zos.	Zosimus, *Historia Nova*

1

INTRODUCTION

In one of his many unrelentingly caustic letters, Jerome described a man who had recently buried the latest of his twenty-two wives in the city of Rome. His deceased spouse had had twenty husbands of her own.[1] Jerome passively witnessed the funeral with bemusement. Later in his missive, the cleric subjected the old widower to all his withering sarcasm and vitriol, attacking from a position of self-assured moral and religious superiority. And yet the image of that day in 384, despite Jerome's mocking disdain, impresses upon the mind an essential question about Roman social life: in the age of a supposedly Christian empire, to what degree did the new religion permeate that most basic of societal units, the family?

To be sure, the question in itself raises fundamental questions about the later Roman Empire and the way in which scholars have recently looked at the period. In the last thirty years, late antiquity has transcended the fuzzy and ill-defined boundary between the ancient and medieval worlds and has become a field of study in its own right. The era is marked by profound and distinctive political, religious and cultural characteristics, which helped to create the basis of Western European society for 1,500 years and also helped to forge the direct successor to the Roman Empire, Byzantium. Our new interest has been largely focused on the social history of the age, leaving behind – if only momentarily – the political and military upheavals which have so dominated Roman history-writing since the days of Gibbon.

In light of these interests, this present study is meant to be a comprehensive, if not exhaustive, examination of the family in late antiquity. It will, out of necessity, be somewhat anachronistic and vernacular: when discussing the late Roman Empire, there will always be enormous temporal and regional variation. Nevertheless, as what will hopefully be a work which will spark further research, it is my intent that this book will serve as an introduction to the topic and provide the basic outlines of familial identity, societal ideals concerning responsibilities and obligations within the kin group, and general notions of comportment and behavior. In short, it is an attempt to parallel recent works on the classical family as well as those concerning the modern European family.[2]

1

Work on the classical family since the 1970s provides both the method-ological and the epistemological boundaries for this task. As with research on late antiquity, history of the family has grown into a thriving discipline: there is an increasing scrutiny of 'private life' in general and the role of the family in particular. Yet for all of the modern work written on this important and ever-expanding topic, relatively little has been produced on the family of the later Roman Empire. This lacuna is all the more glaring given late antiquity's current attraction. The number of sources available, combined with their variety, would seem to make such studies practical, obvious and valuable. And yet scholars have, with a few exceptions, failed to make such studies. The one notable exception, of course, are those who examine the extensive legal codes of the fifth and sixth centuries, but the focus on these codes has mostly been to extrude information about earlier periods.[3] In sum, modern interest in the family has relegated the later Roman era to footnotes or has placed it in larger works discussing the broader changes in European civilization.[4]

The natural result of this omission has been a tendency either to treat the Roman family monolithically,[5] varying not at all from century to century, or simply not to think about differences in the later period at all. Even worse, the study of Christian attitudes and perceptions of sex, marriage, widowhood, virginity, as well as other areas of private life, have skewed what we do know about the family of late antiquity. Recent interest in sexuality and dialogues of the body have stressed the intellectual and social actions of the day.[6] While this is an important field, scholarship on the body has said little about the nature or behavior of the individual within the household. They characterize affective relationships in an essentially unidimensional manner and peri-pherally address issues of children and other relations. Moreover, while these recent works do say something about morality vis-à-vis personal relations with one's family, they tend to focus more on the theological bases behind such attitudes.

In the last ten years, this state of affairs has begun slowly to change. While nascent, scholars have started to focus on hitherto neglected issues of con-tinuity and change in the Roman family. Some authors have touched upon the topic directly, while others have dealt with topics intimately related to kin groups and households.[7] Nevertheless, there is still much that has yet to be explored. Most interest, for example, has tended to focus on the legal record concerning private life, since it is the most abundant single source of information we have on the family, ancient or medieval. While important, however, there are limitations to the legal record and writers on the subject have had to use other sources as supplementary material.[8]

In conjunction with presenting a generalized view of late Roman family life, then, our second purpose here is to give a more balanced, synthesized vision of the Roman family in the late ancient world. As Jane Gardner points out, law does not describe how people behave, nor even what they think. Instead, it gives people the option to behave in a certain way or *not* to behave in that manner.[9] As valuable as Roman law is, it cannot predict, or even reflect, a family's behavior, actions, attitudes or customs – unless specifically attested to in the body of a ruling. And while it provides us with an unparalleled abundance of source material,[10] it is essential that law not be given inordinate historical value by virtue of its quantity. The feelings expressed by a husband in a piece of correspondence, a canon from a local Church council regulating slave–master relations, or the description of a mother's qualities in an epitaph are all threads in a densely woven tapestry.

Finally, this study must address the issue of Christianity itself. As Antti Arjava has asked in his recent study of Roman women and law during this period, to what degree did the religion of Constantine and his successors change the social fabric? Did it, as Christian authors of the day imply, change custom and action in the family or were its effects negligible?

Scope of study

With only a few exceptions, most work done on the classical Roman family has centered on activity in the West and particularly in Italy.[11] This is hardly surprising: Republican Rome by definition refers specifically to the denizens of that city and its environs. Moreover, as most of the literary evidence deals with the great statesmen of that city, our view of family life not only concentrates on Rome, but on the upper classes as well. The imperial period broadens the geographical and conceptual areas slightly. Those studies of family in the Empire interpret that term more loosely: 'Roman' is basically understood to be those people within the borders of the Empire. For the purposes of this study, however, those areas where Roman and Italian colonization was the strongest shall be our focus. That would include Gaul, Spain and North Africa. True, the literature for the most part supports only an examination of the upper classes and that must by elimination be our primary focus; but again, this is hardly surprising, since the literature of the age was produced for and by the cultural and power elite. Even modern examinations of ancient society's lower classes – such as slaves or freedmen – are always made in the context of the aristocratic world.[12]

Epigraphy does allow the scholar to cast his net beyond the shallow waters of upper class existence. The variety of individuals and their places in Roman society are extensive.[13] Yet despite the tens of thousands of surviving inscriptions, their venue is remarkably limited. As public writings, they generally commemorate only specialized, and thus limited, kinds of events. Most common are funerary inscriptions, and it is from them that the vast majority of the epigraphic information about family life comes. The majority of these provide only prosopographical information, although they do occasionally discuss an individual's behavior and its relation to Roman ideals – and in rarer cases, those of a class.[14] So despite the relative wealth of the evidence, inscriptions are of limited value or at least must be examined in limited

3

contexts. They do, however, recapitulate the sense that Roman society extended beyond Italy. When similar societal ideals, religious notions, and liturgical formulae are expressed in places thousands of miles from one another, as well as being expressed in the same language, the idea of Rome as a culture rather than a place is more sharply defined.

Nevertheless, this study's scope will, like other studies on the Roman family, try to be limited to those places where Roman ideas and customs remained most prevalent in the Empire. The differences between the Eastern and Western halves were considerable in innumerable aspects, but even within the Western Empire, we know that regional variation in behavior and beliefs could be considerable.[15] Although there appears not to have been a conscious attempt to maintain a local cultural identity, one scholar has noted that such endurance was almost unintentional.[16] One can, however, speak with some confidence of Italy as a more or less unified area linguistically and culturally, with extensive contact and interdependence spanning back centuries to the early Republic and even further.[17] Southern Gaul, too, has some cultural relation to Italy, since the area was intensively colonized and Romanized in the first centuries BCE and CE. Given that for our purposes, 'Romans' refer to those people who inhabited these core Western regions, the period of time covered in this survey is a second issue. This is somewhat problematic: late antiquity has several different connotations in different fields of study. Roman historians, classicists, Hellenistic historians and Judaic scholars could all give different answers. Common sense would dictate, however, that the first alternative is best, in part since this study centers on areas in the West. Moreover, since most studies of family history seem to cover the 'classical' age of Rome – that is, from the beginning of the first century BCE to the early third century CE – the period after might be properly understood to be late antiquity.[18] Leaving apart for the moment that the third century was an important and critical age in the life of the Roman Empire, we can with some assurance speak of a different and new age when Diocletian in 284 assumed the purple and carried out substantive and long-lasting changes.

But if the reign of Diocletian can be truly considered a new age, at what point are the major political, economic and cultural underpinnings of that new era in place? Certainly, the best known social movement, the recognition of Christianity by the government as a legitimate religion and its acceptance by the bulk of the urban population, was an ongoing process throughout the fourth and fifth centuries.[19] The main focus of our examination, then, will be on the family after 350: the official condemnation of polytheism, the rise of administrations actively involved in Christianization,[20] and crucial theological disputes that defined a Christian ideology all fell after this date. This is not to say that the third and early fourth centuries will be ignored. The development of Christian ideals regarding marriage, divorce, widowhood, children and parenting became clearly enunciated in those years. The role of

Constantine, too, was also significant in the development of an official ideology of the family. But these ideals *vis-à-vis* the new religion were most articulately expressed by the authors of the late fourth and early fifth centuries. It is unsurprising that the great 'pagan response', if we can speak of such a thing, came at the same time.[21]

Of some importance, too, were the marked demographic changes accelerating in the mid-fourth century. Germanic tribes, always on the margins of Roman society, had in preceding centuries caused substantial if not overwhelming problems, and now began to migrate on a large scale into the southern lands of Europe. In the 360s and 370s, a confederation of Visigoths pushed into the Empire, presenting the Romans with their first significant military loss in almost 400 years at Adrianople in 378.[22] Their entrance began a series of movements of northern European peoples, which only ended in the West in 568 with the Lombard invasion of Italy. In practical terms, while their numbers were relatively small compared to the indigenous population, their settlement affected practical matters of governance, organization of the military, the economics of the cities and countryside, and the tenor of religious debate. More imponderable changes included the nature of social interaction, educational goals and means, and moral and religious beliefs. In this context, then, the mid-fourth century acts as an important demarcation point.

The next question concerns duration: how long does this distinctive period of late antiquity last? Again, it is a difficult problem, especially since it also suggests the broader question of when the ancient world ends. In the particular case of Italy, and perhaps of southern Gaul, the society is still identifiably Roman into the mid-sixth century. The imperial bureaucracy, although bereft of an emperor, still functioned tolerably well until the great reconquest of Justinian in the 530s. The senatorial aristocracy, despite some occasional difficulties with Germanic nobles covetous of their lands, retained much of their wealth and ancient privilege under Ostrogothic rule. The great cities of Italy proved to be economically resilient, capable of producing impressive games and subsidizing *literati*.[23] Sicily still produced bountiful harvests and Narbonensis potable wine. Despite the large numbers of migratory peoples settling in all areas of the Roman Empire, they were, as mentioned above, a small minority of the population. In sum, although there were a number of political realignments in Italy, Gaul and the rest of the West, life among the Romans of the Mediterranean was not totally different from that of the fifth century.

The change, at least for Italy, seems to have come in the course of Justinian's dream of universal Empire. From 536 to 552, the eastern emperor struggled with the Ostrogoths to regain control of the peninsula. It was a Pyrrhic victory. In the process of reconquest, much of the countryside had been ravaged. Rome, Naples and other cities were denuded of their population and suffered severe physical damage.[24] The infrastructure of government had largely vanished except for Ravenna, Milan and a few other cities, as the letters of Pope Gregory affirm a few decades later.[25] Those letters also attest the remarkable poverty of the Italian peninsula and the unenviable duty of the Church: attempting to fill the void left by the absence of troops, material and infrastructure.[26] The *coup de grâce* was the Lombard invasion in 568. The Italy of 600 was quite different from the Italy of 500.[27]

The closing date of this study then will be set before these turn of events, roughly the mid-sixth century. There is some support for this in the historiography of family life as well. Both Jack Goody and David Herlihy take the sixth century as a turning point (or more accurately, a starting point) for their larger studies on European family types.[28] More recently, David Kertzer and Richard Saller's edited collection of essays on the family in Italy, which covers the last two thousand years of that country's history, seems to place the demarcation point between ancient and medieval somewhere in the mid-sixth century.[29] Following what is clearly thought of in the historiography and other more general studies as the end of the ancient world, then, the period roughly covered in this study will be 350–550 CE.

Definitions and models

When thinking of family today, a number of notions and images tend to spring to mind. Parents and siblings are the images from youth. If independent, one might think of spouses and children as family. More liberal thinkers might think that the cohabitation of individuals, whether in a sexual or platonic relationship, could be understood or recognized as a family. However the word's meaning might be construed, it is necessary that the term, broadly and specifically in the context of the Roman world, be discussed in some detail.

Although we are primarily dealing with the period after 350 CE, it first seems important to develop a working definition or model of the Roman classical family.[30] It is impossible to speak of changes, whether in a quantitative or a qualitative sense, without speaking of what the family changed from. Moreover, the great majority of work that has been done on the classical period allows for an extensive if not definitive picture. The recent scholarship of the Roman family also stresses certain features that can be tracked over time: these include predominant opinions (at least in the upper classes) about ideal family life, marriage practices, heirship strategies, and the use and abuse of slaves. Therefore, before looking at the families of late antiquity, I must include their predecessors.

The most obvious starting point is an understanding of how the Romans themselves perceived and defined the term.[31] The word 'family' is not a direct cognate of the Latin term, *familia*, at least in meaning;[32] *domus* is perhaps a closer approximation in the sources to what is understood as kin.[33] Moreover, at least in the sources, there is a notable change in the use of these two terms as time progresses. Their meanings, indeed, almost become transposed in the legal sources.

Second, related to the question of Roman definitions of the family is the notion of modern perceptions of what constitutes the familial unit. Quite beyond daily existence and experiences and recent interest in so-called 'family values', there are a number of almost *a priori* accepted ideas when trying to build our own conceptual frameworks. Many of these preconceptions stem from nineteenth-century studies, and much of that work was tied to the politics and social conditions of industrialization. In England, for example, Friedrich Engels attempted to connect changes in the family to the transition from an agricultural economy to an industrial one.[34] Pierre Le Play went even further: he created an entire taxonomy of family types, the most important classification for the modern world being the so-called nuclear family.[35] Such notions of 'nuclear', 'extended', and 'stem' families are modern constructions; and the modern historian finds that such types are not always applicable to the Roman world, even within the theoretically heterogeneous aristocracy. The works of Engels, Le Play and others subsequently, however, did inspire other studies in England, France and America.[36]

Taxonomy of families is also a product of anthropology. Towards the end of the last century and the beginning of our own, interests in kinship structures, marriage customs, matriarchal and patriarchal authority, and many similar behavioral patterns became features for understanding a society. Margaret Mead, David Kroeber, Claude Lévi-Strauss and others created a vocabulary for describing 'primitive' and historical cultures, their particular features and the means by which their members interact. Yet anthropology, too, presumes that the family (and society as a whole) can be classified: the classical Roman family might be called patriarchal, patrilocal, exogamous, agnatic, conscious of extended family and possessing extensive kinship lines. To some degree these labels are roughly valid, accepted even by Romans (or at least, by Roman jurists); but the literary and epigraphic evidence presents so many contrary examples to these constructions that such classifications are not terribly useful, or even germane, to creating a generalized understanding of the family.

Third, when we consider the Roman family, there must be an awareness of the conditions and limitations imposed on its definition. There is considerably more knowledge about the upper classes than about the lower classes. Relatively little is known about regional differences. There may have been common features in Italy and perhaps southern Gaul, but beyond that, even in the Latin West, native systems of family and community may well have endured or even prevailed. Much, too, is based on legal sources, which, despite their indispensability, can present various pitfalls. The evidence is also generally more focused on the male rather than the female, more on the adult than the child, and more on the older adult than the younger one. Indeed, with a few notable exceptions, most of the literary evidence was written by men well into their adulthood. The issue of change over time, of course, is one focal point in this thesis. These factors, as well as other more subtle ones, need to be recognized in any attempt to generate a usable definition.

These three issues, then – Roman understanding of what a family constituted, modern conceptions of family, and the natural limitations of the evidence when categorically defining a family – should remain foremost in any attempt to generate a model for Rome. With that caveat in mind, I want to give brief definitions of the terms that will be used throughout the study.

The word 'family' in this work will refer for the most part to those co-residing individuals associated by marriage or by kinship. Occasionally, it may be used to also refer to other kin not residing in the same domicile, such as siblings, cousins and other relations.[37] The term, then, is based more or less on our own modern concepts of what comprises family, and like us, Romans often understood it to mean more than one thing. In contrast to family is the Latin word '*familia*,' which had a considerably broader meaning. Technically, it refers to all persons and things under the control of the eldest ascendant male in a household, the head of the family (*paterfamilias*). In addition to kin, it could refer to slaves, clients, boarders and even chattel property. As will be discussed in the next chapter, *familia* presumed a certain legal status of those people and things under the power of the *paterfamilias*. This status, as we shall see, did not always reflect the realities of a situation, but *familia* refers to a specific legal definition.[38]

In addition, the word household will often be used and generally has two meanings. In the most literal sense, it refers to the physical house, along with properties associated with it. In a more general sense, it refers to the semi-official entity that represented the family and the *familia*. This was particularly important in upper-class households, where a family and its dependents as a whole could wield considerable influence and even a quasi-official authority. Closely associated with this latter meaning is the word '*domus*'. In the broadest usage, *domus* could be properly considered an agglomeration of related families in some ways similar to the old Roman *gens*.[39] *Domus*, then, could also be extended to past generations of a family. Since, too, in a strictly legal sense, a *familia* survived through the male (agnatic) relations, whereas a *domus* could also refer to a daughter and her descendants as well. In sum, household and *domus* have more elastic meanings than either family or *familia*.

Using these definitions as rough guidelines, it would be tempting to go further and try to construct a basic model of the Roman family. Many concepts have been put forward. Some have opted for a legalistic model, especially since the Romans (or at least upper-class Romans) were obsessed with jurisprudence and, as mentioned above, it is the most abundant single source about the family we possess. But a legal approach provides little insight to the nature of the family, only setting the context within which the family can be defined. It presents the modern researcher with options for constructing types of familial behavior and composition, but the legal record can provide little more. It instead often acts as an 'out-of-bounds' marker. Clearly, the familial unit must be understood in a different context or at least in one that has a richer and broader theoretical basis.

There are also various forms of kinship models, including nuclear and extended families, multi-generational households, and the like. It is clear from the sources that Roman interest centered on the married couple and their children. But there are too many legal, statistical and behavioral factors arguing against its use as an effective model. Roman families, especially during the classical period (100 BCE–200 CE), were often broken up and reformed in what can best be described as serial monogamy and blended households. Siblings, half-siblings and step-siblings could be living in the same household or entirely different ones. Those siblings might be separated by decades in age. Kinship is a key element in defining the family, perhaps the essential one, but there are other factors involved, too.

Sociologists have offered a third approach, preferring to emphasize location and household as a more accurate means of defining the family.[40] A sociological definition also emphasizes the idea of a role or function carried out in the house: that is, people gathered at a specific place to complete a task, whether it be service, commerce or otherwise. Also, by using residence as a model, there is no necessity to make a distinction between the nuclear and extended family nor concern ourselves with relation at all. The problems with such a model, however, are more numerous than those that take a legalistic or kinship approach. In general, it confuses family with residence.[41] Again, the distinction in Roman minds between who was family and who simply lived at a residence is clear. There are other problems with co-residency in the context of our concerns with the extended family model, but it is enough to say here that defining the family in terms of household creates more problems than it solves. It artificially blurs lines of relationship that were recognized then (and now) as being distinct.

After rejecting three different approaches, is there then anything substantive to be said regarding a Roman family model? I believe there is. While it seems difficult to place the Roman family in a definitive typology, mostly because of its wide variability, Keith Bradley has offered a useful alternative to trying to build a model. He prefers instead that the Roman family be identified by certain features. These features do not necessarily form a comprehensive definition, but they provide markers by which we can gauge changes in family structure and behavior. In short, Bradley's alternative is more descriptive than it is definitive. His own list of features of the classical family is perhaps worth quoting in full here:

1. the arranged nature of most marriages, especially those controlled by the world of politics, and the relative unimportance of sentiment in compacting marital unions;
2. the impermanence of the marriage bond and the ease of its dissolution;
3. the frequency of premature death and consequent availability of a surviving spouse to enter a new union;[42]
4. the likelihood that an individual's children would be broadly spaced in age;

5. the likelihood that some of an individual's children would belong to the same generation as his or her grandchildren;
6. the likelihood that husband and wife would either be significantly distanced in age or belong to different generations;
7. the immanence of the belief that marriage and procreation were culturally induced social obligations, not the result of individualistic choices;
8. the creation through serial marriage of networks of marital relationships which extended beyond the immediate household.[43]

To these features, two others are worth mentioning. First, the importance of the ideal family to Romans themselves should be added. The literature and the epigraphy both show an emphasis placed on *concordia* (harmony), the obedience and modesty of the wife, the high status of the *univira* (a woman who had only a single husband),[44] the filial devotion of children to their parents and especially their father, and the financial obligations of a father to his progeny upon his death. Second, the presence of slaves even in modest households made them ubiquitous. The prevalence of slaves (and freedmen), along with their roles as surrogates for sex and procreation, forces us to recognize their function, treatment and status in the family.[45] The essential point of the preceding discussion has been to look beyond definitions and models, and instead try to see how family behavior affected and was affected by social and cultural factors.

Plan of study

To accomplish that goal, we must first examine more closely the classical family. The first part of the second chapter is devoted to this topic. In discussing the classical family unit, we will concentrate on two areas. First, what constituted the ideal vision of the Roman family? Any kind of description will, of course, be largely subjective: various authors depicted the family in a number of ways. More precisely, the ideal family to a poet or a moralist might be quite distinct from the ideal family of a jurist. Different members of the family might be described in different ways as well. Moreover, there were a number of changes within the classical age, a period of approximately three centuries. Certainly, the family of 100 BCE and the family of 200 CE were hardly the same. But when speaking of ideals, the differences may not be as extensive as the realities. Even in late antiquity, literature often espoused underlying classical values. It should therefore be possible to create a synthesis which will allow a comparison with the ideals of the late Roman period.

The second area of concentration will center on the realities of family life and existence. Behavior, customs and attitudes will be the central issues discussed. There is also enough material on the economy of the private home – literary, epigraphic and archeological – to say something of household make-up and division of labor. Letters from Cicero, Pliny, Fronto and others provide some insights and personal examples of the dynamics of marital relations and familial obligations, although they are admittedly told from a male perspective. Historians who relate sensational scandals (regardless of their veracity[46]), philosophers who explore moral conundrums, and poets who discuss a whole range of social and emotional ills all help to define attitudes about personal comportment. Again, there is some degree of change in the classical period, and most of our information deals with the upper classes. But the aim here is to give only a rough overview of the classical family, and not to present another study on that topic. The subtler and deeper questions about the nature of private life in the late republican and early imperial ages need not be explored.[47] Instead, tracing with broad strokes the outlines of the Roman family will provide a guide for its counterpart in late antiquity.

Our attention will then turn to the early Christian family or at least the ideals surrounding them. Information about family life as it actually existed is notoriously patchy. While more attention is starting to be focused on this period – most recently by Halvor Moxnes[48] – it is still largely untouched in the historiography. True, the early Christian age prior to Constantine is not clearly defined by distinctive changes in contemporary impressions of what family meant nor in how it apparently functioned, but significant developments which came to fruition in the fourth century began at the religion's inception.

The age of Constantine, too, is a period of enormous significance, at least legally, and will be briefly explored. While the effects of Christianity on the emperor's social legislation have been rightly questioned of late, it is a significant age in that it represented the theoretical confluence of the Roman and Christian worlds.

The rest of our attention will be exclusively focused on the family of the later Roman Empire. A primary area of interest will be the effect of religion on perceptions of family life and on customary behavior. This is not simply to discuss the family in the context of Christianity, although this will be a central theme in this study. Rather, this means that, with the rise of the new religion in the fourth century, the ideological lines between pagan and Christian were brought more sharply into focus. For the first time, opinions were fully expressed. Such opinions thus offered a new phase in the development of literature relating to the family. There was not as radical a difference in the new religion's attitudes toward marriage and child rearing, for example, as one might at first think. Indeed, in certain areas, there was little, if any, difference at all. Nevertheless, there was a paradigmatic shift in an overall conception of the family and how that shift was expressed. Defining 'Roman' and 'Christian' opinions and observations will be a major endeavor of this work.

The primary focus, however, will be concerned with various familial relationships. One may logically infer that this examination will include, in considerably more depth, many of the issues relating to the classical family. Of paramount importance was the role of marriage in late antique society. The process of contracting a marital union, the marriage itself, and life after marriage will all be explored. Alternatives to the married state, notably concubinage, will also be an important area of interest, not least because pagans and Christians both engaged in the practice. The legal, economic, religious and even biological demands of marriage in late Roman society will be considered. Even in a society where Christian alternatives to marriage first appeared (celibacy and virginity), the married state remained the singularly most important human relationship.

Another issue will be child rearing. The activities of raising and educating a child are the place where there is perhaps the greatest level of disagreement between pagans and Christians. While the latter never really developed a true alternative to the classical educational system, they altered and added to it. Moreover, feelings in the late Roman world about the means by which a parent raised his offspring had also changed. Thus, this particular facet of family life is important.

A third area which has been largely been ignored by scholars, extended family, is also of great importance, largely because of its elusive nature. The fuzziness, legally and otherwise, of an individual to his extended relations, is a constant in the modern mind. Given that the Romans themselves saw the family, *familia*, and *domus* in a number of ways, kin of more distant relation is an issue that needs closer examination. Indeed, the extended family in the classical age needs greater discussion.

A final topic will be the role of the domestic slave in the late Roman household. They, too, were technically members of the *familia*, although their place in the family structure was complicated both by their legal status and their frequent lack of blood ties to the principal family. Their place in the Roman family accordingly raises a number of questions. How did proximity, physical and emotional, affect attitudes and behavior? How, if at all, did Christianization influence opinion? What other factors – cultural, legal, economic or otherwise – helped to shape the understanding of the unfree person within the structure of society's most basic unit of organization?

Having catalogued the changes between the classical Roman age and the later Roman period – and looking at the late antique family in its own right – a final task will be to give some account as to why certain underlying trends in Roman society acted as catalysts or obstacles for such changes. Much of the evolution, as I intend to prove, was illusory. While Christianity tended to place new moral and legal restrictions on the functioning of the family, it failed to create deep-seated changes in the structure and behavior of this unit. Perhaps the classical Roman ideal of family metamorphosed into something somewhat different, but classical practices and customs endured. That will be the theme of this study.

The sources

An important task in completing these tasks will be to look at how the Romans of late antiquity visualized the family itself. Accordingly, late antique literature concerning perceptions of family, the moral and legal duties and obligations of its members, and the conscious and unconscious ways a Christian or a pagan thought about the family's make-up and function will all be of primary importance. Our discussion will include a close scrutiny of the legal records so as to understand, if possible, how these perceptions manifested themselves into an official ideology (in that they became law). The political agendas are less an interest in themselves than they are symptomatic of something occurring on a deeper level in the society. A close parallel in the Church is the slow creation of a body of canon law. It, too, created an official ideology, although it was rarely unified throughout the Empire. Additionally, there will be an examination of Christian homiletics, which often provided ruminations about family, mother, father, daughter, son, widow, virgin, slave, male, female, husband, wife, concupiscence, celibacy, and virginity. The bulk of such work is found in sermons, theological tracts and public letters. Jerome, Ambrose and Augustine are especially useful authors for looking at such things: they wrote extensively and precisely on these issues. The epigraphy, despite its limitations, will also be touched upon: how a family treated its own in death usually indicated how it wanted a family member to be recalled in life. Examples in these sorts of works were often as much ideological constructs as anything else: in the case of Christians, archetypal biblical figures; in the case of pagans, Greeks and Romans of great accomplishment.[49]

There are also more individualized, if not private, works. As with the classical age, we will have to depend largely on epistles, which often cite particular events. Secular and religious figures alike could write intensely personal thoughts and feelings within the body of these unofficial works. Saints' lives, too, are of some value. There are of course inherent problems with accepting the information contained in a *vita* as factual, but they nevertheless offer some interesting inroads to the nature of late ancient society that otherwise would be inaccessible. They are moral pieces, with set rhetorical figures, but they are also products of their age: their authors could not talk of certain kinds of actions or customs in a social vacuum. Saints' lives thus provide some information about types of private comportment. A third source of primary materials lies in autobiographical and semi-autobiographical works. Augustine's *Confessiones* is one of the few truly introspective documents of the ancient world.[50] It not only reports in detail the daily goings on in a well-off home, something not really discussed consistently elsewhere, but also provides reflections, impressions and feelings to supplement the factual data. A similar, if much shorter piece, is Paulinus of Pella's *Eucharisticos*, a poem written about a long and not always happy life. The poetry of Ausonius also offers personal glimpses into the private life of the local aristocracy. Finally, the historians of the age, whether simple chroniclers or more sophisticated and educated literary luminaries, often discuss private affairs, if only parenthetically or incidentally. Some histories, like the *Res Gestae* of Ammianus Marcellinus, are quite fruitful and discuss private life and behavior at some length.[51] While these documents deal almost exclusively with the highest ranks of society and often supply little new information, they sometimes substantiate information found elsewhere. The use of histories, secular and religious, can also provide an overarching temporal context that is often hard to duplicate from other sources.

Common and rarefied perceptions will be contrasted as far as possible with the actual functioning of the family. This will necessitate the separation of the moral opinions of ancient writers from what they commented upon. There is, among the various letters of Christian and pagan authors alike, sanctimonious acrimony and polemic against behavior and intentions which they deigned immoral or improper. The underlying implications of such recriminations often suggest that those authors were speaking from the standpoint of the majority or, perhaps more accurately, from a moral imperative. But there is frequently no substantiating evidence to support such inferences. Even if one accepted that a particular author was writing with the strength of common opinion behind him, the behavior which he castigated still existed or was at least considered possible. The need, then, to parse commentary and the object commented upon is clear. This distinction, too, is also important for understanding the endurance of custom in a nominally Christian age.

2

TWO TRADITIONS

The family, as viewed by Roman jurists and by the upper classes of society, was depicted in the legal codes and literature as almost a microcosm of the Roman *res publica*.[1] Like the Roman penchant for ordered government and utilitarian religious practices, the household supposedly ran like a practical and well-oiled machine under the auspices of the house head, the *paterfamilias*. The reality of domestic life, like the reality of republican politics, was rarely so neat. Conflict between generations, between spouses, and between masters and slaves were common tensions that characterized the social fabric. A deeper examination of the dynamics of Roman family life reveals duties and obligations of a father to his children, a husband to his wife and a master to his servant – precisely opposite of what is often supposed. While the *paterfamilias* might have possessed considerable legal power over those nominally under his jurisdiction, authoritarian or capricious behavior was rarely approved of – at least in classical times. Even those who praised the nature of familial hierarchy drew a parallel between the public world and the private household by laying out the responsibilities of the governors and the governed.

Where the ideal ended and reality began is difficult to say with any degree of accuracy. Scholars continue to offer valuable examinations of the structure and the make-up of families as depicted in the law codes and it is a debate that I do not intend to delve into too deeply.[2] The first section of this chapter is instead meant to describe the family during the classical age of Rome, from approximately 100 BCE to 200 CE. The first part will accordingly sketch a composite picture of the ideal Roman family. It will, in its brevity, be necessarily anachronistic at times and occasionally contradictory: when speaking of a 300-year time span, with a number of differing opinions from a wide range of sources, there are bound to be inconsistencies in any generalized portrait. Our purpose, however, is to permit a comparison with the realities of everyday home life. We will examine the practical issues and problems in the *domus*, as well as the tenor of various power relationships therein. But it is important to remember that the voices we hear from the past are largely wealthy, male ones, whose own interpretations of commonly held attitudes must be weighed accordingly. That notwithstanding, the final aim here is to provide a basis for comparing the classical and late antique families.

15

The second half of the chapter will consider the early Christian family. The contributions of ancient Jewish ideas and customs were exceedingly important for its formation, but Christian thinkers quickly distinguished their practices from those of the Roman and Judaic worlds. 'Christian family', however, is notoriously difficult to define, but it is necessary to explore for much the same reasons as we look at the classical Roman family. We cannot analyse late antique family life in any depth without having a strong understanding of its structural, behavioral and moral antecedents.

The Roman family

Marriage

Marriage was often an event that occurred early in life: the minimum age of union for males was 14 and for females 12.[3] As a general rule, however, our sources generally demonstrate that men tended to be about ten years the senior of their spouses. The epigraphic evidence suggests that the upper classes tended to marry somewhat later than those of the lower born, but as an institution, first marriages were for the young.[4]

A constant in the definition of the Roman word *familia* is the element of the legally recognized marriage, the *iustum matrimonium*. Like most ancient societies, only if both parents were citizens and had been in a recognized contract of marriage was their child considered fully a Roman citizen.[5] It was accordingly not uncommon for the censors to ask if a senator or an equestrian was getting married for the purpose of producing offspring.[6] In a world that drew sharp divisions in society, degrees of freedom, citizenship and place were important: one's status affected his or her legal rights,[7] social acceptance,[8] and economic activities.

Marriage was therefore first and foremost a legal state. Religious ceremonies were incidental. There was usually a joining of right hands, the so-called *iunctio dextrarum*; a sacrifice and feast; and, of course, the traditional carrying of the bride over the threshold. But these were customary: they neither were needed nor required.[9] In the Empire, the only event that sealed the marriage was the signing of the contract in regards to property, dowries and the like (the *pactio nuptialis* and *pactia doctalia*). Dowries were given for a husband to use as he saw fit; should divorce occur, he had to return such property. Gifts between spouses were not allowed, mostly to avoid questions of property ownership in the event of disputes.[10] A marriage, then, was a contract.

The terms of the marriage varied. The union of course implied that there was consent of both partners and their *patresfamilias*, should they be living. Until the late Republic it was not uncommon for the wife to be given into the *manus* (literally 'hand') of her husband. That gave the husband, barring a few legal strictures, *potestas* over his mate. *Potestas* was a legal concept that gave a *paterfamilias* control over legal and economic rights, and in theory even included the decision of life and death over an individual (*ius vitae necisque*). A wife thus gained a new *paterfamilias* and all her property would become his. The legal significance of this action was to make the woman legally a member of her husband's family. Its one advantage (for the woman, at least) was that if a husband died intestate, she would be considered an heir (*heres*). But marriage with *manus* became increasingly rare until it essentially disappeared in the Empire, at least among upper-class partners who wished to maintain control over their own moneys and properties.[11] By 23 CE, it appears to have ended entirely except in cases where it was necessary to hold religious office.[12] Instead, women remained in the *potestas* of their fathers. When a father died, a woman in this state immediately came under the jurisdiction of a tutor (*tutela legitima*) who theoretically directed a woman's legal and economic affairs.

These legal fictions notwithstanding, the conjugal couple was supposed to cohabit and live in perfect harmony: what the Romans termed *concordia*. The concept of *concordia*, like many concepts from antiquity, is difficult to define. Apart from its political implications,[13] the notion of *concordia* seems to have had a broad meaning, partially because of differing interpretations among different authors. At its most basic level, however, the term meant harmony within marriage. Regardless of station or status, the value of *concordia* was shared by all. Although many male–female arrangements were not considered legal marriages (or even marriages at all), the dynamics of affective relationships were often identical to so-called legitimate unions. In one funerary stele, for example, former slaves Aurelia L. l. Philematio and L. Aurelius L. l. Hermia described their relationship as 'companions' (*contubernales*) in the same terms as did freeborn married couples.[14]

The assortment of references to marital accord among social equals is abundant in reference to both husbands and wives. Valerius Maximus, for example, related a custom from the old days of Rome: when a couple had a disagreement, they went to the temple of Viriplaca, literally 'the Placater of men'. There, both related their sides of the argument and worked out the problem in the sight of the goddess. Afterwards, they returned to the '*domum in concordiam*'.[15] Valerius went on to explain how this gave the wife, who was naturally inferior to her husband, a means of resolving critical disagreements. More significantly, there was a clear understanding that disagreements should not occur in the physical house, an indication of its symbolic importance.

The classical period of Roman history presents somewhat more useful insights into the nature of conjugal harmony. In recounting a senatorial debate in 22 CE concerning governors and their wives, Valerius Messalinus argued that they should not be separated from the 'partnership in good fortune and in bad'.[16] Tacitus, in describing his parents-in-law, makes much the same comment:[17] 'they lived in miraculous accord, by mutual care and by serving one another'. Marriage was supposed to be a true partnership, where good and bad were shared, although perhaps not equally. The banished philosopher,

Musonius Rufus, equated *concordia* with the Greek concept of *homonoia*,[18] which implied stability as well as happiness. Further, Modestinus stated that marriage was a crossroads between the human and divine laws.[19] As a divinely approved state, then, marriage required harmony.

There are a few scattered references in the legal texts to the term. In such works, *concordia* has a notably neutral sense: it is presumed that the concept had a similar meaning for both men and women. Paulus refers blandly to *bene concordans matrimonium*,[20] which is a stock legal phrase,[21] and tells us little about the nature of *concordia*. Modestinus in his legal textbook, *Regulae*, for example, echoing Tacitus' words, calls marriage a *consortium omnis*, a sharing of all things in life.[22] The implication that there is a complete sharing, whether in good times or ill, suggests that *concordia* meant accepting personal misfortunes equitably and not being overly joyous at good fortune. Concord or harmony was thus more than good congress between husband and wife; it was a call for equanimity – a characteristically Stoic element in upper-class Roman life.

Despite this ideal, the man's role as husband was generally not considered of great significance in the Roman world. There are only a few references to the role of the husband. In a piece entitled *de Officio Mariti*, Marcus Varro explained that a husband had the choice of improving his wife or with putting up with her faults:[23] 'A wife's vices must either be tolerated or suppressed. He who quashes her faults makes her more accommodating; but he who tolerates them makes himself better.' Although this work was satire, Gellius underscored a man's obligation to endure his wife's flights of fancy, whether good or ill, in order to maintain harmony and decorum in the marriage.

In a more serious vein, Pliny the Younger, when writing of his much beloved third wife, Calpurnia (a woman, incidentally, who was at least twenty years his junior), seems to reinforce this idea that a husband should be both corrective and tolerant of his wife in a loving way. In one particular instance, when Calpurnia inadvertently miscarried in an undetected pregnancy, Pliny took it upon himself to inform her relatives and to caution them against blaming her: 'it was not her fault, but that of her [young] age'.[24] Certainly such age differences reinforced an attitude of paternalism. Indeed, a husband might literally act as a teacher. Pliny mentioned a friend who had so well tutored his wife in literature that her work read like Terence in prose.[25] And a proper attitude was important in nurturing *concordia* in marriage. Pliny recommended Minucius Acilianus to a friend, a young man who offered not only wealth and lineage, but also had a '*senatorius decor*', which apparently to Pliny's mind was well suited to young women.[26]

With wives, insuring a happy marriage was a more exacting task. She ought to be '*lanificia, pia, pudica, frugi, casta, domiseda*'.[27] While her chastity was important, so was the notion of her purity and devotion to one man. She ought to be submissive to her husband, offering unqualified support, '*sine discrimine, sine offensione*'.[28] Moreover, for a woman to have only one husband –

univira – during her lifetime was especially prized among Roman men,[29] although clearly it was not a virtue applied to husbands: there was no concept of *unifemina*.[30] The state of *univira* implied a whole host of other virtues: chastity, devotion, loyalty and, of course, purity.

The so-called *Laudatio Turiae* is the longest surviving passage in any medium dealing with the role of the wife in Rome. It appears to have been based on an actual funerary speech given by Turia's unnamed husband. The identities of husband and wife are not known for certain,[31] but they were clearly wealthy and lived in the last days of the Republic and perhaps well into Augustus' reign. The widower addressed Turia's domestic qualities – *domestica bona* – both as a wife and daughter:

> Domestica bona pudici[t]iae, opsequi, comitatis, facilitatis, lanificiis tuis [*adsiduitatis, religionis*] | sine superstitione, o[r]natus non conspiciendi, cultus modici cur [*memorem? cur dicam de tuorum cari*] | tate, familiae pietate, [c]um aeque matrem meam ac tuos parentes col[*veris eandemque quietem*] | illi quam tuis curaveris . . . ?[32]

But this relatively common litany of virtues is enlarged upon by a number of specific actions, actual events unique to her life. At one point shortly after her father's death, for example, Turia was left to fend for herself in a legal matter (her husband was en route to Macedonia at the time) involving her inheritance. Some unnamed persons had tried to get guardianship over her and her sister and thus get control of the property. Despite considerable pressure, she would not bow and they eventually were forced to give up:

> Cesserunt constantiae tuae neque amplius rem sollicitarunt: quo facto [*reverentiae in patrem*], | pietatis in sororem, fide[i] in nos patrocinium succeptum sola peregisti.[33]

Turia's strength and authority to essentially act as a man were thus legitimized by her loyalty to her husband.

But there were two other general virtues valued in a wife. She first and foremost had to be a good manager in the household: '*Summum est acumen, summa frugalitas*'.[34] That frugality was supposed to extend even to a wife's own person, as Marcus Fronto noted: '*Neque est Gratia mea, ut causidicorum uxores feruntur, multi cibi.*'[35] Such frugality and sharpness optimally extended into the area of household finances, overseeing the proper running of a household, care of guests and other 'domestic' duties. To be sure, these duties were not required, but were nevertheless prized.

Finally, a wife was expected to be intimately involved in all aspects of her husband's life and it gave her impetus to act, often publicly. Pliny tells a sycophantic story, for example, about Calpurnia memorizing his works and sending slaves into court to see how his pleadings were being received.[36] There is an even more dramatic tale. Apparently when Marcus Brutus married his cousin, Porcia, she proved the strength of her love and devotion for her indifferent husband by gravely wounding herself. In an impassioned plea, begging to be considered more than simply someone whom Brutus bedded, Porcia exclaimed that she wanted to share his joys and his sorrows, as well as his secrets. Brutus was reportedly amazed at this and prayed to the gods that he would be worthy of such a wife.[37] The ideal wife might be expected then to help her husband in all his endeavors to the best of her ability and in any way her spouse saw fit. Porcia, incidentally, killed herself when she learned of Brutus' death.[38]

Briefly, then, the evidence illustrates the role of wives as clearly subordinate. But more significantly, that role was more clearly defined than that of the husband. The variety of characteristics a woman should possess, no doubt to insure a working marriage, was more than simply items on a checklist. They allowed a wife a range of actions – frequently independent – when carried out in the name of her husband or out of conjugal duty. In short, a wife was to be a partner, albeit a lesser one, in the institution of marriage.

Concordia might have little to do with love.[39] What it did require from both partners was an understanding: in the case of the husband, of a woman's foibles and, in the case of the wife, of a man's needs. But the literature elucidates an important theme found in the funerary monuments. The wife's role was much more thoroughly described because the success or failure of a marriage ultimately depended on her. As Tacitus concluded, a woman took a greater share of the credit if the conjugal couple had a harmonious marriage.[40] She accordingly also took a greater share of the blame were the union stormy.

Divorce, widowhood, and remarriage

The ease of divorce in Rome was canonized in that society's earliest laws. Whether by mutual consent or unilaterally, a marriage could be brought to an end by either spouse. Once the desire to maintain a marriage ended – that is, the absence of the *maritalis affectio* – it was legally considered at an end. Living together was incidental. While a *repudium* was customarily sent to a wife from her husband or occasionally from a father-in-law to a son-in-law,[41] no legal notice was actually required before the age of emperors. Augustus' marriage legislation perhaps made divorce a slightly more difficult proceeding: there had to be several individuals present to witness a divorce or an intention to divorce.[42] But as modern scholars have pointed out, this was less an attempt to make divorce harder to obtain than it was to make a divorce easier to confirm.[43] Where issues of dowry and property were concerned, the time and circumstances surrounding a divorce were important.

The reasons for divorce could be manifold. If a marriage was without issue, the necessity for a new one became clear.[44] Infidelity (*stuprum*) for wives was one of the gravest offenses that would at least end in divorce, and quite possibly in death.[45] Married men and women nevertheless did commonly engage in extramarital affairs, a topic to which we shall shortly return. Augustus divorced his second wife, Scribonia, for the 'perversity of her habits' – probably a sexual allusion.[46] The very suggestion of impropriety justified divorce in early Rome: Gaius Sulpicius Gallus (*cos.* 166 BCE) divorced his wife for having walked outside with her head uncovered.[47] Publius Sempronius Sophus (*cos.* 268 BCE) divorced his spouse for attending the public games without his knowledge.[48] These all indicate the husband's justification for separation, but they also imply that divorce could be initiated for many causes. A wife or her *paterfamilias* was able to do likewise, although it was probably less common. While a divorce could be initiated on the flimsiest of reasons, no law during the Republic required it.

It was not until Augustus took control that divorce in at least one case was mandatory. His *lex Julia de adulteriis* compelled husbands to divorce their wives in cases of immorality (*stuprum*).[49] In the past, being cuckolded or even the appearance of such a state was grounds for severe punishment. Cato the Elder, for example, in his lost oration, *de Dotalia*, argued that when a husband divorced a wife, he should act like a censor when he decided whether she deserved punishment.[50] What separated Augustus' law from past custom was that it was now possible for a wife to sue for divorce (with financial repercussions) if her husband was caught *in flagrante*, although she could not carry out criminal proceedings.[51]

Apart from supposed legal constraints, however, the power over one's wife could frequently turn ugly. Domestic violence between partners, as has been alluded to above, was apparently quite common. For example, the praetor Plautius Silvanus, for unclear reasons, threw his wife from a window. When Tiberius had the matter investigated, he found that there had been some violence done against her before the murder.[52] More revealing is the crude humor of Roman writers. Petronius, for example, merely confirms with a certain casualness the commonality of wife-beating: Trimalchio, angry at his shrewish wife, found succor by smashing a wine cup into her face.[53] Plautus, too, seems to make light of violence against a wife.[54] It is unclear, however, whether such domestic violence actually resulted in divorce. Since Roman society did not greatly chastise wife-beating and in some cases exalted it,[55] it was unlikely that women used it as a pretext for divorce.

Moreover, the culture took a dim view of divorce as an affront to marital loyalty, *fides*. It was said that frequent divorces and remarriages gave rise to talk, and that a woman who married often upset a lot of husbands.[56] There were practical considerations as well. Unless a woman were married *in manu*, her property remained her own. Gifts between spouses were specifically forbidden save under special circumstances.[57] The only financial gain a husband might expect is whatever dowry was agreed upon in the *pacta dotalia*. He would get use of that dowry for the duration of the marriage. Use (*usus*) did not assume ownership, so if a marriage ended in divorce, the groom would usually have to return whatever property and money that came with his bride. The existence of divorce deeds in Roman Egypt imply that such documents likely existed in Italy in some form.[58] Marriage contracts undoubtedly made many men, who generally saw marriage as a form of advancement, pause in initiating a divorce.

Nevertheless, divorce was common, if not frequent. Some dynasts, such as Pompey, could have five wives in one lifetime. As a general rule, we should think of divorce, at least from the man's perspective, not as an opposite of marriage, but as a means of remarriage. Indeed, the powerful could take great interest in the maintenance of the married state. Even before Augustus' social engineering, Cicero expressed his worries about the survival of the senatorial aristocracy because young men and women of that order did not want to marry.[59] How true such complaints were is hard to determine, but it does not necessarily exhibit an interest in the survival of the single, lifelong union. And indeed, it appears that divorcees, widows and widowers actively sought remarriage, despite the ideal of *univira*.[60] Susan Treggiari estimates that one in six upper-class Roman marriages ended in divorce within the first ten years of marriage and another one in six from death.[61] Given that her figures are correct, that means one-third of adult upper-class women could in fact expect three marriages in their lifetime.

Of course, either party might simply prefer to remain unmarried after a divorce or more commonly after the death of one's spouse. While Augustus had required a certain number of legitimate children be produced before an individual could choose celibacy,[62] there were many who remained unmarried once they had regained their single status. For women in particular, remaining unattached might be profitable. Often husbands left large legacies (*fideicommissa*) for their spouses. Men also frequently left all property to their natural heirs, but granted all usufructuary rights to their spouses as long as they lived or alternatively until those heirs came of age (usually at 25).[63] Given a certain financial independence – along with legal independence – the impetus to remarry perhaps diminished.

A further inducement to eschew marriage in a woman's case would be the unseemliness of the situation. In the early days of Rome, remaining widowed was considered a virtue.[64] But even in the classical period, Roman society tended to frown upon remarriage in many situations, particularly if a widow were past child-bearing years. Alternatively, if a woman had a reputation for remarrying with some frequency or with undue haste, it would reflect badly upon her. The ten-month mourning period for widows, mostly to ensure that there would be no question of paternity, was sacrosanct.[65] A woman who remarried too soon not only pushed the bounds of propriety, but might be suspected of collusion in her husband's death with her new husband. Such was implied by Tacitus and Dio Cassius when Seianus requested Livilla's hand in marriage shortly after the death of her husband, Drusus.[66] The circumstances of marriage, then, might dictate continued widowhood.

For a widower, the reasons for remaining unwed might be different, but they were equally compelling. A husband need not worry about a mourning period:[67] he was free to remarry after the funeral ceremony and occasionally did so. Rather, the first impediment to remarriage was the cultural biases against the stepmother (noverca). Stepmothers were commonly thought to favor their own children at the expense of their spouse's. A widower's decision to remarry might also be based on age. But unlike widows, the age of a widower's progeny was at issue. If one's children were still minors and thus needed care (since legitimate children always went with their fathers in the event of divorce), then remarriage, noverca or not, might be expected. If, however, a man had only grown offspring, particularly if they were male, then it was expected that he would remain unattached. If a man needed companionship, he could either get a slave-mistress, paelex, or a freed one, a concubina or contubernalis. Vespasian, for example, lived with a freedwoman for over a decade apparently to sidestep the dynastic problems so evident in the Julio-Claudian family.[68] The biographer of Marcus Aurelius is clearer: Marcus lived with a concubine to avoid putting a stepmother over his many children.[69] For men, then, remaining unwed could be as compelling as it was for women.[70]

Concubinage was, as a general rule, formed by two free persons, although frequently of different social status. In fact, the epitaphs from Italy show that concubines were almost exclusively freedwomen.[71] Susan Treggiari perhaps summed up the difference between a wife and a concubine best: 'They (were) expected to have the virtues of a wife, but not her pretensions.'[72] That is, in terms of behavior, the dynamics of the relationship were similar to a 'real' marriage. But the entanglements of patrimonies, dowries and other legal or economic considerations were conveniently absent. Indeed, should a concubine produce children – something apparently rare in the upper echelons of society[73] – there was no need to consider them as heredes. Thus, by possessing a concubine, a father need not worry about breaking up a patrimony.[74]

But what of marriage patterns for the broader society? Arguments have been presented by some to show that there was a general decline in the divorce and remarriage rate among the senatorial and equestrian orders over the course of the Empire.[75] Could it be that the changing trends in the upper classes, if they are true, represented an alteration of behavior consistent with the greater populace? The results are at best inconclusive. Iiro Kajanto argued that the lower classes did not in fact marry and divorce to the extent the upper classes did, claiming that they did not have the same kind of social pressures.[76] Others have seen remarriage as an integral part of Roman society in particular and pre-industrial societies more generally.[77] It is not clear whether either case can be argued with any degree of substance, but the patterns of divorce, widowhood, and remarriage are worth examining briefly.

Basically, lower-class marriages fell into three amorphous categories. First, there were slave marriages, which were of course not legally binding unions and were susceptible to dissolution at the whim of a master.[78] Second, there were a bewildering series of 'mixed' marriages, where the status of one or both of the partners had changed either prior to or during the match. The formal union in such cases was *contubernium*, where one partner was either a slave or formerly one.[79] But there were also legally recognized marriages between freedmen and freedwomen or between a freedperson and a free born citizen. These often consisted of the recently manumitted woman and her manumittor. Third, there were marriages between the poor freeborn. It is important to note at the outset, however, that all these fine legal distinctions were treated quite loosely, since they rarely involved people of significance.[80]

The variety of these unions makes it difficult to draw any conclusions about the behavior of the poorer members of Roman society. There may have been a greater marital stability among lower-class families, but it is impossible to be definite. For the classical period, then, the realms of divorce, widowhood and remarriage were largely represented by those who held economic and political power.

Children

The primary reason for marriage in the Roman world was the production of offspring. As much as it was the duty of a wife to obey and aid her husband, it was also her duty to provide her spouse with heirs. Should a child be produced in any way other than through *iustum matrimonium*, the child's status as a Roman citizen, as a legitimate and free person was brought into question. Producing a family had an equally straightforward goal: the transmission of wealth and property in an uninterrupted manner from one generation to the next.[81] Bastard children, on the other hand, were not subject to *patria potestas* and were not natural heirs. From the moment of birth, a child was under the *potestas* of its father or *paterfamilias*. In contrast, a wife had no legal rights over her offspring, although she had considerable moral authority. Indeed, it was said that the chaste *materfamilias* was second-in-command by being obedient to her husband.[82] That moral control could take on dynastic proportions.[83]

Once a child was born, the father decided within eight days whether it would live or would be exposed. Generally a baby was abandoned if it were physically or mentally defective. Given the high rate of child mortality and the preponderance of diseases, this was perhaps fairly common. But a *paterfamilias* might end a newborn's life for any reason, a power in accordance with *ius vitae necisque*. Such reasons might include the legitimacy of the child, or the desire to keep a family small for financial reasons. The necessity of providing dowries, a child's value as productive members of the *familia*, and the relatively low status of women generally also worked to favor infant boys over girls. In one extreme case, the Emperor Claudius ordered his daughter exposed at five months after birth.[84] While during the early Republic and perhaps among the lower classes,[85] exposure meant a child's death, later writers make clear that it was often a euphemism for a child to be (anonymously) taken by another.[86] On occasion such children, raised by others, could regain their status: Flavia Domitilla, Vespasian's wife, was just such a person.[87] But if a child were accepted by the father, he or she was fully a member of the *familia*.

Were a couple without issue, options existed to insure promulgation of the line. The most common means of insuring an *heres* was through adoption. There were two basic forms of adoption: *adoptio*, when a person was transferred from the *potestas* of one man to another; and *adrogatio*, when a male,[88] *sui iuris*, submitted himself to the *potestas* of another. Once the transaction had been completed, the adoptee, whether child or adult, was considered the natural successor and heir of the adoptor. If a man or woman died without any offspring, the rules of such succession (*bonorum possessio*) – most commonly applied in cases of intestacy[89] – created a framework for inheritance by which some semblance of continuity in the familial line could, if not be recreated, at least be simulated.[90]

The rearing of a child, particularly in the first dangerous year of life, was especially important to parents. The extensive medical literature on the subject suggests that at least among the upper classes there was a strong parental concern for the child even from an early age.[91] While scholars have questioned the level of emotional involvement parents had with their infants and their children generally,[92] the epigraphy and much of the literature support a high level of emotional attachment.

Whether such sentiments extended beyond the upper classes, for whom such works were written, is difficult to say. To mention briefly the epigraphic evidence, there were a multitude of references to children, from newborn to *adulescentia*, which expressed heartfelt pain and regret over their untimely deaths.[93] In the first three centuries CE, well over a quarter of the epitaphs were dedicated to this group in Rome (in the later Empire, that number had risen to over a third[94]). To be sure, that may say as much about child mortality as it does about sentiment. But clearly the expression of feeling in an epitaph suggests a cultural model for the treatment of and attitudes towards children, especially when certain formulae and standard terms are used. Even a Greek freedman like Publius Julius Lysippus, for example, could make much of his son, dead at 15, because of his filial piety.[95]

Often, though, affection for a child need not have been diluted by any requirements. Epitynchanus (a freedman?) spoke lovingly of his recently deceased daughter, who had sadly died on her seventh birthday.[96] Another dedication to the 5-year-old, Aulus Egrilius, not only recapitulates such sentiment, but includes a masterful effigy of the child petting a sacrificial goat.[97] Children could thus be appreciated and loved in their own right as well as for the culturally prized characteristics they might display. A child's proper behavior, then, was not a necessity for love; it merely augmented it.

A child's role in the family, however, especially when he or she passed the age of 7, was not purely the position of the loved youth. Like every member of the *familia*, he or she had duties and responsibilities. Since raising children represented a substantial investment in resources for rich and poor alike, their labor was often a valuable commodity. For the approximately 90 percent of the population which was rural, that labor meant help with farms of various sizes and kinds. The lot of urban children of the lower orders no doubt had analogous situations with familial professions. Should a father have many male children, he was completely within his rights to sell them into slavery.[98] He also had the option of placing boys and girls both into some form of indentured servitude or apprenticeship, or simply hire them out – often to a creditor.[99]

Children were also expected to care for their parents under the rubric of *pietas*, which implied both compliance (*obsequium*) and strong family loyalty. It was not quite love, but it was clearly something similar to it. *Pietas* was expected from one's spouse, siblings and parents as well as one's children. Hadrian exiled one man for killing his son as a breach of *pietas*.[100] Piety, if we may call it that, assumed respect and duty freely given. But for children in particular, it had a number of specific tasks associated with it. Taking care of one's parents in old age was especially important. Pliny describes with great emotion, for example, how the matron Fannia died in attendance of a sick elderly relative.[101]

Care for one's parents extended to a responsibility of sacrificing to one's ancestors. In a sense, children, by becoming his successors and by participating in the family cult, assured a father's immortality by the transmission of property and by ritual remembrance. The obsession of Romans of all classes with fitting burials and commemorations implies that children were morally responsible for their parents' inhumations.[102] To be childless, then, was a horrible situation that no married couple wanted to face. Ovid described the sorrow of the aged peasants, Baucis and Philemon: they neither had children to care for them or to bury them.[103]

For children of the upper classes, groomed for public life or for business, there were a host of different responsibilities. The duty to honor their ancestors, for example, often went beyond private worship. Their images and *tituli* – or achievements – were displayed prominently in the home.[104] On certain festivals, a son of a notable family was expected to display the waxen portraits, *imagines*, of his famous ancestors in public processions. Famous generals, ex-consuls, and the like came to life again as actors donned these masks and pantomimed their models. Displaying the glory and deeds of a *familia* was the highest form of honoring and remembering one's ancestors.

There was a more tangible obligation, however. As extensions of their *paterfamilias'* ambitions, offspring were expected to marry or divorce at his whim. This dynastic principle is most visible among the great senatorial families of the late Republic, whose members often married multiple times to either signify political alliances or to further their own political and monetary lives.[105] It was in fact impossible for two people to be married without the permission of the *paterfamilias* and he could order them divorced at any time.[106] Indeed, unless a son or daughter actively objected to the marriage,[107] a father formed and contracted the union. In the realm of marriage, '*si pater iubeat, obsequendam est*'.[108]

Finally, children of the upper classes had the obligation of furthering the fortunes and glory of their family as well as bringing no dishonor upon themselves. As Rome was a society that put great stock in land and property, this meant first and most importantly that the patrimony passed from a father to his son or to his daughter survive unsquandered.[109] It would take too long to enumerate the hundreds of laws concerning conveyance of property here, but we can say that a plurality of the notices in Justinian's *Digesta* deal with wills, legacies, intestacy and related issues. As a whole, they indicate a deep and lasting concern with the transmission of wealth from one generation to the next, and particularly the sanctity of land. Indeed, for the senatorial aristocracy, land was the only socially and, in certain cases, legally acceptable form of accumulating wealth.[110]

In sum, a son or daughter of any class was expected to fulfill whatever order a *paterfamilias* gave, provided, of course, it was legal. We should note in closing, however, that fathers did not always exercise the theoretical control that *patria potestas* afforded them. Two customs were important: the notion of the *bonus paterfamilias* (and his opposite, the *malus paterfamilias*) and the role of the family council (*consilium*). As we have noted, a good *paterfamilias* had to be a good manager of property. But being an effective administrator of chattel – land, property and slaves – was not all. A *paterfamilias* had to behave responsibly in his conduct towards his children. He should, for example, insure that his daughter was married to a good man, one who would neither use nor abuse her.[111] A son, particularly an older one, was not to be beaten without great cause, at least among the upper classes.[112] Mercy was a valued quality: in a treatise devoted to that virtue, Seneca relates favorably how Tarius sentenced his son to luxurious exile in Marseilles when the latter had plotted the death of his father.[113]

The family *consilium*, which seems to have included both male and female members, also acted as a curb against absolutism. Its numbers and membership were not set: in cases where kin was involved, it might include only kin;[114] in issues of household slaves, slaves, friends and other dependants might be on hand.[115] Its existence and power, however, were purely customary. Although quasi-legal, it remained an informal organization and one that rarely *had* to be called.[116]

The *paterfamilias'* decision may have been final, but even the most conservative and ancient supporters of his power looked ill upon a father who ignored the opinion of various family members. To take a semi-historical example, the censors of 307 BCE struck L. Annius' name from the senatorial rolls for failing to consult with his *consilium* before putting away his wife. More significant perhaps was Augustus' use of the Senate as a *consilium* in the matter of his daughter, Julia.[117] As W.K. Lacey points out, the timing of the affair was significant: he had already been named Father of the Country (*pater patriae*) and thus his handling of the situation might be seen as important to the state embodied in its highest body.[118]

In sum, *potestas* had limits, customary and moral. And by the imperial period, there were a number of legal strictures as well. But these were not necessarily seen as a diminution of the principle of *patria potestas*. Rather, there was a recognition that in an ideal society, a father's decisions were tempered and strengthened by reason and mercy, whether from him or from those under his control.

Half-siblings, step-siblings and other children

The frequent rate of divorce and remarriage had a marked effect upon children. Not unlike many Western families today, any one household could include a variety of children whose relationships to one another were bewildering. That was partially due to an understanding that *matrimonium iustum* was contracted to produce legitimate children and hence heirs (*heredes*). So it was naturally assumed that if an individual had agreed to wedlock, as opposed to any of a number of the less entangling options, he or she was intent on creating *filiae* and *filiifamilias*.

But unlike modern society, there was no question where legitimate children would go if a couple should happen to divorce: a Roman father's legitimate children always went with him. Only in cases of *spurii*, illegitimate children, would a child remain with the mother, since the father's identity might be unclear (unless he claimed his offspring publicly[119]).[120] But children born in wedlock were, after all, a father's heirs and members of his *familia*. Wives, unless they were *in manu*, were legally the ends of their lines:[121] women did not technically possess *potestas* and not until the reign of Commodus could they legally designate their own children as heirs.[122] So when a man decided to remarry, he came with whatever offspring he claimed. Were he to divorce a second time, the process would be repeated. In the more common case of widows, a woman choosing to remarry would retain whatever children she brought from her past marriages, but any new children would be her husband's.

From even these basic outlines, one can see the potentially extended framework of a single family. It would be theoretically possible for several step-siblings to be raised by a *noverca* and a stepfather (*vitricus*) with no living parent. It was also quite possible for two full siblings living in different houses. Let us take the example of the Caepiones, which illustrates the convoluted situations that could develop. Gnaeus Servilius Caepio married the sister of Livius Drusus. They produced Servilia, Servililia and Caepio Junior. When they divorced, Livia Drusa kept her children, apparently because Caepio had questioned the children's parentage. She remarried Cato

Solanianus and produced Porcia and Cato the Younger. Cato Solanianus died shortly after his son was conceived and Livia died soon in childbirth. The five children then remained in Drusus' custody, perhaps as an adoptive father, until he was murdered. With no relatives to care for them (Caepio Senior had been killed in the Social War and Drusus' wife had died years before in labor), Gnaea Servilia, the children's cousin once removed, ended up raising them in Livius Drusus' home.[123] This example is a relatively simple one. The examples of Sulla, Marc Antony and Oppicianus display the possible depth of such interrelations.[124]

Of course, within the household, there were a variety of children who had little pretense to kinship but were nevertheless part of the *familia*. Along with legitimate and free bastard children, it was common for *vernae* and *alumni* to be present and fully integrated members of the *domus*. *Vernae* were children born to slaves in the household and were thus slaves, too. It did not matter who the father was: they took their mother's status. Their place in the household appears to have been slightly better than those slaves who had not been born into the *familia*. Rawson indicates that they may well have been given a chance to apprentice in more specialized jobs than normal slaves carried out.[125] More rarely, they seem to have acted as surrogate children,[126] although from the paucity of legal documentation, they did not figure prominently in testamentary issues.[127]

The identities of *alumni* and *alumnae* are more difficult to define. The name literally means the 'nourished', but that says relatively little. They have been variously described as foundlings, foster-children, children of the freed still living in the household, and illegitimate children. In the case of some, clearly the last group was represented.[128] But for our purposes, their origin is less important than how they functioned in the household. Gaius noted that they were one of the few groups that could receive full Roman citizenship if manumitted (as opposed to Junian rights, which was more common).[129] The legal record of *alumni*, in contrast to *vernae*, was one that suggests closer affective ties. Leaving large amounts of property to an *alumnus/a* apparently was equivalent to passing on one's patrimony to a legitimate heir.[130] In fact, they were sometimes described as *heredes*.[131] To legitimate children, they might act as *de facto* siblings: there are various references to foster-brothers or *collactei*.[132] Seneca, with difficulty, describes an old man who claimed to be such a mate.[133] But to adults, they might act as surrogate children, offering love, affection and *pietas*. The term *deliciae* is often used when describing these children. Martial wrote a series of epigrams devoted to *alumni*, most of them in their teens. But even much younger children were held in similar regard: the 5-year-old Seppius, for example, was cruelly snatched from his beloved patron, Seppius Proculus.[134] Occasionally, too, there were pederastic overtones to these relationships. One boy, Glaucia, was especially missed by his former master, having died aged 13. *Epigram* vi: 29 is particularly poignant:

Non de plebe domus nec avarae verna castastae,
sed domini sancto dignus amore puer,
munera cum posset nondum sentire patroni,
Glaucia libertus nam Melioris erat.
Moribus hoc formaque datum: quis blandior illo?
aut quis Apollineo pulchior ore fuit?
Inmodicis brevis et aetes et rara senectus.
Quidquid ames, cupias non placuisse nimis.[135]

In some cases, the object of such affection was eventual marriage.[136] Most of the inscriptions and literature, however, suggest that *alumni* were beloved members of the *familia*, they brought joy to foster-parents and foster-siblings, and they were sorely missed whenever they passed away.

In sum, the children that might inhabit a Roman household could be multitudinous and varied. We must consider the fact that a father's legitimate offspring had a much wider assortment of contacts at an early age than might be commonly thought. Step-siblings theoretically might be only months apart in age, full siblings years, half-siblings decades. *Spurii*, *vernae* and *alumni* all represented family members under one roof with different backgrounds, legal statuses and roles in life. In short, the children of a Roman household were a microcosm of Roman society at large.

Extended family

The notion of extended family was an important one in ancient Roman society and it was recognized in law as a definition of *familia*.[137] In the early Republic and perhaps up until our period beginning around 100 BCE, this recognition was limited to the agnatic line. Legal responsibilities for underage children *sui iuris*, rights to intestate patrimonies, and of course the adoption of the *nomen* and *cognomen* all fell within the sphere of the father's kin.[138] Unless a mother were *in manu* of her spouse (in which case she became a member of her husband's *familia*), her legal rights over her children, the ability to declare her children heirs, and the ability to inherit from her husband were all severely limited. While that changed slowly in the imperial period, the agnatic principle always remained a dominant paradigm.

This does not say much about more distant kin, however. Deference for an elder, particularly if he were male, was expected by Roman society at large. This meant, in part, praising one's ancestors (without perhaps sounding too sycophantic). Sometimes these praises were quite personal, as in the case of Oscia Modesta from her grandson: '*avia carissima educatrix dulcissima*'.[139] Other times, they were more public. Tacitus, for example, in writing the *Agricola*, was doing more than composing a panegyric; it was an act of *pietas* on his part and one which Tacitus acknowledges early in the work: '*hic interim liber . . . professione pietatis aut laudatus erit aut excusatus*'.[140] Favors, in various forms, were also granted between relatives regularly. Pliny, for example, made it his responsibility to repair Fabatus' estate in Campania since he had been staying at the old man's invitation.[141] But favors need not have been given in only one direction. Cicero, for example, took his brother's son, Quintus Iunior, with him to Cilicia as part of his staff in 51 BCE and later arranged accommodation for him (and his own son) at the court of the Galatian king.[142]

Along with favors, blood relations also assumed responsibilities. Cicero, writing to Atticus, asked him to rein in the ebullience of their common nephew, Quintus Iunior.[143] In more dramatic passages of Roman history, such tasks might take on epic proportions: for example, Brutus and his sister's daughter, Lucretia. These duties might be as much a facet of *pietas* as was the respect showed by the young. If a member was in a position to help another member, he or she did so. For older relatives, this meant assuming a modicum of responsibility for younger members of the *familia*. For younger members, respect shown to their parents extended upwards and collaterally.

There are numerous other literary references, many detailing favors bestowed or granted on kin of some great – and often non-lineal – distance. Indeed, if testamentary law is any indication, familial devotion within the *gens* was not unknown,[144] although there is no real anecdotal evidence to substantiate that claim.[145] It is impossible, however, really to state definitively what degree of favor was owed to what degree of relation. Some authors have made interesting observations about various members of the family and have noted how Roman culture perceived their respective roles differently.[146] But such observations remain relatively crude and indeed may indicate ill-defined perceptions among the Romans themselves as to what constituted familial *obsequium*. We must content ourselves with this: while the extended family was important both conceptually and in practice, its role in the overall function of family life remains unclear.

Slaves and freedmen

It is a truism to say that slavery was an integral feature of Roman society, both in the city and in the country. They and their former compatriots, freedmen and women, were employed in all walks of life, from the simple laborer to the emperor's highest ministers. It was an institution that endured not simply because the economy, primarily agrarian, depended greatly on it.[147] Rather, the concept of slavery in law, literature and general belief was universally acknowledged and accepted. Even slaves themselves supported and propagated the institution: they could, to draw on a superficial example, own their own slaves. The state was a normal condition and thus was not questioned.[148]

Slavery was so ubiquitous that frequently free citizens even of humble means possessed a slave or two. It was said, for instance, that Sulla, before his political and financial fortunes changed, lived in poor lodgings with a single slave.[149] Whether true or not, it indicates slavery's existence on all levels of society. On any sizeable estate which was worked by slaves or in large-scale workshops, obviously the number of workers reached into the hundreds. But for the *domus*, in its more literal meaning of house and household, a moderate number of slaves and freedmen constituted an integral part of the *familia*.[150]

Legally, slaves were part of the *familia* in two ways.[151] First, they were members by virtue of being under the *potestas* of their masters; and second, they were mentioned specifically as chattel.[152] Their position in life was thought to be inferior (if not natural[153]), much like a child's status *vis-à-vis* his *paterfamilias*. Thus, if a slave disobeyed his master, he could be beaten or killed, depending on the circumstances. Indeed, should a man decide to have his slave executed, he could have it carried out by a municipal *lictor*, paying only for the material needed to cremate the unfortunate servant.[154] As property, they could be disposed of as a *dominus* wished.

That is not to say that slaves were solely seen as property. Idealists such as Seneca argued that slaves should be treated well since they were human: '*verberibus muta admonentur*'.[155] It was all too easy to abuse one's position as an exercise of power. Much more difficult and more commendable was running one's house well and engendering the respect of one's servants. Atticus, for example, only employed slaves who were raised in his own house – so-called *vernae*. The result was a small, but extremely efficient household staff ('*familia*').[156] Being a good *paterfamilias* was partially determined by the manner in which a master treated and managed his slaves.

Domestic slaves for their part were a varied lot. Many had specific or regular tasks in the household. Wet-nurses, *nutrices*, engendered considerable emotional attachments among their wards, who in some cases had large monuments erected to their former guardians.[157] *Paedogogi*, who were frequently elder slaves, oversaw the protection and basic education of the house's children. *Notarii*, or personal secretaries, were also quite common among the wealthy. There was, of course, a whole host of trained and untrained slaves, but apart from their duties, they were generally expected to be loyal to the *domus* and respect their *dominus*. In one funerary inscription from Locri, both a slave-woman's father and her 'husband' noted, '*Alimma quae in vita sua summa discipulina servavit, . . . pientissimae benemerenti*.'[158] As members of the *familia*, *pietas* was both required and expected.

Freedpersons were similarly employed in the *domus*. Often manumission meant little in the day-to-day life of a newly freed individual. Rarely would their position within the household change, either in terms of their work or even where they lived.[159] The difference of course lay in status. They could enter into business contracts of their own accord, rather than in the name of their manumittor.[160] Freedmen were allowed to contract marriages, something not allowed to slaves.[161] If they had legitimate children, they could leave property to these *heredes*.[162] And, of course, whatever children they bore (whether bastards or legitimate) were freeborn providing their mother was free.

But *liberti* usually owed their labor, or *operae*, to their former masters, agreed upon prior to emancipation,[163] providing such work was not illegal, dangerous or life-threatening.[164] Such obligation ended only under certain conditions, usually when a patron died. But even after the death of a patron, a former slave would often become attached to his household – in the Republic and early Empire, *liberti* usually took the family and clan names of their masters – and thus to that patron's heirs. Failure to comply with a patron's wishes could result in fines, liens against estates and even a reversion to their slave status.[165]

Slaves and freedmen then were unquestionably members of the *familia*, both in law and by custom. They were treated in many ways like children and although they could not inherit as the *heredes* of the *paterfamilias*, they nevertheless formed an integral part of the household. Not related by blood, it was the duty of all slaves and freedmen, along with their masters, to further the fortunes and well-being of their common *domus*.

Discipline

Children and slaves of the *familia* were united in the realities of their subordinate position. Both were subject to the rule of the *paterfamilias*. For sons in particular, correction was nominally done in aid of teaching and raising them to be respectful, law-abiding and self-controlled adults. Unsurprisingly, there were many suggestions from various authors concerning the raising of children, usually in connection with formal learning. Quintilian, for example, in a well-known passage argued that the whipping of students was bad pedagogy, suggesting that it bred a slave mentality.[166] The whipping of slaves, in contrast, was done merely to punish certain behavior: there was no greater plan other than instilling a master's will over his slave's. As Cicero explained, a father governs his obedient children, a master bullies and breaks his slave.[167] Thus, the nature of discipline for both groups was in theory inherently different.

Saller has tried to make the distinction surrounding the issue of a beating proper.[168] It is his contention that the *verbera* had a profound psychological effect on Roman society. The whip was understood as a punishment for slaves and consequently had deep implications for any free person who was subjected to the lash. Because it was an affront to a free person's *dignitas* in fact and symbolically, Saller concludes that while a child might be beaten, it was considered an inappropriate and repulsive thing.

One must question, however, the degree to which *patresfamilias* made such subtle distinctions. Such ideas, even if they were accepted by the majority of the population, remained definitely theoretical. '*Diligit hic natum, virga qui corripit illum.*'[169] The realities of disciplining a boy (and occasionally a girl) were replete with beatings of every sort. One grandfather thought it entirely appropriate to hit a boy if he were pulling juvenile pranks.[170] Seneca compared young children to dumb beasts and at times they had to be treated as such.[171] Pseudo-Plutarch noted that it was in fact incumbent upon a father to make use of a variety of methods, including physical punishment, to curb misbehavior and encourage obedience.[172] And quite apart from Quintilian's admonitions, the violence done to students was accepted and expected: Augustine as an adult vividly remembered his school beatings, still seething at the humiliations.[173]

The frequency with which boys were disciplined is another matter. 'Youth ought to be curbed by reason, not violence', as the saying went.[174] Classical authors advised fathers to be reflective and patient before they punished.[175] Consequently, the tendency to hit one's offspring was frequently reactive and immediate. Unless a son had done something outrageous, he was unlikely to be punished unless he misbehaved in front of his father. There was a certain acceptance that boys had to sow their wild oats. Cicero noted that they ought to be able to enjoy their 'fun and games'.[176] If the kind of pranks Augustine pulled as a boy was any indication of the realities of the earlier period, boys could lie, cheat, steal, destroy public and private property and swindle without fear of parental retribution.[177] To be sure, fathers would on occasion punish their sons frightfully, as in the case of the equestrian Tricho, who killed his son by whipping him to death (Tricho was subsequently murdered by a crowd in the forum).[178] But while these incidents may have occurred, clearly they were exceptional – as evidenced by Tricho's death – and the correction of sons was at best sporadic.

Fathers did have help. As Publilius Syrus noted, the *materfamilias* commanded second through obedience.[179] Obedient or not, women could wield considerable power over sons and daughters alike. Mothers unquestionably had direct control over their girls, training them more or less to be good wives, and this control extended well past marriage. They were generally acknowledged to have an interest in protecting a daughter's property and dowry once married.[180] Daughters were taught to report most everything to their mother, even as adults.[181] But often a Roman matron would take a hand in a son's upbringing, particularly if his father had died. Seneca's depiction of a mother's nurturing character was often at odds with her potentially domineering character.[182] She would normally have a strong say in who her son would marry, even if she were divorced,[183] and could wield considerable pressure if a son did not agree. Sassia was able to bring a charge of murder against one son through the authority of a son-in-law, ostensibly for failing to marry her chosen daughter-in-law.[184] But women had a far more effective weapon for bending their children's wills to their own: their personal, and sometimes considerable, wealth. A son, eager to embark on either a political or business career, could be beholden to his mother for immediate financial aid and the promise of a large inheritance. Julius Caesar had his mother Aurelia living with him in his home, the insinuation being that this was possibly due to her wealth.[185] A woman's power over her children, then, was not one of punishment, but of coercion.[186] Predictably, friction between a mother and a son growing into adulthood was a common event.[187]

When looking at slaves, the confusion over how to raise one's child was unmercifully absent with regards to punishment. We have already discussed how a good *paterfamilias* would punish his slaves in a thoughtful manner and how beating a slave indiscriminately showed a distasteful lack of control on a master's part. As property, however, slaves could be treated in any manner by their owners. There were certain limits. A master could not sell his slave to fight wild beasts.[188] But other means of punishment were available. In investigating a crime, a master could freely torture his (or her[189]) slave.[190] Much more common was some form of beating, often for trivial offenses. Seneca mentioned that a whipping might be induced by a cough at the dinner table.[191] Perhaps more revealing is Tacitus' surprising remark (to Romans, at least) that the Germans rarely beat their slaves.[192]

For more intransigent slaves, there were other options. They could be sold as troublemakers to the mines, a particularly horrible fate for an urban house slave. They could be branded or chained, making their conditions of manumission much worse than if they had been cooperative.[193] In extreme cases, a master could order a slave executed either by his own household or by a municipal judge.[194] Indeed, for certain infractions, the death of a slave was required.[195] Although Stoics might not concur, a master's goal was to keep his servants subordinate, obedient and cowed.

There is one last observation about the treatment of slaves. There was a whispered fear of them. That they made up a substantial portion of the population is well known. Perhaps the casual viciousness with which many were treated was carried out partially in reaction to this fear. Occasional slave revolts and the more common murder of a cruel master likely reinforced a siege mentality among the *paterfamilias*: 'tot hostes quot servi'.[196] If a master appeared unconcerned about any possibility of domestic violence, he was much more likely to survive: 'the master who fears his underlings is their slave'.[197] The Stoic solution, of course, was to treat one's slaves like fellow men and women, separated by status rather than humanity,[198] a notion that Christians quickly adopted. But for most slave-owners, there was an uneasy truce that could only be maintained by complete domination over members of one's own *familia*. As Livy noted, 'suus cuique domi hostis.'[199]

Conclusions

The classical Roman family was a dynamic and mutable unit. While the idealized family included images of the nuclear family, respectful children, and obedient slaves and freedmen, the reality was rarely so neat. Pressures for producing heirs, the inculcation into the household of sexual surrogates, the loose agglomeration of kin and unrelated individuals under one roof: all made the Roman *domus* a bewilderingly different scene than what was presented by moralists such as Plutarch or Valerius Maximus. Nevertheless, several overarching observations can be made.

First, remarriage was a reality and often a necessity. Although *univira* was prized, financial needs and political aspirations among the upper classes in particular could make marriage a transitory thing. Marriage, like a loan or a contract, was largely a business affair that rarely had any initial emotional backing. The process of ending a marriage and forming a new one created a series of relationships which could have political and economic consequences. The ease of divorce was particularly useful to furthering such ends, despite the provisos placed upon marriage dissolution by Augustus. The poor were perhaps less interested in ending marriages and with the advent of Empire, the need for political dynasties decreased. But with the relatively high rates of mortality among partners, particularly male ones, the chance for marriage alignments to both partners' advantage increased with age.

Moreover, there were a series of different relations that a man or a woman could enter similar to marriage, but without its legal and social strictures. They could fill the physical, emotional and psychological needs of its participants while allowing them the freedom to end the relationship should it become advantageous or necessary. Widowhood, whether for men or women, was accepted when a person's social viability ended. For men, that occurred when he possessed legitimate adult children ready to become *heredes*. For women, that meant remaining celibate when she could no longer conceive.

Second, the variety of children that might inhabit a household was multifarious. Those under the jurisdiction of the *paterfamilias* – whether in his role as father, as master or as patron – could be related by blood or marriage, could be legitimate or illegitimate, half-sibling or step-sibling, or could have no kin ties at all. It was common for the sons and daughters of the upper classes to live in a variety of households and for full siblings to live apart from one another. A person might also expect a growing number of brothers and sisters well into adulthood and perhaps after he or she had produced children. While they nominally were under the strict guidance of their fathers, the sons and daughters could often behave with a great deal of autonomy, no doubt exacerbated by the wide social network that began in the house with such a wide variety of youthful compatriots. Children who may have had little or no relation to the conjugal couple were also frequently present, acting as *de facto* heirs and providing an emotional focus for households that possessed few or no children. Their role in the *familia* may have been a consciously idealized one, but it was as real as any son's or daughter's.

Third, slaves were held in relatively low esteem by their masters and the society at large. While considerable emotional ties could exist between the governors and the governed – whether the latter were *nutrices*,[200] *concubinae*, *alumni* or other intimates – taken as a whole the state of servitude was a contemptible one. Discipline was harsh, at times sadistic. They may have been part of the *familia* and fulfilled vital roles in the *domus*, but they were chattel – movable property. Their counterparts, freedmen and freedwomen, fared somewhat better. While there was considerable stigma attached to their position, they nevertheless possessed important personal liberties that allowed them to more fully participate on a level footing with the free members of the *familia*. They performed duties for patrons, but there were limits. They could also contract legal marriages and were given an opportunity to free mates still enslaved. Most important, any child a freedwoman bore subsequent to her manumission was free. They, too, could create their own *familia*.

Christianity and the family

The history of Christianity in the Roman Empire is a long and complicated tale and it is not my intent to discuss it in any great length here. However, the ideas its adherents espoused concerning sex, marriage, adultery, children and a host of other private life issues are of great interest, particularly in the era which will be our primary focus. The production of works on such topics, both in the East and West, first became widely spread in the second century and exploded in the third. Latin literature was dominated by the voluminous work of Tertullian, the African presbyter and Montanist. His apologies and his theological treatises set the tone for future writers in Africa, Italy and elsewhere.

The availability of information on early Christian families is considerably more limited than our knowledge of its classical Roman counterpart and so this brief exposition may seem abbreviated in comparison. As recently as 1995, scholars have bemoaned the fact that knowledge and studies on the early Christian family remain woefully underdeveloped.[201] There are a number of reasons for this relative paucity. The overriding factor has clearly been the general obscurity in which Christian habits were kept. Obviously, this transcended the realm of family, touching upon many aspects of Christian life. As a result, there are relatively few passages about actual behavior in the family. This is not to say that Christians treated their religion like a mystery cult, which required silence. But early critics engaged in hyperbole when describing the movement's secrecy, and their antagonism help both to conceal and distort our understanding of the first Christian communities.

A second problem comes from the men producing early Christian literature. Much of our information comes from early theologians and spiritual writers, who often had other concerns. They clearly did not ignore their own moral precepts, but issues of proper comportment in familial settings tended to be peripheral both professionally and personally: such men often eschewed the entanglements of both family life and (optimally) sexual relations. Overwhelming eschatological concerns made 'a small number of prominent Christian men use . . . their bodies to mock continuity, by the drastic gesture of perpetual chastity'.[202] As Paul wrote to the community at Corinth:

37

The appointed time has grown short . . . The unmarried man is anxious about the affairs of the Lord, how to please the Lord . . . And the unmarried woman . . . is anxious about the affairs of the Lord, so that they may be holy in body and spirit.'[203]

This conscious decision to deny their sexual nature and society's pressures might go to extremes, such as Origen's ill-fated choice of self-emasculation, but such action was the exception rather than the rule. And to be sure, we should not paint with too broad a brush: prominent Christians such as Tertullian did marry and have children. But the value placed on abstinence often relegated issues surrounding family as lesser concerns.

Understandably, the sources are patchy. The surviving literature is not terribly helpful. Early Christian treatises were frequently more concerned with the establishment of an orthodox set of beliefs and, especially in the East, with questions of metaphysics and manner of worship. The Lyonese bishop, Irenaeus, for example, wrote an impressive and lengthy work, *Adversus Omnes Haereses*, but it did not touch upon the issues with which we are concerned here. Even the polemic against the new religion focused on the peculiarities of custom and belief and so is of limited value. Occasionally we get lurid charges of incest and sexual orgies, but these were largely based on standard rhetorical techniques to vilify an enemy.[204]

The epigraphic evidence before the third century is particularly scarce, practically non-existent. The inscriptions that do survive have even a narrower venue than pagan funeral commemorations. There is rarely more in a Christian memorial than a name and perhaps a '*neofitus in Deum*'. Christian ideals — not notably different from Roman ones — rarely appear. Even the iconography on funeral monuments is not as helpful as it could be, when it can be found. As such, inscriptions offer little help in the first centuries CE.

Third, the archeological evidence still remains largely an unknown. Scholars are slowly starting to look at how external factors, such as household architecture and city planning, affected the composition and function of the family.[205] But even the most careful observer must be leery of reading too much into the archeological record. It can supplement what we know from the written sources and can say a good deal about the important issue of living conditions and patterns, but its role, too, is limited.

These conditions taken into account, there is nevertheless enough information to provide a rough outline of early Christian ideas on the family and on behavior within the kin-group. We will accordingly look first at early thoughts on marriage, children and other issues dealing with the *familia*. We will then assemble the few examples we have of early Christian behavior and custom. As with the survey of the classical Roman family, almost all of the voices we hear tend to be male ones, although they are not necessarily drawn from the upper class. In fact, with the possible exception of Tertullian, many early Christian writers tended to be from the middling ranks of Roman society, which in itself presents limitations: Christianity, at least in its first years, was largely a religion for the poorer segments of society. But like the previous section, the purpose here is to provide a basis of comparison when we discuss the family in late antiquity. Again, we cannot analyse the latter in any depth without having a grounding in its structural, behavioral and moral roots.

Early Christian thought

For a Roman, the reason for entering a legal marriage was the promise of producing legitimate children and passing on a patrimony intact to the next generation. Marriage was therefore the beginning of the family, not a goal or end in itself. Judaic thought on this subject did not vary greatly from this attitude. Within the broader context of the Hellenistic era, family and kinship ties in Jewish communities were emphasized not only as an end unto themselves, but as a means of creating and reinforcing a cultural and ethnic identity.[206] More specific parallels between Roman and Jewish construction of family are also visible. Similar to the Roman *coemptio*, where a wife would be 'sold' to her husband, early Hebrew law conceptualized the relationship between husband and wife as that of owner and property.[207] Ancient Hebrew law emphasized, too, the heavily patriarchal character in marriage and the family: only men initially had the right to divorce and in early days had apparently practiced polygamy.[208] Moreover, analogous to the sympathetic notions of family life among Romans, Jews seemed to idealize the institution of marriage as a permanent union by the early first century BCE. The Damascus Document from Qumran, perhaps an extreme example, emphasized marriage as a divine gift.[209] But as a divine gift from the Creation, the institution was also understood as having a primary goal of propitiating the human race. As one Talmudic writer baldly put it, 'He who does not engage in procreation of the human race is as though he sheds human blood.'[210]

In contrast, the joining between a man and a woman, and the manner of that joining, was the most important human relationship to the early Christian. Children, other relations, slaves, freedmen, and the like were all ancillary. The essential pairing for the Christian was thus husband and wife, not husband and *familia*. The peculiarities of the religion's moral core as it developed and diverged from Judaic thought were the primary source for this new emphasis. In general, the interest in remaining celibate, which also metamorphosed over time, kept the focus on the relationship between man and woman rather than on husband, wife and children.

Like so much Christian thought, our story begins with Paul of Tarsus, the Pharisee-turned-Christian convert who was executed at Rome some time around 60 CE. He can arguably be called the first Christian theologian and his works were of tremendous importance to future generations of Christian authors. As an early Christian, he admittedly had little to go on. Jesus had made a few oblique comments on the nature of family life and interpersonal relationships, but little of it was definitive or even that substantive. In marriage, however, he seems to emphasize the contemporary rabbinical opinion on the permanence of marriage. Mark 10: 2–12 is perhaps the most explicit explanation of Jesus' views, where he calls divorce and remarriage by either spouse an act of adultery. Given that Judaic law prohibited a woman from even getting a divorce, it has been recently suggested that Jesus was addressing Graeco-Roman practices as well.[211]

Whether or not that was the case, the emphasis on one body – *sarx mia* – was the ideal.[212] So inseparable were husband and wife that anyone who might come between them would be cursed.[213] Jesus' thoughts were thus in line with contemporary Judaic thought: Qumran's *Genesis Apocryphon* cites an instance where Pharoah was cursed with impotence for two years for separating Abram and Sarai![214] The *only* exception to this permanence, and mentioned only once in the synoptic gospels, would be for 'dismissing' one's wife for adultery.[215] Paul paraphrased what little Jesus had to say on the subject of marriage and divorce and elaborated on those admonitions slightly. To his credit, he was careful to delineate divine imperative from his own thoughts on the subject.[216]

In essence, Paul's interest in marriage was negligible, it being a means to circumvent the inability of men and women to remain continent. As one scholar recently characterized it: 'Paul considered marriage a mechanism by which desire [*porneia*] could be extinguished.'[217] Paul, moreover, clearly considered it a relatively minor subject of discussion, since he mentioned that his comments were only in response to concerns put forward by members of the small Christian community in Corinth.[218] He himself boasted of his own capacity to remain abstinent, but pointed out fairly that 'each has a particular gift from God, one having one kind and another a different kind'.[219] This was at variance with Essene abstinence, which permitted intercourse in marriage only until conception of a child was achieved.[220] Despite the higher spiritual state that may come with sexual self-denial, then, it was not crucial to Paul's vision of salvation. Indeed, warm congress within marriage was apparently something that could be readily praised.

Not even the widowed, whom in the following centuries would be strongly discouraged from remarrying, were forbidden to wed: 'I say therefore to the unmarried and widows, it is good for them if they abide even as I. But if they cannot contain, let them marry: for it is better to marry than to burn.'[221] It is clear then that Paul recognized the power of *porneia* over the human psyche. Moreover, despite a deep respect for the institution of marriage, it was not one that had to be endured under any circumstance. Recapitulating Jesus' apparent exception for divorce (adultery), Paul seems in certain cases to have permitted separation, if not outright divorce, providing that the one leaving remained unmarried.[222]

That is not to say that Paul took marriage lightly. It was the central human relationship, so much so that he considered marriage more important than the bond between parent and child.[223] This was a radical notion to Roman thought and law, where the commonalty of divorce might be in dispute among modern scholars, but was by no means an unusual event. Permanence of course was a virtue, but Romans always placed the *function* of marriage – the production of children – over the nature of the relationship. Consequently, divorce was accepted and acceptable, especially in cases where there was no issue. Among Jews of the Common Era, too, laws permitting divorce despite marriage's idealized status had been extended from serious charges of immorality to something as insignificant as a ruined dinner.[224] Again, this does not say anything about the commonalty of divorce among ancient Jews, but it does confirm the broad parameters under which divorce was permitted. In contrast and perhaps in reaction to such frivolous action (legal or otherwise), marriage for Christians had taken on a transcendent spiritual dimension. But Paul's epistles illustrate that there had been an uneasiness among early Christian communities as to what this commitment precisely meant. His goal was to make clear that a nuptial union was something concrete. By marrying, a man and a woman became one flesh, *'una carne'*.[225] The conjugal couple was thus in theory inseparable, physically and spiritually.

But Paul's ruminations about the nature of marriage went beyond description of its character. In point of fact, he gave advice to both husbands and wives on the proper conduct in wedlock. The joining of a man and wife, like that in the Roman ceremony, was a relationship of unequals. Paul recapitulated the ancient Jewish belief which affirmed that woman was created from man and thus was forced to use him as a mediator between the divine and herself: 'man . . . is the glory of God, but the woman is the glory of the man'.[226] A wife was subordinate to her husband and was expected to act as such: *'Mulieres viris suis subditae sint, sicut Domino.'*[227] Such admonitions, of course, fit in well with the concept of the broader Roman concepts of patriarchal authority. But unlike a Roman marriage, Paul enjoined upon the man a specific duty as well: love your wife as you would your own body, *since* husband and wife were one.[228] A man should therefore nourish and cherish his wife because every man loves his own body. It is not entirely clear what precisely the nature of that love was, but clearly Paul had wanted husbands to treat their wives with respect and avoid both violence and public disgrace. Perhaps this idea was an echo of contemporary Judaic thought, with which Paul was no doubt familiar: 'Concerning the man who loves his wife as himself, who honors her more than himself, . . . of him it is written: thou shalt know that thy tent is at peace.'[229] Paul seems to have taken this sentiment and changed it to make it a necessary virtue for both spouses. Love in Christian marriage, then, was of considerable importance.

This concept of mutual responsibilities transcended the husband–wife relationship. Quite apart from marriage, Paul offered advice for other members of the family as well. Children were the natural by-products of a union between man and woman, although they were not its primary purpose. That is why Paul could accept the Jewish blessing of 'fruitful seed' without deeming it in any way significant.[230] A child's appearance was to be expected, especially since the former Pharisee tried to discourage abstinence within the married state itself: 'and come together again, that Satan tempt you not for your incontinency'.[231] True, Paul did argue in his first epistle to Timothy that bearing children might save a woman.[232] But children in point of fact were of even less importance to Paul's vision of salvation than marriage had been; it was simply that he found it necessary to comment upon the parent–child bond since Christian marriages resulted in Christian children.

His advice, as one might expect, was based on the commandment to honor one's mother and father.[233] Similar to the Roman concept of *obsequium* was the Christian concept of obedience (*oboedientia*). Like the original divine order, Paul claimed that obedience should be given so that a child might live a long life, implying that a father had the power of life and death over his offspring. But again, like the husband to the wife, the father had a responsibility to his sons and daughters. Parents were to insure harmony in the house by teaching them to love Christ and to follow Christian ways.[234] But there was more to the statement: a parent was to avoid '*ad iracundiam provocare*'. The imposition of will at the cost of breaking one's house was the sin of pride. Authority, tempered by fairness, should be the rule. Emphasizing, too, the patriarchal character of this relationship, Paul expanded Jesus' brief references to parents and concentrated on the father as the object of respect.[235]

Significantly, then, the notion of paternal and husbandly obligations was reversed in Paul. Love was an added bonus to the Roman marital ideal, but it was not required in *concordia*. Love for a child, however, should be natural in a parent, regardless of the affections a child might return. In Paul's vision of the Christian *familia*, however, these ideals were turned on their heads. *Concordia* was the rule between generations, and love (through the unity of Christian belief) was reserved for the conjugal couple. Again, love might exist between parent and child, but it was not necessary as long as the child had love and respect for the divine. How this affected (or was supposed to affect) the parent–child relationship is unclear, but it nevertheless offered a somewhat different model of behavior.

Finally, Paul offered some advice on the relationship between master and slave. As with most Mediterranean societies in antiquity, slavery was an integral part of Judaic society. Like Seneca, Musonius Rufus and other liberal Stoics, Paul did not question the institution of slavery, only the manner in which it was conducted. And like Seneca, who thought slaves should be treated as fellow human beings, Paul believed in a mutual respect between *dominus* and *servus*. There was, as he pointed out, neither bond nor free in Christ.[236] Paul, too, admonished masters for treating their servants ill, not because it showed a lack of control and respect on a master's part, but because poor treatment reflected badly on them as Christians.[237] And like the husband and wife or the parent and child, there was a reciprocal quality to this relationship. Slaves had to obey their masters to the best of their ability and with a glad heart.[238] With slaves, Paul offers the promise of equal salvation: they can receive heavenly rewards as easily as the free. Slavery was an institution of man and so ought to be respected in that context. Humanity was an institution of a higher order. Paul's own close relationship with the slave, Onesimus, was a case in point.[239]

But in addition to these specific relationships, Paul also created an important metaphorical language for the Christian community. Separated in age, space and status, Paul unsurprisingly turned to the family as a model to promote unity. All members of the faith were *adelphoi* ('brothers and sisters'), in direct contradiction to those things that did separate them. Indeed, some have gone so far as to argue that this new fictive kinship was supposed to supplant actual kin ties.[240] Further terms abound: God the Father, Jesus the Son, children of God. Paul's formulation of a surrogate family was no doubt aided by Jesus' subordination of family in favor of the divine.[241]

Whether or not these phrases were to be taken literally, their use did have certain ramifications on Christian organization generally and the concept of the family in particular. First, by using the language of family, Paul created a device which future Christian authors could use to 'communicate a Christian theology as well as construct . . . a church community with a certain kind of leadership and certain patterns of interactions between its members'.[242] Of greater relevance to our interests, the creation of such language reinforced the highly hierarchical nature of family relationships, whether in the Roman or the Judaic tradition. Future Christians would emphasize the function of the ideal spouse, parent, and the like within the rigid framework of family structure. Finally, it centralized the role of religion within the family. It was not simply that Christians were to comport themselves morally. Paul had made religion and its dissemination a *function* of family. This was of particular importance in late antiquity. It is also probably why Paul sought in no way to diminish the family's role in Christian life: it offered a natural vessel by which to transmit the gospel and organize the proselytized. Paul's discussion on the nature of family life was limited, but it provided the rock upon which later Christians built their vision of the *domus*. Hermas, a second-century slave who was freed in Rome and subsequently became a wealthy merchant, elaborates on Paul's statements on marriage and children in a series of visions collected in *The Shepherd*.[243] Hermas envisioned a man's familial responsibilities in broader terms. A husband was expected to insure tranquillity and the moral standards within his own household (*oikia*).[244] By explaining to his wife and children the history and dangers of human sin, forgiving them for their past transgressions, a household head could insure moral decency and internal order. Wrongs caused by children in particular were to be forgiven, since that would aid in their moral learning.

There were of course circumstances that might lead to a marriage's end. In agreement with Jesus' statement in Matthew,[245] Hermas saw unilateral divorce acceptable for either party in cases of unrepentant adultery.[246] But Hermas argued for perpetual celibacy until there was reonciliation and forgiveness. Only when the divorced spouse was truly penitent could he or she be reaccepted.

Hermas also advocated something relatively new in parenthood. The responsibility for the moral upbringing of children, at least among wealthier families, traditionally was the lot of mothers and wet-nurses for the first several years of life,[247] and pedagogues and teachers thereafter.[248] In Hermas' opinion, not only must both parents accept the responsibility for a proper rearing and education, but the father for the consequences of failure. This was a far cry from Cicero's claim that a father could not be blamed for the moral failings and crimes of their sons.[249] One early Greek Christian even argued that marriage at a young age prevented a child from sinning and a parent from that sin's moral responsibility.[250]

These basic pre-third-century ideas voiced by early Christian writers in the West were more fully developed and expanded with the appearance of Tertullian. He was the first Christian theologian to write in Latin and his work had enormous influence in Rome, where he resided,[251] as well as the rest of the Western Empire. Receiving a formal classical education, Tertullian used his skills to publish apologies, treatises, and polemical attacks in the defense of Christianity. Although his views on sin after baptism and continuing prophecy would eventually lead him to espouse Montanism, he nevertheless shaped Western Christian thought for many centuries.[252]

A lawyer by trade, Tertullian was a prolific writer with a sharp wit and a sharper tongue. While many of his works were directed against heretics and Roman persecutors, many others were directed to Christians as treatises of proper moral conduct and comportment. His thoughts on the sanctity of marriage, the importance of upright behavior, and his harsh interpretations of the consequences of sin give his work a decidedly different sense than his contemporaries. These are not the sage ruminations of a respected Christian elder, but primers of religious instruction. His forceful, didactic tone is unmistakable and gives his writings perhaps a more practical flavor. But because of his manner – and his own self-perceived obligations as a family man – Tertullian offers the most complete treatment on marriage and sexuality in the West until the fourth century.

Tertullian's take on the family was somewhat more extensive than Paul's, at times interpreting scripture quite loosely. His two major works relating to the family, *To his Wife* (*ad Uxorem*) and *On Monogamy* (*de Monogamia*), make it clear that the single marriage was even more central to his theology than that of earlier Christians writers. As he pointed out, celibacy might be preferable to marriage, but the latter was nevertheless a '*bono isto*' because it was established in creation.[253] The tenor of married life was far more complex than having divine approval, however, and Tertullian spent some time in describing the nature of that state.

Tertullian was the first to thoroughly castigate the Roman ideal of wedded unions as a means to produce children. He rejected the notion of posterity and worldly ambitions as reasons for begetting offspring.[254] Sons and daughters may be the natural result of marriage, but they detracted from one's concentration on the divine and the attempt to achieve salvation. Children were to be endured, but parents to be pitied: *'Vae autem praegnantibus et nutrientibus!'*[255] This was the clearest rejection of traditional Roman marriages that had yet been voiced. Rejecting the notion of children as important in a person's road to paradise was one thing. To reject them out-of-hand as unimportant was quite another and such opinions in the future were only voiced indirectly through the filter of exhortations to chastity. Not even Jerome, who expressed the greatest anxiety about marriage and children in late antiquity, would be so extreme.

Moreover, the confines of marriage were tight. Marriage may have been good, but the right kind of marriages was necessary. A single marriage was permitted – the marriage of Adam to Eve condoned that.[256] A second marriage, presumably for a man as well as a woman, was unthinkable. Tertullian – perhaps consciously, perhaps not – directed this statement to widows only.[257] In fact, his ostensible purpose for writing *ad Uxorem* was to insure his wife knew how to behave in the eventuality of his death. A second marriage was tantamount to adultery, since it was, in Tertullian's eyes, associated with attraction of a worldly sort.[258] Striking a chord which later Christian authors would also echo, Tertullian seemed to be the first author to suggest that widowhood was in fact a form of freedom: 'Why do you reject the freedom that is given to you in returning to the bonds of matrimony?'[259] Freedom here was not the freedom from the obedience owed to one's husband: that was assumed in the natural order of things. This was instead freedom from the sexual demands of one's mate, which a wife could also not refuse. By remaining celibate in widowhood, a woman regained a measure of her purity, since she had rightfully given herself only to one man. *Univira*, then, was an even more important ideal among Christians than it had been among Romans. *Univira* was greatly admired by Romans and Christians both, but *multivira* was especially to be despised by the latter: 'Ought we to marry every day?'[260]

Tightening those confines even further, Tertullian devoted the second book of *ad Uxorem* as a warning against 'mixed' marriages. A woman should never enter into a union with a non-Christian. In those cases, a wife inevitably becomes a slave of her husband and thus must act as a pagan to be an obedient wife.[261] The underlying implication of this section of course was that a wife should be subordinate to her husband, even to the exclusion of her own religious beliefs. That was the real fear permeating throughout Tertullian's writings: he seemed unable (or unwilling) to reconcile Paul's thoughts on the position of wives and women more generally with the dangers associated with heathen worship. The implied assumption must have been that by choosing to marry a non-Christian, a woman had in fact rejected her religion. The only exception that Tertullian granted were cases where two gentiles married and the wife subsequently converted to Christianity.[262] Only then were women both allowed to preserve their marriages and risk their husbands' wrath by practicing Christianity.

The tight bonds of matrimony, in Tertullian's opinion, were to be further squeezed on either side by virginity and celibate widowhood. Fornication within the married state was tolerable, but outside of it was sin. He likened extramarital sex to murder and idolatry.[263] Adultery, then, clearly had wider meanings than just sexual congress between two persons not married to each other. Although concubines were not mentioned, for example, it becomes apparent from a long exegesis on Paul that they were forbidden and, married or unmarried, a man who had one was committing adultery.[264] Refraining from activities or habits that might excite *porneia* was especially important. Nor did women alone bear the burden for discouraging such behavior: men, for example, were expected to dress conservatively and modestly whether married or single.[265] Sexual desire affected everyone.

Tertullian's *Exhortatio ad castitatem* and his earlier works revel in the value of virginity and celibacy. It was not simply that they were required elements of a Christian life. Permanent virginity was given by the '*voluntatem Dei*'[266] and celibacy after marriage was '*ad testimonium fidei*'.[267] That is, these things were signs of one's faith. As if to underline the point, Tertullian threw down the gauntlet of non-believers at his fellow Christians. He noted with disdain (and dismay) that pagans, in the service of evil, took vows of celibacy and chastity in the name of their religion: 'He [Satan] challenges the servants of God by his own [vows of] celibacy as if the two were equal! Even the priests of Gehenna are continent!'[268]

Tertullian, in all, offered a new definition of marriage. It was not a state to be enjoyed for women and men, but endured. Its outlines were formed by the borders of virginity and celibacy. Marriage was a safety zone in which sexual congress could be permitted. Within that zone, a wife's function was to serve her husband to the best of her ability, preferably in his attempt to uphold the tenets of their faith.[269] The husband's rule, it may be inferred, was final, both in the matters of the marriage itself and as it pertained to the rest of the family. But Tertullian was not concerned with the *domus*. He was concerned with fidelity and conduct.

The rest of the human race, then, was a potential wasteland of adultery and *stuprum* surrounding that small refuge. But the oasis of marriage, if it can be called that, was itself also a desert isle. Men and women were trapped by their own carnal desires. Only with the death of a spouse could a widow (or widower?) be rescued, returning to the safe harbor of continence. At that point, a woman could leave her inferior state, a 'second-best modesty',[270] and practice her own virtue.

In sum, Tertullian both accepted and discarded certain aspects of the ideal Roman marriage, although he certainly would not have interpreted his thoughts as radically different from the Christian mainstream. While recapitulating important concepts such as *univira*, condemnation of adultery and *patria potestas*, his writings present a rejection of many other traditional beliefs and behavior surrounding the family as well. His pronouncements on virginity, marriage and widowhood – also beginning to be formulated in the East – would become models for many fourth-century authors in the West. It is unfortunate that such a voluminous writer did not say more about children, extended family and the like. But he would have undoubtedly answered that these issues had little to do with the individual's role as a Christian.

There are a few more references to the role of children and parents in subsequent authors. Of particular interest is the relationship and its characterization. Commodianus, a mid-third-century bishop from North Africa, in his poem, *Instructiones*, made several references to children. In one section, which unfortunately is only partially extant, he discussed the apparent problem of infants forsaken by heaven.[271] He placed the responsibility fully on the heads of their parents, suggesting that mothers and fathers renew their efforts in being good Christians and that presumably – since the passage is lost – a child not be deprived of grace. Such harsh reasoning must be weighed against the real love parents apparently felt for their children. Yes, Minucius Felix agreed, the responsibility of parents were to raise their children to respect and love Christ,[272] but he recognized the loving bond between parent and child (especially the younger child)

> Nam negotii et visendi mei gratia Romam contenderat, relicta domo, coniuge, liberis, et – quod in liberis amabilius – adhuc annis innocentibus et adhuc dimidiatu verba temptantibus, loquellam ipso offensantis linguae fragmine dulciorem.[273]

There was a recognition, then, that in addition to responsibilities, there was a deep satisfaction in fulfilling those duties.[274]

Along with a parent's role as educator, a parent was expected to deal with realities of everyday life. The matter of a dying child, for example, was an area of concern that Commodianus addressed. He argued that the Roman custom of commemorating a son's death, complete with the theatrical outbreaks of emotional excess, was unseemly and inappropriate for a Christian.[275] A parent ought to mourn on the inside. Ostentatious black togas, large ceremonies, professional mourners and loud wailing were the providence of heathen funerals, not those of Christians who had salvation in their eyes. A parent dishonored his child as well as himself by engaging in such histrionics.

Some Christian writers recognized, then, that children were of greater importance than Tertullian, or even Paul, implied. Cognizant of their choices, parents had as much responsibility to their progeny's spiritual state as they did to their own.

Early evidence of the family in Christianity

Having briefly discussed some early ideas on the family, one must ask whether such advice and instruction were followed by Western Christians of the first three centuries CE. The answer is not readily answerable. Even more than discussions of ideal comportment in the familial setting, evidence for actual behavior is scarcer. Much of the evidence for the early Church, largely gleaned from Eusebius, dealt with the Eastern Mediterranean. The brief glimpses of the West from this time refer to the length of a bishop's reign or the occasional religious dispute.[276] These are hardly indications of Christian private life.

A significant problem with the surviving material, in the first century especially, is the differing family types that appear in early writings. As Halvor Moxnes has recently made quite clear, even in the East there was variance: the Gospels seem to deal with rural Palestine and the epistles of Paul and others seem to be largely addressed to a Hellenistic urban population.[277] For the West, the problem is even more difficult. Local variation between Rome, the Italian cities, and other urban centers, was no doubt as great as the differences between town and country. Much more than the classical Roman family, then, where there was at least a unity of expressed ideals in the cities (if not reality), our reconstruction of early Christian behavior will be unfortunately incomplete.

Marriage can only be guessed at, although there are a few specific references to married men and women in the first three centuries. We can affirm first, however, that the permanence and sanctity of a union were of overwhelming importance, whether it be a *iustum matrimonium* or not. Bishop Callixtus of Rome in the early third century apparently allowed for a kind of *contubernium* between upper-class women and lower-class or even enslaved Christians – suggesting among other things a dearth of marriageable spouses.[278] It did not have to be a legal marriage providing it was permanent.[279] And indeed there is some epigraphic evidence to suggest that not only did Christian noblewomen do this in the third century, but that such practices included more than the Christian population.[280]

Because of the high value placed on virginity and celibacy, however, relatively few accounts of actual marriages between Christians exist from this age. More often, there are tales of individuals attempting to avoid marriage or wanting to maintain a celibate state once they were in marriage. But these were Christian *exempla*, celebrated in the *vitae* of saints and therefore invite caution. Particularly in the case of saints' lives written two, three or even more centuries later, there is a question of accuracy. Much more problematic are the attempts of later authors to apply their contemporary Christian values to these figures. These included spurning marriage, an attraction to chastity and virginity, and a host of other anti-social behavior designed to illustrate a saint's sanctity. Lucia of Syracuse's martyrdom, for instance, precipitated by a jilted suitor who subsequently denounced her – and who was parenthetically saved from a life of prostitution – is surely a complete and very late fabrication.[281] The *passio* of Procopius is an even better example, although it contains no information on the family. Eusebius' quite straightforward account of his martyrdom was later supplanted by no less than three fictitious and outlandish traditions.[282] So we must cast a skeptical eye over even those accounts which are believed legitimate. It is clear, too, that the acts chronicled in *vitae* were not representative of common behavior for most Christians.

The life of Macarius of Rome is an early saint's life that seems to have some grounding in cultural reality. His parents seemed to be doing those things well-to-do parents of the Empire did for their children, arranging a marriage contract for their son and holding a large and apparently happy feast at his nuptials:

> Cum autem pueriles excessissem annos, me renuente ac nolente, pater meus desponsavit mihi uxorem, diemque statuit nuptiarum. Interea adornato, cum iam frequentia populi meus hilarior effectus, cunctos invitatos hortatur ad voluptatem conivivii.[283]

While this may have been literary artifice on the author's part,[284] surely the situation could not have been presented if it did not represent familiar circumstances, even to Christians. But even this example and others like it do not reveal much: they are vague and to a certain extent archetypal.

Two other references to married couples in the sources, however, do seem to offer some slight insight into the practical problems of reconciling their religious lives with the demands of social convention. We know that Vibia Perpetua, the famous second-century African martyr, had a surviving mother and a father. It seems, moreover, in contravention to Tertullian's arguments, that her father was polytheist and her mother was a Christian.[285] But their relationship is a mystery: were they divorced, was the mother a convert, did they live together?[286] In the case of Perpetua's parents, however, we are faced with the important, if unanswered, questions regarding a spouse's responsibilities to one's mate. The tension of having a mixed couple was perhaps articulated in the tension between the pagan father and his Christian daughter, of which we will speak more below. But the issue must have been increasingly common as the new religion slowly made inroads into Graeco-Roman civilization.

Our third couple from the second century CE, also unnamed, is found in the *Second Apology* of Justin Martyr.[287] While this couple may have lived in the East (the husband visited, and perhaps lived in, Alexandria), they appear to have been Westerners and were definitely Roman citizens: the legal language of their divorce and subsequent trial argues for citizenship.[288] Their status aside, they had been both originally been pagans, and both, according to Justin, had led sinful lives. The wife, however, had converted to Christianity and given up her impiety. After some time, when her husband refused to convert, she divorced him. Spurned and bitter, he had denounced her to the authorities, but she managed adroitly to avoid trial. We never hear from this woman again, although her vindictive husband did manage to engineer the conviction of the man who converted her.

The wife's actions seem to contradict both Paul and Tertullian's rationales for separation. Justin never directly accuses her husband of adultery, although he does imply it at many points: the verb he uses is '*akolastainein*', which means to be dissolute. But in fact, the only specific accusation he makes is that the husband was 'drunkenly'. Clearly, had the man been adulterous, his wife would have been in the right to divorce him (and Justin would have certainly said so in such a situation).[289] The Christian grounds for divorce are thus not clear in this case. Tertullian, who actively argued against mixed marriages, could not have condoned such a split, either: the case of conversion after marriage was the only exception to a Christian–pagan union.[290] Here, then, in one of our few concrete examples of a marriage, we see that there was a strong separation between the proper course of action and the actual course taken. But again, the affair speaks to the crucial issue of religious conviction versus marital responsibilities.

Unlike some Eastern authors, Western Christians neither found the topic of children worthy of much discussion in the first centuries nor did they idealize the state.[291] As a result, children were even more rarely mentioned in the early sources, but there is something a bit more substantial to the surviving information. One of the best accounts addressing parental responsibilities and inter-generational dynamics was the martyrdom (*passio*) of Perpetua and Felicitas. Originally, the work was believed to be partially autobiographical – apparently penned by Vibia Perpetua – and thus likely to be more reliable. As such, it deals with real events told by the individuals who experienced them. Moreover, its purpose was clearly didactic: it had been addressed not just to brethren (*fratres*) so that they may witness and follow the example of the martyrs, but to young children (*filioli*) as well.[292] Thus, on two levels it was important to the topic of parent–child relations.

First, a rare view into the tension between adult children and their parents is fully visible here. Even though her unnamed father was not a Christian, it is clear that Perpetua treated him with considerable respect and had a deep-abiding love for him. She constantly stated how she felt sorry for his condition and position: '*sic dolui pro senecta eius misera*',[293] '*ego dolebam pro infelici senecta eius*',[294] and '*ego dolebam casum patris mei quod solus de passione mea gauisurus non esset de toto genere meo*'.[295] It seems, too, that she was uncomfortably aware that her contrariness was both improper and unseemly. It was to her father and not to the proconsul adjudicating her case that she tried to explain and make him understand her position. Her father, by contrast, pleaded with her to repent, almost as a child would. He appeared to have the authority to hurt her and make her obey, but could not bring himself to force or harm her.[296] It is clear, too, that she disliked defying her father, especially because he so obviously loved her, but her religious conviction overruled all other concerns. Perpetua acted with the proper filial deference, as was expected, but loved a divine father more – just as Jesus had advised. In sum, the proper feelings of love and respect were contrasted against an inversion of the parent–child hierarchy. *Potestas*, the symbol and expression of male authority, was in this case sublimated.

Second, the *passio* provides us with a broader picture of the relationship between mother and her offspring. Both Perpetua and Felicitas were also concerned about their newborn children. Their interest in caring for their babies was not a desire to preserve their own lives, but to insure that they were healthy and would be raised Christian. Perpetua's father kept his new-born granddaughter, presumably so that she could be brought up by her Christian grandmother and uncle, and Felicitas' baby was to be raised by another Christian woman in her community. The concern for their children's physical and spiritual welfare, then, went hand in hand. Having fulfilled their duties as mothers and as Christians, they could both concentrate on martyrdom.[297] This perhaps was an implication that among women, motherhood came before martyrdom. Indeed, Perpetua expressed real relief that her infant was weaned quickly with no ill effects.[298] The sense of relief, too, that both women felt when they realized that would be martyrs after all suggests that it was not something of which they could be assured. Women, then, even as virginity and celibacy were coming to be prized, were still seen primarily as mothers to their children. That that concern extended to a spiritual caregiving would be further enunciated in the late Roman era and their examples as mothers would be models in the fourth and fifth centuries.

Other information about Christian children and parents is patchy. There have been recent examinations of the role of children in the New Testament, mostly in a metaphorical capacity, but little beyond that.[299] We also occasionally hear mention of a Christian child here or there, as in the case of Octavius' young children that so obviously delighted him or Hermas' pagan sons who reported him.[300] But these brief asides offer little which substantively characterize the nature of the child's role in the family or the nature of the relationship between parent and child. We are left, then, with the stories of Perpetua and Felicitas. What we can construct from their experience, however, is the sense that there is a tension between the responsibilities of Christians as a Christian and their responsibilities to their families. Like the conflicts found in marriage, parents and children both found it difficult to follow the ideals espoused by the notion of reciprocal responsibilities with the realities of life.

Finally, our knowledge of slaves, particularly so-called domestic slaves who were fully integrated into the household, is equally thin. Hermas, as we have mentioned, had been a slave and his former mistress was a Christian who had freed him.[301] But the circumstances of his servitude and his manumission are unclear. A slightly fuller description of a Christian slave's life was that of Callixtus, later bishop of Rome during the reign of Elagabulus. He had been the slave of a Christian imperial freedman, charged with running a bank for Christians. Fleeing when the business failed, he was caught and sentenced by his master to hard labor in the public bakeries. His Christian creditors provided for his release from the flower mill, but Callixtus was soon convicted to work in the mines of Sardinia for fighting in a synagogue on the Sabbath. It was only by the graces of bishop Victor of Rome and an imperial concubine that he supposedly escaped that fate and was later called to the clergy.[302]

This tale, largely colored by the criticism of his enemy, Hippolytus, provides the best early example of the relations between a Christian master and slave. The behavior of Callixtus, if his detractor is to be believed, was hardly exemplary. But it seems, too, that his master, Carpophorus, was less than sympathetic to his slave's failings. Indeed, other Christians secured his release, perhaps intimating a greater concern for the slave, although it was supposedly out of Christian forgiveness that Carpophorus consented. Moreover, at Callixtus' trial before the prefect of Rome, his master tried to claim that his slave was not a Christian, probably as a means of explaining his own behavior to his Christian creditors and furthermore protecting himself from a magistrate not likely to be sympathetic to his religion. These may have been relatively common incidents for a typical *dominus* and *servus*, but they did not characterize the sort of Pauline ideal of master–slave relations.

The vicissitudes of Callixtus' life, however, do underscore an apparently common activity practiced among early Christian communities. As semi-collegial bodies, each local church commonly collected and possessed a fund which clerical officials (usually presbyters and deacons) would use to help the poorer members of the congregation. The most common subjects of such charity tended to be widows and orphans, understandable in a society with little or no public welfare. But there is evidence from early and mostly Eastern sources that such monies were used to effect corporate manumissions of Christian slaves. Ignatius' letter to Polycarp in the late first or early second century is perhaps the best example of this activity.[303] In the epistle, the bishop admonishes Polycarp and others in the Smyrnan congregation not to abuse the process of manumission, but also emphasizes the dangers of doing so at Church expense. If this was an attempt by Ignatius to establish the primacy of the bishop in the congregation, as Harrill has argued, then clearly the issue had broad implications among many Christian communities.[304] True, this was an Eastern bishop writing to an Eastern congregation, but slavery and its associated problems were ubiquitous. Indeed, this was not the first time the issue had been addressed among Christians.

Paul himself had actually addressed the topic when he wrote to Philemon, requesting that the slave, Onesimus, be freed as a fellow Christian.[305] There, the apostle wrestled with the thorny problem of how to take his spiritual protégé out of the bonds of slavery from an equally Christian master and yet not upset the traditional master–slave dynamic. Whether he was successful or not is unknown, but it forced an understanding that slavery might be ended for their brethren in certain circumstances. That the practice seems to have largely disappeared by the end of the third century, however, suggests that the need to free fellow Christians eventually fell out of favor, at least as an institutional activity. As we shall see in later chapters, an overriding factor in its abandonment was an acceptance that one's status on earth had little to do with one's status in the afterlife.

In sum, information about family life among Christians through the third-century West is woefully sparse. From the surviving bits and pieces, it seems as if behavior among Christians was generally consistent with what Christian authors argued, or at least they were cognizant of the issues involved. But perhaps more significantly. It is also clear that the behavior of Christians was not inconsistent with traditional Roman attitudes about the family. The matter of behavior and its relation to the ideals espoused by early Christian authors – in contrast to the later Roman Empire – must remain, however, inconclusive. Barring the discovery of new evidence on the subject, the first three centuries are largely still a mystery.

Conclusions

The first three centuries CE witnessed profound political, economic and social changes in the Roman Empire. The Christian family's metamorphosis during this age – if such a thing can be said to exist – remains fuzzy and ill-defined. But there were several notable developments that indirectly led to a slow evolution in the understanding of *familia*.

First, Christian authors' ideas regarding marriage, sexual relations, slavery and children began to be widely circulated in the West. Apologists such as Tertullian and Minucius Felix not only wrote for the benefit of polytheists – largely to dispel misconceptions about their faith – but also to offer a definitive vision of human affairs. In doing so, they necessarily discussed that most essential social unit, the family. While the role of the family would eventually be set up by theologians of late antiquity almost as a negative model to the Christian ideal of personal comportment, they firmly established that within the bounds of marriage, spouses and parents were without blame.

Second, while these writers did not offer a true alternative to the Roman 'model', they nevertheless raised a number of epistemological issues about the sanctity of marriage, the immorality and dangers of adultery and divorce, and responsibilities to children and slaves. And despite the heavily patriarchal tone and nature of these early works, they also offered in theory a broader range of idealized behavior than the Roman counterpart. Behavior, as Tertullian was at great pains to point out, was only half the battle: one had to behave in the proper way for the proper reason.

Third, families were an integral part of Christian society. They recapitulated broader notions of authority in heaven and on earth. The head of the household controlled his family like the early Hebrew and Roman patriarchs, at least in theory. But on a more practical level, it is also important to note that it was by kinship, by *obligatio* and *obsequium* to the *paterfamilias*, and by marriage that Christianity grew. Even Paul recognized the value of the household structure as a useful unit for transmitting and extending Christian worship: 'it [celibacy] would have broken the subtle chain of command by which his own teachings were passed on to each local community through the authority of local householders'.[306] Martyrs such as Perpetua notwithstanding, Christianity needed the family as much as families needed Christianity.[307]

Finally, like the classical Roman family, there was considerable tension between the ideals espoused by early Christian luminaries and the living up to those ideals. Problems were highlighted and exacerbated by the existence of mixed families, where some members were Christian and others not. But even among Christians, there was considerable conflict. What may have caused such discord in these latter cases is difficult to say. Certainly broadly held beliefs and customs in Graeco-Roman society must have played a part, but to what degree and under what circumstances is impossible to definitively discern. For our purposes here, we must content ourselves with the fact that such enmity within the family did exist and Christian beliefs frequently complicated these entanglements.

3

CONSTANTINE AND THE CONFLUENCE OF TWO TRADITIONS[1]

Tunc et memoriam Constantini, ut novatoris turbatorisque priscarum legum et moris antiquitus recepti, vexavit.[2]

Prologue: legal developments in the third century

In the year 211 CE, Septimius Severus died and his two sons, Geta and Caracalla, took joint control of the Empire. Within a year, Caracalla had murdered his younger brother and reigned alone. As his father before him, the young emperor sought to strengthen his base of support by lavishing favor upon the army. In order to deal with this added pressure on imperial finances, Caracalla extended citizenship to all free peoples living in the Empire in 212 CE.[3] By doing so, he could collect the Roman inheritance tax, the *vicesima hereditatum*, from all free persons. Only fragments of the actual decree survive from a papyrus in Egypt:

> Therefore, I grant Roman citizenship to all [subjects] throughout the Empire except for the *dediticii*, while preserving all local citizenships. For it is fitting that all should bear the [state's] many burdens as well as sharing my victories.[4]

Thus, with one act, Caracalla had wiped out the confusing patchwork of different legal rights, multiple citizenships, and the like. It was an excellent administrative decision for an Empire that, in fits and starts, had been enfranchising many non-Italian peoples into the political and social hierarchy for well over two centuries.

In place of the old system, legal differentiation was based on a simple twofold division among the Empire's free citizens: the *honestiores* and the *humiliores*. These statuses, 'the more honorable' and 'the more humble', actually pre-date Caracalla's *constitutio*: we already possess a number of references to them in the early second century CE.[5] Where the demarcation between the two statuses lay, however, remains a little vague. Originally, leaders of the municipal councils, the decurions, comprised the lowest members of the class of *honestiores*.[6] Thus, this group included the senatorial aristocracy, the equestrian order, military officers,[7] and various members of the imperial bureaucracy.

It is not clear whether Caracalla's enactment had a profound effect upon third-century social legislation. But it is important to note that there were currents in Roman law that made hazier distinctions between all those who were not high-born. These fuzzy delineations under law between the powerful and the weak would become significant in late antiquity.

Specific legislation on the family is somewhat scanty for the third century and has been severely redacted by later Roman jurists. Most post-Severan rescripts are sadly sterile of innovation and sought primarily to support pre-existing legal doctrine. In particular, the legal reforms of Augustus were often extended; an irony, since Augustus' social legislation was roundly despised, especially in the first century CE.

There were, however, in legal practice large changes in the relation of a male to his spouse and his descendants. The *senatusconsultum Tertullianum* made it law that women who died intestate should be succeeded by their children.[8] This decision probably represented a legal *imprimatur* to already existing practices in society, or at least among its wealthier members. Children's legal standing during this age also developed to their benefit. A series of laws aimed at protecting children and minors in contractual obligations were passed along with several *senatusconsulta* to preserve their patrimonies.[9] Finally, the situation of slaves in third-century law seems to have improved, but only slightly. There were new safeguards against their mistreatment.[10] More importantly, a slave who had been sold with the intent of being freed at a certain point in time became free at that time, even if there was no formal manumission.[11] And in certain cases, a slave could make a legitimate will, given that he had received a master's consent.[12] These gains in law, however, must be weighed against the reality of day-to-day life, where such laws were often unknown or ignored.

In sum, then, the third century offered very little in the way of new or radically different policies surrounding marriage, children and other affairs concerning the *domus*. The importance of maintaining stability of the family and regulating its operation were goals sought by an essentially conservative government seeking to preserve civil order in a period of political fluidity. By reaffirming the basic tenets of classical law and Augustus' social programs, the emperor and the imperial bureaucracy played it safe. Modifications and clarifications continued, but overall these acts merely embellished the *status quo*. Finally, enforcement, even among the rich, was patchy. Emperors had other things on their minds.

Constantine and the new world order

Until recently, it had been a truism that with Constantine came a blanket support of Christianity. The emperor became the *de facto* patron of the Church and set about granting it special privileges, as well as passing a series of religiously motivated laws concerning the family. Recent work, however, by Judith Evans Grubbs and others has called many of these assumptions into question.[13] She in particular has sought to distance the role of Christianity from Constantine's legal reforms.

Certainly a significant question is the issue of impetus. Did Constantine see himself as having a Christianizing influence on social legislation and, by extension, Roman society, or did his reforms reflect a more deeply rooted tradition consistent with imperial goals? Inspiration is perhaps less important than the actual passage of these laws, however. A better question to ask is whether they reflected general trends in the Empire, or whether they represented a new mode of conceiving the family and thus an attempt to regulate its composition and function.

Constantine's social legislation

Introduction

From the time of his victory at the Milvian bridge until to his death in 337 CE, Constantine actively concerned himself with issues of betrothal, marriage, divorce, children and slaves.[14] There are approximately 100 pieces of legislation which deal with family life surviving from his reign – a sizeable percentage of his legal activity – and no doubt there were many others which were not promulgated in later collections of Roman jurisprudence. While the tenor and direction of these laws may have been something new, however, certainly a legal renaissance did not begin with Constantine. Simply by scanning the *Codex Iustinianus* and the *Digesta*, one can see renewed activity in all areas of civil and criminal law during the reign of his predecessor, Diocletian. The emperor's enactments may have endured longer and now be better known, but Constantine in this area was once again Diocletian's successor.

Many of the traditional legal concepts such as *patria potestas* and the favoring of agnatic relatives are reaffirmed. But many trends in legal thought from the earlier imperial age, particularly concerning better documentation and observation of legal transactions, are often rejected in his edicts. Those items which catch our eye – notably the harsh rhetoric and the vicious, frequently extravagant punishments for transgressing the law – say more of the age than they do of imperial legal objectives. Certainly, these things represent something new in law,[15] but they do not apply *per se* to his strictures on the family nor necessarily represent Christian opinions concerning punishment.[16]

Christianity, too, was not always diametrically opposed to many of the social aims that the Empire sought to foster.[17] Divorce was discouraged, the husband and father was seen as the head of the family, and children were considered inferior in station but worthy of special treatment. So one should be hesitant to say that *because* a law was consistent with earlier imperial policy, it was inconsistent with Christian thought, custom or behavior. Conversely and by extension, one should not assume that an apparently 'Christian' constitution was somehow irreconcilable with traditional Roman ideals.

There is no one generalization to be made of Constantine's social program.[18] Evans Grubbs is right in questioning religious influences on the emperor, but she probably goes too far when she states, '[Constantine was] an innovator and overturner of laws perhaps, but not, I think, of custom.'[19] While he was mindful of custom – and Christianity, too – Constantine was not bashful in offering new reforms in the area of family law, custom and behavior.

The married state

Constantine's work on *iustae nuptiae* and other unions is especially notable. Most visibly, the legal power of a wife diminished significantly. The rules regulating a wife's right to action no doubt started out as a series of laws aimed at protecting younger women, mostly those who were still *adolescentes*. *CTh* iii:5:3, for instance, offered under-age betrothed ladies the right to keep unregistered pre-nuptial gifts from their fiancés. The emperor also enacted legislation that kept *matronae* from being dragged into public for debt problems.[20] But Constantine also sharply limited their capacity to act of their own accord. One law, which may have been only in effect in Africa, mandated that husbands represent their wives in legal proceedings.[21] It did not specifically *require* a woman to have her spouse plead in her stead, but the language of the law could be interpreted this way. More significantly, Constantine ordered in 322 that women could no longer bring their own actions.[22] It is unclear whether this law was ever enforced in the West,[23] but it certainly represented a new and indeed radical retreat from classical and imperial jurisprudence. Such original, if reactionary, legislation is indicative of much of Constantine's activity. The emperor may have been reinforcing the traditional authority of *patria potestas* in public matters, which would make these laws somewhat more understandable. But since Constantine seemed to limit that same authority in other legislation, his motivation is ambiguous. In either case, there is no definitive legal antecedent for the emperor's edicts.

This pattern of action is clearer when reviewing more general edicts on matrimony. Constantine sharply narrowed the kinds of marriages – *iusta matrimonia* or otherwise – that could be contracted. New prohibitions generally applied to spouses who came from widely differing social classes. Marriage in both the Republic and the Empire was of singular importance to families, always made with a strong sense of social standing. That did not mean Romans felt it necessary to legislate against the majority of question-able matches: should a couple (and their families) wish to live with any presumed *odium* (disgrace), that was their affair.[24] In fact, with the exception of the Augustan strictures against senators and their sons (and later their daughters[25]) and a third-century law condemning the marriage of a *libertus* and his patroness,[26] there were practically no prohibitions of any unions at all. Quite the opposite at times: with the passage of the *senatusconsultum Claudianum* in 52 CE, for example, *contuberni* between free women and slaves were recognized as a legally contracted, if inferior, state.[27] In sum, jurists found other affairs upon which to expound.

The extension of the *s.c. Claudianum*'s provisions during the early years of Constantine's reign affirmed restrictions only against those individuals who had broadly different social backgrounds. One set of constitutions suggests that the emperor wished not only to modify the principles slightly, but to change the sense of those principles – at times, radically.[28] *CTh* iv:12:1, for example, forced those women who had become the *contubernales* of slaves to lose their freedom and take the status of their husbands. Some have thought that this had a Christian impetus, but there is no credible evidence to support this.[29] The language of the law, '*Si qua autem mulier suae sit immemor honestatis*', does not necessarily refer to all free adult females, but only to those who were of high status – *honestiores*.[30] The law is instead consistent with classical juris-prudence allowing marriage between low-born women and their former slaves.[31] In this rarefied sense, then, *CTh* iv:12:1 is more accurately a logical extension of Augustus' proscription against marriages between Senatorial families and *infames*. Moreover, it seems to have been targeting those women who had taken up residence with slaves whom they did *not* own. Indeed, Constantine shortly thereafter even permitted free women the old privilege of entering into *contubernia* with slaves of the *domus Caesaris*.[32] The woman's children, although illegitimate, would be considered free with Latin rights. Very little was new in these laws.

Nor was a reduction of status easily accomplished. In a fragmentary law, the emperor reconfirmed an involved procedure to notify a woman of her impending diminution to slavery.[33] Seven Roman citizens were required to witness a written document, the *denuntiatio*, and it had to be delivered to the offending woman three times. Only later, when legitimate and non-legitimate marriages were delineated, did Constantine tried to forego this lengthy process.[34] The need for notification, presumably for the sake of expe-diency, was no longer required. Surprisingly, it was not until the reign of Honorius that the emperor's experiment in being legally expeditious was rescinded.[35] How well the law functioned is questionable, but the action was indicative of a government willing to reject legal precedent when need suited.

And by 326, slave–free woman relations became more restrictive. In a law that can only be characterized as moralistic, Constantine prescribed the death penalty to free women who cohabited with their own slaves.[36] Despite some question about the non-legal language of the constitution and its abridged nature,[37] there are no other apparent reasons for the issuance of this law. If any other motives were involved during the law's conception – such as a reaction to a specific case[38] – they are not obvious and were likely ancillary concerns. As a practical matter, Constantine's stricture was certainly unworkable: it allowed and even encouraged any and all individuals to denounce the suspected offender. The death sentence for the woman as well as the slave perhaps underlies the seriousness with which the government viewed this violation, but again, death and other harsh penalties had become the norm.

The law represents something quite new in terms of the relations between the nominally private *domus* and the role of the state, however. In issues of family name and honor, particularly in reference to women, the government had previously treaded carefully and lightly. Only with the Augustan *lex Julia de adulteriis* were criminal actions to be pursued against a woman, and then only by her husband or his relatives. That *delatores* (informers), whom Constantine found personally distasteful and detestable,[39] should have the opportunity to denounce a woman of high standing hearkened back to the remarkably unpopular denunciations of the first century CE. The government thus insinuated itself into an area that was largely considered private. While such action was not wholly unique, Constantine's decision was nevertheless extraordinary.

Evans Grubbs has speculated that the law sought to prevent children born of such unions from claiming a free status.[40] Certainly this provision exists, but that is likely to have been only a secondary concern of this constitution:[41] we can hardly conclude that it only prohibited specifically clandestine affairs between free women and their slaves. Technically, that may hold legal water, but it overlooks a basic assumption the framer of this law was making: he believed that such a relationship, *because* of its nature, would naturally have been secret. So much is implied when the author finishes with: '*Qui vero ex lege disiuncti clam denuo convenerint congressus vetitos renovantes . . . poenam similem sustinebunt.*'[42] It is difficult to provide the precise reasons behind *CTh* ix:9:1's passage and it would be presumptuous to posit a direct Christian influence, but Constantine offered the first comprehensive marriage stricture in three centuries.

One last law of considerable importance, at least for those who wish to tie a Christian agenda to Constantine's program, was *CTh* viii:16:1, which officially ended Augustus' penalties for those who chose not to marry or had no children while married. These strictures were detested from their inception, and no doubt they were often ignored, so it is possible that Constantine recognized the long-standing opposition to the law from the populace at large and from the upper classes specifically. But the annulment of the Augustan proscriptions in 320 could also have been influenced by Christians or at least Christian ideals, since there seemed to be little other incentive to change the policy. If indeed this was the case, it was a piece of legislation that had an eye cast to the future.[43] Either way, it was a bold move for a government that had some stake in the financial windfalls of Augustus' law.

Oddly enough, in contrast to his many laws on marriage, Constantine said little in specific reference to the status of the concubine. Possibly the fact that his mother and Minervina, with whom he had a relationship, were both concubines, was some reflection on this. But it is more than likely that he considered the concubine's role socially acceptable, as did the general population. We possess one fragmentary law on the matter and its meaning is not entirely clear.[44] The language could imply a complete interdiction on *concubinae*,[45] but more than likely Constantine was trying to prevent already married men from having what amounted to a second wife. The abbreviated nature of the passage makes it impossible to say much more about the emperor's interest or intent concerning concubines, but it is unlikely that he attempted to outlaw their existence. If indeed that was the intent, it was an abject failure.

Constantine's legislation on marriage, then, covered wide and varied interests. At times, his laws seem to greatly extend already prevailing imperial legal ideas, but he also offered laws to prevent what he and his court saw as morally objectionable or unseemly unions. It goes too far, however, to suggest that he was concerned mostly in keeping with custom. Custom may have frowned upon certain kinds of unions, but it was also customary to let Roman society regulate itself in these matters. His reforms were likely seen as intrusive and unwelcome, although only Julian forty years later tried to moderate them. Emperors in the past might have legally discouraged what they perceived as immoral behavior, but they were careful not to combat it directly. Not so Constantine. His needs dictated his actions, whether in the legal sphere or elsewhere. This attitude is equally manifest in his long political career.

Assuming that there were no legal impediments to a marriage, the early fourth century saw several laws regulating the way in which a marriage might be contracted. These constitutions raised the affianced state to a contractual level, where there could be legal repercussions should a betrothal be terminated by one or both of the partners. Were a betrothal consummated in an actual marriage, the particulars of pre-nuptial gifts and the *pacta dotalia* were of no concern to the government. If, however, a betrothal ended abruptly, either because of one or both parties backing out or because of death, the matter was often brought to the attention of the imperial judiciary. A number of surviving *libelli* in the *Codex Iustinianus* address these issues, as well as opinions concerning such eventualities in the *Digesta*.[46] Constantine thus logically enacted general rules that tried to summarize and answer the major problems of a broken betrothal. While the laws could have been supported by clerics and other influential Christians, who placed great value on betrothals,[47] the impetus clearly came from elsewhere.

There were essentially two matters upon which Constantine legislated: the first was the status of gifts, official and unofficial, when the betrothal was summarily ended. The second dealt with the length of time a betrothal could last before it could be broken with impunity – a statute of limitations, as it were. In the surviving laws, the imperial bureaucracy tried to cover almost all contingencies.

In 319, Constantine passed the most encompassing of his laws. *CTh* iii:5:2 precluded either party from breaking off the engagement, no matter for what reason: the question of a person's character had to be taken into account *before* the marriage was contracted. Should an individual decide to subsequently back out of a legal union, not only must all gifts be returned to the rejected party, but also any gifts he or she had given would be forfeited.[48] The second set of laws, *CTh* iii:5:4 and 5, were originally part of the same law.[49] These edicts basically allowed a woman to break off the engagement and marry another if the prospective husband failed to marry her within two years of the betrothal.

Christianity's influence in the promotion of betrothal here was probably slight. Constantine's laws concerning this state were entirely pragmatic. His broad pronouncements on the status of betrothed individuals offered judges – *praeses* and *iudices* – quick and relatively easy guidelines for deciding matters involving failed betrothals.

Constantine was bolder in his enactments concerning divorce and set Roman jurisprudence in a new direction. True, only one major enactment survives from his reign, *CTh* iii:16:1, but it is of enormous significance.[50] One scholar has tried to argue that this law was written by a cleric because of its unusual language.[51] It is unlikely, however, that this is so given this edict's peculiarities.[52] The matter is made less likely since some provisions clearly were at odds with earlier or contemporary Christian thought in the matter of divorce.

Unlike past laws, Constantine was specifically targeting unilateral divorce. It would still be some time before the government tried to prohibit divorces where both parties agreed that a marriage should come to an end. Briefly, the law severely limited the legitimate reasons for initiating divorce. Before, there were only one or two laws that *required* an individual to separate from his spouse, and in most cases those reasons involved the infidelity of a wife:[53] almost any reason for divorce by either party was valid. With Constantine's law, however, unilateral *repudium* was curtailed.

The reasons, moreover, for ending a marriage were different for husband and wife. A man had to prove that his wife was guilty of adultery, acted as a procuress, or was a sorceress – all of which were criminal offenses. If he divorced her for any other reason, he had to return her dowry and was forbidden from marrying again. Moreover, if he did remarry, the first wife had the right to come into his home and take the second wife's dowry for herself. A woman wishing divorce had the harder lot. She also had to prove criminal charges against her husband, but she faced impoverishment and exile to an island should her reasons remain unproven or deemed insufficient. Adultery was not a legitimate reason for divorce. Instead, she had to show that her husband were either a murderer, a sorcerer, or a defiler of tombs. Should she prove any of these cases, she retrieved her entire dowry and '*demum laudata*' (ultimate praise). Oddly enough, it does not appear from the language of the law that any of these infractions, whether made by the husband or the wife, were grounds for *requiring* divorce. But since the fact of a wife committing adultery required that a *repudium* be sent and subsequent criminal charges be brought, it may be inferred that such was the case for these offenses as well. This is arguing from negative evidence, however.

Dismissing for the moment a cleric's role in Constantine's new guidelines, what was the likely impetus for its passage? Evans Grubbs, following earlier opinion,[54] thinks that despite some problems with interpreting this enactment, there was some Christian influence in the law's creation.[55] Assuming that Ablabius, a high-ranking Christian in Constantine's court to whom the law was addressed, actually drafted *CTh* iii:16:1, one can assume that the minister wanted to reduce the frequency of a religiously condemned action.[56] There are certain problems with this hypothesis, however. That Ablabius had Christian leanings is clear, but the nature of his Christianity, like that of his master, is open to debate. There are only two references to his religious affiliation, both of which are ambiguous.[57] The most basic fact upon which his theory is largely based is thus open to question.[58] This does not preclude a possible Christian influence in this law's passage, but such arguments must rest more on the content of the law itself.

Turning to the substance of *CTh* iii:16:1, there are, it would seem, two different issues involved here. First, there is the larger question of limiting the grounds for divorce. This unquestionably represents something new in Roman jurisprudence. Second, and perhaps more intriguing, there is the matter of the actual grounds for divorce itself: that is, why were these particular items singled out?

As to the first issue, that of limiting unilateral divorce, there is perhaps some basis for seeing a Christian influence. While a single and long-lasting marriage was an ideal shared and espoused by both classical Roman and early Christian writers, certainly the former did not expect younger widows and widowers to be found in great abundance. In fact, Augustus' law on inheritance, whether followed or not, would have tended to discourage the single marriage since it required the production of several children to fully inherit. As for early Christians, it is not entirely clear whether their ideals found frequent or constant expression. Wealthy women in late antiquity occasionally put away dissolute husbands.[59] On the other hand, many women also remained unattached after their divorces or their husbands died. So one can perhaps make an argument for Christians being more interested in living up to certain religious ideals. Whether that translated into actual behavior modification is largely impossible to tell. The available material from Egypt – notably out of our sphere of interest – argues against this: divorce documents prove that both polytheists and Christians ended marriages.[60] The matter of limiting divorces may have been inspired by Christian thought, but this is far from clear.

As to the specific grounds for divorce, it is possible, for the most part, largely to dismiss Christianity's influence in *CTh* iii:16:1. Looking first at a husband's causes for divorce, we can see older, non-Christian concepts at work. The matter of adultery was nothing new: *repudium* had been mandatory for such a transgression since the first days of the Empire. The third charge of procuring was more or less a variation on the adultery theme. Not only would it imply that a wife herself was likely committing adultery, but that it was being done with her husband's consent. This, moreover, had all sorts of unpleasant implications for the other female members of the *familia*. The moral stigma would then fall on the *paterfamilias* and the *domus* as a whole. Later constitutions seem to make this connection clear.[61] Finally, sorcery was a crime against which the government long inveighed. Tiberius in the first century CE (and moralists even earlier in the Republic) was leery of the occult: we know of two *senatusconsulta* in the early imperial age (16 CE and 52 CE) and an imperial edict (69 CE) which expelled astrologers from the city of Rome.[62] Constantine's other legislation concerning polytheistic officials, who appear from context to be associated with sorcery, view them with suspicion.[63] By 357, Constantius sentenced most soothsayers to capital punishment if found practicing their respective arts.[64] It seems, then, that men only divorced their wives for practices long condemned by the government.

As for a woman's grounds for divorcing her husband, old Roman ideals are again in evidence. The first charge, divorce because a husband committed homicide, needs little comment. Homicide in itself was a capital offense for a majority of the population;[65] trying to conceal a murderer's actions meant complicity in Roman law, and was itself punishable.[66] Sorcery has just been discussed. Finally, the defilement of a tomb was considered a serious crime at least from the first century BCE: it was covered under the *lex Julia de vi publica* (18 BCE)[67] and Ulpian argued that the act was properly a crime of *infamia*.[68] Thus, disturbing a tomb could carry pecuniary as well as capital punishments.[69] It is possible that with the rise of Christianity came a stronger prohibition against this crime, but ruminations from earlier Christian apologists admit that they and polytheists honored the dead and their resting places with equal piety.[70]

In sum, *CTh* iii:16:1 at best has only a slight relation to Christianity and the ideals it espoused. It is more likely that this law should be viewed in much the same light as his laws surrounding the condition of marriage. His concerns are not entirely clear, but his legislation was clearly more assertive than that of his predecessors. Constantine's law on divorce seems to have more in common with *CTh* ix:9:1 concerning the cohabitation of free women and their slaves than it does Christianity. As the emperor sought to prevent marriages that he deemed unsuitable, so, too, did he seek to stop divorces he also found morally or socially unacceptable. And once again, he found it necessary to legislate on issues that had previously been regulated by Roman society. In the general area of contracting, engaging and dissolving marriage, Constantine was in fact a rather forceful *turbator*.

Children and family

Constantine's legal formulations governing the status of children seem to have continued an imperial trend concerned with bettering their status. This is not to say that these edicts improved a child's upbringing or physical treatment in any measurable way, although certainly his pronouncements tried to address those issues. Instead, the government was more interested in pursuing a policy aimed at protecting the patrimonies of minors and doing so with greater diligence. As a whole, Constantine produced more legislation on children and related topics than any other single social issue and, indeed, we have more surviving constitutions on the topic than from any other emperor's reign.[71]

One of the common ways in which family size was regulated was through exposure and the sale of children. How extensive these practices were is impossible to gauge, and in the case of exposure one assumes that if a child were healthy and its parents could afford its upkeep, they would keep and raise their baby, male or female.[72] But the custom of parents ridding themselves of problematic newborns continued well into the medieval period.

As for the sale of children, it appears from the few references to its occurrence that enforced servitude was a relatively uncommon affair for the freeborn. Since the first century it had been illegal to sell a free child into permanent slavery, no matter how much his or her family might need the money. Yet happen it did and not always by a parent's choice. In one revealing letter, Augustine described the ravages of slave traders in and around his city of Hippo.[73] The bishop noted that traffickers in slaves almost always preferred children, and not always the newborn. They apparently used a combination of kidnapping, purchases from parents and the use of local agents (who in turn got their 'stock' from a variety of sources) to acquire their product. Augustine was particularly incensed at parents who, in violation of an otherwise unknown law (or laws), had been selling their children in perpetuity rather than the legal twenty-five years.[74] The sense of the letter was that these activities were short-lived, if unpleasant affairs. But while the event itself may have been of limited duration, no doubt this sort of grab-and-run operation had been a standard practice among slavers.

The infrequency of the sale of free children is confirmed later in a *novella* of Valentinian III, published in 451, which attempted to heavily regulate the practice.[75] In the law's introduction, the emperor acknowledged that people were selling their children in Italy, due to a famine that had been plaguing the countryside. To maintain some sense of order until the crisis passed, the imperial government tried to keep buyers from taking advantage of the situation by reselling the children or taking them out of Italy.

There are several laws dealing with children and poverty, as well as other, non-legal evidence of government support. Eusebius, for example, described how Constantine instituted a system to distribute grain on the local level through the metropolitan churches.[76] It is unclear as to whether it was a short-term program, although it or something close to it was still in effect in the following century.[77] Constantine thus used the Church's infrastructure to better, and presumably more honestly, distribute food to the needy. But since the distribution only came annually, unlike the grain and pork distributions at Constantinople and Rome, its effect on relieving hunger is unknown.

Whether or not the Church succeeded in convincing parents to keep their children is also unclear.[78] There had been a long-standing opposition to exposure of children among Christian authors, beginning of course with the well-known attack by Justin Martyr: he implied that exposure meant condemning children to slavery and a life of prostitution.[79] Augustine claimed that it had also been a long-standing practice for the Church to liberate children who had been taken into slavery, either by sale or by some other means.[80] There appears then to have been a widespread denunciation of exposing and enslaving children, although there are no surviving proscriptions in early Church canons.[81] It is difficult to ascertain whether Constantine was inspired by Christian thought or not.

Nevertheless, he did enact several constitutions that tried to discourage the sale and exposure of children. *CTh* xi:27:1 and 2 both seem to address specific emergencies in different parts of the Empire.[82] They made provisions for parents who were driven by poverty to get rid of their children. In the first case, the government voiced its belief that exposure of newborn children had dramatically increased. To combat this trend and to prevent starvation, the emperor directed that clothing and food would be issued to all those who applied. The second law in 322 was concerned with another famine, apparently raging in Africa.[83] The fear here was that parents were selling their children in great numbers to raise money and to avoid feeding them. Again, Constantine ordered local officials to provide food from imperial stocks. In both cases, once the crises had been averted, the programs would end.

But is it possible that these or similar initiatives may have been envisioned as long term? Famine was common enough in the ancient world and no doubt both the urban and rural poor frequently had problems feeding their own families, although again this is arguing from negative evidence. If indeed Constantine's directives were conceived as permanent initiatives to combat hunger, one must question why they began at this point. Christian influence is one possible motive, but as we mentioned above, the government supported the activities of the Church through increased legal rights and various tax breaks. There could have also been an attempt on Constantine's part to institute something like earlier relief programs. But while the *alimenta* scheme of the second century did try to support children in need, its purpose was to insure enough citizens to man the legions.[84] A third alternative might be related to the recovery from the third-century's financial woes. But Constantine's military and bureaucratic reforms, along with those of Diocletian, put enormous pressure on the central government's financial resources. Indeed, Constantine had to institute a new tax, the *collatio lustralis*, to pay for the new programs. It was extremely unpopular and Zosimus even claimed that parents had to sell their children *because* of the new tax.[85] It seems likely, in sum, that these attempts to alleviate poverty were stopgap measures.[86]

The emperor also took steps to prevent violence towards children. In one law of 318, Constantine had outlawed the killing of one's child (along with the murder of any of one's close kin).[87] While a father's *ius vitae necisque* had in theory endured in classical jurisprudence, it had been an abandoned practice for centuries. It would seem, then, that Constantine had simply sanctioned what had already been common practice for a very long time. But the law's orientation is not entirely clear. While it was practically impossible for a *paterfamilias* to legally kill his own, whether as an adult or child, it does not seem to be directed specifically at newborns (whom this law would presumably best protect). It is possible that the law in fact standardized punishment for *parricidia*: the author states that all other forms of torture and execution were to be rejected in favor of the *culleus*, wherein the guilty party would be sewn up in a sack with wild animals and thrown into the water. Thus, while *CTh* ix:15:1 may have offered a modicum of protection through a harsher sentence, it did not make parricide in itself a new crime.[88]

The emperor, however, did offer other incentives to halt the sale and abandonment of children. Classical law had up to Constantine's time stated that the loss of *patria potestas* did not come with a decision to expose a free newborn.[89] Should the opportunity present itself, a child could claim his inheritance or, alternatively, a father could recover his son or daughter. In 331, Constantine issued a law transferring *potestas* from the father to the man who had retrieved the abandoned baby.[90] The child's savior moreover had the option to raise the child as his own or as a slave.[91] It is not clear whether custom dictated the return of children to their natural parents where possible, but examples of the issue coming up in legal disputes implies that – with a relatively few minor provisos[92] – a child incontrovertibly belonged to the natural father. Constantine was therefore probably trying to discourage exposure by legalizing the finality of the act. Once a child was abandoned, it was gone for good.

Two years earlier, the emperor offered a similarly stringent constitution concerning the inviolability of a freeborn child's free status, even if sold into servitude. In a law addressed to Italy in 329, Constantine ended this right in the specific case of newborn infants.[93] The emperor legitimized their sale, thus condemning them in theory to a legal enslavement. The situation was not necessarily as permanent as abandonment, however. If parents wished to recover their child, they could do so if they paid restitution. That took the form of either money or a similarly suited slave.[94]

CTh v:9:1 and 10:1 were surely trying to dissuade parents from giving up their children in any way. Rejecting custom and legal doctrine, Constantine made it plain to parents the consequences of their actions. Combined with this negative reinforcement were measures that tried to soften those problems that dictated the removal of a child from its home. There was therefore a conscious policy on the government's part. Why Constantine did so is not readily answerable. The possibility of Christian influence is attractive, but difficult to confirm. The alimentary laws seem to suggest otherwise, but the laws concerning sale and exposure point more directly to the new religion. If anything, it appears that Constantine's legislation inspired greater opposition to exposure and sale of children by the Church, rather than the other way around.[95] Exposure was only specifically outlawed in 374, which was more in keeping with actual Christian thoughts on the matter.[96] It is even possible, though not very likely, that Constantine wanted to ensure sufficient numbers of free poor available to preserve skilled labor in the Empire. If that were the case, then his legislation on sale and abandonment could be seen in conjunction with his numerous laws enforcing public services and making many trades hereditary.[97] Whatever his reasons, the emperor clearly set out a program that attempted to offer greater safeguards to poor children by dissuading their abandonment.

In conjunction with his legislation about a child's physical state, Constantine enacted a series of laws that addressed issues of inheritance. Given that marriage patterns and life expectancies in ancient Rome frequently resulted in young men and women inheriting from a dead parent before they reached their majorities, minors were naturally the target of extortion, swindles and other forms of fraud. So it is perhaps unsurprising that Constantine's ministers, like Roman jurists in the past, legislated more on the issue of patrimonies than any other single subject.

Many of his attempts to regulate minors' patrimonies had to do with their legal guardians, *tutores* and *curatores*. The former, who protected children (boys under the age of 14 and girls under the age of 12), were singled out, although both were frequently mentioned together. As a basic rule of thumb, Constantine directed that most losses of a patrimony or other property owned by anyone under 25 were the financial responsibilities of the guardian. One set of laws lists five Constantinian rulings indemnifying minors (*pupillae*) against various contingencies.[98] These included losses of gifts made to a child, insurance against children and guardians being sued as co-owners, and any loss from emphyteutic tenures.[99] Moreover, even in situations where the complicity of a *tutor* or *curator* was suspected in debts that may have accrued through the fault of a minor or his deceased benefactor, the guardian had to prove his innocence in court.[100] In sum, Constantine tried to insure that a patrimony remained more or less inviolate until an heir's majority.[101]

Similar types of laws, as earlier discussed, were being enacted in the third century. That patrimonial problems for minors continued to be addressed in the fourth and fifth centuries implies the constant threat to children. The only major difference between these laws and previous ones were their general nature. Like his laws on betrothal, Constantine tried to cover all possible problems, trying to react to novel methods of fraud. That such edicts did not stop being issued after his death suggests the ubiquity of the problem.

The emperor also made inheritance an easier affair for all involved. The frequently strict rules governing a legitimate will gave rise to frequent complaints of *inofficiosis*. Under a new law, if a *paterfamilias* wished to divide his patrimony between his children and grandchildren, it was no longer necessary for the will to be completed in the proper manner.[102] In an edict further simplifying the procedure, Constantine deemed the flimsiest soldier's will, even if written in the dirt, valid.[103] These and other regulations tried to make the transfer of ownership smoother. In sum, Constantine wanted to make it easier for one generation to inherit from another and to do so in a relatively uniform manner.

Finally, the emperor gave minors a more active say over their recently acquired property. If a father had the right of usufruct over estates left to his children by his deceased wife, he could not do anything to endanger or greatly change that property.[104] Another ruling gave minors greater latitude in dealing with lawsuits that tried to reclaim money.[105] A third law also gave under-aged adults just entering their majority special privileges in trying to recover monies from their former *tutores* and *curatores*.[106] And perhaps most important, on permission from the government, a minor could apply to have full authority over his or her property.[107]

Constantine's laws concerning minors and their property, then, tried to insure protection and control in deference to their age. Like the emperor's edicts trying to discourage the sale and abandonment of children, it seems clear that these laws sought to keep the *familia*, in the broadest legal sense, safe and intact.[108] In that context, Constantine's legislation on children was fully in keeping with the aims of his predecessors. The interests of the state, as emperors in the previous century had found, were partially based on the stability of the family. Constantine's program was more about maintaining that stability than it was about religion.

Slave familia and familiae

Surviving legislation on the status of slaves from Constantine's reign is comparatively scarce. Despite the paucity of material, however, there was one significant piece of legislation, which helps underscore general attitudes about the nature of slave unions and families as they developed in the Empire.

But as a general rule, the tenor of master–servant relations were kept as they had been, much to the detriment of the enslaved.

The place of slaves within the household is a topic of some debate. The only definitive characterization is that a slave's treatment varied with each owner. Certainly, corporal punishment and even death could be meted out by an unsatisfied master. But the degree of violence perpetrated on a slave also depended on his or her station. The more intimate or important the position of a domestic, the less likely they were to be treated like chattel. On the other hand, as Horace made clear, one could 'walk alone' with his slaves at his side.[109] They were as easily ignored as they were punished.

Constantine made it clear that only a wanton, deliberate attempt to kill one's slave would make a master liable for murder charges. A constitution of 319 stated plainly that should a slave die during a beating, even if rods or whips were being used, the owner was not guilty of murder.[110] A second law further elucidated that these rules applied to all slaves and not simply those owned by large property holders and public institutions: it specifically refers to household slaves.[111] While these laws did not allow a disgruntled slave-owner to 'dispose' of his property with impunity, they did offer considerable latitude in the matter.[112] However unpopular they may have been, these constitutions reconfirmed the violent and hierarchical relationship inherent in forced servitude.[113]

This unequal association was further enforced by a law which may have been in effect only in North Africa, although it was issued in Cologne.[114] The constitution permitted a freedmen to be enslaved if he behaved inappropriately towards his patron. This was not a unique ruling: there are surviving laws from the third century that made similar provisions.[115] Constantine, as with his laws on beating slaves, was reconfirming a basic tenet of imperial law and of custom.

In the issues surrounding status, however, Constantine may have been somewhat more liberal. In 331, Constantine rescinded a no longer extant law, which he may well have enacted, that permitted children of a free father and slave mother to maintain their freedom if no claim for recovery came from the mother's master after sixteen years.[116] Whether it was Constantine's original ruling or not, he modified it significantly. Now there would be no statute of limitations for recovering children of any such unions, nor would they be considered free. Instead, the father would have to make restitution to the mother's *dominus*, either financially or by replacing the child with an equivalent slave. The law does not address cases where the master prefers the child to compensation. But once again, Constantine was reaffirming an old rule: in the case of illegitimacy, children took the mother's status. They were slaves until their masters freed them. The one novel ruling we have from this emperor concerns slaves who were members of the *familia Caesaris*. For more important imperial slaves and freedmen, there was an enjoyment of status and privilege not afforded to the mass of Rome's free population. But those bureaucrats (*cubicularii*, *castrenses*, and *scriniarii*) were few in number. On the other hand, the emperor employed huge numbers of slaves on his extensive estates, imperial monopolies and other institutions which required the support of unfree labor (such as the army). The number of slaves owned and employed by the emperor must have conservatively been in the tens of thousands.[117] The emperor's *familia*, then, was sizeable.

Of that number, most were slaves who worked as farmers on imperial estates. Constantine addressed a law to Gerulus, the *rationalis* (chief financial officer) of Sardinia, Corsica and Sicily, concerning their status.[118] The emperor made provision that in the sale of imperial lands to private individuals, the division had to insure that slave families would not be broken up in the transfer. This included both the patrimonial (that is, the private) holdings of the emperor as well as those which belonged to the state. The Latin in the constitution's interpretation could even be understood more literally: '*privati*' could refer to estates owned by the emperor personally or alternatively they could extend to the patrimonies of *all* private citizens. Certainly the rhetoric of the law might suggest that the latter was the case – '*Quis enim ferat liberos a parentibus, a fratribus sororis, a viris coniuges segregare?*'[119] – but it would be difficult to see the government advocating such an egregiously impractical and contentious policy. While the law is specific to the province of Sardinia, however, it would not be hard to believe that this law was meant to apply at least in provinces where there were extensive imperial holdings – notably Sicily and those that made up the diocese of Africa.

As a piece of social engineering, the government was doing little more than protecting a familial group that had been recognized by society at large for centuries, placing his official *imprimatur* on a well-established custom. As a legal initiative, however, Constantine had instituted a bold change, rejecting a key element of classical law of peoples (*ius gentium*). Now, slave families were considered legally the equivalent of free families. As individuals, these spouses, parents, siblings and children would have fewer rights and options in Roman society, but their marriages and kin relations were deemed legitimate. Perhaps for that reason alone, the word '*privati*' could be interpreted in the broader sense. This edict represented, then, a true turnaround in slave law.

Furthermore, the law made reference to specific circumstances: '*In Sardinia fundis patrimonialibus . . . per diversos nunc dominos distributis . . .*'[120] If it was written in reaction to an actual set of events going on in Sardinia, the outrage expressed in this constitution would then imply that slave families *were* being broken up. The imperial government was thus reacting to unusual or at least frowned-upon behavior. It might have been legally permissible, but it was clearly reprehensible.[121] If we assume moreover that this law was drafted by the central government, then the recipient, Gerulus, was likely being upbraided for the uproar apparently caused by his administration. The law ends with '*Et in vigilia, ne per provinciam aliqua post hac querella super divisis mancipiorem affectibus perseveret.*'[122]

71

Constantine's laws surrounding slaves seem in sum to represent many of the basic long-held beliefs and customs of Rome. His legislative activity, which is admittedly scarce, unfortunately reveals little about imperial policy or prevailing opinions. The emperor reaffirmed the subordinate position of the unfree within the *familia* and society in general, but the slave's role within the household cannot be determined from his laws. He did recognize a new classification of family, however, and one that could not in theory be broken up by the status of its constituent members. Constantine in this case was not doing anything startlingly bold for Roman society, but he showed himself willing to be both flexible and forceful when circumstances called for it.

Conclusions

The extent of Constantine's social legislation has only been touched upon here. But there are several significant observations that are directly relevant to events surrounding his reign in particular and the larger parameters of late antiquity.

First and most important, Constantine was the first emperor since Augustus to legislate so broadly and so extensively on the family in particular and social issues more generally. We have tried to demonstrate here that the Evans Grubbs' thesis is substantially valid: the relationship between Christianity and the emperor's legislative activity is tenuous at best and we should look elsewhere to explain the impetus for his legislation. More accurately, the emperor's edicts were formulated as a means of addressing a number of problems surrounding private life that had been touched upon helter-skelter by third-century emperors. But perhaps more significantly, Constantine legitimized the frequent use of imperial policy to regulate social behavior. Whether or not he was successful in enforcing his program is not at issue. The emperor's actions provided a model for future emperors, and ones whose policies could be clearly connected to a Christianizing influence. Constantine may not have discarded all custom, but he served as an *exemplum* for imperial successors who did envision more doctrinaire ideas for social change.

Second, and connected to this first point, Constantine was an innovator and an overturner of both laws and customs when need dictated. While he certainly tried to reinforce long-held or institutionalized beliefs, he was also quite willing to introduce new ideas that were antithetical to classical and early imperial jurisprudence. He found it legitimate to regulate matters that had previously been left to the *mores* of Roman society to dictate. He had no compunction about rejecting large portions of Augustus' social program and forcing his own vision of proper comportment on an undoubtedly leery populace. Unfortunately, we have no social critic like Ovid to comment on Constantine.

Third, his program seems to have been more or less consciously constructed. While many of his laws were no doubt in reaction to specific events or immediate needs, there is a sense that his enactments essentially tried to answer once and for all social issues that had been plaguing the government's legal system for at least two centuries. His administration in particular seemed interested in tying up legal loose ends that had been poorly dealt with during the political crisis of the previous seventy years. Constantine was not trying to Christianize the Empire nor was he necessarily trying to preserve long-standing Roman tradition. He was, to use the vernacular, playing catch-up.

Whatever his short- and long-term goals, the emperor left his mark on Roman law. In both the *Codex Theodosianus* and the *Codex Iustinianus*, his laws figure prominently in their own right and in the multiple references to them by later emperors. In that sense, as in so many others, Flavius Valerius Constantinus was a bridge between the Principate of imperial Rome and the Dominate of late antiquity, finishing what Diocletian had started. The social legislation of his reign made Constantine the last of the third-century emperors and the first of late antiquity.

4

MARRIAGE

Introduction

One pursuit in the next several chapters will be to delve more deeply into the sociological and cultural changes of fourth and fifth centuries CE that went hand in hand with the rise of Christianity. The religion had found a new champion in the emperor, but that did not mean its travails were ended. As the history of synods and ecumenical councils of the period demonstrate, arguments over the definition of orthodox Christianity often erupted into violence between various partisan factions. Nor were their disagreements limited to violence against their fellow Christians. Their anger was often focused against pagans and Jews, who saw their rights and protections under the law slowly vanish.[1] Not even the emperor, who usually understood the need for civil peace, could offer effective physical protection to their property and their persons.[2] If persecution had been a *modus vivendi* of polytheistic Roman society in the third century, many of the new religion's proponents saw violence as an equally effective means of dealing with enemies. Augustine tried to put the best face on such violence in his *De civitate Dei*: '*ut autem etiam inimici diligantur, exercent eius benevolentiam aut etiam benificientam, sive suadibili doctrina cum eius sive terribili disciplina.*'[3]

Since this new religion frequently used strong-arm methods for controlling religious diversity, which regularly duplicated the Roman polity's earlier attempts to halt Christianity, one of the areas we must first examine is the official tenets which the Church tried to promulgate concerning the family and its constituent parts. The ruminations of Christian *literati* on issues of virginity, marriage and widowhood provided the conceptual framework for creating sanctioned procedures on these issues, but frequently their thoughts did not match actual policy embodied in fourth- and fifth-century canon, let alone imperial, law. This distinction is significant. A fitting analogy might be the relationship of legal opinion to actual legislation.

It is in the context of this distinction that we ought to consider much of the surviving religious treatises, sermons and letters. Unquestionably these types of literary exercise had different purposes, both rhetorically and substantively. A private letter speculating on the relative worths of consecrated virgins and unmarried girls, for example, certainly cannot be comprehensively compared to a full-blown tract on the same subject. But as voices in a larger debate trying to define the nature of Christianity and Church doctrine, they help to interpret the direction and formulation of that debate. It is important that we consider the final results, which are visible in the canons of Church councils, even though they offer only half of the picture.

But there must also be an awareness that canons were not the same as laws. The Church in theory could only extend their rules to Christians who chose to accept these regulations.[4] The only means by which it could enforce these canons was under the threat of penance and extended or permanent excommunication from the 'body of Christ'. Moreover, as we shall see, canon law was at times at odds with Roman civil law. While there was a sporadic progression towards unity of Church and state in the matters of family regulation, there was never complete agreement. We are lucky in one regard, however. Unlike imperial constitutions that often survive in a historical vacuum, visible and direct links between current events, religious tracts and the creation of local or ecumenical councils are discernible. Not only did the ministry of the heresiarch Jovinian in the 380s and 390s, to cite one example, affect synods in Rome and Milan, but it also inspired Augustine to write *On Good Marriage* and *On the Sanctity of Virginity* (*De bono coniugali* and *De sancta virginitate*).[5]

In creating a synthesis of Christian views on marriage, children, and the like, then, as well as considering how they fit into broader societal opinion and custom, it will hopefully become apparent that, at least from a theoretical perspective, Christianity had some effect on Roman ideals. The tenor of family relations and behavior was supposed to be quite different from that of their classical counterparts. Serial monogamy was in essence forbidden, the child's role in the family was largely redefined, and the Church and state often intruded into private affairs where no institution had previously dared to tread. The Roman family at the latter stages of Empire found itself, in short, to be a much more public association than in the past, or at least subject to greater public scrutiny.

The institution of marriage

Augustine within secular and Christian thought

Like so much of our information about the family in late antiquity, much of what we know about marriage outside of the law begins with Augustine. For him, the *familia* began with marriage, the *copulatio* of a man and a woman.[6] Indeed, with the exception of one or two radical opinions from marginalized clerics, very few Christians had any objections to the state of marriage. The anonymous Pelagian author of a letter on virginity did not represent the majority of opinion, Christian or otherwise, when he compared it to an evil condition.[7] Characteristic of his studied asceticism, Jerome had come close to impugning the institution of matrimony, but only in an attempt to combat the radical theology of Jovinian.[8] His behavior was understandable in the face of a man who had denied the spiritual differences between virgins, widows and the married.[9] For the most part, however, the wedded union was an accepted and honorable state, and one which most were reluctant to denounce. Indeed, canon law had attempted to make a marriage legitimate by requiring a priest's formal blessing *after* the ceremony.[10] For traditional Roman society, marriage had been the heart of the *familia*. For Christians, it was a sacrament that had been sealed in the relationship between Adam and Eve.[11] As Augustine wrote, '*Prima itaque naturalis humanae societatis copula vir et uxor est.*'[12]

Indeed, Augustine's treatise on good marriage outlines many of the virtues of matrimony as seen through a lay Western Christian's eyes. To him, marriage was a singular honor for the individuals involved; more than one marriage, especially in the case of divorcées, was expressly condemned.[13] Like Jerome, he gave full expression to his ideas as a result of Jovinian's teaching. Augustine was also sensitive to the discomfort that many clerics and a fair number of parishioners felt concerning the subject of marriage. But unlike Jerome, the African bishop did not voice his misgivings about the wedded state. Instead, he chose to extol its value to the human condition, direct and indirect. There was a real companionship that naturally developed and went beyond the bonds of procreation, the '*naturalem in diverso sexu societatem*'.[14] Moreover, it turned carnal desire into something positive: the begetting of children. Finally, it encouraged a couple who had become parents to be more modest sexually.[15]

Adam and Eve were at the heart of Augustine's theories on marriage. The Fall did not make marriage a necessary state, as Jerome had argued.[16] Rather, the first couple had been as men and women today, procreating by sexual intercourse, but not subject to lust.[17] Original Sin may have changed the nature of marriage after the human race was ejected from Paradise, but the institution was honorable. The sin of Adam and Eve had instead changed the way spouses had to behave towards one another. There had to be a certain wariness between the two, that they not be given over to the throes of lust. The act of intercourse itself, because it was propelled by desire, resonated with the first sin.[18] That was, however, a distinction between marriage and the acts carried out within marriage: both were natural, but the former was unquestionably good. This allowed Augustine subsequently to argue that virginity and widowhood could be more honorable states than marriage without disparaging matrimony.[19] This kind of subtlety always eluded the caustic thoughts of Jerome.[20]

The wedded union, therefore, was fully accepted as a part of human life and human society. The desire to be married (*concupiscentia nuptiarum*) was part of the natural order of man and woman that transcended the Fall.[21] In this sense,

Augustine's ideas were probably more representative of secular ideals of marriage than those of the ascetic clergy. Antony's life and the *Apothegmata* of the desert fathers may have inspired some lay Christians, but few tried to fully emulate (or surpass) their innovative feats of self-denial. A certain continence in marriage – which included abstinence during holidays and Sundays, during *menses* and pregnancy, and during penance – was more than sufficient: '*pater et mater esse meditantur.*'[22]

For non-Christian Romans, of course, the matter was not an issue. They had no need to praise (or castigate) marriage, because it was never compared or set in opposition to virginity and widowhood. Rather, each state was seen as a successive stage, at least in the case of women: virginity occurred prior to marriage and *viduitas* after. *Virginitas* to Ammianus Marcellinus, for example, was not the state of virginity, but the state of girlhood: '*adulta virginitates*' were contrasted with married women (*nuptae*).[23] Virginity in the Christian sense of the word was, to a non-Christian, simply one attribute of being a maiden. Permanent *virginitas* could never be seriously considered as a viable alternative, and therefore pagans felt no need to write extensive treatises on the relative worths of the wedded state and celibate one. The nominally Christian Luxorius perhaps expressed their sentiment best: '*Numquid non mulier conparis esse potes?*'[24]

And one need only look at the surviving funerary inscriptions to see that little had changed in the expressed ideals that surrounded Roman marriage. For example, an extensive epitaph to Aconia Faltonia Paulina in Rome makes use of the same concepts to describe the traditional virtues for a traditional matron: '*sibi maritum praeferans {sic}, Romam viro, | pudens, fidelis, pura mente et corpore, | benigna cunctis, utilis penatibus . . .*'[25] The rear side of the monument's base notes that whatever fame and honor she possessed came from her husband, Vettius Agorius Praetextatus.[26] Moreover, late antique epitaphs employed language that was consistent with funerary monuments of the classical period used for wives burying their husbands.[27] Nor did Christian ideals, when expressed on the funerary inscriptions, vary greatly from their pagan counterparts. On the sarcophagus of Flavius Iulius Catervius, for example, decorated with Christian motifs, his wife, Septimia Severina, uses language indistinguishable from traditional Roman epitaphs.[28]

When we look at marriage as it is described in law and literature, then, we must be constantly aware that the distinctions we draw between Christian and pagan did not easily apply. As we shall discuss below, both had identical concerns in the formation and consummation of a legal union.

Contracting a marriage: the example of Honorius and Maria

Before discussing the nature of married relations and the wedded state, we ought to look first at the formation of the marriage. The issues of gift-giving, dowries, and other particulars that went into a match, even if it were relatively humble, were of great importance to the couple and to their respective families. One need only look at the voluminous amount of legal material on dowries to understand that Romans had an ongoing obsession with the details of marriage.[29]

Before a *iustum matrimonium* could occur, considerable preparations had first to be made. Contracting a betrothal between two individuals after all was also a contract between two families: that is why both the Church and Constantine punished families which in an unwarranted fashion broke off engagements.[30] The process of negotiating and drawing up a contract, offering betrothal gifts and of course determining a dowry could take considerable time.

We have one detailed, albeit poetic example of the process. It is abbreviated and certainly anachronistic, but it bears describing in detail since it addresses many of the concerns prospective spouses and their families may have had. The poet Claudian commemorated the marriage of the Emperor Honorius to Maria in an *Epithalamium* of considerable length and great subtlety.[31] Like Martianus Capella's pedantic and extravagant opus, *de nuptiis Mercurii et Philologiae*, Claudian is given to lengthy flights of fancy: we must assume that only the thinnest outlines of the event have any relation to reality. Moreover, his use of mythological motifs and *topoi* to accentuate the drama of his verse presents a further caveat. The thoughts and actions of his characters – they are too stylized to call them historical persons – must thus be viewed and interpreted with care. While we have no way of knowing whether Claudian's portrayals even approximately represent these individuals, certainly their behavior and thoughts drew their impetus from idealized notions of what constituted proper courting, betrothal and marriage.

The actual and quite Christian marriage probably occurred sometime in February of 398.[32] Maria was the daughter of the *magister utriusque militum*, Stilicho, who ran the Western Empire for thirteen years. There was, however, already a blood connection between the two: Honorius and Maria were first cousins once removed.[33] Since they were not immediately wed upon Honorius' accession to the throne, we may assume that Maria was probably still a minor at the time, and only by 398 was she of a legal marriageable age. The wedding was thus one of political alliance and primarily aimed at reinforcing and extending the Theodosian line. But Stilicho's plans were an unquestionable failure. As Kenneth Holum cynically noted, 'Stilicho employed his western protégé to stud with Maria . . . , but Honorius failed even in this function.'[34] Upon her death, Maria's younger sister, Thermantia, was hastily wed to the ineffectual emperor. No issue resulted from this union, either, and upon Stilicho's execution in 408, the second wife of the Western emperor was divorced and sent packing to live with her mother in Rome.[35] Apparently, Honorius was not particularly fond of either wife.

In contrast to the sketchy reality of this dynastic alliance, we have Claudian's description of a union forged by Love, but cognizant of the niceties of family honor and respect. Claudian's readers are first made privy to the love-struck thoughts of the young emperor. Honorius is a man impatient to be married: already, before marriage, he calls Stilicho father-in-law (*socer*).[36] He arranges to send betrothal gifts of great value and antiquity.[37] He moreover protests to himself and to his audience that his pursuit of Maria has been honorable and proper. He has not forced himself upon a married woman: '*non rapio praeceps alienae foedera taedae*'[38] Despite his impatience, he has acted as a man ought when pursuing a marriage instead of an emperor who could command that union: '*fastidia supplex deposui gessique procum.*'[39] He has even sent representatives of high rank to Stilicho as agents trying to petition for the marriage, paying proper respect to the father and his family.[40]

But in addition to his affirmations of correct behavior, Honorius argues that Maria is rightly owed to him. It was Honorius' father, Theodosius, who had given his niece and adopted daughter, Serena, to Stilicho to wed, and so Maria is owed in return: '*faenus mihi solve paternum, redde suos aulae.*'[41] Indeed, Stilicho himself is aware of this transaction: the general's troops speak directly to the *genius* of Theodosius, informing the long-departed emperor that his servant's debt and duty to his old master have been repaid.[42] Moreover, Serena had cared for Honorius when he was just a boy and was thus her *de facto* foster-child. As such, Honorius reasons that it is right and proper to marry Maria, since it is assumed that such children should marry their adopted siblings: '*Quid iuveni natam non reddis alumno.*'[43] So in terms of behavior, respect and family situation, Honorius believed his status as husband unimpeachable.

In contrast to the emperor's pining, Maria appears blissfully unaware of the marriage negotiations and the preparations for the actual event. The bride-to-be is instead sitting at her mother's knee, gaining the proper moral education: '*Illa autem secura tori taedasque parari nescia divinae fruitur sermone parentis maternosque bibit mores exemplaque discit prisca pudicitiae.*'[44] Indeed, Maria is only made aware of her wedding when Venus herself announces it to her, emphasizing her isolation from the rest of human society. As a private citizen – as opposed to an empress – so much is expected of Maria: young girls ought not to be freely consorting with men. But Venus is the one who decides she can no longer '*vilior . . . privatos paterere lares*', since regal obligations await her.[45] Such duties, of course, include passing the crown down to future generations of rulers.[46] It is Claudian's closing wish that a little Honorius, sprung from Maria's womb, might sit on his grandfather's lap.[47] Venus acts as the matron of honor (*pronuba*), and it becomes the responsibility of the goddess and her retinue to prepare the empress-to-be for her wedding. They prepare the wedding chamber, they dress the bride in a traditional gown and veil, and send her forth to meet her awaiting husband in a gleaming chariot. Honorius rushes to meet her and waits impatiently for the sun to set.[48]

The poem ends not with the actual wedding, but with the celebration after the wedding. The guest of honor is, unsurprisingly, Stilicho; the bridal guests, the army. Instead of bearing weapons and armor, Rome's soldiers have dressed in white and anointed themselves with fragrant spices. They toast not the bride and groom, but the bride's father. Hailed as the *'fortunatissime patrum'*, it is the wedding party's greatest hope that Stilicho's own son, Eucherius, shall surpass his father and that Thermantia, his second daughter, shall make as good a match as Maria.[49] Claudian's sycophancy for his patron focuses attention away from the bride and especially the groom, but the importance of the two fathers, Stilicho and the departed Theodosius, nevertheless emphasize their roles as the prime movers in their respective children's marriage.

From this brief recounting of this poem, we are given glimpses of several important issues surrounding the contracting of a marriage. First and foremost, Claudian emphasized tying a knot more tightly between the *familiae* of Stilicho and Theodosius. The love that the young emperor had for Maria notwithstanding, this was a match that had important consequences for both families (quite apart from those for the Western Empire). It seems, however, that more was incumbent on the suitor than on his intended spouse: the prenuptial gifts all come from the groom-to-be. Perhaps this was expected, since a new husband would have control over the dowry, no doubt sizeable in wealthy families. Certainly the laws from late antiquity surrounding gift giving all point towards the suitor or husband recovering such gifts should the union go awry.[50] While no doubt gifts traveled in the opposite direction, they were more likely to have been incidental to any prenuptial agreements and were probably of lesser value.[51]

Moreover, there is an awareness of past and present obligations on both parties' parts. Honorius recognized the duties to and respect for his mentor, since it was under his tutelage that he had grown to adulthood. Stilicho was aware of the favor that Theodosius granted him by that guardianship and by giving Serena to him in marriage. But the implied calm demeanor of the old general, in contrast to the burning desire of the young man, also suggests a father who carefully weighed the benefits of such a marriage. The reader never hears his final approval, perhaps to emphasize Maria's willing participation in the joyous event. Whatever the reason, Claudian created a delicate balance between obligation and sagacity.

Finally, as respective *patresfamilias* of their respective households, the two men are fulfilling their responsibilities for contracting the marriage. Ambrose advised in a letter to Sisinnius that a son should not get married without a father's permission. The bishop went further and noted that a man had to choose his daughter-in-law (*nurus*), since it both exalted the prospective new bride and made her subservient.[52] This power was even canonized in late Roman law: Honorius himself issued a constitution stipulating the permanence of a *pacta nupta* made by the head of the *familia* for his daughter.[53] Joining both houses together by a further bond of matrimony may well have been influenced by the *materfamilias* or perhaps by other close kinsmen, for there are certainly examples of that. Augustine's mother, Monnica, for instance, had been the key player in putting together a match for her son.[54]

But in that case, her husband had already died and Monnica was clearly too old to have been under the influence of any guardian or kin.[55] Ultimately it was primarily the father's duty to oversee a proper match was made, and his decision was more often than not the decisive one. The references to Theodosius also implied that Honorius was faithful to the will of his father, a dutiful *filiusfamilias*.

The passages concerning Maria also merit attention. While we are given a rather grand view of the unmarried woman's life in the home, her role is hardly inconsistent with cultural attitudes – Christian and otherwise – concerning unwed daughters. Witness the similarities between Maria's preparation for her wedding and that of an unnamed girl in one of Ausonius' more ostentatious poems, *Cento nuptialis*: both brides are as resplendent as Venus.[56] Maria's mother, moreover, was clearly responsible for her child's moral upbringing: the young woman is interested in learning and practicing '*prisca pudicitiae*'. Claudian, moreover, stated that Serena made personal provisions for her formal education, too. Under her mother's guidance, Maria '*Latios . . . volvere libros desinit aut Graios*',[57] making sure she was as well versed in literature as she was in womanly virtue. That she should receive such learning is not unusual, either: in Chapter 6, we will discuss the education of children by mothers. But the fact that Maria receives all this in isolation of other people might strike us as odd.

Certainly, high-born Roman women of the classical era, both married and single, did not totally shut themselves off to outside contact with people. While unmarried daughters were undoubtedly watched by mothers, fathers and slaves with keen eyes, there were no parallels to the virtual solitary confinement which their earlier Greek counterparts endured.[58] Young boys and girls under the age of 12 both attended school in the imperial age, sometimes together.[59] As 12 was legally the earliest time that girls could wed, young women who had reached this age would often be considered *adolescentes*, with certain adult responsibilities. While their education was directed towards more domestic duties in preparation for running a household, this did not mean that unmarried girls were suddenly secluded from public life. The distaff and loom were objects for the ideal woman of the early Republic, not for the high-born lady of the imperial age.[60]

Yet from the admittedly few oblique lines of Claudian's poem, there is an underlying understanding that Maria *has* been secluded. Her purity was undoubtedly her most important quality, not only for herself, but for her marriage. Christians in particular were quick to emphasize this fact. For example, in one sermon, Gaudentius emphasized this idea by extolling the power of the virgin Mary to protect the *pudor* of young girls, through their chastity and their seclusion.[61] Indeed, Jerome stated in his letter to the noble woman Laeta, which dealt with a girl's proper upbringing, that the more secluded a girl was, the better her spiritual state would likely be.[62] In our semi-mythical poem's case, Serena alone is responsible for Maria's upbringing.

The young woman was unaware of the machinations of her family, even those things that directly affect her. It is, after all, an immortal god who enlightened her! No doubt much of this had to do with her prospective role as empress, but such seclusion was not inconsistent with Christian opinions on pedagogy for young women. So if we can draw any conclusions from Maria's situation, we must emphasize an emergent standard for unmarried girls within the *familia*, especially if they were wealthy and betrothed.

Actual examples of betrothals and any accompanying conditions that went with them are somewhat harder to find. We have a few scattered references to them in the surviving literature, although most come from the East. The Roman senator Symmachus engaged his unnamed daughter to the son of his lifelong friend, Virius Nicomachus Flavianus. The son, Nicomachus Flavianus junior, received over 80 letters from his *socer* on a wide variety of subjects.[63] Moreover, the couple's daughter, Galla, may well have married Symmachus' son, since he calls Virius *prosocer*.[64] Galla may have been only the step-granddaughter of Symmachus, but a letter to Stilicho in 400 or 401 seems to imply that the senator was concerned about possible charges of incest.[65] In any event, the two were married and perhaps had a son who was later consul in 446.[66] Symmachus incidentally described the intricate and lengthy negotiations of other couples as well.[67]

These complicated family machinations are telling. The primary purpose of these matches, like the marriage between Honorius and Maria, were first to make advantageous matches for furthering both families' fortunes. Both Symmachus and the elder Nicomachus were pagans and so perhaps united by their hostility to Christian hegemony.[68] Both had served in the highest offices of civil government, including the consulship, and both had supported the polytheist rhetor-*cum*-emperor, Eugenius.[69] Second, also like the nuptials of Honorius and Maria, there was a desire on Symmachus' part to reunite the lines of the family: '*iugendae per filios necessitudinis*'.[70] Not only did this supposedly strengthen the standing of the family, but also reconcentrated the family's wealth. Finally, Symmachus' concern about the status of the marriage underscored a concern about possible financial and legal ramifications as well.

The father's control over whom his children married was clearly the most significant issue in contracting a union. Ambrose, reaffirming the power of the father to make or break a marriage, offered a revealing story of his power. One young girl had run to the altar where a service was in progress, begging to be made a virgin of the Church. When one of her relatives attending the service demanded to know whether she would have stayed unmarried if her father were still alive, she rather cold-heartedly answered that perhaps he died so that she could become a virgin.[71] In the absence of a living father, the responsibility of course would fall to a *materfamilias*. Assuming that she did not preach to her own child the virtues of remaining a virgin – which was a distinct possibility among Christians in Italy[72] – she would have to fill in where her husband was absent. One old widow, for example, in attempting to get her daughter *out* of a vow of virginity, asked a deacon, Felix, if it were possible to wed her with a suitable husband.[73] The involvement, then, of a parent in the betrothal of a son or daughter proved that marriage remained a family affair.

Disconnects: canon and imperial law

Marriage in the classical age was first and foremost a legal state, and any religious ceremonies were incidental. This is not to belittle the importance pagan rites may have played in the formal union, but to emphasize the contractual nature of the relationship.[74] Throughout the history of Rome, from at least the fourth century BCE until well after the Western Empire's political demise, there could be considerable legal and financial implications for the wedded couple and their respective families. Divorce and widowhood, as we shall discuss in the following chapter, merely amplified those issues. While this component of marriage never changed, the growth of Christianity in the fourth and fifth centuries nevertheless had a direct, if patchy impact on marriage law, as well as redefining – at least for Christians – what constituted a *iustum matrimonium*. The goal here, then, is to see what changes were effected and what new ideals – if any – replaced or supplemented classical ones.

By means of introduction, however, much of what we have already discussed in the legal arena before the age of Constantine, was theoretically still authoritative in late antiquity. The great collection of Roman law, the *Corpus Iuris Civilis*, was compiled in the early part of the sixth century CE. Made up of the *Digesta* (a selection of legal opinions stretching back to the Twelve Tables of the early Republic), the *Codex Iustinianus* (a pandect of important laws), assorted *Novellae* and the *Institutes* (a legal textbook), this corpus was meant to be the definitive edition of Roman legal thought.[75] This was no small task for the lawyers who undertook this project: they apparently drew on approximately 2,000 different legal works.[76] But they were given the power to select, delete and change the wording of the large number of laws that had accumulated over the centuries.[77] The *Digesta*, as a collection of legal theory, was perhaps the most difficult task before the legal commission under Tribonian's presidency, and it is clear that substantial editing must have occurred. So while it is difficult to define in what way many laws and juridical opinions had been changed, their survival into Justinian's civil laws implies that they were to some extent considered valid up to their formal codification.

The editing and compilation of early and classical law notwithstanding, there was also considerable legal activity on the part of fourth-, fifth- and sixth-century emperors, and much of it concerned the family. As in the early fourth century, we must affirm that in the following years, Christianity was by no means the definitive influence on legislation regarding private life. Nevertheless, unlike the extensive social engineering of Constantine, we can see within imperial constitutions a clearer sensitivity to Christian opinion in many areas. The 26 laws of *CTh* ii:8, for example, concern and regulate all public holidays, with particular attention paid to the newly canonized Christian ones. More relevant to our interests, additional strictures on marriage were introduced with a clear religious impetus, as well as new guidelines for divorce and widowhood. The divergence between the classical Roman family and the Christian one perhaps had its seeds in Constantine, but budded and blossomed more fully under his successors.

Finally, not all such legal initiatives were geared to the West in general nor to Italy and Gaul in particular. While constitutions issued by emperors might be easily taken as *leges generales*, the reality was that often a law applied originally only to the area which an emperor controlled. An oration of Libanius, for example, noted sadly that a law of Valentinian II concerning inheritance rights of illegitimate children did not apply to the Eastern Empire.[78] Moreover, it is not always clear whether laws directed at a single city, province or diocese, had wider application within the Empire.[79] The promulgation of imperial constitutions in the *Codex Theodosianus* and *Codex Iustinianus* imply their universal application at the publication of these compilations, but not at the time of their original issuance. In only the case of the earlier code, then, published in 438, can we perhaps agree that some Eastern laws were held good for the Western Empire. Still, as a general rule, such constitutions will be drawn upon sparingly. The area and scope of the laws discussed, then, do not represent the entirety of late antique legislation, but one portion of it.

As with Augustus, emperors of late antiquity found themselves legislating frequently on social issues. But much of their activity had no relation to Christian doctrine and belief. We can state initially, however, that movement towards broadening the definition of family continued.

First, the role of the wife, as a full member of the *familia*, crystallized finally into a solid form. As *materfamilias*, her discretion over disciplining her children, in control of her spouse's property should he die, and protection from exploitation by her husband's male kin became – in law at least – unquestionable. For example, a 392 law from the East, but presumably applicable to the whole Empire, stated clearly that a woman had to be accorded the same honors and dignities as her husband.[80] While the law's language is somewhat vague, previous legislation had already granted those rights in a more tangible – albeit more narrow – way. Constantius had almost forty years earlier granted the tax-free status of clerics to their wives.[81] Moreover, a woman's power and status, as we will discuss more fully below, extended to her control over her children.[82] Like a *paterfamilias*, for example, a mother could reclaim a gift given to a child if that child had somehow wronged her.[83] Finally, a wife's standing in inheritance from a spouse was upheld. In 426, Valentinian III addressed a law to the Senate of Rome indicating that whatever an individual left to his or her spouse would remain that spouse's, even if he or she was under the *potestas* of another.[84]

Second, we see a continuing diminution of the status of any person who married below his or her social position. Unlike Constantine, who often tried to actively legislate against such marriages, his Western successors seemed to have accepted a broader definition of the marriage: *contubernium* and *matrimonium* meant increasingly less in terms of legitimacy of the union. That did not translate into a neutral position concerning the contubernial state, however. Inevitably, those individuals, particularly women, who chose to cohabit with those beneath their status faced a loss of position. A woman, for example, who allowed herself to become enslaved through *contubernium* with an unfree man, relegated her children, presumably those she brought into the marriage, to the servile state as well.[85] Another law meant to apply to all the West stipulated that women who had married purple-dye fish collectors (*murileguli*), would be consigned to their husbands' status.[86] There are further examples of such laws,[87] but these two should indicate the continuing trend in Roman attempts to discourage unions that might be considered unseemly without actually outlawing them. A *contubernium* was a legitimate union, but an inferior one with legal sanctions.

Finally, there was a continuing trend in family law, initiated by Constantine, that tried to ease procedures surrounding marriage. The stipulations regulating a marriage, as would be clearly laid out in a contract, had, in law at least, to be strictly followed.[88] Failure to abide by the provisions set out in that agreement or irregularities in its language could result in the quick dissolution of a marriage. No doubt these things were tools for spouses or their families or even (in theory) a third party to break off unwanted marriages, although Constantine tried to limit sharply the circumstances for unilateral divorce.[89] One of his laws, for example, entitled a betrothed woman to keep half of any gifts should her fiancé, having given her a kiss as a pledge, die before marriage.[90] Whatever the reasons, emperors of the fourth and fifth century relaxed rules surrounding gifts, dowries and the formation of a legitimate *iusta nupta*. Oddly enough, however, most of the legislation on these issues came out of the Eastern Empire and thus may not have been enforced in the West.[91] A law of 380, probably issued by Theodosius, for example, implies that gifts could be given to spouses as well as other, more extended relatives.[92] This move towards a certain informality also extended to betrothal gifts. Julian made it easier to give land to under-age girls who had become engaged.[93] And another law, issued by Honorius, reconfirmed a spouse's right to a dowry if his or her mate died, without interference from close kin.[94] Of perhaps greatest importance was a law, apparently circulated empire-wide, that stated a couple whose marriage contract contained irregularities could still be considered legally married, and any children would be legitimate.[95]

This last law of Theodosius II and Valentinian III offers a good introduction to a government seemingly more and more sensitive to Christian concerns when it came to family issues. The Church, for its part, had tied the legitimacy of a marriage to the approval of a priest: a canon from the fourth synod at Carthage stated that a married couple had to be presented by their parents for a priest's blessing.[96] And according to Possidius, Ambrose's biographer, the bishop of Milan had recommended a bishop's services in approving and blessing the actual marriage contract![97] Of course, there were, from the early fourth century, a number of laws concerning clerics and the Church: they included special privileges for clerics and judicial powers for episcopal courts.[98] Emperors would also occasionally grant general amnesties to criminals on important Christian holidays.[99] By the fifth century, the imperial government actively involved itself with regulating the clergy: Valentinian III, for example, started pushing for the supremacy of the Roman bishop in the West.[100] Along with these special considerations, emperors sometimes applied what they perceived as Christian-based morality to the married state. While it is hard to generalize, the 'Christianization of marriage' laws took two directions. First, they dealt specifically with the status of matrimony itself. Second, there were increasing numbers of laws aimed at protecting and glorifying virginity as well as discouraging divorce and re-marriage. As we shall examine shortly, some of these were inspired directly by canon law, although Church regulations were often at odds with even staunchly Christian emperors.

Turning first to the status of marriage, let us consider Roman marriage patterns. As a general rule, Roman law and custom permitted endogamy to a certain degree, providing they were relatives of at least the fourth degree who were neither ascendants nor descendants.[101] The closest fourth degree relationship would thus be a first cousin. An exception, of course, was the famous story of the Emperor Claudius who, wishing to marry his brother's daughter, Agrippina, persuaded the Senate to pass a law permitting such a union.[102] Also, there had been a long-standing tradition, in the legal litera-ture at least, of a man marrying his brother's widow.[103] There were no legal bars, of course, to marrying entirely out of one's kin group, and despite the legality of certain types of endogamous union, marriage patterns seem to indicate a tendency towards exogamy.[104] Of course, in the case of foreigners and sometimes even with Romans, the right to marriage (*conubium*) would be lacking and thus such unions could not be recognized as *iustum matrimonium*. But by marrying within one's extended family, certain patrimonial benefits occurred: dowries stayed within one family, wealth which had been divided among one generation might be reconcentrated amongst common grand-children and it could strengthen the prestige and station of a *domus*. So, in a sense, Roman law did encourage a limited kind of endogamy within the free Roman population.

As a parallel, early Christians seemed to encourage endogamy within their own community and we have already discussed the use of the metaphor of family among this group. We have the famous statement of Jerome, who suggested the value of Christian women marrying and converting polytheistic husbands.[105] But the realities of the situation appear to have been significantly different. Kate Cooper has convincingly argued that the works of Jerome and others concerning a wife's role in a man's religious state were more rhetorical artifice than they were an accurate reflection of real life.[106] More striking is Michele Salzman's study on aristocratic women. Using the available prosopography, she surveyed the surviving literary and epigraphic evidence.[107] She found that of the 319 aristocrats she sampled, only a small percentage were married to spouses of another religion.[108] So in practice at least, Christians tended to marry within their own community, not unlike the ancient Jewish sects such as the Essenes or those at Qumran.[109] In the sense that we can speak of them as a quasi-kin group, we can argue that, too, they were endogamous.[110]

These practices tended to be codified in the Church by certain marriage proscriptions. Some of the earliest extant canons, drawn from the council of Elvira in late 306, tried to regulate the marriage habits of the Christian community. These canons, of course, never had the force of law, even in the fifth and sixth centuries CE. In theory, the only power the Church had over its own members, as mentioned above, was the threat of penance and excommunication. Nor were the Elviran canons fully recapitulated in future synods of late antiquity. Considering the large number of local, regional and ecumenical councils that were convened in the fourth and fifth centuries, this suggests that these restrictions had much to do with a young religion struggling to identify and define itself. This trend towards endogamy thus likely came out of an earlier tradition of a smaller and more tightly knit Christian community. Nevertheless, we should briefly summarize them.

As a general rule, these proscriptions seemed to be directed against those persons who might endanger the spiritual well-being of the laity who intended to marry.[111] So it is unsurprising that canon 15 of Elvira, 'Concerning the marriage of a gentile' (*de coniugio eorum qui ex gentilitate*)', specifically prohibits the marriage of Christians to pagans. The language of the title itself has an almost racial quality to it: the word *gentilitas* in late Latin could mean barbarian or foreigner as well as heathen.[112] Nor was this all. If Christian parents knowingly approved of or arranged a marriage to a non-believer, they, too, would be subject to excommunication.[113] But we know, despite its relative rarity, of Christian women who *did* marry pagans. The most famous example of a 'mixed' marriage was the union of Augustine's parents. His father, Patricius, had been a polytheist for most of his life, and only near his death did he accept baptism at his wife's urging.[114] In contrast, Monnica, Augustine's mother, and her entire household were Christian.[115] Monnica had accepted what Jerome suggested and converted her spouse. Nor were Augustine's parents unique. Apparently, sometime in the 380s, some small villages in the foothills of Aemilia in northern Italy happily permitted marriages between Christians and non-believers.[116]

But the council of Elvira did not only single out polytheists. Women were forbidden to marry both Jews and heretics.[117] Certain types of *infames* were to be avoided: women should not marry dandies (*comati* or *viri cinerarii*: literally, men with long or permed hair).[118] The only specific instruction to men required five years penance if they committed adultery with polytheists or Jews.[119]

As with most canons, these sorts of restrictions on marriage had little immediate effect on law. It was not until March of 388 that the first surviving constitution preventing Christians from marrying a certain group (Jews) appears, and it may have only been enforced in the East.[120] The only other law before that time which was in any way related to this kind of marital exclusivity was a 343 ruling of Constantius, redeeming Christian women sold into brothels and mandating only that Christians buy them.[121] This was hardly a strong endorsement of the canons of Elvira. Nevertheless, while the connection to Church law was tenuous at best, there can be little doubt that inspiration for both constitutions was at least nominally Christian.

The law barring the marriage between Christians and Jews deserves closer attention, however. The time of its passage was delicate politically. Theodosius, probably the initiator of the law, was just about to head West to secure political support for an increasingly puppet-like Valentinian II. The Eastern emperor's political support in the West, despite family ties to Spain, was apparently slim. Before he could leave, however, Theodosius learned that the Christian community at Callinicum had burned down the local synagogue. When the emperor directed the bishop to rebuild the Jewish temple, Ambrose convinced him to rescind his order.[122] It is within this context that we can perhaps interpret his law. In an attempt to keep the two communities separate, Theodosius may have seen his stricture as a useful expediency. But it also no doubt appealed to many zealous Christians, like the communities at Callinicum and the one which would later murder the polytheist philosopher, Hypatia, in Alexandria.[123] Furthermore, by classifying such a union as an act of adultery, and one which any person could bring charges, the emperor made intermarriage with Jews a criminal act. The government could therefore become fully involved in maintaining the separation. So while *CTh* iii:7:2 had its origins in Christian issues, it was a product of politics as much as doctrine.

The effect of this legal separation is unknown, but both the Church and the state passed other restrictions the contracting of marriages. Marriage between close kin had always been looked upon suspiciously by the Church. Incest was a common theme harped upon in early Christian apologies, a concern that seemed to grow with the religion. By the mid-fourth century, not only were clerics supporting new strictures on incest, but were actively promoting government policies to broaden the term's definition.[124]

Moreover, Christians in the past had been nervous about charges that they themselves practiced incest. The use of *frater* and *soror*, even between spouses, apparently led to all sorts of misunderstandings: Minucius Felix had to give an impassioned defense of Christian propriety.[125] Apologists therefore would often make it a point to condemn the practice.[126] The crime was frequently associated with cannibalism, to which early Christians, participating in the Eucharist, were obviously sensitive (and suspect). For religious authors of late antiquity, on the other hand, incest was seen as a direct result of the Fall: Augustine included it in a litany of miseries which befell man because of Original Sin.[127]

The parameters of what constituted incest are not entirely clear. As a practical matter, incest for Christians was not simply an issue between ascendants and descendants, since lineal breaches could be a concern: under the threat of death, Constantius rescinded the Claudian rule permitting uncles to marry their sibling's daughters.[128] Such unions had always been rare, although Ambrose criticized Aemilius Florus Paternus' desire to marry his son, Cynegius, to his granddaughter by an unnamed daughter.[129] Rather, close collateral relations, even where no blood tie existed, were discouraged. Sometimes, there was a mixture of both: one early canon, for example, excommunicated permanently the former father-in-law who married his son's wife.[130] But as a general rule, there seems to have been a retreat from those marriages within one's own family that had been in theory accepted by Roman society.

The proscriptions generally ran against individuals marrying multiple siblings or siblings-in-law. Of the six surviving canons from various Western synods, four include such restrictions. A synod held in Agde (on the Mediterranean coast near Narbonne) offered an extensive list of prohibited unions, providing the basis for a similar regulation in a synod held at Epaon in Burgundy some years after.[131] Most regulations were more limited in scope, however. An early fifth-century synod held at Rome, for example, ruled that a man could not marry his deceased wife's sister.[132] A council held at Orleans in 511 recapitulated that ruling, and added that he was also barred from marrying his brother's wife.[133]

One piece of imperial legislation seemed to run along similar lines, although the timing of its passage does not even roughly correlate to the time of similar canonical activity. A law of Constantius, evidently for enforcement in Gaul, prohibited a man from contracting a marriage with either his former wife's sister or marrying the former wife of his brother.[134] Any children from the union would be considered *spurii*. But the law was published in April of 355, some fifty years before the synod held at Rome in 402 and fifty years after Elvira.[135] In other words, there is no clear connection between official Church policy and its imperial counterpart.

Nevertheless, the corresponding imperial laws can only be understood in the context of Christian thought. *CTh* iii:12:2 begins with an explanation that it was considered perfectly normal for such unions to occur in the past: '*Etsi licitum veteres crediderunt . . .*'.[136] There is little evidence that such behavior still continued in late antiquity.[137] And yet there was at least an understanding that marriages between former in-laws could legally occur. It would be logical to infer, then, that a desire to regulate no longer practiced customs related to a deeper change in the moral climate. The final question to ask then is whether we can associate this change with Christianity. Constantius, of course, granted a large number of varied privileges to the clergy.[138] He also attacked paganism at several junctures, outlawing certain types of sacrifices in 341 and 353 and ordered a general closing of polytheist temples in Italy and Africa.[139] Libanius even stated that Constantius ordered the destruction of a number of temples.[140] That the emperor was a vociferous supporter of Christianity is thus undeniable, although his religious leanings were decidedly Arian in nature.[141] Unfortunately, it is not possible to tell whether Arian and Athanasian partisans differed on issues surrounding marriage and the family, although given the nature of their disagreements, it is likely that they were minimal if they existed at all.[142] Given this admittedly circumstantial evidence, combined with Constantius' earlier law outlawing marriage between uncles and nieces,[143] it is a reasonable assumption to argue that Christian concerns about incest inspired the passage of these laws.

There were two other laws on incest, both published in the East, one of which was quite lengthy. One constitution, published in 396, makes mention of a no longer extant earlier law which outlawed marriages between first cousins (or cousins of the fourth degree).[144] When and where it was issued is unknown,[145] but evidently it ordered burning in addition to the confiscation of all the guilty parties' property.[146] *CTh* iii:12:3 authorized a lesser punishment for marrying one's cousin – along with nieces and former siblings-in-law – that was financial in nature. Nevertheless, marriages between cousins of various degrees, which had existed even in late antiquity were for the first time banned. But did the rejection of a long-held Roman practice come from a Christian impetus?

As mentioned above, the synod of Agde outlawed a number of incestuous unions, including first cousins.[147] This canon recapitulated another passed in the East in the fifth century. But this still divides the constitution from official Church law by almost a century. Since the law was promulgated first in the Eastern Empire, it is logical we should enlarge our search to include Eastern authors as well. We have, as it turns out, at least one Christian in the late fourth century who did condemn such marriages. Basil of Caesarea wrote in one letter that he supported various imperial bans on various incestuous marriages, including those between cousins.[148] The letter was written in the late 360s or early 370s. It is not clear from the language of the letter whether an actual ban on cousin marriages had been enacted, but let us assume conservatively that it did not. If we therefore deduce that the law referred to in *CTh* iii:12:3 was written after 363, but before 395 (and possibly before 379), then we see a much closer association between the mystery law and Christian condemnation of first cousin marriages.[149] Again, the evidence is circumstantial, but it does provide a correlation of time and space between religious opinion and imperial law.

In sum, then, we can state that some imperial restrictions on marriage were related in one form or another to Christian concerns and controversies. To be sure, direct connections are impossible to demonstrate and indirect ones are difficult to define as well. But the preponderance of past Christian opinion on incest, the Christianizing policies of fourth-century emperors in other areas, and the prevailing politics of the period all suggest that the connection was there.

Thus, the legislation of the fourth and fifth centuries reveal a paradigmatic shift in laws dealing with social affairs. A tangible, if not comprehensive, Christian influence on family issues became more prominent in especially the late fourth and early fifth centuries. That period corresponded with some of the most fertile Christian thought in the West. The imperial government did not discard Roman civil law, nor did it have to. Social legislation had provided a vessel for transmitting Christian concerns and issues to the wider population of the Roman Empire. What did it matter that Roman law was still largely classical, if its heart was Christian?

The negative example: Melania the Younger and Pinian

As with betrothal, it is perhaps worthwhile looking at one marriage which was clearly idealized and about which we know a fair amount. While we must once again deal with aristocratic *familia* for any in-depth look into private households, the marriage of Melania to Pinian is in some ways atypical for aristocratic life as well. In principle, of course, they represent a contradictory example of typical family life. They were largely celibate for most of their lives and chose poverty as a means of extricating themselves from what they saw as a cycle of worldly temptation and sin. Unsurprisingly, they are commemorated in Melania's Christian *vita*.

Like Claudian's highly stylized account of Honorius and Maria's wedding, the life of Melania the Younger is also a work that must be viewed carefully. To begin, there are several surviving accounts and partial accounts of her activities. They appear in both Greek and Latin, and the manuscript tradition is complicated and confused.[150] This has resulted sometimes in a considerable difference of details surrounding Melania's day-to-day affairs. Since many of the accounts seem to date from the tenth century or later, there are also questions as to the quality of information being related.[151] Second, Melania and Pinian's married life also says a great deal about the *de facto* destruction of their own *domus*, what Susanna Elm would term the 'gradual dissolution of the traditional family structure.'[152] As such, it is in many ways a work antithetical to the presumed norms of behavior and culture. It is accordingly more a source of negative evidence than anything else.

Most important, of course, is that as a *vita*, the work has certain rhetorical and substantive goals consistent with its literary genre. As a general rule, *vitae* were not necessarily inclusive as biographies: 'extraneous' events – notably comprehensive accounts of the subject's life – were frequently absent. Rather, they tended to be anecdotal, for several reasons. First and foremost was the desire to display the purity and holiness of the said saint. This was manifest in his or her ability to control sexual desires, but also frequently included were constant and occasionally novel ways of mortifying the flesh. Second, hagiographies were testaments to the saint's faith in Christ. It was by divine grace that these individuals could gain control over themselves as well as perform great works and miracles. Finally, *vitae* had an ostensible pedagogical purpose. A saint's life was in itself a 'how-to book', offering inspiration and direction for anchorites, eremites and even lay Christians. So much is clear in Melania's life when we look at her relationship to her husband. The young saint literally instructs Pinian on how to pursue the ascetic life, as well as giving advice to the nunnery she founded. A *vita*, then, was a roadmap from the earthly city to the heavenly one.[153]

The recounting of Melania's relationship to Pinian is thus centered around their spiritual kinship. We are only told a fraction about their married life in the *vita*, yet enough to see a number of important developments in the Roman institution of matrimony. Both Melania and Pinian were scions of enormously wealthy and important families. Melania's father, Publicola, had been the *praetor urbanus* in Rome in 374,[154] and may have also been *consularis* of Campania sometime in the late fourth century.[155] He had been sole heir to the fortune of his mother, Melania the Elder.[156] Melania's mother, Albina, came from similarly illustrious roots. Pinian is described as coming from a consular family, and while this is not easily confirmed, his father had certainly been the *Praefectus urbis Romae*.[157] Their wealth stretched across the extent of the Empire, spanning Europe and Africa. At one point, the hagiographer mentions the fact that Pinian's annual income alone, without his wife's properties, amounted to 120,000 *solidi*.[158] If we accept Olympiodorus' statement that the wealthiest Senators had incomes of 4,000 pounds of gold per year (288,000 *solidi*) and that middling ones had 1,500 (108,000 *solidi*), then the two were moderately wealthy Senators, but fabulously rich overall.[159]

The two were married at a relatively young age: Melania was 14 and Pinian was not quite 17. The youth of these individuals was apparently a factor in their living arrangements: it seems that Melania continued to remain in her father's house even after the marriage had been consummated.[160] When she tried to run away, she feared not her husband's wrath, but the reaction of her parents.[161] It was not until her father died that Melania seems to have taken up a permanent residence with her husband. Even then, her mother was always with them, accompanying the two on their trip throughout Africa and the East, and eventually settling with her daughter in the same cloister. Her mother was buried in the *Aposteleion* she had built for her monastery.[162]

The marriage itself was rocky at first. Melania wanted no part of its physical aspects, and both begged and tried to bribe her husband to leave her a virgin.[163] Her disdain for marriage partially confirms what might have been inferred about the marriage: it had been arranged by the minors' families. It is clear that she had to be forced into the marriage. Melania's pleas, however, were to no avail. Pinian's motives for marriage were also quite clear. It was his desire and intent to have at least two children. Only then would he be willing to accede to her wishes for chastity.[164]

Melania took it ill. On several occasions, she attempted to run away. Clearly these were the acts of a willful and desperate child, and it appears as if her parents were still responsible for her discipline precisely because of her behavior. It was only after respected clerics told her to be patient and obey the wishes of her husband that the young woman acceded to Pinian's demands. The actions of another young woman, Ecdicia, who had decided to become a widow without bothering to consult her very much living husband, would not be an issue in this marriage.[165] But even her initial attempts of asceticism were met with distress by various members of her family.

Feeling the need to leave at least a single heir, Pinian's plan came to naught. Their first child, pledged as a virgin, died when she was just a few years old. Their second child, a son, died shortly after birth. Depression set in for both *coniuges* and it was Pinian who finally lost the war of wills. Fearful for his wife's health, which seems to have been degenerating rapidly, he agreed to respect Melania's wishes for a chaste life. Apparently, then, Pinian had had some real affection for his wife, or he surely never would have capitulated. He was 24 and she 20.

Their marriage after this decision apparently went for the better. Melania took to calling her husband her spiritual brother – '*adelphos*'. They began by performing charitable works together and slowly ridding themselves of their considerable wealth. Such behavior was clearly looked upon as asinine and disastrous by family and peers: at one point Pinian's brother, Severus, along with members of Melania's family, tried to retrieve the patrimonies which the couple intended to liquidate.[166] As technical minors, both Melania and Pinian could be legally prevented from divesting themselves from their property.[167] They persevered, however, and with the assistance of the Empress Serena, proceeded with their plans. By the time they settled in Jerusalem they had disposed of most of their wealth. And through a combination of adversity and travel, the two lived in harmony, or *concordia*, until Pinian died in 431. They had been married for almost thirty-two years.[168]

Pinian and Melania in some ways had a typical aristocratic marriage, with the exception of their joint celibacy. To be sure, they had married contemporaries who also took vows of chastity: Iniuriosus, for example, a wealthy man of senatorial stock, was convinced to live chastely with his bride on their wedding night.[169] Perhaps closer to Melania and Pinian's story, Paulinus of Nola and his wife, Therasia, both committed themselves to chastity after the death of their son, Celsus.[170] Even so, clerics advised against permanent celibacy, at least in a marriage's initial years. In fact, Augustine argued that denying one's partner was considered a sin, albeit a venial one, because it had the potential for leading to greater sins.[171] He had foreseen the difficulties: in one letter, Augustine found himself in the unenviable position of trying to convince a couple who had taken an oath of continence not to forswear it.[172] Those older couples who had achieved a lasting celibacy might well be praised,[173] but it was not something to be entered into lightly nor immediately. No doubt this was the sort of warning Melania received from those clerics she respected, advising her to capitulate to Pinian's demands. It incidentally reaffirmed the ideal of male dominance in the marriage contract. Christians may have held men and women to the same moral standard and rigors as spouses, but it was still an unequal arrangement.

Their youth, or *adolescentia*, created additional problems for the couple, although it seems as if pre-adult marriages (if not quite this young) were common enough. Their situation was therefore by no means unusual. Of greater interest were their living conditions after marriage. They were intimate and had consummated the marriage. Moreover, as discussed in the second chapter, marriage specifically meant beginning one's own *familia*, if not *domus*, in a separate living facility for aristocrats of the classical period. Yet Melania dwelt in her father's house and apparently under his strict supervision. Perhaps Pinian existed under similar circumstances. What are we to make of this action? Does it imply a Christian influence, wherein there is closer scrutiny of a child's behavior until he or she reached legal adulthood? Is this an example of fuller control over marriages contracted between elites? Or, finally, could this be an example of a new trend in family composition and living patterns?

These questions are not easily answerable, although we can surely eliminate the last possibility. While there may have been trends towards the multi-family and multi-generational households in the rural areas of the Western Empire, there is no evidence that it was a common feature among urban populations, particularly among its wealthier denizens.[174] Most of the Roman aristocracy allowed their children their own houses, lands and household staffs. In the case of Symmachus, for example, his son was living on his own *before* he was married, and was possibly still under the age of 25.[175] Nor was it uncommon, it appears, for widowed mothers to live or travel with their children. As John Chrysostom mentioned, it was traditional for Roman widows to be the guardians of household property and finances.[176] We know, for example, of the travels of Augustine's mother; although before she reached Milan, she was more accurately chasing her son, rather than traveling with him.[177] So it is difficult to document a trend towards extended family households in the great families of late antiquity. Melania's living situation prior to her father's death, then, seems to have had its origins elsewhere.

That both families were Christian, moreover, does not imply that the two were concerned with Melania and Pinian's moral rectitude. Indeed, there are specific instances where both families were appalled by their overzealous behavior. At one point, Melania had to beg her aunt to keep her hair shirt a secret from her parents.[178] Pinian's brother, Severus, tried to keep his younger brother from squandering his inheritance on charity.[179] If their families were concerned about their religious state, they no doubt felt that their children's positions and actions were too severe. More to the point, their conduct had seemed childish and rash. Their petulant plan to starve themselves unless their parents acceded to their desires underscores this point.[180] Melania may have had her own chapel, but religion appears to have been a secondary concern to her family. Having grandchildren, on the other hand, was her father's stated goal.

The idea that Melania's continued residence in her father's house was related to her high position in society may have the most merit. Although she had consummated the marriage and had had a child, her parents seem to have had considerable say in her continued status as a minor. Melania's father was admittedly concerned with their place in society, apologizing on his deathbed for his preoccupation with other men's opinions. It may be that he gave up on trying to convince them, but surely before that time, he found his daughter's actions not only self-destructive, but unseemly. Running away, behaving strangely at the public baths, and bribing friends, retainers and slaves to hide her behavior were hardly the actions of a high-born, if young, Roman matron. Of course, Melania's situation may have been an isolated incident. Her demeanor and single-mindedness may have dictated her parents' actions. So although it was a distinct possibility, there is not enough evidence to state categorically that this was standard behavior among the aristocracy, or even urban populations.

Melania's residence must remain a mystery. Yet there were other issues involved in their marriage. While Melania capitulated to her husband's desires for children, it was half-hearted at best. Only on the urging of various holy men did she agree. The importance of the man's role in a marriage was thus being marginalized here. To the majority of lay Christians, such behavior would have seemed as inappropriate as it would to polytheists. Augustine had argued that the Fall had relegated women to the control of their fathers and spouses, thus recapitulating the basic patriarchal structure of the Roman family.[181] Only Jerome had encouraged wives to act contrary to the wills of their husbands, if only to force pagan mates to convert.[182] But once Pinian agreed to his wife's wishes, it is clear that he had become the subordinate partner in the relationship. Melania acted as advisor and director of their actions. She properly commemorated him at his death, but it is important to note that she did so as her brother in Christ, not as her husband.[183] Certainly, such a turnaround had a remarkable rhetorical effect on the readers of Melania's *vita*, as it no doubt intended. But while it may have sparked admiration for the young woman – and perhaps for her husband – it was not a model for behavior within the family. The friction between the couple's respective families and between each other amply illustrated that.

The *vita* of Melania was admittedly less about Christian marriage than it was about sanctity. Nevertheless, from their negative example, and supplemented with additional material, it provides some positive evidence. First, with Christian marriage, like Roman marriage, came a belief in conceptual hierarchy. Marriage had been confirmed in the Creation as a sacrament,[184] had changed in the Fall, and would remain in its present form until the end of time. Wives were right to keep their eyes heavenward, but they were unquestionably subject to their husbands.[185] Jerome had of course emphasized the drudgery of a wife's lot – notably to the detriment of God – but even he had reaffirmed this basic fact.[186] That Melania rejected this concept would have undoubtedly raised eyebrows of disapproval from many lay readers.

Second, the function of procreation, also like its Roman counterpart, was the most important and positive rationale for marriage. *Proles* were the primary natural and legitimate purpose of marriage.[187] The Church sought to protect that. Even Jerome had expressed his outrage that married couples might use contraceptives or abortificants to avoid the gifts which marriage provided.[188] No Western Christian would go as far as John Chrysostom, however, and say that there were no more need for children since the world was fully populated.[189] Augustine could reject such claims blithely, waving away the specter of worldwide abstinence simply because the Church preached continence and celibacy.[190] In fact, with complete sincerity, Augustine could argue that intercourse was good for the health of the human race.[191] He knew from his own experience as a father that sexual congress could not be easily controlled. Marriage put desire to good use.[192] Pinian, even at first, was not opposed to continence, but only *after* he had children.

Third, marriage was something that could not be thoughtlessly ended. One did not run away from it, nor could it be considered a commodity, to be dispensed with if something better came along (whether it were a better spouse or a calling from Christ). As matrimony was a blessed state of sorts, divorce, except in the case of adultery, was unthinkable. Indeed, divorce did not end a marriage, it merely suspended it. Only death broke the bonds.[193] Even when adultery occurred, which apparently was never a problem for Melania or Pinian, the wedded state was not to be thrown away lightly. Forgiveness was a viable alternative to ending the relationship.

Finally, faithfulness in marriage was required. *Fides* had been an important concept in the classical period, although more often than not, being faithful to one's spouse was a wife's responsibility rather than the other way around. A husband, in contrast, could be expected to partake of a number of sexual adventures, ranging from *paelices* to homosexual liaisons. Such behavior was decidedly rejected in the Christian marriage, where both spouses were held to the same moral standards. Unlike Roman law, wherein women were not allowed to charge their husbands with *stuprum*, moral censure for adulterous husbands was as strong as it was for women in the late antique Church.[194] Marriage may have been an unequal partnership, but both parties were beholden to the other. There would be no double-standard in this regard.[195]

Problems in marriage

Adultery

The boundaries of marriage, as well as the actions of the unmarried, in the classical world were only restrained by the limits a man chose to place on them. Horace had eloquently bewailed the rampant infidelity in Rome in 23 BCE.[196] A husband might be divorced for his failings and suffer some financial loss, but he would almost never be criminally censured as his wife might be.[197] So the issue of continence in late antique marriages is a fruitful issue to discuss. Simply put, did the Church's call for marital fidelity resonate with any great success among Christians of late antiquity, let alone the considerable population of non-Christians?

The evidence is mixed. It is true that adultery was condemned by, or at least castigated by, secular authors in late antiquity. Ausonius had written a number of epigrams, viciously lampooning several people, possibly real, who had transgressed their marital vows. One Eumpina, for example, not only was faithless, but also tried ineptly to poison her husband.[198] The African poet, Luxorius, castigated the sterile Proconius for prostituting his wife in order to have children.[199] But these artful and crudely humorous criticisms are similar to the satire of earlier, classical Roman poets. Their existence perhaps illustrates a general opprobrium associated with adultery, but tells us little of the why. Quite apart from poetry, there was, as mentioned earlier, considerable discussion of the act in the surviving legal texts as well; but it, too, basically paralleled the jurisprudence of an earlier day. While adultery may have therefore been decried by all segments of Roman society, Christian and otherwise, the condemnation in the secular literature came from a long-standing literary tradition.

Perhaps more revealing are two brief references as to why individuals chose *not* to break up a marriage. One offers a man's perspective and the other a woman's. We first have the misgivings of Paulinus of Pella. In describing his somewhat wild youth, he made it a point never to sleep with a married woman nor, for that matter, with any free woman.[200] He mentioned two over-riding concerns. First, he claimed that he did not wish to injure that which was not his, although somewhat later he admitted that he could have dealt with the inevitable moral reproaches. Second, and this seems closer to truth, he wanted nothing to ruin his own *fama* nor his reputation. His station in the world, even as a *iuvens*, could be seriously jeopardized by so much as a *reus criminis*.[201] From the concern about his name, we can further assume that blame could easily affected his *domus* as well.

Augustine in his autobiography related the second demurral. When Augustine's father gleefully announced the discovery of his son's erection at the public baths, his mother became extremely agitated.[202] Fearing the worst, Monnica entreated her son not to engage in any sexual activity, but especially not to sleep with any man's wife.[203] Augustine specifically stated that he thought such advice was womanish, *muliebris*, indicating that this was what might be considered a woman's argument for forswearing adultery. Unlike Paulinus, who feared for his place in society, Monnica feared for the chastity of an *uxor* and for her son in committing such an onerous sin.

These two opinions concerning adultery at first appear odd. A husband might logically be expected to be the center of such objections given Rome's *paterfamilias*-dominated ideology. As one of Augustine's exasperated parishioners asked: 'Can't a man do what he wants in his own house?'[204] Both Paulinus and Monnica's imaginary wife place their concern in different corners, however: Paulinus as the lover and Monnica as the faithless, but victimized, woman. True, they expressed the viewpoint from positions they might conceivably be in, but there is not even an acknowledgment of the cuckolded husband. No doubt if a husband expounded on the same subject, even though he had recourse to both civil and criminal law, he would have considered his position of primary importance. Shame would fall on his wife, but that would only compound the shame upon him: the *lex Iulia* had termed it an *iniuria maior* to his honor.[205] But these issues are considered by neither Paulinus nor Augustine's mother. A paramour might be justifiably murdered if he was found *in flagrante* (although we have no examples of this from the West[206]), but a greater danger came from the damage done to place in one's own *familia* and the society at large. This perhaps says little about adultery's commonality, but it does represent a broad spectrum of opinion concerning the many repercussions of an illicit affair. If adultery was not *de rigueur*, at least feelings about it were.

Actual cases of adultery also give us a mixed picture. The most highly publicized accounts from late antiquity were the adultery trials found in Ammianus Marcellinus' narrative, which revealed the affairs of a number of influential Romans in the late 360s. At least ten persons of senatorial stock, five men and five women, were prosecuted and nine were apparently executed for their infidelities.[207] These simple facts alone, however, should give us pause. While criminal proceedings could, and occasionally were brought against a wife, they were almost never brought against a husband. Yet three senators and the *vicarius Romae* were tried and executed.[208] The law had never made any provisions for such actions, although, as John Matthews has noted, one imperial enactment ordered more severe treatment for senators convicted of serious crimes.[209] This law assumed, however, that the death penalty was imposed on the guilty, but the punishment in earlier times for the condemned was not necessarily death.[210] Moreover, Constantine had reiterated and augmented Augustus' provision that only close kin or a husband could bring a charge of adultery against a wife.[211] It stands to reason that in the event of such an action against a man, only a woman's close male kin could bring a criminal charge.

There are further problems with Ammianus' narrative. These accusations were mixed in with charges of poison and magic that, as Peter Brown has suggested, revealed a deeper division between the polytheist and newly Christianized aristocracies.[212] In the case of Aginatius, for example, he was convicted both of adultery *and* sorcery.[213] The use of the black arts, particularly in cases where they could be used against the emperor, had since the time of Tiberius been a crime of *maiestas* and so carried a death sentence. Julius Festus Hymetius, for example, fearing a harsh punishment from the emperor because of a sensitive political matter, had apparently consulted a diviner and was prosecuted for it.[214] There is thus some confusion as to the actual reasons behind many of these trials. Furthermore, in the cases of Anepsia and Avienus, the accusations and trial went on for several years.[215] In other words, these cases were not necessarily sensationalistic, short-term affairs. Their statuses were undoubtedly subject to the political ups and downs of the day and the stated facts of the accusations may have had little basis in reality.

But the most problematic issue with Ammianus' account is the lack of any great detail. We hear of the injustice done to Flaviana and Claritas by their executioner – and his subsequent punishment – but we hear nothing of their actual crime.[216] Only in the case of Anepsia do we get an impression of her initial innocence, but her behavior subsequent to the accusation is much better documented. Moreover, the language itself was vague. Phrases like '*ex coetu amplissimo*' do not even make it clear, in fact, that a person's sexual activities were technically adulterous. The paucity of detail may well have been due to Ammianus' personal unfamiliarity with the specific events,[217] but we have no way of judging the truth of the allegations nor whether, supposing they were false, the acts at least represented an interpretable mode of behavior.

The combination, therefore, of the unusual legal procedures, the political nature of these trials and the lack of any corroborating evidence make any use of these events somewhat limited. Whether the named individuals actually committed these acts is impossible to say. We can offer only one small observation. The attitude of Ammianus, as well as that of the Roman world he portrayed, clearly did imply that such transgressions were more offensive among the aristocracy than among the lower classes. If these allegations *were* true, and the historian's narrative suggests they were largely false,[218] then it was proper for the elite to be censured and severely punished. Judicial violence may have meted out fouler methods of execution to the *humiliores*, but the end result for the guilty was still death.

We do know of several confirmed incidents of adultery in the later Roman Empire, albeit not as sensational as those discussed by Ammianus. I will examine three, mostly to illustrate its variety. Augustine had boasted that his mother, Monnica, was a *univira* and had been the ideal wife to her husband, Patricius.[219] In contrast, his father had at least one extramarital sexual relationship and perhaps more.[220] Indeed, there is at least a suggestion that they were ongoing: '*expectabat enim misericordiam tuam super eum, ut in te credens castificaretur.*'[221] It is not entirely clear with whom he had sexual relations, but his actions were apparently common knowledge within the *familia*. It may well have been that the household gossip, which strained the relationship between Monnica and her mother-in-law, had to do with Patricius' infidelities. Whatever the case, his peccadilloes seem to have been short-lived and neither husband nor wife considered a divorce.

There was also the above-mentioned husband of Fabiola, who, according to Jerome, '*tanta . . . vitia habuisse . . . , ut ne scortum quidem et vile mancipium ea sustinere posset.*'[222] In their case, his sins were so severe that Fabiola actually divorced him. Fabiola's husband seemed to revel in every kind of sexual exploit, whether it was carousing in the brothels of Rome or throwing himself upon the nearest available slave girl. Indeed, on one occasion his behavior was so egregious that it had evidently scandalized the entire neighborhood and precipitated the separation. Jerome never tells us precisely what the crime is, but we can assume that it must have been fairly sensational, even for this man. Clearly his reputation for debauchery was as renowned as it was continuous.

Our final example is found in a novel of Majorian from 459. A certain Ambrosius allegedly slept with the wife of another man and was punished for his crime.[223] The individuals involved must have been of a fairly high station if the *consularis* of Suburbicarian Tuscany adjudicated the case. Although it is never clearly stated, the matter seems to have ended in divorce for the woman and her husband. Ambrosius was convicted and sentenced to a temporary exile. The event stands in sharp contrast to a similar case related by Jerome from late fourth-century Liguria. The *consularis* of that province (perhaps Ambrose?) had tried a case of adultery wherein the lover was tortured into confessing and was subsequently executed.[224]

We see three modes of behavior presented from these examples as well as three very different interpretations of the misdeed. In the first case, Patricius' acts seem to have been deemed a common case of adultery in Augustine's eyes. Augustine found the behavior inexcusable and yet there was a certain tired acquaintance with such actions. Patricius had, after all, not wanted to divorce his wife and was generally a kind man. He made it a point to provide for his son and family, and it is clear that he gave his wife considerable latitude in running the house and raising the children.[225] Although he had a hot temper, Monnica never made an issue of his infidelity and so maintained domestic harmony. His actions clearly were not agreeable, but they were at least familiar and thus tolerable. And he did finally end his extramarital activity. Perhaps when Patricius finally converted to Christianity after his wife's dogged insistence, his infidelity ceased.[226] Perhaps, despite the insinuations of Augustine to the contrary, he had stopped sooner.

In contrast, Fabiola's husband's infidelity seems more representative of a young man who never quite achieved the sobriety that marriage was supposed to bring. It was fairly common for men to sow their wild oats in their twenties and only think about marriage as they approached thirty. Augustine had been such a man, as had Paulinus of Pella and Prudentius. Engaging a low-class concubine was quite normal, for they could be jettisoned as unwanted cargo when the need for a marriage commitment presented itself. To be sure, some men had trouble in shifting to monogamy. Constantine, for example, had Constantine II by a concubine in 317, three years after his marriage to Fausta. Such behavior could not have been that uncommon. That is perhaps why canon law forbade men from having wives *and* concubines.[227] In the case of Fabiola's husband, he clearly had trouble with the shift to responsible citizen. His marriage failed not because of his unfaithfulness, but because his actions were so blatant. As Caesarius of Arles observed in one sermon, adultery was all the more despicable when it was public.[228]

Finally, we have the case of Ambrosius, which describes the issue from the perspective of the lover. Here was a man who was portrayed as having little regard for what he had done. His crime against the chastity of the marriage bed was typified and magnified by his unwillingness to accept temporary *relegatio* gracefully. His escape from exile perhaps represents something more than a simple disregard for the law. If that were the sole reason for his behavior, then there would have perhaps been an account of a lengthy series of appeals, such as Cassiodorus provides in the case of Aetheria and her former husband.[229] It may well have been, of course, that Ambrosius did not have the financial resources for such a legal battle, but the sense we get of Ambrosius from his actions, if they are recounted accurately, is that of a man who seemed to feel he had done nothing wrong. Divorce could be presumed to have ensued, and perhaps the unnamed husband would press a criminal charge against his wife. But Ambrosius did not likely expect punishment, or at least one so severe in his eyes, or he would not have fled. He no doubt expected leniency since '*confessus Ambrosius in nefario crimine*' and may well have done so without judicial torture.[230] No doubt, too, that one's station in society was a powerful mitigating factor. The aristocratic Paulinus of Pella had, after all, feared no legal repercussions from adultery; it was, as we said above, the fear of a damaged reputation.

As is hopefully apparent from these examples, all profess an implied attitude that not only adultery was a reality in late antiquity, but that it was a common one at that. Patricius represents the 'successful' adulterer; successful because his actions did not transcend the boundaries of social convention. As Augustine had pointed out elsewhere, an adulterous husband discovered did not rush to throw out their wives or accuse their mothers of crimes.[231] Fabiola's husband, of course, was the 'unsuccessful' adulterer, due to his inability to keep his infidelities an intra-*domus* affair. Finally, Ambrosius was the shocked paramour, incapable of accepting punishment for what must have seemed a commonplace transgression to him. All were portrayed as being guilty and described with a certain shocked tone, but neither Augustine nor Jerome nor Majorian's legal officers expressed particular surprise. While there are few other concrete examples of adultery, three such disparate sources offer a sense of its pervasiveness in late Roman society.

The relative paucity of even anecdotal evidence for adultery, however, might suggest that its practice was as limited as divorce in late antiquity. The complaints of a Salvian, for example, regarding the sexual licentiousness of the time, may have been nothing more than polemic in an age of relative chastity.[232] As one scholar observed about the medieval period, which is as equally applicable to late antiquity, 'it is difficult to confirm whether adultery was as widespread as many historians believe'.[233] There are, it is true, a fair number of oblique and vague references to unnamed adulterers in the tracts and sermons of various Christian authors.[234] But we must disregard many of them, largely due the general nature of the references. More often than not, they were moral *exempla* employed to achieve a didactic end. The tendency to make comparisons of such behavior to biblical archetypes presents a further warning sign. Therefore, such claims of adultery may have had little basis in reality.[235]

Nevertheless, the difficulty in assessing the prevalence of this practice is perhaps best addressed by looking at some general admonitions against adultery which survive from the age. They also suggest that the practice was fairly widespread. That Caesarius was forced to lock the church doors so that angry parishioners could not leave during sermons condemning their actions gives some indication both to the presence of the problem – mostly from husbands with wandering eyes – and its sensitive nature.[236] The bishop was infuriated to overhear sniggering among members of his church concerning their sexual exploits, as well as 'business trips' when they were away from their wives.[237] Nor was Caesarius' experience or frustration unusual. Augustine expressed similar misgivings amongst his own flock.[238] He expressed a certain familiar annoyance at the daily confidential complaints from hapless wives about their unfaithful husbands.[239] Indeed, to Christians at least, even the appearance of adultery and *stuprum* was common enough: a puritanical Jerome wrote to an unnamed mother and daughter living in Gaul on precisely these issues.[240] Admittedly, Jerome's heightened sense of propriety might have been unrepresentative of society at large, but certainly the issue of appearances, good or ill, was a general topic for comment. Ammianus Marcellinus, for example and in contrast, noted with some wonder that the Emperor Constantius II's well-known fidelity to his wife was so strong that even the insinuations of a disgruntled servant failed to raise suspicion.[241] Adultery was to all these men a common, if not an approved occurrence.

In sum, there is ample circumstantial evidence to show that adultery was ubiquitous, if not frequent. Indeed, the basic Christian tenet that a husband should be as faithful to his wife as she to him made the basic assumption that men *were* commonly sexually active before and during marriage. As Robin Lane Fox noted, for example, the term *virginius* – a male still a virgin at his wedding – is a rare phenomenon on Christian inscriptions.[242] Adultery clearly did not end in divorce in many cases, and the pressures of Roman society dictated that such affairs should be kept discreet. Exposure would lead to a general condemnation in the community, not only because the acts were in themselves castigated, but also because the exposure was equated with an added sordidness. Indeed, there may have been a small, but direct relationship between the prevalence of adultery and the infrequency of divorce. If an individual were to send a *repudium* for the generally approved of reason of adultery, that person would in essence publicize a spouse's infidelity. Augustine after all heard only secret and anonymous complaints. Moreover, husbands, too, might want to keep such things secret: Rufinus, in his late fourth-century translation of Sextus' *Sententiae*, had expressed an undoubtedly common sentiment in noting that a divorce revealed a man's inability to control his wife.[243] Keeping one's reputation in society, then, would tend to keep extramarital affairs in the closet. Thus, as we shall see in the following chapter, divorce was low and infidelity is difficult to document.

Domestic violence

In addition to the problems associated with adultery, life in the married state could potentially be less pleasant. Optimally, harmony should have been maintained in the household, what Augustine termed '*reverenter amabilis*'.[244] The sad reality, however, appears to suggest that domestic violence was not only limited to children and slaves. *Concordia* in the classical family might have had little to do with love, but it did insist on a certain respect for each partner in the relationship. Were a union stormy, *concordia* was absent and the failure lay both on husband and wife, although admittedly more on the woman.[245] Clerics had less to say on the matter, although relations in Christian marriage were viewed initially by pagans as possessing an 'austere sexual morality'.[246] A wife was naturally subject to her husband due to the Fall, but Augustine suggested that if a husband were physically abusive towards his mate – something never addressed in the many variations of the Pauline justification for divorce – a woman had a right to terminate the marriage.[247] Domestic violence was never singled out by other authors in the West, although some Eastern authors implied that it was a legitimate concern.[248] The concept, however, of a *naturalem in diverso sexu societatem* was an idea with which most of the regular clergy could agree.[249] Marriage led to sexual modesty and thus to a theoretically peaceful relationship. And even though the wife was subject to the husband, Paul admonished men to love their mates and to be good to them.[250]

A passage in Augustine's *Confessiones* gives us pause on this score, however. Violence against wives apparently was a common enough feature in many marriages, if not necessarily a frequent one. In a long discussion on the virtues of Monnica, the African bishop mentioned the general condition of husband–wife relations in describing the one between his own parents:

> Denique cum matronae multae, quarum viri mansuetoris erant, plagarum vestigia etiam de honestata facie gererent, inter amica conloquia illae arguebant maritorum vitam . . . Cumque mirarentur illae, scientes quam ferocem coniugem sustineret, numquam fuisse auditum aut aliquo indicio claruisse, quod Patricius ceciderit uxorem, aut quod a se invicem vel unum diem domestica lite dissenserint.[251]

Augustine's remarks are as illuminating as they are startling. Not only was such behavior common, but it was, with certain short-tempered husbands, expected! Moreover, he was trying to show just how virtuous his mother was by her ability both to maintain *concordia* in a marriage with a potentially violent man and to keep spousal disagreements – were there any – to herself. The sense of the passage clearly expresses a well-known tendency (if not necessarily a widely practiced one) for husbands to beat their wives.

It is possible that Augustine's reporting applied only to the small town of Thagaste or perhaps to the general area of North Africa. We certainly hear of no divorces that were brought upon by physical abuse anywhere in the Empire, although that is of course arguing from negative evidence. But there were other isolated instances of abuse which seem to suggest that Augustine's impression of marriage was applicable to the greater Roman world. In a long letter to his parents, Hypatius and Quieta, Salvian along with his two sisters made vague references to his father's behavior towards his wife while describing his severity towards his children.[252] This may have been due to his hostility towards Christianity, as Salvian implies, but Hypatius had also converted some years before. Whether such behavior included violence is not specifically stated, but it does seem to have been the case with his children. There are other, more concrete examples as well. Apparently, women could on occasion undergo forced starvation by their husbands as well.[253] In extreme cases, emperors such as Constantine had their wives killed over domestic disagreements.

Perhaps more significant, however, was Theodosius II's decision in 449 to allow divorce in the case of wife-beating.[254] The law may well have been based on a real case, although there are so many other provisions in this constitution that it is impossible to tell. And while it certainly does not speak to the frequency of domestic violence nor the kind of violence inflicted upon a spouse, it at least shows that it was an actionable offense and thus had happened with enough regularity to be addressed. Even more telling is Justinian's revocation of Theodosius' law: wife-beating was punishable by a relatively light fine.[255] Justinian's decision was clear indication that domestic violence was common, or at least that it was thought to be common.

We cannot definitively say that physical abuse happened often in marriages nor that most wives at some point experienced violence at the hands of their spouses. And to be sure, we should not recapitulate late antique stereotypes of weak women, in need of protection.[256] But these examples do indicate a familiarity with violent behavior. Christian authors said little about this feature of marriage, although from their discussions of marital relations, one could extrapolate that such behavior was unneeded and was condemned. Indeed, when Augustine spoke of the need for domestic 'correction', he spoke solely of children and slaves.[257] There was unfortunately no recourse in law for divorcing abusive husbands until 449, so violence was borne by a wife up to that time to the best of her abilities. Would the townswomen of Thagaste have been so eager to be divorced were it legally feasible, or would that, too, betray the confidence of the *familia*?

Conclusions

As with Roman marriage, affective unions, from their inception to their dissolution, were at the very heart of Christian views on the family. The nature of virginity, marriage and widowhood were objects of constant comment, partially because they were, as Augustine put it, three different manifestations of purity.[258] Christian authors did not offer radically new notions of married life, but they did place new emphases on the conduct of spouses. While they did not, I think, offer a true alternative to the Roman 'model', they nevertheless addressed a number of epistemological issues about the sanctity of marriage, the immorality and dangers of adultery. Imperial law, as we described, tried to follow suit, if only in a sporadic, ragtag way.

The matter of pagan marriage is somewhat more difficult to judge. The scattered references we have among the literary and epigraphical sources suggest that idealized sentiments concerning affective ties had not greatly changed from the days of the late Republic. But we have also seen how stock words and phrases shifted and changed meaning over time and between religious affiliations. *Univira, pudicitia, fidelis* and other terms resonated as strongly among Christians as they did among Roman society generally. If we can speak, then, of a common parlance, then those who rejected the new religion may have nevertheless found a common sentiment. Peter Brown has argued that the aristocracy of late Roman society, Christian and pagan, had created a common language of visual symbols in the culture.[259] Classical elements were redeployed instead of being rejected out-of-hand. Such supposedly disparate elements could be seen together, for example, in the Calendar of 354, which included both Christian and traditional Roman *dies festiales*.[260] Concepts such as *fides* or *viduitas*, too, appear to have had the same malleable and redefined quality. In the case of marriage in late antiquity, both in its inception and its description, it is more than likely we are witnessing yet another parallel.

Despite the visibility of Christian ideology, however, the wedded state in late antiquity did not seem to be heavily affected by the ideals which the Church, the state and many theologians avowed. That is not to say that the family of the later Roman age had remained the same as that of several hundred years before. It seems, for example, that affective ties between husband and wife were considered a more important component to a successful marriage than before.[261] But for the most part, the same pressures on the married union remained: the production of children continued to be emphasized, the social stigma apparently attached to divorce kept adultery and domestic violence strictly an internal familial affair, and patterns of male sexual behavior before marriage encouraged extramarital affairs after they had contracted *iusta matrimonia*. Thus, it is still possible to speak, for the majority of the Western Empire's population, of Roman marriages rather than Christian ones.

5

ALTERNATIVES TO MARRIAGE

In the classical age, alternatives to marriage were generally not permanent things. Virginity, in the literal sense of the word, simply meant the age of girlhood, where they were legally incapable and physically unprepared for the responsibilities and duties of marriage. Divorce in that period was almost always seen as an avenue to remarriage rather than an end in itself. Permanent widowhood for men and women was not entered into lightly. A woman's fecundity was generally at issue, despite the value placed on the virtue of *univira*. Only when she passed the period of reproduction was widowhood seen as worthy and laudable thing. Widowers, of course, had no such problems. Many nobles and emperors remarried relatively late in life, although it is true that many found themselves concubines instead of wives (or on occasion, in addition to their spouses). In short, marriage still remained the center of one's relations.

To a large extent, the financial, cultural, and biological pressures in late antiquity did not greatly change. Nevertheless, Christian thinkers and the Church encouraged things like virginity and widowhood as praiseworthy ends in themselves. In Chapter 4 we discussed how the Church created a hierarchy of feminine sanctity based on these states. All states were good, but virginity was the best. Moreover, they actively disapproved of the practice of concubines, especially if a man were already married. The concept of celibacy received added praise and remarriage, and while not fully condemned, was seen as unnecessary and potentially sinful. In this chapter, then, we shall examine these alternatives to marriage and see what forces drove the practices of divorce, remarriage, and widowhood. As with marriage, the impetus for arranging and engaging in alternative unions or forgoing them altogether were dependent on a number of interrelated factors.

Divorce

Divorce and the Church

Let us begin with a few general comments about Christian attitudes towards the dissolution of marriage. Church authorities looked ill upon both divorce and remarriage. The only legitimate reason for divorce in their opinion were cases of infidelity. If divorce because of adultery did occur, however, it did not mean that an individual was free to contract another marriage. Divorce meant voluntary and permanent celibacy. In the case of the widowed, particularly women, as we will discuss in more depth below, the matter was less clear. Certainly, Christian authors argued the relatively high state of the honored widow, but providing there were no improprieties, remarriage was an option. Even in the religious community, young widows were often expected – if not encouraged – to remarry. But a sexual ranking had been long established. Permanent virginity was the highest moral state, followed by the perpetual chastity of *viduitas*, and finally the married woman. Any attempts to relativize this scale, as the monk Jovinian had in the late 380s and 390s, were quickly quashed.[1]

This scale manifested itself unabashedly in canon law. Divorce in particular was discouraged. It was bad enough to divorce because of adultery, but at the council of Arles, the Church made it necessary to excommunicate men who divorced their wives in favor of another.[2] Even were she an adulteress, he had to remained unmarried.[3] Some years before, the bishops assembled at Elvira made the same provisions for women leaving their husbands.[4] Moreover, the charge of adultery had to be substantiated. As in criminal law, one canon passed at the council of Vennes in western Gaul, ordered that the charge be proven or the accuser risked excommunication.[5] As a further deterrent, one council ordered a man be excommunicated along with his wife should he have married another man's wife.[6]

But unlike Roman law, there was no imperative for a man and a woman to be divorced *because* of an adulterous action. In fact, Church policy emphasized reconciliation in the married state.[7] Adultery had a standard penance time of five years and beyond that, the act was deemed forgiven.[8] Even a husband who committed multiple adulteries could receive communion on his deathbed if he promised to mend his ways should he recover.[9] The eleventh synod at Carthage ordered a comprehensive rule, based on the Pauline admonition: either remain divorced or be reconciled.[10] Indeed, the African congregation was so interested in making this a standard policy that they took the unusual step of petitioning the emperor to pass a law enforcing their canon. There is no evidence that either Honorius or Arcadius acceded to this request, and judging from future imperial legislation, it is unlikely that they ever did.[11] Nevertheless, the concept of reconciliation was important.

This emphasis on forgiveness and rapprochement, however, should not be mistaken for even a tacit consent of adultery. A husband who knowingly allowed his wife to commit adultery would be permanently excommunicated, although if he subsequently divorced her, the punishment would be commuted to ten years.[12] No doubt a wife's situation in similar circumstances would be more difficult. Moreover, reconciliation did not abrogate an individual's responsibility to atone for his or her sins. Doing penance unsurprisingly required the approval of a spouse first.[13] That penance usually meant abstinence for some period of time, even years, made the matter more complicated. Forgiveness may have been good for the strength of the marriage and the *familia*, but that did not erase the transgression. Finally, the term *adulterare* seems to have broadened in meaning. Adultery was no longer a term referring to sexual congress between a man and a woman not legally joined: it could mean any illegitimate act of fornication. That is perhaps why a man who had no wife and instead had a concubine could be admitted to communion, but a man who had both could not.

Divorce and the law

Remarriage for dynastic purposes meant that divorce continued in imperial households well beyond the life of the Western Empire. Even for emperors, the procreative desire to continue their lines remained strong. Constantius, Gratian, Valentinian I, Theodosius, and Honorius, to name only fourth century emperors, all had at least two wives. True, death and occasional executions also created opportunity for contracting new unions, but as a whole, divorce remained a legal remedy under many circumstances. When we look at Roman jurisprudence on these subjects, we see a number of parallels between canon law and imperial constitutions. Similar restrictions were placed on divorce, but more tangible penalties were offered by the imperial government.

The severe divorce law of Constantine, *CTh* iii:16:1, which we examined in Chapter 3, had a relatively short life span and was modified by his nephew, Julian. In what precise ways, we cannot know, although one anonymous author implies that a divorce was easily – *licenter* – accomplished and that women were divorcing their husbands frequently.[14] No doubt he was greatly prejudiced by his own religious beliefs, but it may be that Julian had simply restored classical laws respecting unilateral divorce.[15] The emperor's modifications, however, permitted Honorius and Constantius III to offer a more comprehensive divorce law which also touched upon the issues of adultery and remarriage.[16] Briefly stated, it held both the husband and the wife equally accountable for proving the grounds for unilateral divorce. It is not precisely clear what those grounds were, but they included adultery for the woman – still a prosecutable crime – and serious crimes such as *maiestas* for both.

The penalties imposed were, however, very much unequal. Were a woman not able to prove her accusations, she would lose her marriage gifts, her dowry, her rights of rank (*postliminium*), would be barred from ever remarrying, and finally suffer deportation.[17] If she had merely proven defects in her husband's character, a wife would lose her gifts and dowry, would be barred from ever remarrying, and presumably be liable for accusations of *stuprum* should her husband wish to bring them.[18] If on the other hand she proved her charges, a woman could regain her dowry, keep her gifts, but was barred from remarrying for five years so as to ensure there were no other motives involved in the action.[19] In contrast, a husband who had failed to prove his case only had to return the dowry, although he was barred from ever remarrying.[20] Proving faults in his wife permitted remarriage after two years, although he still had to give back the dotal property. But if he proved his charges, a man could keep the dowry, recover his antenuptial gifts, and could marry another woman at his discretion.[21]

There have been suggestions that this law had a Christian impetus to it. But the change in divorce law and its punishments seem to have the same interpretive problems as Constantine's divorce law. It is difficult to see what were the precise issues involved in its passage. Clearly, treasonous behavior and crimes of that magnitude could be attributed to the not so enlightened self-interest of an ever suspicious imperial government. Moreover, the differences in punishments for men and women, as in *CTh* iii:16:1, reflect a strong Roman patriarchal tradition. It can be traced clearly to classical law and indeed to the laws of Constantine. In sum, the law has no real connection to Christianity, except possibly that Christians disapproved of divorce. But the unpopularity of divorce may have also been an important factor in the broader population.[22]

Instead, the timing of the law may help to tie its passage to current events. The constitution's issuance came on the heels of an important event in the West. Two weeks before its recipient, Palladius, received the new regulations, Galla Placidia had been made *augusta*.[23] Constantius III and Placidia were unquestionably insuring Valentinian III's succession to the Western throne after his uncle Honorius died.[24] The couple's mutual interest in seeing their son as Western emperor, however, belied problems within the marriage itself. If we are to believe Olympiodorus, it was an arranged marriage that had not been wholly agreeable to Placidia.[25] Moreover, Constantius' behavior during their marriage had been miserly and had been conspicuously avaricious, much to Placidia's chagrin.[26] Most significant, however, was an incident that apparently occurred very close to her elevation to *augusta*. Ravenna was visited by a certain Libanius, a mysterious man from the East, who made a remarkable claim: he could defeat the barbarians by magic, without any use of armies.[27] There was evidently some support for this man, even in the court, and perhaps Constantius himself. Placidia was not impressed by Libanius, and was so upset at the support for his proposals that she threatened her husband with divorce – apparently a legally permissible action under Julian's modifications – unless the magician were executed. In wake of these events, *CTh* iii:16:2 could be viewed in a slightly different light. The law may well have been protection for Constantius' position. By reintroducing stringent divorce laws and by making his wife an *augusta*, he made his own marriage less vulnerable. Moreover, if the emperor's security in the Western government had been threatened by his actions to accumulate wealth, strengthening the bonds of his marriage to a Theodosian empress became even more imperative. Legal niceties may not have always been followed, of course, but the new emperor's position had to be unimpeachable for his own long-term support. Constantius died of an unspecified illness six months later.[28]

We should not wholly discount a Christian influence, however. Two final observations are worth making. First, Constantine's famous law on divorce had two different aspects to it: a general castigation of unilateral divorce and the actual reasons by which it could come to pass. We furthermore suggested that at least in the case of the former, there may well have been a Christian influence at work. This can be readily said of our 421 law. Certainly the specifics of the law are difficult to interpret, but the condemnation of divorce on one spouse's part is clearly reiterated in *CTh* iii:16:2. Indeed, during the reign of Justinian, a multiplicity of reasons for unilateral divorce appeared, but so, too, did strictures on mutually agreed upon separations.[29] Even so, the strength of Christian influence was not always absolute. After our time, Justinian's successor, Justin, once again permitted divorce by mutual consent.[30]

Second, Honorius and Constantius III's law on divorce attempted to reintroduce elements of Constantine's strictures into the West. There was no doubt a perception among some Christians that Julian's modifications *had* allowed immoral behavior because of his polytheist loyalties. It is possible that further laws governing divorce were passed between the late fourth century and the law of 421, although none survive.[31] We cannot directly tie such sentiment to the formulation of this constitution, but clearly this was the first major piece of legislation to deal with the thorny subject. It would go too far to dismiss a Christian persuasion entirely.

Moreover, a subsequent law points more clearly to its influence. Theodosius II had presented a whole new set of reasons for unilateral divorce.[32] Some eleven years earlier, the emperor had experimented with permitting unilateral divorce for any reason, and this new law had abrogated the first.[33] One particular item in *CJ* v:17:8 is of great interest: for the first time since legal impediments had been put in place 120 years before, a woman had the right to divorce her husband for adultery. We cannot be entirely certain that this law was promulgated in the West, but a *novella* of Valentinian III implies that it may have been. The young emperor decreed that all of Theodosius II's legislation would be accepted in the Western Empire.[34] It moreover stipulated that the two would always be in accord, implying that it was his intention to make this standard policy for the future: '*isdem quoque legibus temperetur*'.[35]

Assuming *CJ* v:17:8 was enforced in the West, the law includes two decidedly Christian elements. First, other reasons permitting a divorce included a provision that condemned a wife for attending, without her husband's knowledge, the circus, theater or arena.[36] All three were public entertainments against which Christian authors had long inveighed as being immoral:[37] the Church passed a number of canons condemning the circus in one form or another.[38] The perception, then, of impropriety or indecency, as defined by Christian morals, suggests a Christian influence. The overall sense of the law, then, is that at least general outlines of the religion's condemnations were present. Second, by allowing women to sue for divorce on the grounds of adultery, an equality for men and women in this regard reflected an equality espoused by Christian authors and Church canons. Divorce, of course, was not required in Church law, nor was it required for women in civil law, but the option was now there.

A final law concerning adultery from the West illustrates evidence for the religion's indirect influence in the realm of divorce. In the province of Tuscany, the *consularis* there had ruled on a case involving an individual who had committed adultery with another man's wife.[39] Honorius had required that persons charged with adultery immediately go to trial.[40] We have also discussed in the last chapter the case of Ambrosius, which merited the Emperor Majorian's personal attention.[41] According to the minutes of the *novella*, the young man had been convicted of committing adultery, which resulted in divorce for the married couple. Rogatianus, the judge in this case, had sentenced the man to *relegatio*, but apparently of temporary duration. Ambrosius, however, did not stand for even that light a punishment and fled from exile. Having botched the job, Rogatianus appealed to the emperor. Majorian ordered a new general regulation that sentenced convicted adulterers to permanent exile and ordered the imperial fisc to confiscate their property. Moreover, should the convicted escape from exile, he would be subject to the death penalty.

While *N. Maj.* ix:1 deals mostly with adultery and its punishment, the sanctity of marriage and the tragedy of divorce are referred to several times. The language is notably non-legal in character: '*alieni doloris iniuriam*', '*ut maculam pudoris exincti et eius summam criminis*', and '*genialis tori . . . castitatem*'.[42] The word *castitas*, in fact, is rarely found in legal documents: it only appears in edicts dealing with involuntary violations of chastity. Indeed, its use was more common among Christian authors, and referred either to a steadfast faith or even sexual abstinence *within* marriage.[43] The use of the word in Majorian's decree implies that the law was at least in part motivated out of (presumed) moral indignation. Adultery may have been the enabler of divorce and that had been a tragedy, but the reason for the divorce had been clearly justifiable.

A final point ought to be made about the legal activity surrounding divorce. The number of laws actually passed in the fourth and fifth centuries remained relatively low. Only in the sixth century does their seem to be an increased interest in regulating the practice, and then only in the East. One must be careful, then, in suggesting that there was too much of a connection between imperial law and Christian ideals. Indeed, the lack of activity over the centuries implies that for most of the time, emperors and their ministers were unconcerned with the issue entirely. When we look at divorce as it apparently functioned in the real world, we perhaps begin to understand why.

Divorce in practice

Equality among spouses, even among Christians, was never conceptualized in the ancient period as an ideal worthy of following. As we saw in Chapter 4, late antique authors considered the hierarchical relationship between man and woman – and so by extension husband and wife – as natural and unalterable. Nevertheless, Christian authors felt that the dominance over one's wife or children did not mean that a man was free from the moral constraints that bound a family and society together. In that sense, a husband was beholden to the same strict moral code as a wife. The use of concubines, the affairs one might have with free and enslaved individuals, and the patronage of prostitutes were all forbidden. As we have seen, in the mid-fifth century, a woman could sue for divorce on account of adultery as easily as a man.[44]

Divorce would seem central to the question of sexual monogamy. The Church permitted it in the case of adultery, although clerics emphasized reconciliation rather than termination. The emperors continuously fine-tuned the grounds for and the means of ending a marriage, never really being completely satisfied with these efforts, but in general they continued to permit divorce for a wider number of causes. We have of course several cases of Christians divorcing spouses in our period of interest, but the wrangling over marriage dissolution raises an initial important question about the wedded state in late antiquity: how popular was divorce? Was it, as the Ambrosiaster author claimed, a daily occurrence that happened with ease and without regard for its consequences?[45] Or did its decline apparent in the early Empire continue to the days of the fourth and fifth century?

The would-be political dynasts in the first century BCE made divorce a viable and common means for making strategic alliances in the power vacuum of the late Republic. Once the Julio-Claudian clan had effectively co-opted all real power in the Roman world, however, the pressure for making important marriage alliances apparently subsided to some degree.[46] Accordingly, the incidence of *divortium* seems to have decreased. Many of the divorces we know of from that period, moreover, were in the ruling house itself. M.-T. Raepsaet-Charlier's now-standard study of the senatorial class from 10 BCE to 200 CE reveals that of the 562 attested *senatrices*, only 27 were confirmed to be divorced.[47] This of course says nothing of the greater mass of the Roman society, not even among the *equites*, but there is strong evidence to support divorce's unpopularity among the wider population. In a carefully reasoned essay, Iiro Kajanto has indicated divorce's rarity among the lower classes largely due to a lack of financial and political pressures visible in the upper classes.[48] It is possible, although there is no statistical evidence, that the decline in marriage dissolution amongst the upper classes partially occurred in rough conjunction with the infusion of new members into the aristocracy. The marriage habits of senatorial *parvenus* thus may have slowly percolated up into the Empire's elite. An analogous explanation has been offered for the Christianization of the senatorial and imperial ranks in the fourth century.[49] The commonality and relative ease of divorce in the *haut-empire*, in sum, does not attest to its frequency.

A similar survey of divorce in the late ancient world yields similar results. Drawing upon the first and second volumes of the *Prosopography of the Later Roman Empire*, which covers the period of 260 to 527 CE, there are approximately 13,000 entries. Slightly less than half those entries are from the West. Of that considerable figure, there are only six confirmed cases of divorce.[50] By adding possible divorces, the number rises to a still-minuscule twenty. Moreover, ten took place within the imperial household and all but one of those seems to have been initiated specifically to forge new dynastic alliances. By looking more closely at those twenty confirmed and possible divorces, we find that only the marriage of Fabiola was dissolved because of adultery and other sexual transgressions.[51] Nor did a couple necessarily stay divorced. Agapita in the early sixth century claimed that she had been tricked into leaving her husband, Basilius, to sell some property, and subsequently returned to him.[52] The production of children was still seen as the root of marriage, despite some Christians' claims that it was to prevent sin. After reviewing the constant refinements to divorce law and the considerable moral objections raised by Christian authors in the last two chapters, these figures and circumstances seem somewhat thin.

We are left then with two possible alternatives to explain this low number of divorces. First, we can argue that it represents a continuation of Roman behavior from an earlier day. The low numbers would therefore reflect an on-going reluctance to end the legal state of marriage (I say nothing of affective ties) and could be traced back to the early Empire. The second explanation assumes that Christian morality was taken to heart by at least the senatorial and imperial aristocracies and they accordingly changed – or at least adjusted – their marriage patterns. The incidence of divorce, seemingly even lower than in the days of the Julio-Claudians, could thus underlie the effectiveness of the Church's stand against the capricious termination of a *iustum matrimonium*.

The latter explanation would be difficult to prove, however. To begin with, the numbers, even if not fully reflective of the actual patterns in the general population, are not large enough to establish any clear-cut trend in behavior. The rate was always low. Second, the kind of divorces that are attested to in late antiquity would in general not be approved of by the Church. Only in the case of Fabiola was divorce justified, but she had clearly violated both canon law and Paul's admonitions in choosing to marry a second time. If an individual was going to be divorced, they had to stay divorced or to be reconciled.[53] In contrast, divorces, for the majority of our cases, facilitated a better or necessary marriage. The two other separations about which we are given any details were those of Agapita and Basilius mentioned above, and the near-divorce of Galla Placidia and Constantius III. In the case of the imperial couple, there may have been subtle reasons for Placidia's threat of divorce, but adultery, as we shall see, was not the reason offered nor was it even implied.[54] Finally, the individuals annulling their marriages were both Christian and pagan. If the Church's objections to divorce were primarily aimed at Christians, why did believers continue to engage in it? Conversely, if the moral arguments were supposedly directed at them and assuming that they were successful, why did non-Christians take them to heart as well?

In contrast, an explanation suggesting a long-term objection to divorce has more basis in fact. First, there appears to have been a general societal rejection of divorce in late antiquity.[55] The rejection of divorce by Christians did not represent anything new. Second, when we look at marriage dissolution in late antiquity, we can see similarities to divorces in the early Empire and even in the last century of the Republic. Half of the divorces from the later Roman period were acts of political expediency in the imperial family and usually done as a prelude to making other, more advantageous matches. Galerius Maximianus, for example, divorced his unnamed first wife to marry the daughter of Diocletian, Valeria.[56] Only in the case of Honorius and Thermantia did both spouses remain unmarried, partially because the political purposes for which it had been forged had abruptly ended. In comparison, Raepsaet-Charlier's study shows that of 27 attested divorces, 15 took place in the emperor's household.[57] Moreover, the divorces of the late Republic seem also to have been to reforge new marriages for political and economic gain.[58] Sulla, as mentioned in Chapter 2, went through five wives before he died. Marriages were thus subjected to the same external dynamics in the late antique age as in the classical. Third, the means of divorce were similar. Frequently, banishment was used among the emperors as a kind of *repudium*. Valentinian I, for example, in 369 exiled and divorced his wife simultaneously for making an illicit property transaction.[59] So, too, did Honorius banish Thermantia, albeit to Rome.[60] Comparable methods had been used by Augustus and Caligula. Finally, as we have said, the few annulments that took place outside of the imperial family were pursued by both Christians *and* pagans. Lacking the same sort of dynastic obligations as the *domus Augusti*, non-imperial divorces were nevertheless diverse. No ideological constraints seem to have affected the decision to terminate a marriage or at least not strongly enough to prevent their actions. In sum, divorce had always been low in the Empire, but the pressures which caused them were by no means removed with the accession of Christianity.

It seems then that the considerable discussion among Christian authors and, to a lesser extent, in imperial law about divorce did not accurately reflect reality. The author of Ambrosiaster spoke as an opponent to the polytheist revival under Julian, happily engaging in hyperbole, rather than an objective social commentator. As with the classical age, the contrast between ideal and reality was clear. Augustine no doubt would have been happy to paraphrase his own line about incest: even though divorce was permitted in law, the behavior of most people was better than their laws.[61]

Widowhood and remarriage

Church encouragement

The *vidua* in classical Rome was respected, if not necessarily venerated. Widows had been singled out in ancient Judaism, however, as possessing a purer spiritual state than married or divorced women. They, along with virgins, were the only women a priest could take to wife. But no literature grew up around them nor did they ever possess any institutionalized status.[62]

Christianity, on the other hand, placed considerable emphasis on *viduitas*. Unlike the ancient Jews, the clergy created a corps of widows both in the Eastern and Western parts of the Roman Empire, sworn to perpetual chastity, although a formal order of widows seems to have died out sometime in the West during the fourth century.[63] *Viduitas* was thus classified as a state more blessed than marriage, although not as blessed as virginity.[64] But we should state initially that the choice to marry again was never curtailed. While the Church wished to emphasize permanent chastity whether someone was divorced or widowed, the government never saw fit in this period to actually forbid multiple marriages.[65] To be sure, multiple marriages were looked on as unseemly, and not just by moralists: Luxorius in late fifth-century North Africa, for example, viciously lampooned the widow, Paula, who was about to wed a fourth time.[66] But the fact that she was criticized of course meant that she could remarry as often as she wanted. And it did occur: if we are to believe Jerome, sometimes to the point of the absurd.[67]

If the death of a spouse occurred, however, men and especially women were encouraged by the clergy to remain widowed for the rest of their lives. This is not to say that people shunned widowhood out-of-hand, since even from the earliest times of the Republic, Romans felt that multiple marriages were improper and unseemly. Indeed, the early Republican cult of the goddess, Pudicitia, admitted only women who had been married once.[68] But as we shall see, like the classical period, there were legal reasons for avoiding subsequent marriages. Men of course were under far less pressure to stay widowers and there were practically no time constraints upon their remarrying. Not even the Church could fully create a concept of *unifemina*, although Jerome had expressed his misgivings about widowers incapable of remaining continent.[69] Yet exhortations to the widowed, particularly to women, were numerous, whether they came in the form of letters, sermons, or full-blown religious tracts.

To Christians, widows were admittedly a curious phenomenon: as Peter Brown aptly put it, they were 'disturbingly amphibious creatures'.[70] They were not virgins, nor were they married. They could take no orders, with the possible exception of deaconess, but by consecrating their widowhood to Christ, they had in essence transcended the simple laity.[71] They participated in Church functions, performing various social services, mostly supporting the poor and the sick. This is perhaps why so many clerics spent considerable time explaining their role in society and in the Church, while at the same time depending on wealthier widows for financial and political support. Jerome in particular focused his energies in that direction. As rewards for the importance he placed on their position as widows, he received as much financial help as was necessary to continue his biblical translations and exegetical work. In short, Jerome was a kept man.

Of course, most widows wielded no such power. As weaker members of the Christian community, they were frequently included amongst the rolls of the orphaned and the sick – what Eliza Doolittle's father might call the 'deserving poor'. The fourth synod of Carthage, for example, had institutionalized significant support for young and sickly widows.[72] They were worthy of being sustained, Jerome reasoned, if not protected.[73] If we accept, then, that the Church did provide widows with material sustenance in their state, the question arises as to *why* did it emphasize widowhood's importance initially. Did it, as Lightman and Zeisel have argued, take at its root the Roman (or perhaps Mediterranean?) concept of *univira* and graft it onto a Christian uneasiness towards multiple marriages?[74] Or had the Western Church taken Tertullian to heart, viewing marriage as the training ground for continence and widowhood as the actual battle?[75]

Certainly the question of repeated marriages, as we have already discussed, had raised Roman eyebrows for many centuries. If we are to believe Jerome, most pagan widows flaunted their new-found freedom, made up to look like prostitutes, going out in public and fraternizing freely with all.[76] A single remarriage might be expected,[77] especially if a woman were young and had no children; but any more than that and people, no matter their religious persuasion, would talk.[78] If she already had children, Christians could see no valid reason to remarry and implied incontinence was the likely culprit.[79] A second issue had frankly to do specifically with age. Once a woman had passed her childbearing years, the need to contract a marriage was considered unnecessary. If she could produce no offspring, legitimate or otherwise, the exercise would be deemed pointless. When menopause occurred, however, and when the ancients thought it occurred, is not entirely clear. The mid-fifth-century Roman seems to have set that age arbitrarily at 40, at least according to a Church canon and a novel of Majorian.[80] Certainly, fertility range was likely much lower in the ancient world than it is today, but a constitution of Justinian noted that women even over 40, however rare, were capable of producing children.[81] Age, however, begged the point. Whatever the reality, new marriages were condemned when fecundity was at an end.

But if a woman had some number of children at the death of her husband, she had gained the right to act as their legal guardian and was moreover encouraged to do so.[82] Indeed, the sense we get from many late sources is that widowed *matresfamilias* acted more or less as guardians over the entire *familia*. Suzanne Dixon has already effectively demonstrated the considerable power a mother could have over her offspring, not the least of which was financial.[83] Many Church leaders gave that control a semi-formality by lauding the widowed state. Women, for good or for ill, had after all been seen as the traditional caretakers of the home in Roman society, whether they were wealthy or poor.[84] The specific duties as guardian, however, were not so clearly defined by the Church. They were not spelled out as clearly as *tutela* had been in Roman law.

Nevertheless, there were two essential attributes that Christian authors seemed to emphasize relating to this role. The most important was a proper moral comportment. This not only reflected well on the widow, of course, but on her entire family. Jerome, for example, complimented the mother of Chromatius and Eusebius, who aided her sons in the holy life by virtue of her continence.[85] In another letter written to the wealthy widow Furia, he noted the peculiar glory of her pre-Christian ancestors who '*secundos nosse concubitus*', and by which her family had from antiquity been especially distinguished.[86] Yet by virtue of their *viduitas*, these women were more than simple ornaments to their houses. They apparently possessed some degree of autonomy – so much so that Jerome had to warn wealthy widows against traveling about on a palanquin, proceeded by a phalanx of personal eunuchs.[87] Without naming names, he went on to point to one (apparently Christian) Italian widow who had been traveling through the East keeping questionable company and putting on elaborate banquets. No doubt these examples belied something of the freedom and power such widows could possess, but it was not a power undeserved. They were expected to take care of their parents if they still lived[88] and had to provide for the upkeep of their children:[89] '*Vidua populos regit, vidua ducit exercitus, vidua duces eligit, vidua bella disponit, mandat triumphos.*'[90] A new marriage would destroy this: '*Superducit mater filiis non vitricum, sed hostem, non parentem, sed tyrannum.*'[91]

The second attribute related to their positions as guardians of their *familiae* was the virtue of hospitality. It was not enough to take care of one's own. As matrons running their own houses, they were also supposed to provide succor, material or spiritual, to all who asked for it. The widow from Zarephath who fed Elijah during a plague was frequently drawn on as an archetype.[92] A widow's largesse indeed should extend beyond the traditional duties of guest-friendship, and ought to be applied to all who might need her assistance. Thus, the clergy could advise women to give wealth to the poor: a widow could give sustenance to the needy through the Church structure and thus become a patron of the Church and the poor simultaneously.

A woman's role in the family, as a former *coniunx* and as the *materfamilias*, was thus raised significantly beyond the single virtue of *univira*. That may have been at the heart of a widow's sanctity, but it acted as a foundation for her own behavior in the family and on behalf of her family. By keeping a tenuous balance of humility and independence, a *vidua* might greatly expand her role in the *familia*. By denying her body any further sexual contact, she transcended her strict position as a woman. A virgin had always done so, but the married woman's transformation was clearly more dramatic. By a conscious choice of neutering themselves, they trod dangerously close to the world of men.[93] While their legal role was still limited, the Church had in effect raised the widow's status to a veritable *paterfamilias*.

For those who had been widowed, especially women, the Church was relatively practical, and offered both the carrot and the stick to keep their status permanent.[94] Given the continuing marriage patterns of the Roman populace, especially among the aristocracy, young Roman women usually married men at least several years their senior.[95] Augustine, to draw on anecdotal evidence, had, at the age of 30, put off his arranged marriage for two years until his betrothed was old enough to wed.[96] Thus, more of the widowed were undoubtedly women. Many of Jerome's wealthy and aristocratic correspondents in Rome had been widowed, and at a young age. The pressure placed on them to remain widows was no doubt accentuated by the Roman ideal of *univira*.[97] *Univiritas* in a Christian context, however, meant a devotion to Christ for the rest of their natural lives.[98] Discouraging remarriage after the death of the spouse was directed almost exclusively at widows.

But the encouragement, at least by official Church statements, was relatively small. We have already mentioned the fourth synod of Carthage, which had ordered that support ought to be provided for young and sickly widows.[99] It does not say what that support should be, whether it was financial, material or simply moral. We know from Eusebius, however, that the third-century Roman church alone supported 1,500 widows and the oppressed (*thlibomenoi*), so there was apparently action behind such injunctions.[100] Second, a canon from the council of Sardica implied that bishops should be making legal petitions for widows, *pauperes* and *pupilli*, rather than for their own self-importance.[101] The African assembly, in contrast, decreed that an archdeacon or archpresbyter should oversee the care of widows, along with orphans and *peregrini*.[102] In many areas, too, local bishops tried to create solidarity by forming a quasi-official body of sworn widows.[103] They took a vow of perpetual *viduitas* before a bishop and received a special insignia.[104] Anyone who violated her, even with her permission, would be punished. It is not precisely clear what that punishment was, but the sense of the canon is that it would have gone beyond the normal penance and excommunication.

In contrast, there were a large number of canonical rulings that were meant to discourage widows from violating their status. The fourth synod in Carthage also condemned adulterous widows to excommunication.[105] The only leeway that the Church offered was to the widow who committed adultery, but subsequently married: then she could be readmitted to the

Christian community after five years of penance.[106] Some churches went further and punished widows who simply had questionable relations with a man.[107] If she were the former wife of a deacon, priest or bishop, retribution extended to the man who married her.[108] The clergy was beholden to these restrictions as well. A cleric who married a second time would be demoted in the Church hierarchy, and would be defrocked entirely if he took a third wife.[109] Any layman, to take the reverse situation, who took a widow to wife, would be ineligible for ordination.[110]

The Church, in contrast to Christian thinkers, did what it could to keep the widowed unattached. Certainly, they could not control those women who had taken no vows to perpetual celibacy, but for those who had, it used the power of communion to assure their chastity. Theologians, on the other hand, encouraged women to make that elusive pledge. They could not keep widows, particularly young ones from remarrying (especially if they had no children) nor could they wholly condemn it. But by offering widows a certain raised status, the clergy tried to deliver such women into the Church and thus make them subject to the regulations of canon law.

Choosing widowhood

Like the classical period, there was a good chance that a spouse, more often a woman, would find herself single after a relatively short period of marriage. Divorce was a potential, if distant possibility, but given the mortality rates of the period, men and women of a relatively young age faced the choice of widowhood or remarriage. Marriage patterns, as we have seen, usually left a ten-year disparity between spouses. Men, commonly waiting until their late twenties to contract a marriage, could be expected to die while most of their offspring were under-age. Patricius, for example, had died while Augustine, probably the eldest, was only 17.[111] More often than not, then, women made up the ranks of the widowed. Jerome had, after all, managed to gather around him a remarkable and powerful group of wealthy widows, some of whom had become so after a few short months of marriage. Paula, Fabiola, Marcella, Furia and other women, many with no children, had all chosen permanent *viduitas* after the deaths of their husbands. To be sure, death could come early to women as well, particularly in childbirth. Ausonius in one of his epitaphs described the young Anicia, wife and mother, dying at the age of 16.[112] Once a spouse was lost, for whatever reason, a person was faced with a new problem: whether or not to marry again.

For the Church in late antiquity, as we have seen, the answer was clear. It was best not to remarry. Widowhood was a higher ideal to follow. Given that the circumstances were fairly honorable, however, many clerics were not so absolute in their condemnation of second marriages. Augustine, for example, had disapproved of it, but did not consider it a major sin.[113] Overall, however, remaining unmarried and celibate after a first marriage had ended was the ideal. The imperial government did not care, except in assuring that children from a first marriage were financially protected[114] and that a woman wait for a proper period before remarrying.[115]

Which opinion represented a closer approximation of life after marriage is a matter of some debate. It is true that the same reasons for remaining unmarried after becoming widowed or divorced probably in the classical world undoubtedly existed for the late antique world as well. First among those was protecting the inheritances of children, particularly those who were still under-age. The legal record is replete with constitutions insuring a child's rights as an *heres*.[116] Were a man or woman with children from a first marriage to wed a second time, there would be natural concerns both about support and about patrimony. Indeed in the early sixth century, the case of Archotomia, discussed in greater length in Chapter 7, dealt precisely with these issues.[117] Her former daughter-in-law apparently refused to support her children, who were living with her son. That the daughter-in-law, Aetheria, could successfully appeal a decision brought against her gives us some indication of how complicated and drawn out such disputes could become.[118] The threat to children's rights, then, was a legitimate fear and no doubt this affected a person's decision to contract a second marriage.

Moreover, at least in the case of husbands, the intense dislike of the stepmother (*noverca*) endured into late antique literature. Her status, if such a thing is possible, seems to have further diminished in late antiquity. The fear of putting the evil stepmother over a child continued, as well as the concern that she would favor her own children over those of her husband's first marriage. Indeed, Sidonius Apollinaris had argued that Nature herself acted the stepmother, '*novercaretur*', because she so poorly prepared her child, humanity, for the physical dangers of this earth.[119] Stepfathers, too, were distrusted. Jerome had pointedly called a *novercus* an enemy to his new wife and a tyrant over his new stepchildren.[120] But as early as the second century CE, stepmothers were also considered loose women.[121] Theodosius II had spoken of introducing lewd women (*impudicae mulieries*) into the household, much to the detriment of a child.[122] Theodosius here had been talking about concubines and perhaps *paelices*, but it also seems to have included new wives as well. The empress, Iustina, was a suspect *noverca* because she had become empress through her sexual charms and had supposedly plotted the death of her stepson, the Emperor Gratian.[123] The characterization of their poor relationship was accentuated by the favor the empress showed to her own son, Valentinian II. Certainly such fears did not keep emperors from remarrying, although affairs such as Fausta and Crispus' could also erupt on occasion. But did the problems associated with patrimonies and step-parents prevent or deter remarriage for the society at large and if so, to what degree?

These are not easily answerable questions. We would have trouble saying one way or the other whether remarriage was common. Certainly there are many examples of both men and women doing so. Perhaps a better question to ask is what options a divorcee or widowed individual had and construct a broader assessment of behavioral patterns from that perspective.

First, of course, a person could stay widowed. More often than not, women rather than men would be faced with this choice. For the Furias and the Paulas of the world, it was much easier to choose *viduitas* because of their financial independence. But despite the advantages widowhood supposedly afforded women, the realities for most women were not so pleasant. At the very least was the sense of loss. Even Christians were aware of its harsh emotional consequences. The widow of Alfenius Ceionius Iulianus *signo* Kamenius, for example, described with real feeling how sad she was to be cast into *viduitas*, left alone to raise several small children: '*Te dulcis coniunx lacrimis noctesque diesque cum parvis deflet natis, solacia amisisse dolens casto viduata cubili.*'[124] Similarly, the widower of Philomethia, a crippled man (*patrem debilis*), was dealt a sudden and cruel blow (*subita suprema*) at his 30-year-old wife's death and left to take care of five children alone.[125]

More significant were the financial troubles associated with the permanence of widowhood. Even Christians admitted it was a burdensome existence.[126] Widows, along with orphans and the destitute, were considered individuals most in need of material assistance from the Church. If a woman were raising children, it was even more difficult should she lack any significant income. There are many references to the harsh conditions these women suffered. One well-born woman from Cologne, for example, was so poor that she essentially sold herself 'to the wives of barbarians' in order to eat.[127] In fact, a widow's lot was so commonly believed to be poor that Ambrose actually upbraided those rich widows who had dared to compare themselves with the downtrodden.[128] They could, moreover, be the targets of legal harassment and extortion: one widow in the fifth century was sued by her daughter-in-law's father (*consocer*) after the death of her own son and grandson.[129] Nevertheless, as a group, they seemed to endure such circumstances and apparently did not remarry in great numbers for the sake of financial security.

On the other hand, we know that some number of Christian widows and widowers did not stay so. The merry widow of Luxorius' poem was starting on her fourth husband, her mourning clothes barely put away.[130] Of more concrete examples, we also know Constantius II had three wives and he was widowed at least once from his second marriage.[131] The Emperor Honorius likewise lost his spouse and quickly remarried; so, too, did his sister, Galla Placidia. We must thus readdress our initial question of whether remarriage was a common feature and instead ask what made some people remain widowed.

The decision to remain celibate after marriage, I believe, can be found in a letter of Augustine to the deacon Felix concerning a widow and her child.[132] During her daughter's life-threatening illness, she had pledged the girl's virginity to the Church should she survive. The girl had recovered, but the widow now wanted to know if her child could be released from her vows and still go to heaven. The old woman had offered her own widowhood as a replacement. But the reason for the widow's change of heart was significant: her elder son, from whom she had hoped to see grandchildren, had died suddenly. She had thus wanted her daughter to contract a marriage and multiply. The essential component of any marriage remained the production offspring and heirs. Once that had been achieved, one could pursue widowhood without fear of having a family dying out. That had been the concern of Pinian when he married Melania. And that had been the concern of their families when the two decided on chastity and started to give away their possessions: Melania's father had begged her to have more children.[133] Having no children at all was a danger and for many it was an offense to *pietas*. As Ausonius had mused, '*casta puella anus est*'.[134]

To be sure, there were other reasons affecting the decision to remain widowed or opt for remarriage. Some did, no doubt, take the wishes of the Church seriously, as in the case Marcella, who was left a widow and childless after seven months of marriage.[135] No doubt others chose widowhood because of the independence it might afford.[136] Men, too, no doubt tended to remain widowed too if they had children, although we have no examples similar to that of Marcus Aurelius.[137] Conversely, some also remarried solely for the purpose of getting children, as apparently was the case with Constantius II when he married his third wife, Faustina.[138] So again, the choice of *viduitas*, more than any other factor, was therefore conditioned by the issue of children. As Ambrose had written, where there were children, there was no need for a second marriage.[139] It would not go to far to hypothesize a correlation between childless widows and widowers and decisions to remarry.

Of course, the ideal of a celibate widowhood was another matter altogether. An individual might abstain from a second for patrimonial or other reasons, but still engage in affective and sexual relationships. The place of the concubine, as we have noted, did not end with Christianity nor with Christians. Men continued to use them: Jerome had sadly wished old widowers would control their sexual proclivities.[140] The concubine's role as a temporary or surrogate wife, however, seems to have slowly changed over time. While she still played a significant role in the lives of young and unmarried men, she is referred to less and less in relation to the widower. Pope Leo, for example, had referred in one letter to those penitents who had cohabited with concubines, referring solely to young men.[141] Sidonius Apollinaris, moreover, had written of one anonymous young man's dalliances with a concubine in a manner that suggested that this was typical, if unfortunate behavior of the young.[142] The Church had played it safe at times by permitting the possibility of an unmarried man having a concubine if she acted as a spouse (and of course that there was no actual wife!), but this seems to be directed towards those who had never been married.[143] Indeed, Luxorius at least had made fun of one old man who had chosen to keep a number of mistresses in a virtual harem.[144]

Nevertheless, the option was there and some widowers apparently found it a means of answering whatever emotional or physical needs they required without any legally and financially entangling unions.

But *vidui* were not the only ones to partake of surrogate partners. A mid-sixth-century Latin epitome of Justinian's novels mentioned the *concubitores* of widowed women.[145] We hear, more significantly, of older widows who would adopt young men, frequently freedmen, who would quickly become their lovers. Jerome reported to his correspondent, Rusticus, about some of these goings-on at Rome:

> Novi ego quasdam iam maturioris aetatis et plerasque generis libertini adulescentibus delectari et filios quaerere spiritales paulatimque pudore superato per ficta matrum nomina erumpere in licentiam maritalem.[146]

Nor do these appear to be pagan women: the term *filios spiritales* implies that they had taken these youths on as godchildren. This made matters all the worse, since the social and religious significance of spiritual sponsorship made such fraternizations tantamount to incest.[147] Such was the rhetorical point of Procopius' rumors about Antonina (still married to Belisaurius!) and her godson, Theodosius.[148] While Jerome may have been shocked at the unseemliness of such old women with young *concubini*, the situation appears to have been similar to the older widower who took a young concubine. Jerome went on to claim that there were others, presumably not slaves nor *liberti*, who habitually slept with virgins and widows. Whether or not this represented typical behavior is unclear, but certainly testament to such action suggests that widowhood was not always equated with celibacy.

The Church's attempt to regulate and encourage *viduitas* thus met with only partial success. It was predicated on a deeper cultural and biological commitment to propitiating the *familia*. Even some of the clergy understood and at times accepted this fundamental desire. But the Christian ideal of widowhood was not always matched by the actions of the widowed. The need and desire to maintain emotional and physical ties with the opposite sex further eroded the moral authority of Church teaching in this regard. In short, the permanency of widowhood was beholden to the same pressures that had existed for centuries.

Remarriage

The second choice for the widowed or divorced was remarriage. Given what we have said about widowhood, however, we can see that a second marriage was normally considered a necessity for the childless. For those who had been divorced, remarriage might be even more important. It was possible that all sorts of unpleasant rumors might erupt about their post-nuptial lives, as had been the case with Honorius and his half-sister, Galla Placidia.[149] Even in the case of a remarriage, rumors surrounding a divorcée might surface. Valentinian I apparently was a little too quick to marry his second wife, Iustina, after he divorced his first one, Marina Severa, and caused quite a stir.[150] For such individuals, then, the taint of disapproval lingered. But this disapprobation was undoubtedly connected to the broader impressions of divorce in Roman society. And it is important to note that the Church's attempt to keep even the righteously divorced from remarrying was for the most part an abject failure. The council of Agde had thrown in the figurative towel when it allowed remarriage – subject to the approval of the local bishop – for the cuckolded spouse.[151]

For the widowed, on the other hand, no such blemish existed. If they were young and childless, the moral censure of the Church was necessarily low key. Indeed, the furor over the *number* of marriages a person could contract in later Byzantine law indicates the relative ineffectiveness of religious dissuasion.[152] As long as women, at least, waited one year and did not cross the bounds of incest, the opprobrium would be so small as to be almost non-existent. Only Jerome had dared to suggest that second marriages were akin to prostitution, but his position was so severe that even his own friends criticized it and he subsequently retreated from that position.[153] For honest and upright Christians *vidui* did remarry, and usually for the production of *proles*. But children also were frequently a parent's social security. As Augustine noted, they offered some protection in one's old age.[154]

Little more need be said about remarriage, since we have already discussed the reasons why a widowed individual would enter a second union. But there are three final observations regarding multiple marriages. First, we know that in many cases – men in particular – children from a previous marriage would not necessarily stop someone from marrying again. The son-in-law of Symmachus, Nichomachus Flavianus, for example, had not only been married previously, but had a daughter from that union.[155] The emperor, Theodosius, too, had married a second wife, Galla, after his first wife had bore him two sons. The reason for contracting such matches is not immediately apparent and certainly they varied from case to case. What is clear, however, was that they would not have been made if there were any financial or inheritance problems associated with a second union. Remarrying with children, then, was probably more common to Rome's elite.

Second, remarriage for women did not necessarily mean that these unions represented the formation of new *familiae*. We see in the admittedly unusual circumstances of the imperial house, for example, several emperors and would-be emperors in the fourth and fifth centuries marrying into the *domus Augusti* to lend legitimacy to their own positions. Their wives had been married previously, but retained the status of being imperials. Zeno, for example, was as much emperor because of his marriage to Ariadne as was her second husband, Anastasius. Some even adopted the family name. Numerous other men during the same period, not in line to become emperor, had also married into the imperial house to the practical demise of their own households. These imperial *augustae* were special cases, but their multiple marriages indicated their high status.[156] So at least in a dynastic setting, serial monogamy was a way of extending the existing family lines (*stirpes*) rather than creating a new one. More significantly, a broader study of Roman polyonomy, where a change in the naming patterns of late antique persons incorporated the *nomina* from both parents, indicates a greater importance placed on the cognatic line.[157] Sidonius Apollinaris had stated in fact that every man owed much to his mother and her family.[158] Even a cognate line of succession could be accepted: the widow who had pledged her daughter's virginity had wanted to continue her family's line *through her daughter*.[159] A man's *familia* of course would include all his dependants: wives, living and dead, his children, slaves and freedmen. But it seems possible that a woman of high enough position could be master of her own *domus*, assuming that her husband and *paterfamilias* were dead. Sextus Petronius Probus, for example, had by his marriage been unofficially adopted into the powerful Anician family according to the verses of Ausonius.[160]

Finally, and connected to the first two points, remarriage presented an opportunity for creating new lines of relation. A parent or grandparent who was not related to a child by blood might nevertheless accept such offspring as his or her own. Symmachus, for example, had called Galla, his little step-granddaughter, *nepticula*, even though she technically bore no relation.[161] The roles of the step-parent and grandparent were thus not always hated, perhaps indicating that they represented more of a literary *topos* than it did reality. Other *noverci* and *novercae* took the opportunity to claim and care for step-children as well. Maximianus Herculis, for example, had evidently claimed his stepdaughter, Theodora, as his own.[162] Ausonius' son-in-law, Thalassius, to cite a final instance, was apparently a good father to his wife's son by a first marriage.[163] At times, it is true, the appearance of a step-parent could destroy the harmony of the *familia*, a fact promoted by clerics to discourage multiple unions. But they said little of those situations where a second marriage nurtured and fostered the family.

Legal issues surrounding widowhood and remarriage

Roman law in the later Empire officially made widowhood an honorable state. It had long been respected in Roman society, as we have stated, but respect in the culture was translated into a more tangible form. To begin with, they were afforded protections that had not existed previously. Along with virgins, they were protected from *raptus* by special punishments for the offenders.[164] Indeed, virgins and widows were often cited together, intimating a certain congruity between the two in the sense that they deserved special respect.[165] Valentinian I, after all, exempted both virgins and widows from the plebeian poll tax (*capitatio*) in 368, presumably to encourage their continued status.[166] Moreover, so that no onus would fall upon widows, Valens and Valentinian II forbade all clergymen from visiting their homes under the threat of banishment. Nor could a cleric leave money to a widow.[167] Finally, if a woman publicly declared that she would remain widowed, she could act as a *tutor* or *curator* for her children, providing she was an adult.[168]

There were exceptions, of course. Majorian, clearly concerned about the lack of available manpower in Italy, specifically outlawed childless widows before the age of menopause.[169] On the face of it, the novel seemed to have some similarities to the social legislation of Augustus. But by the time of Justinian, however, this law had been rescinded. Majorian's legislation can thus be seen as a response to immediate problems than as a long-term, far-reaching policy. It also did not work.

On the other hand, the government did not so value widowhood that it tried to preserve the state above all else. In general, the only restriction placed on preventing remarriages was the time placed between them. As had always been the case, a man could remarry immediately after the death or divorce of his wife. Later Roman divorce laws had put a few strictures on divorces were a man found culpable in some way, but these were minor.[170] Women, on the other hand, were held to a stricter standard. At best, they had to wait a year before remarrying if they were widows, so there would be no questions of a posthumous child's lineage. In cases of divorce, where other motivations may have been at work, Honorius and Constantius III, as we have discussed, made women wait up to five years to remarry.[171]

There also were rewards if a woman waited and respected the proper period of time. A 382 constitution first passed in the East, but later enforced in the West, permitted a widow who remarried to dispense any gifts she saw fit, providing she protected properties for her children.[172] Honorius also ensured that a properly remarried widow would be assured of lifetime usufruct on any and all properties she brought into the marriage.[173] Conversely, penalties could be imposed on women should they choose to remarry before the allotted period of time. One law, whose provenance is admittedly Eastern and thus not applicable in the West until 438, charged a widow with *infamia* and imposed potentially large financial losses upon her property should she marry within a year of her husband's death.[174]

Having briefly discussed this legislation, we must consider whether these laws were Christian in character. Certainly those laws which respected the state of widowhood had specific ties to Christian authority. The rough equality of virgins and widows, the exceptional punishments for their violation and the deference paid to their position all indicate a conscious decision on the government's part to give them a special, if not an entirely privileged, status. That there were Christian interests being addressed in these laws would seem self-evident, especially since Christian sentiment was often specifically expressed. Whether or not they accurately reflected actual opinion in the late Roman world is a matter addressed below. The matter is far less clear, however, with the rules for remarriage. Guardianships, charges of *infamia*, provision for children of a previous marriage and concerns about passing along patrimonies were all issues with which classical law had dealt. They could only be Christian to the extent that Christians did not object to them, and certainly in some cases, they may well have raised objections. The Church, after all, had in general discouraged *all* remarriages.

In sum, however, we can perhaps make a fine distinction. Widowhood was, to a certain extent, a respected state in Roman society, and Christian writers raised its status even higher. Late Roman law recognized and was influenced by the Church's attempts to place value on *viduitas*. Remarriage, on the other hand, was decidedly discouraged. Despite the state's attempt to regulate the speed with which multiple marriages were contracted, the government was reacting to issues raised in classical law. The status of widows was perhaps Christianized; the means by which they could conduct their subsequent lives certainly was not.

In conclusion, then, an infrequent, if not comprehensive, Christian influence on these issues became more prominent in especially the late fourth and early fifth centuries. The imperial government did not discard Roman civil law, nor did it have to. Social legislation once again provided a vessel for occasionally transmitting Christian concerns and issues to the wider population of the Roman Empire.

Other states

Concubinage

Since we have discussed concubinage in relation to widowhood, we should discuss its role more fully. The concubine did not disappear with the rise of Christianity, nor did she disappear among Christians. Canon law had permitted her place in certain circumstances. But these regulations say more about the man who had a concubine than the concubine herself. Certainly, her position must have been seen as precarious among the clergy and many ended up attacking the institution as being synonymous with prostitution. One could see their point: a woman's ostensible reason for being so connected to a man was sexual rather than procreative. And the primary result of marriage, Christian or pagan, was to produce legitimate children. As Pope Innocent had paraphrased Genesis in the early fifth century, God had put humans on earth to engage in marriage and multiply.[175]

Many of the reasons for having a concubine instead of a wife remained the same in late antiquity as they had centuries before.[176] They provided an effective role for men who did not wish to be burdened with the problems associated with legitimate or additional children. *Spurii* were not natural heirs under the law, so problems with transmitting patrimonies did not exist should a man die intestate. This was important, especially in cases where a man already had legitimate children. *Concubinae* could, moreover, be discarded by younger men once they had contracted a marriage. Paulinus of Pella, for example, made it a point in his youth to sleep only with slave mistresses (*paelices*) from his own household until his parents found him a wife.[177] This sort of behavior by men, however, could only be viewed by the Church as synonymous with divorce and remarriage.

Yet there might be mitigating circumstances for a woman who had chosen to live with a man rather than marry him. Augustine described in some detail his own experience with a concubine. Perhaps unusual, perhaps not, he remained faithful to her in a monogamous relationship for thirteen years. He had a son by her, Adeodatus, whom he claimed and raised as his own. Indeed, he mentions that children were unlooked for in such relationships, but they were loved nevertheless.[178] And in fact, he kept his son with him in Milan after his concubine had returned to Africa.[179] Augustine may have been overly sensitive to his responsibilities, but Adeodatus was lovingly accepted by his grandmother as well.[180] His own experiences no doubt influenced his attitudes towards concubines as a Christian author. He did not see the black–white distinctions of the relationship as a Jerome or an Ambrose might. Clearly, he agreed, concubinage in its basest form was adultery. But if a woman only took one man and consequently remained continent after the relationship had ended (as his own apparently had, the woman choosing voluntary widowhood[181]), it was difficult to call her an adulteress.[182] Augustine went even further and argued that if a concubine's only purpose for her relationship with a man was to beget children, she might be of a higher moral caliber than those Roman matrons who only married to satisfy their lust! Nor was this simple theorizing on Augustine's part. His parishioners were made fully aware of these subtleties as guidelines for their own behavior.[183]

At times, even the Church had to practice appeasement. The council of Toledo was perhaps most accepting of the institution, permitting a man to receive communion if he has a concubine but no wife.[184] A synod in Rome, too, tacitly permitted a man to have one under the same circumstances.[185] More often, though, the Church seemed to direct Christian men, presumably young men who had not yet been married, to wed their concubines. At council of Elvira, a relatively conservative meeting, the Church permitted unmarried individuals who had sinned to receive communion if they subsequently married and did penance.[186] Even in cases where a consecrated virgin had illicit sexual relations, she could eventually be permitted back into the Church if she married the man and performed a long period of penance.[187] It seems then, at least with younger people, who were no doubt seen as being more susceptible to sexual desire, the Church tried to minimize or even do away with concubinage by encouraging alternatives to the state.

For older persons, as we have indicated, the Church and its clergy took a decidedly harder line. For them, there was no reason for remarriage and production of children, and thus no reason for sexual intercourse. Jerome held up the example of virtuous old widows to shame widowers into similar circumspection: *'atque utinam praeconia feminarum imitarentur viri et rugosa senectus redderet, quod sponte offert adulescentia!'*[188] The council of Elvira had taken a particularly harsh line: if a widow sinned, she would have to do five years penance; if she married another, she was excommunicated.[189] African bishops, too, were unforgiving on this point.[190] The council of Arles was perhaps most unequivocal: illicit intercourse resulted in excommunication.[191] When contrasted to the more conciliatory line with younger persons and concubinage, a discernible if not comprehensive policy seems to have developed.

There was nevertheless no discernible ideal, Christian or otherwise, for the concubine in late antiquity. She was part of the *monde véritable*, whose existence was at best an unpleasant necessity for the unmarried man. Both he and his concubine could be excused for their relationship under certain circumstances – mostly if they acted for all intents and purposes as husband and wife. Anything short of that and he was an adulterer in the Church's eyes (especially if he already had a wife) and she little more than a prostitute (*meretrix*). But that was perhaps as it should be. As Ausonius asked in one epigram: *'Nam nisi moribus his fuerit, casta modesta pudenter agens, dicere abominor, uxor erit?'*[192]

Virginity

Finally, with regards to virgins, relatively little needs to be said. Virginity, almost by definition, was something outside the cultural and legal bounds of the family. Indeed, it was a conscious denial of the concept and reality of kinship: a woman (and on occasion, a man) purposely ended her line for a greater good. Nevertheless, by denying kinship, it represented a true alternative to the married state, the *familia*, and by extension, traditional Roman society.

As we have already implied, once a family's future had been established, many parents and widows did find it in their interest to pledge one child to perpetual chastity. Even the wealthy had wished to ensure the goodwill of the divine when they promised a daughter's (or occasionally a son's[193]) virginity to the Church. It also had the practical benefit of ending the troublesome task of raising a dowry and other similar forms of maintenance.[194] Melania and Pinian's daughter had been dedicated to God, as had the widow's daughter in Augustine's letter. As long as the line continued, then, a family could afford to be generous in this manner. A cynical and unhappy Duchess of Marlborough had called this practical compromise possessing 'an heir and a spare'.

Of course, both Jewish and Roman traditions had long emphasized the importance of virginity, running along roughly congruent lines in stressing its value.[195] But they had seen virginity as a laudable state prior to marriage, not an end in itself. Christianity instead enlarged on these ideas, and exerted enough influence that laws were passed by various emperors to ensure a dedicated woman's protection. An early law of Constantius II, presumably published in Rome, prescribed an unspecified punishment for the rape of a virgin consecrated to Christ.[196] A similar law, with equally vague language concerning punishment, was issued for the provinces of Italy and Africa three years later.[197] Eastern emperors also passed laws forbidding forced marriages upon virgins – let alone any sexual violation – punishable by death.[198] Indeed, the Church itself permitted under-age girls to take the veil of virginity in such situations[199] and even punished its own clergy if they participated in any way with a *raptus* marriage.[200] In fact, the only exception the law made for such affronts on women were in cases of mentally deficient individuals, and even they would have their property impounded by the fisc and forced into permanent exile.[201] Finally, and most extensively, the Emperor Majorian in 458 issued a *novella* that gave women who were consecrated to Christ a series of rights to distribute their wealth as they saw fit.[202] The very nature of laws like these indicates the prevalence of Christian concern among the imperial bureaucracy or at least a partial attempt to accommodate them. To be sure, they were by no means all-encompassing and they may well have been an inaccurate representation of current Christian thought on the subject. But surely we can see a tendency to protect the Church's interests and address its concerns.

More of course was said about the regulation of virgins in the Church. The importance placed on continence and celibacy in Christianity has already been discussed, but it is sufficient here to say that the inviolability of the virginal state, whether consecrated to God or not, was sacrosanct. Several different canons stated that any woman breaking a vow of virginity would be punished.[203] The ecumenical council at Chalcedon in 451 also stated that dedicated virgins and monks would be excommunicated if they married.[204] True, there was some room for forgiveness. Elvira permitted communion at death for a fallen virgin who had done sufficient penance.[205] A synod held in Rome was a bit more relaxed. If a veiled virgin wanted to continue in her order, she could do so after an extended penance of many years.[206] There were also distinctions among virgins: an unconsecrated virgin who had committed adultery and subsequently married could be allowed communion after one year, *without* having to do penance.[207] And women who had taken their vows of virginity before the age of 25 – the age of their majority – and had married before taking their final vows, could be received back into their communities along with their husbands after atoning for their transgression.[208] But these were all extenuating circumstances. For the most part, a voluntary violation of one's virginity was a very serious thing.

Yet the role of virginity as an alternative to family always remained small in Roman society. We have already discussed some of the pressures placed on parents to keep their daughters from choosing to remain untouched, especially when they represented the only way in which a family and a *domus* might continue. Dedicating a child's virginity to Christ was generally a luxury that only families with many children and not enough money could afford. Nevertheless, it was an option that Roman society had never entertained and in that sense, it truly became an alternative to the choice of marriage and family.

Conclusions

There is much we have necessarily ignored in our discussion of virginity, widowhood and celibacy. Many of these same religious authorities offered advice, practical and otherwise, on how to successfully pursue sexual chastity. But their ruminations are somewhat beside the point: they were for the most part only valuable to those individuals who had decided to dedicate themselves or their children to a life absent of future marriages and its inevitable consequences.

More interesting and more germane are the questions raised by Christianity and how Roman society reacted to them. As we have attempted to demonstrate, the ideal of the chaste widow never marrying again remained in large part an ideal. Nor did the divorced care much for Christian calls to permanent celibacy. Reproductive, affective and sexual pressures promoted alternative forms of behavior. It is impossible to quantify the practices of remarriage, taking a concubine or other similar actions, but clearly the commonness of these cultural and biological tensions have to be added to the equation. Ambrose had claimed his brother, Satyrus, thought that seeing the defilement of a widow was worse than his own death.[209] The sentiment was perhaps noble, but many chose such a path and probably did not feel violated.

6

CHILDREN

The natural and expected outcome of marriage was of course the production of children. As we saw in Chapter 2, both the Roman and Christian traditions saw children as inevitably following from an accepted union, although they differed on the significance of the event. As with marriage, widowhood and virginity, Christian writers looked at the parent–child bond with a somewhat leery eye. They saw the potential dangers of sin that might bubble forth from the deep waters of the human soul and did their best to prevent them. Fears of negligent behavior on the part of mothers and fathers dominated their concerns, but these men also sought to delve more deeply into the nature of these interpersonal relationships.

The child

A new status?

In comparison to the considerable written material surrounding conjugal relations, there was considerably less attention paid to children and their proper upbringing, both in secular and religious material. Part of this was due, of course, to the fact that children were largely marginal members of Roman society, mere apprentices in the guild of humanity. They needed to be trained, educated, coddled, and chastened before they could logically be expected to participate in worldly affairs. But another reason was due to the way the Romans themselves defined childhood. Technically, anyone under the age of 25 was a minor, although, in practice, marriage was a better indicator of one's majority. Certainly, there were gradations of youth: *iuvens, adolescens,* and the like. But the fact that there were adult 'children' who were married and owned property created problems in the law.[1] We have already discussed some of the familial, financial and legal problems that the under-aged Melania and Pinian faced. It is not surprising, then, that most of the legislation concerning minors dealt with people whom our society would consider adults. The age of 20 seems to have been particularly significant, especially for children under the guardianship of a *tutor* or *curator*.[2] One of the results of this concentration was a notable lack of legal thought concerning individuals in their formative years.[3]

Nevertheless, as one scholar argued a quarter of a century ago, there is more than enough evidence to explore childhood in late antiquity and beyond.[4] Only Thomas Wiedemann, however, has offered a somewhat original interpretation on the role of children in the ancient world.[5] The voices of minors, of course, were even more muted than those of women in antiquity, so he concentrates on adult attitudes towards children throughout the whole history of the Empire. Briefly, Wiedemann argues that several factors led to a demarginalization of children as Rome's Republican past grew more distant. As the political ideologies of the citizen soldier and indeed the whole definition of what it meant to be 'Roman' faded, so, too, did opinions that children – who were incapable of defending the state – were useless members of society. With the rise of Christianity, which placed emphasis on every human soul, children were considered fully members of the human race.

There are problems with this thesis, however. As one critic noted, it says perhaps more about the changing ideology of citizenship than it does about the experience of childhood.[6] Moreover, by emphasizing high mortality rates as an explanation for parental indifference to young children, Wiedemann overlooks the distinctions in childhood that Romans themselves made.[7] We certainly know that high mortality rates did not disappear in late antiquity and anecdotal evidence is personally offered both by Augustine and Paulinus of Pella as to the commonness of life-threatening childhood illnesses.[8] Wiedemann's arguments concerning the effects of Christianity, however, are perhaps more significant. Forgetting for the moment that the perception of children by adults in the early Empire was not as wooden as is generally presumed, the role of the Church in redefining the role of the child and the parental responsibilities to offspring are worth investigating further. Did the child's place in the family and in society become more important?

Part of the answer comes with the change in Christianity's status within the Empire. Once the Church became fully recognized in the early fourth century, there was a qualitative shift in the religion's proselytizing activities. To be sure, they continued and occasionally martyrdom was the result for missionaries who saw it as their duty to educate and convert the heathen. Even in the more pastoral regions of intensively Christianized Italy, apostles of the faith risked death: in the Tirol valley, for example, several met their demise at the hands of enraged pagans in the 390s.[9] But with a large and growing number of Christians in at least the urban centers of the Empire, the need to practice and convert intensively and in secret had ended.

One of the many effects of Christianity's newfound patronage and favor included a significant shift in initiation patterns. For most lay Christians of the early Church, baptism represented the highest level that they could reasonably attain: a state of grace and a remission of all sin. It should not strike us as surprising, then, that baptism was an event which occurred in adulthood and often near the end of one's life: to sin while in the state of grace was considered the vilest of crime. Many of the accounts we have of martyrs, by way of illustration, describe how they were baptized just before their deaths.[10] The story of Constantine's deathbed baptism, of course, is the most famous example.[11] But with their elevation to a favored minority, these so-called clinical baptisms (from *kline*, meaning bed) declined and Christians began to be christened at an earlier age, in many cases all the way back to childhood. It was not yet a sacrament routinely administered to infants, since an individual in theory had to be familiar with the basics of Christian belief before baptism could occur.[12] These basics seemed to have included knowing the Nicene *credo*, a few prayers, and a small amount of Christian history.[13] But once someone had been a catechumen, especially if he or she were an adult, that person, as Ambrose put it, was expected to 'put on Christ' and become 'full' Christians through baptism.[14] Living in limbo – that is remaining a catechumen – was considered an unacceptable and cowardly state by the start of the fifth century.[15]

While many catechumens well into the fifth century were adults, the Church made it a point to have the children of their parishioners go through catechism. Augustine described how he had done so when he was a boy. When seized by a life-threatening ailment, he attempted to secure permission from his mother to be baptized.[16] While his mother resisted and he recovered, Augustine's plight would not have been uncommon for the under-aged population of Rome. Indeed, had his health degenerated, Monnica had been prepared to permit baptism. Given the relatively high rate of mortality in children, then, many parents would have likely been less sensitive than Monnica to the dangers of sin after being symbolically cleansed. To the extent that catechism was an education, the Church certainly emphasized the education of all its own children.

But this only applied to the extent that it secured a child's baptism. Official Church policy seems to have been geared to insuring that children had been duly baptized by an orthodox cleric, although even that was not always necessary.[17] Canons of the early and mid-fifth century concerning children largely deal with their baptized state. In an issue peculiar to Africa, for example, one canon ordered a consultation with the Roman see surrounding former Donatists receiving communion in Catholic churches.[18] Apparently, they had been baptized in Donatist communities, but only at their parents' behest rather than their own. Were they to be rebaptized or not? There were more universal problems, however. Because of the increasing numbers of children forcibly dislodged from their families by slavers and the social disruptions caused by the arrival of Germanic peoples, there were apparently a large number of individuals who were unaware of their status. The sixth synod of Carthage, under the presidency of the archbishop Aurelius, took the unusual step of ordering immediate baptism for children who had been separated from their families and consequently unsure of whether they had been baptized or not.[19] Pope Leo, partially as a response to Vandal incursions, oversaw another council for the bishops of Sicily and ordered summary baptism, subject to a lack of corroborating evidence.[20]

These issues hardly speak for the centrality of children, either in the family or in society at large. At best, it implies a concern for their souls, but this certainly did not extend to their physical well-being. There were two other major areas in which the Church legislated, however. One series of canons dealt with children of the clergy, mostly binding them and their parents to tighter moral standards than lay families. They are accordingly somewhat specialized, and thus need not concern us greatly.[21] The other policy that seemed to be reiterated in canon law were strictures against the sale and exposure of children. Trafficking in minors had been objected to as far back as the second century, for reasons we have outlined in Chapter 2. So it is unsurprising perhaps that one of the earliest canons we have proscribed permanent excommunication to parents who sold their children into slavery.[22] But of greater effect was a different kind of deterrence, a principle that was first voiced in Constantinian legislation: reaffirming the finality of such transactions should parents rashly sell or expose their children. In accordance with the Emperor Honorius' law,[23] the council of Vaison passed two canons institutionalizing this permanence.[24] Canon nine ordered that all exposed children should be taken to a church, and if they had not been reclaimed within ten days, they belonged to the finder. Canon ten, moreover, condemned as murderers those parents who tried to recover their exposed children and slandered the finder. These provisions were recapitulated in two subsequent Gallic synods from our period.[25] The permanence of sale and exposure, then, would hopefully deter rash decisions to get rid of one's children.

Concerns for a child's status in these relatively specified circumstances are difficult to assess. Certainly, they did not represent anything new: exposure of children early on was considered synonymous with slavery and prostitution, as well as opening up the potential for incest. But more to the point, they seem to speak less for children as children *per se* than they do about the status to which they would be lowered. To be a prostitute (*meretrix*) or perhaps a slave in the circus, whether adult or child, was a degrading status.[26] The condition of prostitution and the possibility of an incestuous coupling, then, were the real concerns, and clearly the action of exposure reflected more poorly upon the parent than the child. It seems, too, that these concerns were shared by the imperial government. Little wonder, then, that Valentinian III sentenced to the public mines both fathers and masters who turned their daughters into *meretrices* and gave such young women the chance to appeal to local governors, advocates for the citizenry (*defensores*), and bishops.[27] Age was in reality of no consequence. Only now and then did the vaguer fear of a child's death through exposure prick the conscience of those who enacted canonical and imperial legislation.[28]

Of course, sales of free children had been technically illegal since the early days of the Empire. That did not change until 391 CE. Even at that point, the

Emperor Valentinian II insisted that it could only be a temporary sale, done out of familial need.[29] Indeed, when Valentinian III in 451 seems to have finally permitted such transactions in Italy, he insisted that they were only made because of the horrible famine that had swept the countryside and accordingly took measures to insure that such children could be easily recoverable by their parents.[30] There are some other scattered references to the legality of the practice,[31] but there was a clear policy as old as the Empire outlawing or at least discouraging the barter of free individuals. So while Christians might have been unique in their condemnation of the practice of exposure, certainly their opposition to the sale of children was hardly original.

Apart from canon law, however, the Church did take upon itself two tasks that specifically dealt with children. The first was the care for orphans. Quite apart from providing material assistance for such children, so-called guest-houses, or *xenodochia*, were set up by local parishes (and later by private individuals and the imperial government), which gave shelter as well as aid to all who were needy. By the fifth century, institutions specifically designed for parentless children were established. These orphanages had the dual purpose of caring for destitute youths and preparing a ready reserve of boys for the clergy.[32] One of Augustine's great hopes and great failures, for example, was the young bishop Antoninus, who had been placed on the dole (*matricula pauperum*) and raised in a monastery.[33] But as we well know, the care for destitute children, at least free ones, was also nothing new. The *alimenta* scheme of second-century emperors and the stopgap relief programs of Constantine in the fourth century offered similar assistance to poor and orphaned free children. To the extent that local churches received in return a steady supply of trained young men for their growing parishes, however, one might argue that the Church had been considerably more successful in their recruitment programs than had been the Antonines. Christian coffers were repaid in talent: such children were investments, not simply charity cases. Eventually, they would make up the ranks of the clergy. Finally, children were not alone in receiving assistance. Widows, the physically disabled, and the poor generally were eligible for help. Children were important so far as they were a subset of the needy.

The second task for which the clergy took great responsibility was securing the freedom of children who had been stolen (or bought) by slave-traders or kidnapped by barbarians. Despite its illegality, there was apparently a thriving trade in free boys and girls. This of course was quite different from a general manumission of Christian slaves that had caused considerable consternation within the early Church.[34] While evidence suggests that the slave supply actually increased in the fourth century, demand for slave labor exceeded supply.[35] And with Rome's wars of conquest long past, the regular flow of slaves had ebbed over the centuries. The Empire was therefore partially thrown back on its own resources. If we are to believe Pope Gregory in the late sixth century, for example, there had been a long established supply of slaves coming from Gaul into Italy.[36] The Church's answer to the enslavement of poor free children was obvious: secure the freedom of free citizens, no matter their sex or age. Augustine on more than one occasion impressed upon his parishioners the need to keep coffers full for just this purpose.[37] Nor were the poor the only targets. Sometimes even the children of the high-born were not immune from capture and enslavement. In either 443 or 448, the bishop Theodoret – later author of the *Historia Ecclesiastica* – related how he became involved in securing the return of a young girl, Maria, to her family. Having been captured by the Vandals and sold along with her own house slave to a trader, Maria was sold again into servitude in Cyrrhus. Sympathetic individuals in the city secured her release and handed her over to Theodoret, who in turn reunited the girl with her father, Eudaemon.[38]

Prices for slaves were not cheap and so made securing their freedom that much harder. Constantine had early in his reign set an arbitrary value for any escaped slave at the considerable sum of 20 *solidi*.[39] Children might cost less, but we know of one young Gaulish boy who was sold in 359 for 18 *solidi*.[40] For this reason, the government in the sixth century permitted local churches to pawn church property as a guarantee for freeing slaves.[41] More common than a spectacular mass manumission of captives, such as the bishop, Acacius, secured in the East, were small-scale transactions.[42] Augustine relates in one letter how slave-traders had been stealing and buying both children and adults in the neighborhood around Hippo.[43] A young girl had been rescued thanks to Church coffers, but she seems to have been an exception.[44] What was particularly upsetting to the bishop was that the slavers were shipping them off overseas. But even if a cleric had the money, a slaver was not necessarily willing to ransom his captives. Small wonder that Augustine expressed his deep disgust at seeing slave-traders sitting in his own congregation![45]

While children may have been the focus of these endeavors, however, they were not the only ones. In that same letter, Augustine also noted that a man had sold his feckless wife into slavery and a young bookkeeper from a local monastery had been kidnapped.[46] Ambrose had to defend his decision to sell Church property in order to free many captured soldiers and citizens in war-torn Illyricum and Thrace.[47] The Church, then, like its policy concerning exposure, was not directed at children *per se*. Rather, it attacked the reduction of status of any free person, whether under-age or adult, who had been enslaved against his or her will. Should an individual wish to freely indenture or fully sell himself, that was one thing.[48] So, too, was the long-accepted institution of temporary debt slavery. And, of course, the status of *colonus*, a person technically free but tied to a piece of land, had existed for centuries. But involuntary and permanent servitude for any freeborn person was unquestionably condemned.

Church action, then, matching Church canon, created no truly new concept of childhood that emphasized a specialized status. Much of what the clergy decreed and executed could be traced back or compared to earlier Roman concerns. For those actions or beliefs that might be considered exclusively Christian, we can see upon closer examination that they extended to all persons, children and adults. Even more than women, children were at the periphery of society, albeit clearly within its boundaries. In this sense, the demarginalization of children is, in sum, a myth.

Making it to adulthood

Pulling away for a moment from the theoretical constructs of children and their places in the world, let us look briefly at the lives of minors. A young person's lot for the most part was fraught with difficulty and danger. Even among the wealthy of the ancient world, child mortality was shockingly high and medicine was primitive. A recent find in Lugnano, Italy, testifies to the potential of disease, even in small and relatively isolated communities. There, sometime in the mid-fifth century, forty-seven late-term fetuses and young infants succumbed to malaria one summer and were buried in a special gravesite at an abandoned villa.[49] Disease and death could strike with a quickness and ferocity that made childhood a tenuous thing.

Assuming that a child survived the assault of diseases, to say nothing of exposure, there were other pitfalls. As we know from the legal record and the accounts of many writers, the ever-present threat of famine loomed with an alarming regularity. There were usually only two alternatives for most of the population. The first alternative was, of course, starving. Libanius noted during one famine in 384 that the poor of Antioch were reduced to eating grass.[50] Such conditions could not have been unusual elsewhere. The other choice – that is, as an alternative to death – was waiving one's freedom. The likelihood of indentured servitude or even slavery was a possible, if not inevitable event in a poor child's life. At times, as in Italy of the 450s, it was so severe that the government actually allowed parents to sell their free children in the hopes that both would survive.[51] Sometimes, even when there was no emergency, children could be thrust into slavery without their parents' knowledge or consent. As Augustine noted, they could be simply kidnapped by slave-traders.[52]

The offspring of the elite fared better, but not so much so that childhood (*pueritia*) was ever considered a prized experience. While the image of childhood can only be perceived through a glass darkly, the experience, as Augustine noted, was not generally a pleasant one.[53] As in all eras, the expectations of parents, other relatives, slaves and teachers must have overwhelmed children at times. The ever-present threat of physical punishment may have been deemed necessary by adults,[54] but no doubt created a constant low level of anxiety for many. Augustine had even noted the similarities between the fear of a slave and that of a son.[55] Prudentius' observation about his own childhood, '*aetas prima crepantibus flevit sub ferulis*' could no doubt be repeated by any of a number of young men.[56] Education, at least education past the elementary level, was doctrinaire, intensively paradigmatic, and often enforced by corporal punishment. Even Christian teaching at home was usually no more than tedious rote memorization.[57]

This is not to say that life for children, even poor children, was unrelentingly bleak. But it should give some indication as to why an ideal of childhood never really developed, either among polytheists or Christians. They were fully human beings in the sense that they had souls, but so, too, were women and slaves. Parents clearly loved their children and were saddened by their deaths: the epitaph by the poet Luxorius for a little girl, Damira, can leave no doubt in anyone's mind.[58] But the harsh realities of surviving into adulthood kept the culture from ever developing a romance for the child's condition. In this sense, the ideals and realities of childhood, as seen by both Christians and non-Christians alike, remained much the same.

Children and education

Before we discuss the nature of parent–child relations, we should also perhaps say something of a child's formal education, especially since the theoretical responsibility came under the provenance of a *paterfamilias*. It is not necessary to delve deeply into the educational system and parental expectations in late antiquity: Henri Marrou's magisterial study on that subject is still in many ways the standard.[59] Several brief observations should be sufficient.

First, traditional education was still seen by Christians and polytheists alike as a means for advancing the careers of the elite, whether those vocations be political, literary or religious. Christians may have rejected heathen beliefs, but they were loath to reject its contributions. By the start of the sixth century, we do see a more generalized condemnation of Roman literature and culture among religious authors, but this was by no means a universal opinion.[60] Like the abstract language of artistic symbolism, a classical education represented the shared experience of one thousand years of culture. Cleric and layman employed both standard literary conventions and the historical and mythical *exempla* of Graeco-Roman culture in the commerce of learned communication – what Peter Brown described as the collusion of *paideia* and power.[61] Not until the age of Gregory the Great did the need for an educated elite devolve so greatly that Cassiodorus (thoroughly trained in a classical education himself) could offer a viably alternative Christian educational program in his *Institutiones*. Even in his sweeping and sophisticated vision of a Christian education, Augustine was simply unable to reject most of the liberal arts, particularly grammar and rhetoric. It is hardly surprising that late in life, the old bishop was still irascibly answering questions about Cicero's style and meaning.[62]

Second, Christian education, such as it was, was exceedingly basic and limited both in its scope and its goals. Paulinus of Pella mentions how, early in youth, he learned the ten forms of ignorance and sin that led to damnation, implying there was some sort of simple mnemonic device such as music or rhyme to remember them.[63] More often, however, children were encouraged or coerced into memorizing passages of Scripture, frequently a dull pursuit.[64] Occasionally, a work such as Avitus of Vienne's poetic epitome of the first books of the Old Testament were directed towards children.[65] But familiarity with the Bible did not have any utilitarian purpose in the same sense as a secular education: one did not learn the methods of communication from scriptural *exempla*. For that, only a traditional program would do. Indeed, Ennodius of Pavia apparently continued his secular education *after* entering the Church at the young age of 20.[66] Unless a child was from his or her earliest years destined to be a cleric or a virgin, then, Christian learning was mostly for spiritual edification.

Episcopal schools or *domus ecclesiae*, usually functioning as *de facto* monasteries, did exist in some of the larger cities. There, boys and young men probably received professional training in specialized jobs, such as *notarii* of various sorts and professional speakers of scripture (*lectores*). Children in a monastery might have had a slightly more formalized education, since they were being purposely groomed for the cenobitic or anchoritic life. John Cassian noted that the monastery itself was a training school for children (*iuniorum schola*) learning the hermit's life.[67] As such, it tended to be more properly an apprenticeship than pedagogy, since the boys were training to be ascetics. This included the menial tasks that all monks carried out as well as learning physical self-denial. Basic training in the scriptures and reading the letters and treatises of a few select authors were all that could be reasonably expected. But even that is not definite, since some, such as Eucherius in his description of a monk's life, never mentioned biblical study.[68] Only in the case of young boys was it necessary to teach them the rudiments of reading and writing and the sources are significantly silent about how that was accomplished.[69] While provision was usually given in the rules of a monastery for reading or writing, it was not necessarily provided.

Third, as one might conclude from these two previous points, Christianity never fully created an alternative educational program in the ancient world. Augustine tried and failed to create one in his *de doctrina Christina*. As such, their notions of pedagogy and appropriate learning material varied from place to place, and often from person to person. A layman might see no problems with a classical education, nor might a bishop such as Sidonius Apollonaris. Indeed, Paulinus of Pella in his eighty-fourth year could sincerely proclaim his gratitude for the old-fashioned education he received.[70] On the other hand, the great hermits of the desert had worn their open suspicion of classical learning and culture as badges of honor. Having never developed a truly new concept of learning, Christians concerned about such things were often left in an educational vacuum. No doubt many relied on a classical program for their children without fully being comfortable with its pagan trappings; but it is clear, too, that many were simply oblivious to the concern entirely.

Finally, we get, from the few references to general education in late antiquity, a brief glimpse into the life of a child as well. Augustine, of course, put the worst face on his schooling, although he was clearly an adept and capable student. But Ausonius, writing to his grandson of the same name, advised him to have fun between his hours of study, reasoning that: '*studium puerile fatiscit, laeta nisi austeris varientur, festa profestis.*'[71] Perhaps more sympathetically, he comforts his grandson, telling him not to fear the glowering teacher nor his cane. Paulinus of Pella, the younger Ausonius' brother, also described something of his education. His parents gave him his first lessons, making learning a game as Jerome suggested to the noblewoman, Laeta.[72] He learned Greek before Latin from the family servants with whom he had happily played, clearly not an uncommon phenomenon. And the fourth-century 'Will of Piglet' (*Testamentum Porcelli*) represents a concrete example of a light-hearted school exercise, one which was a favorite among children.[73] The learning process, then, at least in its earlier stages, was supposed to be fun and enjoyable. It is perhaps for that reason a child's first teacher was called the *magister ludi*. But even as the elite child progressed through his education, the need for happiness, relaxation and leisure were considered important factors in his mental and physical well-being. That more than anything suggests an awareness of youth's special needs.

The child in the family

The preceding section may have seemed to imply that Christianity offered no new conceptual ideals concerning children and parenthood and that societal attitudes and behavior remained unchanged from the classical age. This is not quite true. While Christians did not perhaps preach a new centrality to the notion of 'child' or conceptualize childhood differently from before, they did nevertheless create a somewhat new framework for the parent–child relationship. Unlike the Roman concept of *patria potestas*, which, in its purest unadulterated state, was only tempered by family sentiment and *mos maiorum*, Christians insisted obligations between parent and offspring be reciprocal. True, Christian authors, especially ascetics who had raised no children of their own, might be insensitive and impatient towards the young. Jerome hardly painted a sympathetic picture of children or of procreation generally when he asked Furia rhetorically: '*An vereris, ne proles Furiana deficiat et ex te parens tuus non habeat pusionem, qui reptet in pectore et cervices eius stercore linat?*'[74] But such personal distaste should not be mistaken for a general condemnation of children as such. Even the curmudgeonly Jerome could offer sincere advice on how to raise young girls to be holy women.[75]

To be sure, neither Christians nor Roman society at large in any way idealized childhood as something sweet or guileless or even enjoyable. As we have already noted, beatings and hard work were common realities for most youth, with sickness and high mortality rates for all. Augustine asked the citizens of the heavenly city: *'Quis autem non exhorreat et mori eligat, si ei proponatur aut mors perpetienda aut rursus infantia?'*[76] But the bishop's own foray into primitive behavioral psychology had also demonstrated that children were anything but innocent. He observed with great interest the jealousy and fury that could develop between siblings over a mother's attentions.[77] Children had not escaped Original Sin and the tantrums they threw were indications of their guilt. Not even a baby therefore was free from committing sin. The capacity to reason and eventually use speech when an infant grew into a youth (*iuvens*) merely made that child cognizant of his place in the family and in the world. But life in human society and within the family was a stormy one.[78]

Within this context, clerics in late antiquity necessarily emphasized the subordinating hierarchy of human society. That children were inferior and subject to adults was taken for granted. To their parents, a child owed respect and duty. But more important or at least more clearly enunciated were the duties incumbent upon a parent. Briefly, both mothers and fathers were supposed to carefully monitor their children's progress and behavior, and to raise them to be good citizens and good Christians, a common responsibility (*cura communis*).[79] Exposure was heavily censured, both by the Church and in law, and in fact was eventually outlawed in Justinian's day.[80] Raising one's child was in itself an *obligatio* consistent with familial *pietas*. That *obligatio* included moral instruction (both from parents and the Church), careful supervision of a child's contact with non-kin (including contact with slaves and other household retainers), some practical education on proper comportment, and physical correction in cases of a child's unwillingness to accept these responsibilities. There was also a division of labor, so to speak, in the general duties of the father and mother. The former was a figure of *auctoritas*, charged with preparing his progeny, particularly his sons, to survive, function, and perhaps even prosper in the world (*mundus*). A mother, on the other hand, was charged with instilling in her children spiritual and religious direction, augmenting the father's tutelage and insuring their salvation in the afterlife. The amount of information we have about each parent and the clear division of labor between the two makes it worthwhile to look individually at paternal and maternal roles in the late Roman family.

Fathers and their children

Despite the occasional far-flung fits of rhetoric describing how parents moved heaven and earth for a (usually ungrateful) child,[81] there was a general acceptance of a parent's responsibility for his or her offspring in the moral realm. Catechism, for example, seems to have been a staple of a Christian child's upbringing, displaying a practical concern for his or her spiritual state. Religious education outside of the home could even be afforded to young girls.[82] In the post-Constantinian world, as we have mentioned, fewer and fewer Christians were 'neofitus iit ad deum'.[83] And as we have just mentioned, Christian *parentes* were supposed to divide their duties. For beyond educating one's offspring, male or female, each parent had special obligations peculiar to their sex.

But before we discuss these responsibilities, something should be said about the nature of the father–child relationship. As in the classical world, sons and daughters were subject to the will of their father and more generally to their mother and elders. Antti Arjava has recently argued convincingly for the duration of *patria potestas* and the encompassing authority a father had over children who had not yet reached their majorities.[84] Proper filial respect for a father's position was also deemed crucial and this was fully embodied in the law, permitting for example a father to rescind an emancipation if his progeny had somehow wronged him.[85] A child's capitulation to a parent's will generally reconfirmed the basic hierarchy inherent in human relationships. As a woman was subordinate to a man, so, too, was a child subordinate to a parent. But while the former union had a dangerous sexual component to it,[86] a child–parent bond was somewhat more pure in its construction and its operation. A child might be contentious and that was a problem and a sin in itself, but the dynamics of the relationship at least were not charged with the deadly voltage of human lust. Instead, the focus lay on the obeying the wishes of an elder out of piety and duty.

Pietas of course had been the traditional characteristic shown to a father as well as a mother from a child. Respect and compliance – *obsequium* – were naturally owed to parents and underscored the harmony and order of the Roman family, Christian or otherwise. Certainly that concept did not change with the rise of the new religion, since emphasizing the fifth commandment, honoring one's parents, was a common theme found in numerous sermons, religious tracts and letters. Indeed, a number of clerics, mostly in the East, had constructed a conscious parallel between *pietas* to one's parents and to the divine. Augustine noted that piety meant performing acts of compassion, what he called *eusebeia*.[87] He believed that possessing *pietas* for the Father meant assuming servitude (*servitus*). By extending Augustine's comparison – and he clearly implies it – there is no doubt that a certain kind of *servitus* was owed to a parent as well.

Respect may have been considered crucial, but it was not necessarily easy to instill such virtue. Christian scholars, in apparent agreement with Roman opinion generally, seemed to have viewed children more or less as wild *bêtes noires*, requiring considerable energy to indoctrinate them into human society. Greed, ambition, guile, anger, and insolence were all innate in a human being's make-up from birth.[88] This is not to say that children were bent on evil. As one character put it in a fifth-century Roman play, a young man was apt to be more disagreeable than genuinely wicked.[89] In fact, each stage of life meant assuming a new positive quality. Innocence should be the essence of one's infancy, reverence for childhood, patience for adolescence, and courage for youth.[90] To bring a child to a point where he or she acted more or less in accordance with the rules of society, let alone the precepts of Christ, was therefore a process not unlike training a dumb beast.

Of course, at times, particularly in the case of men and their sons, irresponsible behavior seemed to be encouraged. Paulinus of Pella's father, despite being Christian, encouraged his son to take up hunting in the forests around Bordeaux, as well as other unspecified luxuries, much to the detriment of his secular and religious studies.[91] Indeed, a father's attitude and response were in Christian eyes considerably more dangerous than a child's misbehavior. On one trip to the public baths with his father, to cite a more graphic example, a teenage Augustine could not prevent himself from becoming sexually aroused. Instead of being angry or embarrassed, Patricius was unabashedly ecstatic and expressed crassly that he hoped for a few grandchildren soon.[92] Although Augustine was mortified and ashamed by the incident, his own opinions concerning illegitimate children suggest that Patricius had not expressed a sentiment that was purely pagan.[93] Often the production of heirs, as we have seen, took on greater importance than legitimacy. The behavior of young men, then, had to be carefully monitored and regulated. Sexual play in adolescence was the most dangerous vice and accordingly most heavily discouraged by a father. But violence, rowdiness and a general disrespect for authority were general problems that a father might have with a son. The optimal end to fatherhood, as we shall see, was a responsible, financially secure young man who was married and had a family of his own.

Contact between fathers and daughters is not as broadly attested to in the sources, so it is difficult to see the degree and the manner in which they interacted.[94] It was much more common for a girl to be under the direct authority of her mother, especially in her early years of life, as we shall discuss more fully below. One must assume that the issues of controlling an unruly daughter was not generally a pressing problem: there are very few examples of such behavior. Earlier, we mentioned Melania the Younger, who did flaunt parental authority, but her case was unusual in two respects. First, her behavior was non-destructive: she did not steal or commit adultery or generally bring embarrassment upon herself and her family.[95] And second, her behavior was excused by both the author of her *vita* and even by her father at his death because she was, in their eyes, morally correct. But by the sense of outrage at her behavior – from parents, other relatives, and even household slaves – it seems that Melania's transgressions were atypical.

Lacking better evidence, we have to assume that a father's had two essential goals in raising a daughter. As with any sons, a father was of course interested in passing on his patrimony to his daughters. Girls as well as boys were natural heirs to their father and this did not change in late antiquity. Should a father die intestate, property would be divided up evenly. There were, however, few requirements as to what a father *had* to leave a child. The one exception to that rule seems to have been the requirement that father's leave a dowry for every daughter at least one-quarter the amount of an intestate inheritance.[96]

His primary concern, however, was seeing to the proper marriage of a daughter. This seems equally true among Christian and pagan fathers, although with the former there was some pressure to consecrate a daughter as a virgin, especially if he had more than one. The irrevocability of such dedications supposedly raised a family's spiritual state by such an act (to say nothing of the daughters', who usually had as little to say in the matter as they had in marriages), but more pragmatically raised its social status within the Christian community.[97] Nevertheless, marriage for daughters was both more common and preferred. That fathers were primarily concerned with marriage of their daughters is reinforced by the fact that girls tended to marry in their teens: Melania had been 14 and Augustine, at the ripe old age of 31, had to wait two years before he could marry his under-aged bride-to-be.[98] The age differentials between spouses also made it incumbent that fathers act before they themselves died: Augustine's mother had had to make the marriage arrangements. Even in the later Roman Empire, when Christians and pagans alike seem to wait longer before making such unions, women were still invariably young.[99] For that reason, and perhaps because Romans had a strong sense of the law, both dowry and marriage contracts were duly drawn up, witnessed, signed and often deposited in public or religious institutions. In general, husbands were thought better suited to this task: Sidonius Apollinaris had described in a letter to the bishop of Marseille how the mother of one young girl had made a disastrous match with a man of modest means and ill intent.[100] On the other hand, the fact that the mother was forced to make the arrangements because she was a widow once again speaks to the fact that men often did not live long enough to oversee the marriage of a child, daughter or son.

Fatherhood, at least on this basic level, was therefore more limited in the matter of daughters. Much of the evidence about the relationship simply does not exist. If we accept, too, that daughters came mostly under the provenance of mothers, then we should not be too surprised that the record is thin.

Christian models of paternal behavior in regards to sons were surprisingly half-formed. The obvious archetype between father and son might at first seem to be Father and Son. They were two manifestations of the divine, who related in harmony and perfection as one. The Father had sent his Son to free the just of this earth from the evil, both as a moral and political obligation.[101] But the use of this exemplar was minimal, mostly due to its complicated and occasionally contradictory nature. To start, the Father was himself a potential rival to a father, as Jerome made eloquently clear: 'they do not leave a father, they find one.'[102] Moreover, there was an epistemological gap within the literature itself. On the one hand, fatherly affection was generally crowned by forgiveness of one's children for past transgressions, as in the case of the prodigal son.[103] But forgiveness was not the function of the Father, but of the Son. Finally, and perhaps most basic, there was no real interaction – social or otherwise – between Jesus and Yahweh. So as a paradigm for the parent–child relationship, Creator and Christ did not really provide a sound theoretical analogue. Other biblical father–son combinations were occasionally mentioned[104] and in the Middle Ages a cult of Joseph developed,[105] but as a whole even these were unsuitable metaphors for the father-son dynamic.

What, then, were the techniques used to raise a child, especially the wild son, to be an upstanding member of society and an individual possessing *obsequium* and *pietas* for his parents and elders? Instilling the *auctoritas* of the Roman father in the past had been a relatively difficult thing. While fathers did in reality beat their children – and especially one's sons – it had deep social and psychological implications. By enforcing his discipline with corporal punishment, the *paterfamilias* had equated his own heirs with slaves. The whip, even in late antiquity, was a symbol of the inherently violent system of unfree labor. As Quintillian had argued many generations before, beating children inevitably bred a slave mentality.[106] In point of fact, subjecting children to corporal punishment was a common enough event and even Stoic philosophers had pointed to its occasional necessity.[107] Such action, particularly when repeated, showed a startling lack of control on a parent's part – it was inappropriate and verged on the barbaric.[108] Augustine's behavior as an adolescent, to cite one example, showed its relative ineffectiveness. While, on the one hand, he complained about beatings he received as a child, he nevertheless found pleasure in stealing and destroying other people's property.[109] The belief among fathers that such behavior was healthy, or at least expected, made discipline especially difficult for adolescents.

In contrast to a stated distaste for violence against children, or at least against free children, Christians authors saw no moral problems with using physical punishment as a means for correcting and molding the behavior of offspring. A constant theme in many of Augustine's writings is the issue of corporal discipline. He had endured the blows of teachers and parents while a child, and it had affected him enough to recall this discipline with honest hate.[110] But the stinging laughter of his parents when he complained about his treatment also made him understand, as an adult, that being beaten was necessary as a means for correcting behavior and often as a just punitive action. Even if a parent employed a double-standard for his child and for himself – and this small, but significant point was not lost on Augustine – that did not excuse that child's bad behavior.

Such opinions were consistent with the action of the clergy in a number of varied situations. Although excommunication and other forms of spiritual retribution were supposedly the only punishments the Church could impose, the growth in power of episcopal courts changed that. Augustine mentions in one letter that it was common for bishops, or at least North African bishops, to order floggings for those who had transgressed Christian law.[111] Indeed, without the benefit of a trial, outraged clerics in Thagaste viciously beat one wealthy layman who had had sex with a nun.[112]

But what was of greatest concern to Augustine? What did he think crucial to instill in children for their adult years? Odd as it may seem, his great fear, expressed weekly to his flock, was that young men, so untrained and wanton, would squander their inheritance. In several sermons, Augustine railed against the danger of using one's wealth to indulge his desires.[113] He saw it as a tool to indulge in the worst vices. Of course, this was not pure idealism on the African bishop's part. It was money, frankly, that the poor and the Church could put to better use. In one particularly distasteful passage, Augustine coldly rebuked those fathers who held onto inheritances for heirs who had died. If a son were dead, he mercilessly reasoned, why not give his share to the almshouse?[114] Apart from the value squandered money could be to the Church, however, the concern for maintaining a patrimony given by a father or mother was apparently a sign of adulthood and responsibility, and one which was shared more broadly in late antique society. Paulinus of Pella noted that once he was married, he settled down and took to managing his estates and those of his wife's in earnest.[115] In that sense, these were inherently conservative concerns. Continuity in family property was clearly a virtue in Roman society, be the family polytheistic or Christian. Ausonius could brag that his father neither added to nor lost any of his family's estates.[116] Paulinus of Pella claimed his only interest was in maintaining the level of luxury to which he had been accustomed.[117]

Thus, as in the classical period, a father was primarily instilled discipline for a greater good. But as Augustine had noted, this was also done to keep a son on the straight and narrow.[118] Too often would teenagers (*adulescentes*) amuse themselves with '*pila pyrgus, accipiter canis, equus arcus*'.[119] Wanton and destructive behavior had to be kept in check, not only for their own souls, but for the sake of their families. The blackness of adultery and *stuprum*, even if it had no legal repercussions, could nevertheless stain the good name of a notable *domus*. Moreover, the indiscretion of youth could also result in financial ruin and that, too, could damage the *familia*. That Theodoric had to order a special pardon for a young man convicted of raping a virgin, which included future actions against his family property and against libel, indicates the potential problems that could result.[120] A child might be a common problem (*sollicitudo communis*) as well.[121]

The father, then, was supposed to insure his children behaved not only as responsible heirs, but also as responsible citizens. But did that in fact happen? We have seen that Augustine's father actually relished the thought of having grandchildren, illegitimate or not. And Paulinus' father had encouraged his son to neglect his studies for hunting, so that '*ex quibus optatam possem captare salutem'*, even though he understood such laxity was wrong and harmful.[122] Augustine nevertheless mentioned that it was uncommon for parents to complain of their children's bad behavior.[123] This might suggest that children were better than common opinion (including Augustine's) had held them in, but it is equally as likely that secrecy about any disagreements or misbehavior protected a family's reputation.

On the other hand, punishment might be silent as well. The whip was but one of several weapons that a father might bring to bear. The most powerful, of course, was the power of the purse. A *filiusfamilias* owned nothing in his own right, with the possible exception of his private savings (*peculium*), and was thus completely beholden to his father for his financial future.[124] Indeed, a *peculium* was often nothing more than an allowance for his children. A father might even in theory sell a son into an apprenticeship or emancipate him as a means of getting rid of him. Discipline, when it was carried out, could therefore be quite severe.

Many fathers, however, did try to instill more than fear of the whip and disinheritance into their offspring. Paulinus' father had tried to act as a resource for his son, advising him on management of his properties, and was presented as a model for good behavior.[125] Sidonius Apollinaris' good-humored criticism of a fictional reprobate, to cite another example, was framed as a commendation to his son for avoiding the company of evil men.[126] And Symmachus had made it a point to tutor his own son in grammar, rhetoric and oratory, intimating involvement and concern.[127] These fathers seemed to have had the best interest of their sons at heart and provided practical advice for their betterment. These examples are furthermore distinguished partially because of their concern for worldly affairs. There is no mention in any of these passages, nor for that matter in the works of Augustine, Ambrose and Jerome, to suggest that fathers were responsible for the religious upbringing of their children.[128]

Fathers therefore had to instill discipline in the pursuit of maintaining the system of familial patrimonies and the broader social order.[129] This was thought utilitarian, however, since from there, all other responsibilities to a parent flowed. Optimally, a son's father became a wise and valued mentor rather than a strict authority figure.[130] Financial provision for a mother once a father died would be honored by a dutiful and loving child, despite legislation ensuring such fidelity.[131] So, too, would living arrangements: we have many examples of widowed mothers moving in with their children.[132] And a son out of *pietas* and *obsequium* would gladly carry out whatever his father desired, be it a marriage or a chosen vocation or fulfilling a father's vow to enter the Church. Mastery over one's own behavior, then, was perhaps the best mark of adulthood and permitted a person to focus on more serious worldly and spiritual matters. In sum, responsibility to one's property was responsibility to one's *familia*, to society and to the heavenly city. One wonders what reasoning Augustine must have used with those who owned nothing.

Mothers and their children

If discipline of a physical kind was intimately connected with a father's duties in raising his offspring, we must naturally inquire about those of a mother. The archetypal mother for Christians of course was the Mother of Christ. But in many ways, Mary was also an unsatisfactory model for women who had given birth. She may have been the most important mother in all of history, but she also bore Jesus without Original Sin. As Averil Cameron has pointed out, 'the Virgin of late antiquity was neither the *mater dolorosa* nor the domesticated maternal figure of more recent times'.[133] Instead, she was often depicted in the company of young women and in the second coming she would return with her army of virgins (*comitata virgineis*) following close behind.[134] Augustine crowned her the 'associate' of virgins, their invisible patron who demanded obedience and respect.[135] So while Mary's nurturing nature might epitomize the good mother, she had little to do with mother-hood itself. Indeed, Jerome went further by dismissing the relationship of mothers and Mary altogether: '*Habeant nuptiae suum tempus et titulum: mihi virginitas in Maria dedicatur et Christo.*'[136] Rather, Jerome went on to conclude, the role of married women is to produce children – *crescite et multiplicamini.*[137]

First among a mother's duties, then, was to be prolific. Once a child was born, Christian authors exhorted Roman mothers to what must have seemed a strange request to upper-class contemporaries: do not make use of *nutrices*. In a society where wet-nurses were ubiquitous, and were commonly included among members of even a modest *familia*, such a demand would have been tantamount to giving up on domestic servitude entirely.[138] *Nutrices*, after all, usually took care of their wards well past the age they stopped suckling.[139] Indeed, there was a saying that the grief of a nurse came right after a mother's.[140] Nevertheless, to Christian authors, giving a child over to another for nourishment indicated a mother's lack of concern for a child's well-being.[141] Perhaps the blandishment came from a belief that this somehow indicated a lack of proper motherly concern or instinct. After all, Ambrose in the same breath extolled women to wean their own children – which implied that they first had nursed them – *and* to love them.[142] Such sentiments were firmly rooted in the classical tradition: Plutarch had explained rather charm-ingly that women's breasts were high up on the body so that women would have to hold and cuddle their children while feeding them.[143] More importantly, however, this may have been related to scientific theories pos-tulating that children took on something of the nurse's character, indicating – among other things – the generally low regard for the disposition of slaves.[144] Whatever the reason, it appears that these admonitions may have had an effect: we only have two surviving inscriptions of nurses in sixth-century Italy.[145] Comparatively, we have a large number of inscriptions in earlier periods.[146] Whether this relationship was causal is difficult to deter-mine, especially given the paucity and patchiness of the sources. It is possible that this change was also a result of non-Roman influences, but that, too, cannot be confirmed. Nurses undoubtedly survived well past the fifth century, but their role seems to have been significantly less prominent, at least in a commemorative context. Were it the Church's decision, no child would strain on a mother's nipples which had forgotten their milk.[147]

But the emphasis on breastfeeding was tied to the broader question of a woman's duties to her children. One of Augustine's criticisms was that women worried too much about being mothers and not enough about their children.[148] Drawing upon the story of Solomon's decision concerning a baby's parentage, for example, he noted that the two women represented two kinds of mothers. The one who falsely claimed the child was hers personified the woman concerned with the status of motherhood, rather than its inherent responsibilities. That is why she agreed to Solomon's decision to split the child in two. The second mother, however, cared more about her children's welfare than her own status. Devotion to a child's safety and well-being, then, was the general ideal.

That safety began with ensuring a child was raised as a Christian. Ambrose told mothers to teach their children to be *non in terra, sed super terram*.[149] When Augustine had been a boy, it had been Monnica who had overseen his spiritual education. Paulinus of Pella had been taught about sin and vice by his mother at the same time he was first learning the alphabet.[150] That a woman should be responsible for the religious upbringing of her children may at first appear strange, but in Rome mothers had traditionally raised both sons and daughters in their first years. A Christian mother, however, was clearly expected to go further, if only in the religious sphere. Indeed, her devotion to children passed beyond life. A saintly woman might try to get a deceased son or daughter buried close to a martyr and continually pray for her child's soul.[151] Motherhood, then, placed a great responsibility on a woman: she was in large part to blame for a son or daughter's spiritual and religious failings. In that sense, her importance far outweighed that of a father.

If, moreover, we can argue that boys came more or less under the purview of a father's control, a girl certainly fell under her mother's. Jerome's letter to Laeta concerning her daughter Paula's upbringing is addressed solely to the mother, despite the fact that the woman's husband, Julius Toxotius, was very much alive.[152] This had not changed from the classical period, when girls not only received their education from their mothers, but also continued to report to them, even after marriage.[153] But unlike Claudian's poem commemorating the marriage of Honorius and Maria, Jerome more fully elucidated the kind of upbringing and education a daughter should receive.

Jerome offered Laeta much practical advice for her daughter Paula's early years. He began by recommending handmaids and attendants who were not too familiar with worldly affairs so as to limit any contamination done to an impressionable daughter. Paula's special handmaid should be modest in character, although Jerome tried to prevent any girl having a favorite *ancilla* to confide in. Her godparents, of course, should be both figuratively and literally sober. Her teachers should be not be too young, but should be well versed in all subjects and at all levels of learning.[154] To facilitate learning before lessons, however, Jerome suggested a set of block letters be given to the little girl and teaching her an 'ABC' song. As she learned to read and write, Paula should receive her mother's approval by positive reinforcement: enjoyment, rather than punishment, should be part of a young girl's education.[155] And as she got older, her daughter should be made to memorize passages of the Bible for her spiritual enlightenment, as well as being introduced to serious exegesis.[156] Cyprian, Athanasius and Hilary were all approved non-canonical authors,[157] an incidental indication of the continued value placed on a bilingual education.

Paula's movements outside the home were, of course, to be carefully chaperoned, preferably by the mother herself. It was important for Laeta to guard against the sins and evils of the world for an individual incapable as of yet of defending herself. The young girl, then, ought to accompany her mother to church weekly and to night vigils. She should be kept away from the public baths and the apparently boisterous slave weddings (*nuptiae servolorum*).[158] Boys naturally were to be kept away, as were coiffed dandies (*cincinatti*). A girl should not eat in public, not so much because she had to shun human contact as to avoid certain lascivious foods. And if her mother ever left Rome for country estates, she was by no means to leave her daughter at home.[159]

Paula's personal demeanor was to be equally reserved. She should wear conservative clothes denoting her status as a virgin. Silk, brocade and fleece were to be shunned and wool favored. Indeed, Jerome in a fascinating recapitulation of very old and conservative Roman ideals advised her to become skilled with the distaff and spindle, in part to make her own clothes. She should not wear make-up or jewelry, nor have pierced ears. Paula ought also to try to govern her own tastes and desires when old enough, espousing the ideal of Christian self-denial. Jerome, however, was aware of a young person's limits: Laeta's daughter should not, therefore, try to duplicate difficult feats of asceticism. The virgin's life was something to be worked towards, not thrust at with one blind lunge of faith.[160]

Overall, Jerome's letter emphasizes two essential duties of parenthood in general and motherhood specifically. First, he recognized that parents needed to keep much closer supervision over their children. Even in a moderately well-off home, *nutrices*, slave-girls (*ancillae*), pedagogues, guardians (*custodes*), and other free and slave attendants would be watching over and indeed raising the children of the house. It had been Paulinus of Pella's nurse who had carried him over treacherous mountains and braved ocean storms to get him to Carthage.[161] Little Maria mentioned above had been enslaved along with her *ancilla* playmate.[162] The omnipresence of such individuals, as valuable and accepted as they were, could be potentially dangerous. It was relatively easy for parents, in a cleric's mind at least, to abrogate their responsibility in raising their own. Because slaves could be so feckless and dangerous, a mother thus not only had to pick carefully those who would have contact with her children, but also had to be on hand constantly to ensure they were not exposed to the evils of this world.

This naturally relates to the second duty of a mother, already mentioned: the religious education of a child. A mother's greatest instinct was to be protective of her offspring, what Jerome's old grammarian, Donatus, characterized as 'materne'.[163] The highest manifestation of that concern and care was to insure that her daughters and sons both received not only close scrutiny, but also close moral guidance. And, as we said before, a mother's calling might be considered higher than a father's, since his realm only extended to proper behavior for human society. It is significant that mothers were not only responsible for their daughters, but also had the unenviable task of instilling a basic Christian belief and practice in her sons as well. Indeed, in several canons of the period, emphasis was placed on the mother's responsibility in matters involving children.[164] Certainly, this was not an idea that had any polytheistic roots. In the Roman past, there had been an equal division of priestly roles: the household cult of the *lares* and *penates* was overseen by the father and the cult of Vesta by the mother. A child's sex determined who would instruct the child in ritual and its meaning. But within the Christian household, it did appear as if the *materfamilias* was the prime mover.

One need only look at the example of Monnica to see the lengths a mother might go to ensure a child's salvation. Not only did she arrange for Augustine's religious education as a boy, but constantly took care to follow up on his catechism.[165] She warned him against committing adultery and tried to get a priest to talk to him after a fearful dream that her son was slipping from the Christian faith.[166] Monnica had later pleaded with him in Carthage to return home to Thagaste and return to his faith. The young rhetorician was forced to sneak out of the city at night for Rome.[167] Undeterred, she followed her son to Italy and contracted for him a betrothal with a rich, but under-aged Christian girl in the hopes that he would finally be baptized.[168] When Augustine finally converted, Monnica was ecstatically happy, and the brief time they had left together was engaged in lively religious discussion.[169] Five days after their last discussion, she fell ill and died. Perhaps her mission in life had been accomplished and she could die content. But the implication here is important: a mother's religious nurturing for a child did not end with his or her majority.

The single-mindedness of Monnica was undoubtedly an extreme, but there were other comparable acts. Melania the Elder had insured that her son, Publicola, was educated and instilled in him a high moral character.[170] Paulinus of Pella's mother was first to acquaint him with virtue and cardinal vice.[171] Augustine had also praised Anicia Faltonia Proba and Anicia Iuliana, grandmother and mother of Demetrias, respectively, since they had decided jointly to dedicate the young woman as a virgin.[172] In another letter, he advised the matron, Iuliana, against the dangers of Pelagianism with reference to the upbringing of her daughter, implying that the mother had the greatest control over the religious life of the newly veiled girl.[173] In still a third missive, it had been a mother who had promised her daughter would become a virgin if she survived a life-threatening illness.[174]

Women, then, especially aristocratic women, came into the fore of Christian writings in the late fourth century largely due to the influence of religion within the family. Averil Cameron has remarked that despite their important roles in ascetic movements, the vast majority of women, even those of the senatorial classes, were not so committed to the ascetic lifestyle that they completely rejected their traditional roles as wives and mothers.[175] That is why perhaps many women such as Melania the Elder or Anicia Faltonia Proba chose a middle course, blurring the distinction between household and monastic house. Indeed, many of the great houses of late antiquity were converted to cenobitic institutions at their owners' deaths.[176] In that sense, women could pursue the Christian ideals of proper comportment without discarding their reproductive abilities. If a mother were a widow, so much the better.

Widowhood, of course, also meant that mothers would take on a whole host of responsibilities, mostly those that would be taken on by a father. We have, of course, already discussed the contracting of marriages, an issue plainly visible. But that was frequently the beginning. She was expected to maintain the estates and pass on the patrimonies to her children. A mother might also be expected to insure offices for her sons. Cassiodorus, for example, praised the unnamed mother of four sons from the Decii family: she raised and nurtured them, increased the size of their estates, and made sure that each of her boys served as consul.[177] He had similar praise for Amalasuintha's skills as a mother.[178] The widowed mother, then, was judged by her abilities to fulfill the duties of both parents.

In sum, mothers, like wives, had the harder duty. How appropriate that Jerome in one letter should advise his friend, Rusticus: '*Matrem ita vide.*'[179]

Domestic help

One tenet that was almost impossible for any parent to follow was the Christian admonition against slaves overseeing the education and upbringing of children. They were certainly suspect for a number of reasons, as will be discussed later, but the omnipresence of unfree labor made it impractical not to use them. It might be the equivalent of asking a modern parent not to use electricity. *Servi* were a basic power source for making the household operate. That slaves might be expensive did not negate the fact that many were widely owned, at least in the cities. Augustine had claimed that they served in all but the most humble houses.[180] In the homes of even the slightly affluent, slaves were often many and had specialized functions.[181] Doing away with *nutrices*, in particular, was no doubt deemed pointless and wasteful. They were valued and important members of the *domus*, frequently forming strong emotional bonds between their free young masters (*dominelli*).[182] Indeed, they were even held as retainers far past their usefulness strictly as wet-nurses: one old *nutrix* had been so valued that she was fully accepted, '*honorabatur*', as a member of the family she had served devotedly.[183] Sidonius, too, had mentioned a fully grown daughter of his nurse who had eloped with the slave of another, implying the old slave was still with him.[184] If the Church made any headway in stopping the use of wet-nurses, it was only in its success of degrading the value of the position.

The best that could be hoped for was an awareness of how the unfree members of the *familia*, adult and child, made an impression on the heirs of the *paterfamilias*. Instead, they could be employed in other productive ways. To call the *servi* of the household spies – despite the general consensus among ancient authors that slaves knew all the secrets of the family[185] – would perhaps be too harsh. Rather, they optimally acted like monitors, capable of instilling discipline as much as reporting untoward activity. Melania had, after all, tried to bribe her slave-companion not to tell her parents of her behavior in the public baths.[186] Monnica's old nursemaid-companion quite properly oversaw the behavior of her wards: '*Unde etiam curam dominicarum filiarum comissam diligenter gerebat, et erat in eis coercendis, cum opus esset, sancta severitate vehemens, atque in docendis sobria prudentia.*'[187] It is possible in this context to understand the concerns of the Church fathers. Jerome's warnings about letting slaves be too familiar with a child and Ambrose's rejections of *nutrices* were not strictures against using surrogate parents when necessary, but against abrogating parental responsibilities through the use of surrogate parents.

Adult children

The role of parents in the lives of their adult children was considerably more complicated. As already discussed in Chapter 2, marriage patterns and life expectancies made the possibility of a living father at adulthood not a very likely thing in the ancient world. There is little to indicate that the demographics of late antiquity were qualitatively different from the classical period, or at least discernibly different. Large numbers of public men had fathers who had died while they were still in their minorities: emperors such as Valentinian II, Valentinian III, Arcadius and Honorius; clerics including Ambrose and Augustine; and notables like the orator, Libanius, and the patrician, Flavius Inportunus. Like the aristocracy of the classical age, of course, men were more liable to meet with capital punishment for political reasons, and so were more at risk of dying sooner than more humble men. But these individuals represented only a small minority of the population and the relatively late age of marriage for men was clearly the most significant factor in determining whether a man would be the father of adult children.[188]

That said, there were some who did live long enough and took an active role in their children's lives. We have already discussed the role that parents, especially fathers, had in making marriage matches. Those matches to a large extent seemed to have been ends in themselves, especially if we accept Antti Arjava's argument that *patria potestas* in the late antique world generally lasted only as long as a child was under-age.[189] The senator, Symmachus, for example, seems in 401 to have set up his son independently at the age of 18, the date of the younger man's praetorship and marriage.[190] The fact that Pinian and Melania could petition the government to act as adults implied that as adults, even with living fathers, they could control their own property and persons.[191]

But clearly, a father, particularly a wealthy one, could play an active role in their children's lives. Men like Symmachus and others in the highest classes of Roman society, engineered for their children those honors and offices commensurate with their station. One of the proudest moments in Boethius' life, for example, was when he secured two consulships for his two sons.[192] The *magister militium utriusque*, Aspar, too, assured a high military post for his son, Ardabur.[193] In addition, fathers of adult sons seemed to have enjoyed something like an advisory role. Paulinus of Pella had mentioned how his own father had counseled him in his late twenties.[194] Not only had his father been a model for Paulinus to emulate, but he honestly called him a friend and companion. When he died shortly after the poet's thirtieth birthday, he felt as if his house had been ravaged and plundered. A father's role in his adult son's life, in theory at least, thus seemed considerably more gentle and retiring than when that son was still a youth.

Of course, many more mothers made it to see their children wed and produce their own offspring. Their range of control over such children, however, is deeply debated. They possessed no *potestas*, either in their own right or over their offspring and as such had little legal authority to control their actions. But where the law ended, social custom began. A widow was often the *de facto* guardian of her child: indeed, if she forswore remarrying and was of age, she could even possess legal guardianship.[195] She would provide and raise her offspring, and it was to the mother that suitors and their families went for marriage negotiations. Thus, as in many other cases, the legal imperatives in these circumstances did not necessarily match the realities of everyday life.

Moreover, the financial pressure that wealthy widows could bring to bear on both sons and daughters could be considerable. Women like Anicia Faltonia Proba, the widow of the richest man in the West, Petronius Probus, wielded enormous authority over her children as well as over thousands of men and women of her *domus*. Monnica had been providing Augustine with an allowance at Carthage, and he implied that she could have pressured him to change his way of thinking.[196] In spite of such power, however, it seems that a woman's primary goal was to see their offspring married. Monnica, in addition to her interest in Christianizing her children, had the pragmatic goal of providing them with appropriate matches. Anicia Juliana, the last surviving member of the Theodosian house, had had her son, Olybrius, married to the niece of the emperor, Anastasius, hoping that he would be emperor one day.[197] Whether their goals for their children went beyond matchmaking is difficult to say. It seems as if many women were interested in doing the same things as fathers of adult children: Melania the Elder, for example, insured that her son, Publicola, served as praetor of the city.[198]

A mother's role as religious instructor was no doubt strengthened when she decided upon permanent widowhood. Were she to live with her children, which we shall consider shortly, a woman would have the added advantage of overseeing a proper moral climate, whether Christian or otherwise. Many women, such as Macrina, ran their households almost as monasteries.[199] That interest could even extend to grandchildren and other members of the household. So unless a Christian woman were to make a permanent pilgrimage to the Eastern Empire, and this seemed a popular past-time for Rome's religious 'jet-set', a widow might be expected to guarantee the religious fidelity of her children as long as she lived.[200]

Of course, when speaking of such goals, emotional power must also be considered, although that is a more difficult effect to gauge. There are relatively few examples of such evidence. We have already discussed the power Monnica had over Augustine, both as a child and as an adult. We know, too, that Constantine's mother, Helena, had considerable sway over son, securing the conviction and execution of her daughter-in-law, Fausta.[201] Certainly, such power transcended mere religious affiliation: in the highest circles of society, it could easily assume a political function.[202] But as a means to an end, the affective bond between mother and child was in some cases as powerful as any financial incentive. Obviously, the degree to which a mother could impose her will upon a child varied in every case, but emotion seems to have been a tool used much more heavily by mothers than by fathers. Undoubtedly, this was in large part due to the lack of a mother's legal authority over her children.

But in addition to the 'selfless' activities a mother might provide, many widows chose to live with their children, whether daughters or sons. And indeed, they could be an imposing presence. Patricius' mother, shortly after his marriage, promptly had all the slaves beaten. This was ostensibly to control the behavior of their domestic staff, but it seems clear that the old widow also sought establish her dominance in the household.[203] Indeed, as in many pre-modern societies, intergenerational tension seemed to have existed between mothers and their sons' wives. This was in part due to the nature of the *domus* itself: women were charged with the running of a household. In wealthy households, that included the management of household slaves and considerable finances. Were a mother present in her children's home, she would by custom and practice assume dominance in such matters. Augustine reported how his own mother remained quiet and subservient in her mother-in-law's presence.

But caring for an aging and possibly dying mother, as frequently was the case, represented nothing new in late antiquity. In the classical period and either further back, parental care could be tied to broader notions of familial *pietas*. Turia, as we discussed in Chapter 2, was praised for her filial piety.[204] And again, this devotion of course transcended religion: Christian and pagan alike valued and esteemed parents. Indeed, this particular form of piety does not seem to have been the exclusive provenance of mothers. Widowers such as Paulinus of Pella's father lived with their children as well. It was simply more common for women to do so since they frequently lived well past their husbands' deaths.

In sum, the parents of adult children still took an active, if somewhat less direct role in their offspring's lives. Although legal adults, with all the accorded financial and civic responsibilities, sons and daughters were nevertheless beholden to the opinion and desires their parents might have. When the young man, Romulus, physically attacked his father in a fit of pique, he was immediately brought before a court to pay for his actions.[205] Everyone from King Theodoric down heartily condemned the man's actions. The anger was not simply due to the attack itself, but because it was deemed a crime against nature. Under such cultural and legal condemnation, even an adult child ignored the wishes of a father or mother with great care.

Conclusions

Late antique opinions concerning children and the parent–child relationship seem to suggest much closer attention paid to a proper upbringing. This included a personal supervision sufficient to correct poor behavior, a strong interest in a child's basic moral education, and a certain responsibility placed on the parent should that child fail to live up to the expectations of family and society. Specifically, a father groomed a child for this world and a mother trained it for the next. Neither education could be successfully instilled without the other. Augustine would no doubt have explained this as another inextricable mixing of the earthly and heavenly cities. The child as a concept, then, was not suddenly thrust into the center of human affairs with the rise of Christianity. True, the under-aged were as imperiled from the threat of damnation as those who had reached their majority. And as human beings with eternal souls, children had merited a new kind of attention and care. But this did not fully raise them to the status of adults nor even to the status of adult women. They were still half-formed individuals, who needed guidance and correction if they were to enter successfully the earthly and heavenly cities.

Even though the child as concept was largely an unchanged quantity in the late Roman world, the way in which the parent interacted with a child did seem to metamorphose. Christian parents in particular seem to have actually accepted responsibility for the rearing of their own children. A child could not be watched and controlled every moment of its life, but mothers and fathers of the age recognized that they were to a large extent morally responsible for the successes or failings of a child. To be sure, the degree of change undoubtedly varied with each family. If we are to judge by Augustine's childhood, for example, it seems as if he lacked a fair amount of paternal direction. Moreover, we have similar examples of parents taking a deep-abiding interest in the well-being of their children from the classical period. Plutarch's biography of Cato the Elder is an excellent example, although it may have been largely fictional.[206] These men and women needed no ideology to be engaged with progeny. These facts aside, certainly with Christianity there was a much stronger emphasis placed on parental involvement. And with more invasive parental care, hopefully a child would grow into a responsible and pious adult.

7

THE EXTENDED FAMILY

Introduction

The extended family has been generally ignored in recent studies of the classical family, an almost tacit acceptance of the notion that the Romans considered family, as we understand the term, a nuclear one.[1] This in part is due largely to the living patterns of family throughout the Roman Empire: Brent Shaw has shown that the nuclear family had been the general model of organization since the late Republic.[2] In previous chapters, too, we have tried to show that in both the classical and late antique world, emphasis was placed on what we call immediate relations. Whatever the precise reason, extended kin have not been greatly emphasized. Be that as it may, there was an equal notion that *familia* transcended the nuclear model, and could include quite disparate kin and non-kin alike. Domestic slaves and freedpersons of course were among the most visible members in a household, and we will discuss their role in the following chapter. Yet we know that extended kin frequently played a role in family life and in some cases dictated behavior and custom. Accordingly, our aim in this chapter is to make manifest the nature of relations between those individuals whose sanguinity may have been distant and had infrequent contact with one another.

Like the classical period, material on the extended family is sparse for late antiquity. More importantly, however, the references we do have to relations of a more distant sort are vague and ill defined, offering no real indication as to what specific obligations and affective ties might have existed between more distant kin. Since day-to-day contact with aunts, uncles, grandparents and cousins of various degrees was often occasional at best, no guide for behavior ever really developed or at least was never fully elucidated in the surviving literature.

The legal record helps us little, although it does underscore two essential concepts which prove to have been long-standing. First, there was a general understanding that the senior members of a family were somehow responsible for regulating the behavior of their younger relations. The one law we have in this regard, written to the Senate of Rome in the late 360s or early 370s, permits older kinsmen to punish their younger members (*adulescentes*) by the right of paternal authrority (*iure patrio auctoritas*).[3] But it is likely that this constitution was simply extending *patria potestas* to those individuals who had already become *de facto* fathers of more distantly related kin.[4] Antti Arjava, for example, has noted that *parentes* in particular could legally mean either fathers or, more generically, 'relatives'.[5] In most cases, however, this responsibility did not extend to any sort of legal liability: a constitution of Honorius clearly stated that all kin, kin by marriage, *amici* and other members of the *familia* did not share in the guilt of a criminal relation.[6]

The second concept reaffirmed in law was the full acceptance of the cognatic line for purposes of transmitting an inheritance. Constantius in 349 set out a complicated procedure for receiving an estate from a maternal grandfather as an heir.[7] Valentinian III actually made girls *heredes* of their maternal grandmothers should their mothers be deceased.[8] Perhaps most significant of all, should a wife die intestate, her property in the event of childlessness would go to the next closest kin in her family, along the rules of *bonorum possessio*.[9] While the cognatic line still did not equal that of the agnatic one in law, it had nevertheless gained some rights for the purpose of inheritance which had not existed in classical law.

A last legal point of admittedly unclear significance surrounds the crime of *parricidium*, which technically was the killing of a close relative. Justinian in the *Digesta* reaffirmed and extended the *lex Pompeia* from the mid-first century BCE, making it a capital crime if someone killed any of a whole range of individuals who had some sort of familial connection.[10] The list of *parentes* is long, but seems to have been limited to those kin who were either close in relation or alternatively might be expected to be in close contact with a core nuclear family. The cutoff point seems to have been at the fourth degree of sanguinity: second cousins, great aunts and uncles and even more distant relations, for example, were not included. The fact, too, that patrons and patronesses were covered suggests that family – as opposed to *familia* – may have been fairly well established, at least in a legal sense. Whether that can be extended to a broader societal conception of family, extended or otherwise, in late antiquity is problematic at best.

The Church offered even less guidance on relations between extended family. In the case of canon law at least, it had been content to regulate marriage, divorce and exposing or selling children. Admittedly, within the realm of the *iustum matrimonium*, as we have discussed earlier, the Church did declare anathema uncle–niece and first cousin marriages. But we also know that in the case of the former, there is just one surviving example of such a match in late antiquity, and it was only a proposed union. In that case, Ambrose dissuaded the marriage between such close kin, not only attacking its immorality, but also on legal grounds as well.[11] Beyond this small and relatively insignificant contribution, there is little more. The fourth synod at Carthage had stated that the elderly were to be honored more highly among parishioners, but that really says more about respect for age generally than age in a familial context.[12] There was, in short, no real interest among Christians to offer blandishments about extended kin.

We are left having to bring together the few disparate pieces of evidence and see if there were any set rules or ideals for dealing with one's more distant relatives. We do have several references to men and women interacting with relations outside their immediate family, but two individuals in the West stand out: the poet, Ausonius, and the early sixth-century Pavian bishop, Ennodius. In the case of the former, Ausonius had composed a number of poems on the subject of family; but in particular the *Parentalia*, which was a series of short laudatory verses to many of his immediate and extended relations. Ennodius, however, we know of through his extensive epistles to his widely spread family, many of whose exact relation to the bishop is unknown. His letters offer us a practical guide showing how family related to obligation. There are also a few other references from varied sources which help flesh out the extent of connection, but the writings of these men shall be the focus, if only to see familial ideals expressed in Ausonius and the practicalities of dealing with extended kin in Ennodius.

Two extended families

Ausonius was a man whose poetry often gravitated to his family. Among other works he wrote a piece commemorating his father (*Epicidion in Patrem*), one to his father on the birth of his grandson (*Ad Patrem de Suscepto Filio*), one to his son (*Pater ad Filium*), and two works concerning his grandson (*Protrepticus ad Nepotem* and *Genethliacos*). As such, Ausonius is one of the few writers from this period who thought not only about the range of family relationships, but also tried – artistically of course – to characterize – often tersely – the nature of those relationships. He is thus quite removed from the mindset of Paulinus of Pella and Augustine, who remained primarily concerned with the nuclear family group. Of course, Ausonius is primarily concerned with his more immediate relatives as well, but his poems do occasionally venture past the simple relationships of spouse, parent and child. In *Ad Patrem de Suscepto Filio*, for example, Ausonius attempts to assuage fears his father might have had about being marginalized as a grandfather.[13] That is a telling comment in itself about the relationships outside the nuclear family. But it is his great work on a much broader scope, the *Parentalia*, which delves most widely into the extended family.

The poem was one of Ausonius' most ambitious. It offered a variety of meters within its overarching structure and presented a range of emotions as it addressed different individuals. As a whole, the *Parentalia* was in essence a commemoration of Ausonius' various deceased relatives. Some of the relations were extremely close, such as his parents and his wife. But some of his praises were sung to people with whom the kin relationship was tenuous at best: his niece-in-law, Veria Liceria, or his son-in-law's mother, Pomponia Urbica (*consocer*), are but two examples. We should state at the beginning, however, that as a practical matter, it would be difficult to associate certain qualities with specific relations. More often than not, Ausonius described his distant relations in intimate terms. Hence his maternal aunt (*matertera*) was more like a mother to him and his grandniece and nephew like his own grandchildren.[14] These analogies should not seem too unusual, since rhetorical convention as a general rule tended to apply parallels of parenthood and childhood to other relations. As Maurizio Bettini argued, this was a recurrent pattern in Roman literature, delineating paternal and maternal relations and underlying a more pervasive division between agnatic and cognatic lines.[15] To put it more simply, authors associated a certain paternal severity with a father's relations and maternal affection with a mother's.[16] But the necessity of having to create a language of analogy also implies that extended kin were not conceived of in their own right. And while this division was not precisely reproduced in Ausonius' poem, there are enough comparisons of this sort to warrant a careful skepticism of any relation's role.

Nevertheless, there are several worthwhile observations to be made which concern the importance of the extended family. First is the existence of the poem itself. Ausonius explained in both his prose and poetic prefaces that he wrote this work out of sense of devotion to the dead.[17] The *parentalia* was in fact an ancient holiday wherein the dead were remembered over a week's time. Ovid wrote in some detail about its celebration in February, one which, in the words of W. Warde Fowler, gave a 'glimpse of the gentler side of Roman family life'.[18] Family would often gather in front of a beloved's funeral monument and have a sort of feast, which would of course include the spirits of the deceased. Augustine, however, seemed to think that the holiday had sunk in his day to drunken debauchery at the graves of relatives and preferred All Soul's Day, its Christian counterpart.[19] The latter became a significant part of Church commemorations and no doubt was instituted as a replacement for the *parentalia*:[20] there was a strong sense of duty in both holidays to the dead. Remembering them in verse, then, was an act of piety on Ausonius' part. Honoring them in a formal act of ritual remembrance was in his mind the foremost duty owed by a survivor: '*gaudent conpositi cineres sua nomina dici:/ frontibus hoc scriptis et monumenta iubent.*'[21]

Second, and perhaps more significantly, there seems to be no discernible pattern in which Ausonius' relatives were commemorated. Despite the effort of his most recent editor to construct a logical order, only the very barest of organization can be discerned.[22] While the structure of the poem may have had a great deal to do with its metrical cadences, there is nevertheless little attempt to place relative value or worth on individuals beyond his immediate family. Ausonius' father and mother come first and second, respectively, but his wife, in contrast, is ninth on his list. Indeed, one of his sisters, Aemilia Melania, was next to last.[23] The actual text of these verses do not really clarify the situation. Love and respect are expressed in each, and occasionally something of a person's character, appearance or actions. Those with whom Ausonius had more than a passing acquaintance could be commented on more fully, but the sentiment and tone remained more or less the same. The feelings intensify only for those he knew intimately. While the individual poems varied in length and meter, the content was thematically constant.[24]

Finally, it is clear that Ausonius had not met each relative mentioned in the *Parentalia*. This becomes apparent in his remembrance of his *consocer*, Julianus Censor: '*tu non adscito tibi me nec sanguine iuncto.*'[25] Nor apparently did he know his uncle, Clemens Contemtus. This immediately raises a difficult question not readily answerable: why did Ausonius choose whom he did? If we accept the proposition that he probably left some relatives he *did* know out of his poem, then one explanation perhaps arises. The process of selection would have to be directly related to Ausonius' personal feelings and obligations. He chose those whom he respected – or felt he ought to respect – and who had touched his life in a tangible way. The degree of that connection no doubt varied, but those he knew or knew of had at some point contributed directly to his life and that of his private affairs. That would no doubt also explain why Ausonius did not choose to commemorate ancestors, mythical and otherwise,[26] of the distant past. His poem was a tribute to memory of the dead, not a celebration of his family's glories. If funerary *imagines* survived into late antiquity, their faces would have remained unseen in this context. This was an homage made by the living.[27]

Before we draw any conclusions about extended kin from Ausonius' poem, let us also consider the large family of Magnus Felix Ennodius. While the bishop was also fond of writing poetry, both sacred and secular, we know of his relations mostly from his extensive collection of personal and public missives. Like Ausonius, he was a master of style in his day and as such, was frequently called upon by friends and relations alike for help in literary and educational matters. Many of his letters, then, deal with those issues, although as a patron of sorts to his family, Ennodius offered other help in that context as well.

To begin with, Ennodius had used his family to advance his own standing in the world. His kinswoman, Cynegia, had married Flavius Anicius Faustus Iunior Niger, who wielded extensive authority in the government of Theodoric.[28] Because of the senator's literary skill, Ennodius had written a large number of letters to him, praising Faustus' work and often requesting his help.[29] Indeed, his help was apparently so valuable that he called Faustus another father, which implied almost a mentor–protégé relationship.[30] While it is not clear whether Faustus helped to secure his episcopal see, it is significant that the noble was Praetorian Prefect of Italy at the time and actively involved himself in Church affairs.

As for his own acts of support among kin, the record is more clear. In the case of his two nephews, Parthenius and Flavius Licerius Firminus Lupicinus, the Pavian bishop took direct responsibility for overseeing their education. In 504, he secured both boys' entrance into the school of the grammarian, Deuterius, in the city of Milan.[31] Lupicinus was apparently the younger of the two, since Ennodius wrote to his mother to inform her of her son's (slow) progress. Parthenius, on the other hand, seemed to have been particularly adept, and Ennodius sent him to Rome in 506 to study rhetoric.[32] The bishop went out of his way to be solicitous of his education, sending with the young man letters of introduction to several senatorial luminaries in the city as well as to Pope Symmachus.[33] Nor did Ennodius' assistance end at providing an education: in 509, he chastised Parthenius for pursuing city pleasures at the expense of his education.[34] There was thus a broader sense of moral responsibility to these young men as well. And we know that the bishop's help in such matters extended beyond his nephews, in at least one case. Camilla, a kinswoman whose relation to Ennodius is not known, also sent her young son to him for a religious – and presumably a moral – education.[35]

Ennodius' pull in the court of Theodoric was also used to further the fortunes and status of his relations. Beyond his connections with Faustus, the Pavian bishop cultivated other connections in Ravenna. He had, after all, composed a turgid panegyric to the Ostrogothic king in 507 and corresponded extensively with a number of Roman and Germanic officials at court.[36] Accordingly, when several relations had sought his help in their personal affairs, he had no compunctions about appealing to his superiors. Ennodius had asked the Praetorian Prefect of Gaul, Liberius, for example, to lend financial aid to that same Camilla who had sent her son.[37] Parthenius had apparently requested that his uncle use his influence in court so as to keep some property his mother had left him.[38] Ennodius seems to have considerable pull in Church politics as well. A blood relative ('*sanguine catena*'), Helisaea, apparently living in Aquileia, wanted Ennodius to use his influence to regulate the advancement of some of the clergy there.[39]

Perhaps most significant for the purposes of familial relations, however, was an affair no doubt as embarrassing as it was complicated. Another kinswoman of undetermined relation, Archotamia, had evidently sought Ennodius' help in the matter of her grandchildren.[40] Her son had, for reasons that were not made clear, gotten a divorce from his wife, Aetheria, sometime in the first years of the sixth century.[41] Aetheria, a *clarissima*, had remarried and had allegedly been cheating her children from her first marriage out of money and support. Archotamia had sued on her grandchildren's behalf and the case was notable enough to merit King Theodoric's attention.[42] The case was initially decided in the grandmother's favor and it seems from Ennodius' letter that he had lent her moral support and had lobbied her position in Ravenna.[43] The precise nature of that support remains unclear, but it apparently was not strong enough. A short time later, on appeal from Aetheria's second husband, Theodoric ordered the case to go into arbitration.[44]

With the exception of his two nephews, practically all those whom Ennodius helped were extended relations. The vagueness of their precise connection is curious and implies that their affinity must have been distant indeed to be omitted. By means of comparison, Ausonius had named a number of his relatives as *affini*, suggesting that outside a defined circle of relatives (as defined by the laws of *parricidium?*) their precise relationship was not of great importance. That makes the help Ennodius provided for these quite distant relations all the more intriguing. The tenor of Ennodius' letters often seems to suggest that he felt acutely responsible for the well-being of his kin. The word *obsequium*, with its obvious connotations, never seems to be used, but there is nevertheless the sense of some kind of obligation. *Pietas* is also rarely mentioned, although that concept, too, must have played some role. If it were a case of a patron and clients who happened to be kin, a circumstance which would almost surely be precluded by sanguinity (at least on a formal level), then there had to be some sort of reciprocity involved. As a man with some power, on the other hand, it would be Ennodius' duty to his *familia* to aid its members any way he could. Perhaps his vocation of cleric may have been a further inducement to help.

Other references in the surviving sources to extended kin are not as clear. Shaw has assembled the funerary epigraphy for Rome and Italy for the later period, which demonstrates a low percentage of commemoration to and from extended kin.[45] There is a fairly large number of patron–freedperson relations mentioned, but that connection, as we have seen, was conceived of as almost a parent–child relationship. In most of Italy, however, the lack of any commemorator being mentioned on a grave represents a plurality of the surviving inscriptions. Since the simplification of funerary commemorations can be directly attributed to the rise of Christianity, this should not seem too surprising, but it does also skew the reliability and use of such material. Nevertheless, since other studies from earlier periods show a roughly analagous distribution, it seems likely that the value of extended sanguinity was subordinated to concerns with more immediate kin.[46] So much can be expected in most societies, but it rearticulates a basic unfamiliarity among Romans as to how far piety and obligation went in regards to extended blood relations.

Other references in the surviving literature generally mirror what we have seen in writings of Ausonius and Ennodius. There are many references to extended relatives being brought into ruling hierarchies, whether secular or clerical. Emperors, of course, had brought extended family into the government since the days of the Julio-Claudians and certainly continued to do so well past our period. But clerics often did the same thing: Augustine, for example, sponsored his nephew Patricius' induction into the clergy at Hippo.[47] Indeed, Gregory of Tours noted with some contempt that a rival to his claim on his see was preposterous, since he did not come from the right family![48] With the possession of power, then, one assumed a responsibility to further the careers and well-being of his or her relatives, no matter how far removed.

Of course, having a kinsman in high places lent him an ability to act authoritatively in matters of one's family: we need only look at Ambrose and Caesarius of Arles' missives to their siblings about proper comportment.[49] Sometimes, that power could lead others to assume it, as when Caesarius' nephew, Teridius, apparently wrote to his cousin, Caesaria the Younger, in his uncle's name![50] Much more common, however, was a tendency to simply associate oneself with the influential or notable relative. Cassiodorus, for example, claimed the sister-in-law of Boethius, Proba, as a relative (*parens nostra*) – an interesting connection, although tenuous at best.[51] The relationship, then, between a powerful relative and his or her kin, whether extended or not, was expected to be reciprocal. A great man or woman was supposed to help all who claimed blood ties, and those who asked for help (and even those, perhaps, who did not) were expected to be properly deferential.

Conclusions

The surviving source material unfortunately tells us relatively little. A vague sense of obligation and community within the family existed, to be sure. We can state that the definition of extended family seems to have been circumscribed by actual contact someone may have had with kin. Were contact to end, so, too, would the relation. If it never existed in the first place, then blood or no, a relative would have been outside the orbit of family. To take a much more intimate bond, it is significant as it is sad that once Paulinus of Pella's daughter escaped with her husband from the Visigoths, she had in essence disappeared from his world and hence was never mentioned again in his *Eucharisticus*.[52] In contrast, even his two sons who left him were still close by and he could mourn their untimely deaths. Paulinus' daughter was not only lost to him; she was no longer a consideration.

The ill-defined nature and fuzzy perceptions of obligations and responsibilities to extended kin lead us inexorably to the same conclusions we reached concerning classical Roman ideals on this subject. The inability of the sources, no matter their type, to define even broadly a set of behavioral or customary paradigms surrounding the extended family implies Romans themselves were not clear as to what constituted proper familial *pietas* or *obsequium*. Perhaps the prevalence of the nuclear family model, at least in the attested literature and epigraphy, prevented the culture from defining such roles.

Christianity, largely because it had nothing invested in the unity of the extended family, did not help to clarify them. The metaphorical language of family, which early Christians had embraced and writers in late antiquity used carefully or rejected, had no use for aunts, uncles, grandparents, and the like.

Even the lip service given to respect for the elderly in canon law, whether in the family or outside of it, was nothing more than a thinly reworked affirmation of opinions held in society as a whole. In sum, there were no symbolic, theological or even practical reasons for Christianity to address the issue of extend kin.

There was, however, one peculiar phenomenon found among the aristocracy that transcended the bounds of the nuclear family. For unclear reasons, the most important members of the senatorial aristocracy started to look to the far past to construct – or perhaps reconstruct – extended family lines. *Domus*, in the broadest sense of the word, could be properly considered as an agglomeration of related families in some ways similar to the old Roman *gens*.[53] Indeed, the late antique rhetor, Festus, writing about the Aemilian clan, stated: '*gens Aemilia appellatur quae ex multis familiis conficitur.*'[54] It is odd and intriguing, then, that suddenly the great families of late antiquity – including the Anicii, the Decii and the Fausti – started identifying themselves with the great families and figures of the Roman Republic. Tiberius and Gaius Gracchus, Gaius Marius, the Furii and the Cornelii (among others) suddenly found adopted descendants centuries later. Did this half-conscious self-delusion function solely as an ennobling device for families whose roots were not so illustrious? Certainly that was possible with an aristocracy that had to constantly bring new members into its ranks to survive. But there might be another possibility as well, especially since these associations were made by the most powerful and enduring families of the era: the aristocracy of late antiquity may have seen in a mythical past a thin spider's web holding together the strands of large and widely spread kingroups. If it was this latter possibility, even in part, then Roman antiquarians created an artificial mechanism to help maintain family cohesion. That would be the strongest argument yet for the fragile and diaphanous nature of extended kin relations.

8

HOUSEHOLD SLAVES

Even the poorest of men, claimed Augustine one Sunday morning in 426, might own several slaves.[1] Indeed, to illustrate his considerable powers of asceticism, Sulpicius Severus had noted that St Martin owned only one slave while in the army.[2] The continued presence of slaves in late antiquity was in small part due to an acceptance of the institution of slavery in Church teaching. Although all humans were equal in that all had souls, various Christian authors had made a connection between Original Sin and the punishment of servitude. It paralleled the relationship between *ius naturale*, under which all human beings fell into the same category, and *ius gentium*, which made legal distinctions between various peoples. But more than the acceptance of unequal status as natural in a post-Fall world, the Church itself actively supported the institution in its attempt to moderate the effects of slavery. And because it did so, many of the things clerics preached against – namely sexual and physical abuse – were almost guaranteed to occur.

We have already noted in Chapter 2 that all privately owned slaves, especially slaves who served within the *domus* itself, were members of the *familia*. For the most part, they had no kin ties to the masters of the household, although the birth of bastard children with free fathers (and more occasionally, mothers) was certainly common enough. The fact that they lived and interacted with the core family every day and in a myriad of ways invites two questions: what was the nature of the master–slave relationship in late antique society and how did it differ from the classical period? While there appears to be ample evidence to answer both, research on domestic servitude in the late Roman Empire has been relatively small.[3] The practice of employing and maintaining slave labor in the Empire's agrarian economy never died out in antiquity. Indeed, slaves are attested to in the West well into the seventh century. But, for the most part, as an institution, slavery survived in the urban areas. This chapter, then, will attempt to discuss both the nature of domestic servitude in general and how the institution functioned within the context of the family.

Agricultural slaves and *coloni*

It is not the main purpose of this chapter to expend much space discussing slavery broadly, but the distinction between the country and the city slave is significant. The great Italian *latifundia* of the middle Republic were relics of a long-gone age, even if the use of slaves on estates continued at a significant level. Garnsey and Saller have argued that tenant labor was already being favored extensively on large holdings by the first century BCE.[4] A scant century later, agricultural authors were urging the rich to use *coloni* as a means to run their extensive estates better.[5] Some scholars have gone further and have argued unconvincingly for a complete collapse of slave labor in rural areas during the early years of the Empire.[6] While this view may be precipitous, it is hard to deny that there was a degree of decline in Italy and perhaps in other areas of the west. Quantifying or even qualifying that change, however, is not easily accomplished.

Agricultural slavery, however, did survive into late antiquity and its use, if not dominant, was at least widespread. Melania's Latin *vita* describes a *massa* which was farmed by 400 slaves.[7] Moreover, when she and Pinian were first intending to liquidate their considerable assets and donate the proceeds to charity, this caused widespread dissension among the slaves on their estates in suburban Rome.[8] Occasionally, too, large-scale supplies of slaves were windfalls of military victories. After the defeat of Radagasius in 407, for example, his men were auctioned off as slaves, and they were so numerous that they were sold for one *solidus* apiece.[9] Such mass sales of labor, however, were rare compared to earlier periods in Roman history.

Instead, *coloni* were clearly favored in Italy and elsewhere. While technically free persons, *coloni* were by law tied to the land. They were in essence indentured tenant farmers and the direct ancestors of the medieval serf. Early in the centuries of our era, they seem to have dominated the workforce in the countryside. Rutilius Palladius, author of a fourth-century poem on farming, makes no reference to slaves at all.[10] When Count Gildo revolted in Africa, the government under Stilicho's control ordered a general levy of senatorial and imperial estates in Italy, clearly inferring a recruitment of tenant laborers.[11] While the law never mentions *coloni* by name, they must have been the target: Honorius shortly thereafter tried (and failed) to enlist households slaves from the very homes of senators![12] But the status of *coloni* declined from the early fourth century on and probably did not greatly differ from the status of unfree laborers.[13] They no longer had the option to renegotiate their status as they had been permitted in the past, although they were admittedly tied to the land rather than its owner. To be sure, not all tenant farmers were similarly indentured. It seems that in the prefecture of Gaul, for example, the process of registering *coloni* permitted them some movement not enjoyed elsewhere in the west.[14] Nor did they always feel beholden to their *dominus*. *Coloni* farming the estate of Thogonoetum in North Africa, to cite one extreme instance, threatened to leave as a group if a certain bishop were given license to minister to them.[15] Nevertheless, their status was not much better than slaves and certainly their day-to-day lives were comparable to the point of being indistinguishable from one another. One law, for example, held a man responsible for any discrepancies in his financial records, even if they had been taken care of by a slave or a *colonus*.[16] The degree to which *coloni* overshadowed *servi* in rural communities, of course, is unlikely ever to be known.[17] While the ratio of slave to free labor may not be definitively gauged, however, Ramsay MacMullen has taken much of the surviving evidence and has made a comprehensive regional survey. He concluded that the use of slave labor, outside of the cities (and to a lesser extent, outside of Italy), was not a large-scale practice in the late Roman Empire.[18]

Domestics

Christian thought and institutional constructs

This narrows our study of the issue suitably, since it is the slave within the *familia*, the so-called domestic slave, which is our focus here. In the urban areas of the Empire, there is no question that unfree labor remained a visible thread in the social fabric. Slave traders were not only active in importing human labor from central Europe and Asia, but also within the bounds of the Empire. The Church's self-designated role in slave matters also indicated the institution's survival and vibrancy. But when we examine Christian attitudes towards slaves and slavery, especially in regards to those who had certain affective ties or at least feelings of loyalty to their *familia*, it was society rather than religion that dictated Christian opinion and action.

To begin with, slaves and masters may have been equal before the Church and God, but in this world they were to maintain their places in this world's social structure.[19] Like the Stoics, the Christian hierarchy had accepted the existence of slavery as a normal and natural institution in the imperfect earthly city. It is interesting to note in the letters of Ambrose, for example, continuous allusions to slaves and to the enslaved state. In a letter to Simplicanus, to cite one instance, the Milanese bishop played constantly with the concepts of slavery and freedom, drawing parallels between the physical and spiritual states of both.[20] Slavery may have not been natural to man's original condition, but was accepted in his fallen state. Indeed, Augustine went further and argued that slavery was a direct consequence of man's Fall.[21] Slavery was thus one of many punishments for Original Sin. Despite this quite active acceptance of the institution, however, the Church found it necessary to comment upon its condition and to create a slightly different mindset about the role of the slave in the *familia* and how he or she functioned within the free world. Some of these ideals, as manifested in its official policies, tried to better the state. On the other hand, many of their canons and directives simply mirrored imperial trends towards the regulation of slaves and freedmen.

The Church took a decidedly unremarkable attitude towards the legal standing of slaves. An unknown synod at Carthage stipulated that neither slaves nor freedmen could come forward as accusers of clerics in episcopal courts, except in their own defense.[22] Rules of evidence thus roughly approximated those found in Roman law. Moreover, the sixth synod of Carthage made a formal request that the emperor permit emancipations of slaves in the church, thus putting Christian places of worship on a par with pagan ones.[23] A canon from the council at Orange reconfirmed the legitimacy of these manumissions by excommunicating any person who tried to re-enslave an individual set free in this fashion.[24] And the Church also permitted its members to deal with their own slaves as any master might: a late regulation allowed bishops to sell slaves who were intent on running away.[25] Nothing out of the ordinary is addressed in these rules and each suggests the clergy was comfortable with the legal and cultural institution of slavery.

With the acceptance of slavery came also an acceptance of violence towards slaves. Corporal punishment, reasoned Augustine, was necessary to maintain the harmony of the *domus*. A *paterfamilias* should be concerned that all his dependants look to their souls and that they worship and serve God. Therefore, those who destroyed the household's peace, he further argued, needed correction either by word or by whip as a means of helping them. As his first duty to the heavenly city, the head of the house had to govern according to Christian laws. If violence were needed, just as if it were needed with one's children, so be it.[26] Thus, like Seneca 350 years earlier, Augustine saw the greater good of caring for one's slaves.[27] Unlike the Stoic, however, he employed different means. To put it in a rather more cynical way: those in late antiquity beat their slaves with as much abandon as their ancestors had in classical Rome, but only Christianity rationalized an ideal to justify it.

The Church, however, concerned about sin and possible impropriety, offered several uniquely Christian rules about slaves. An early canon attempted to make masters enforce a ban on polytheist idols within their own households.[28] Of course, in cases where a *dominus* might have owned many slaves, it was potentially dangerous to forbid their possession, so the canon further stipulated that masters should live some distance away from their pagan slaves. By avoiding slaves' quarters, at least a *paterfamilias* might remain free of spiritual pollution in his own physical *domus*. The concept of symbolic purity in the household, as mentioned in Chapter 2, however, was an ancient concept going back to the early Republic. Another fascinating canon acquitted masters from any wrongdoing in the event of a slave committing suicide.[29] Suicide was severely criticized in late antiquity by a number of Christian thinkers as a mortal sin and perhaps there was concern among slave-owners as to the apparent responsibility they may have had in its commission.[30] The concept of spiritual separation once again was an important issue here. A final example from the early sixth century was a prohibition against female slaves and freedwomen from serving in a cleric's house.[31] All these

Church rules of course say less about slaves *per se* than they do about how slaves related to their masters. Moreover, these were issues that all had a practical interest in maintaining and minding one's slaves. In contrast to thinkers like Cato, who had advocated the abuse and discarding of slaves, Christians saw their own role in the master–slave relationship as significant. Finally, like the other canons cited above, they all imply an inherent acceptance of the institution. Christians had to work within the same confines of social division as non-Christians.

The Church as a mediating influence

That all said, the Church did try to humanize the relationship between free and unfree. More accurately, they tried, as the Stoics had centuries before, to moralize about the condition.[32] One of the earliest canons ordered seven years penance – without communion – to any woman who killed her *ancilla* intentionally by striking her, five if it had been unintentional.[33] Of course, such a rule was less severe than Constantine's law, which ordered a master be tried for homicide if the resulting death had been intentional.[34] Nevertheless, the Church had implied through this canon that deliberately killing a slave was the moral, if not legal equivalent of murder. Moreover, protection of slaves seems to have gone hand-in-hand with rights that had apparently been extended to slaves some centuries before. The Church confirmed their rights as owners of their own property – that is, their *peculia* – and could generally dispose of their wealth as they desired. We have a ruling of Pope Gelasius, for example, which confirmed the slave, Ampliatus, had the right to leave his holdings to his sons.[35] The Church, too, approved of and encouraged slave marriages, although many thought the ceremonies themselves were of a decidedly questionable nature.[36]

The greatest change was in the role of a church as a place of refuge. As with the ancient temples of Greece and Rome, the clergy made their houses of worship sanctuaries for all those in dire need. A general admonition had been passed at Orange, ordering all Christians to respect the rights of an individual who had taken refuge in a church.[37] Sometimes sanctuary was granted to those who had committed a crime, such as one canon that applied to men who had conducted a *raptus* marriage.[38] More often, though, sanctuary was given to slaves who were fleeing their masters, whether it was temporary – such as avoiding a physical punishment – or something more permanent. The councils of Orange and Orleans had both passed canons protecting the rights of slaves to claim sanctuary in a church.[39] To be sure, even if a church's walls were respected, it was not an all-encompassing protection: slaves had to go with their masters if they claimed them, although the *domini* had to swear not to harm their runaways.[40] It seems, however, that the concept was quickly adopted and respected. Theodosius II had permitted slaves *refugium* in a church, as long as they were unarmed.[41] Thus, not only could the powerful, such as Symmachus, successfully take refuge from the emperor himself,[42] but *servi* evidently sought and received safety from their masters on holy ground. We know, for example, of a Neapolitan monastery that was particularly popular for slave refugees in the sixth century.[43]

The Church as a supporter of slavery

Keith Hopkins, in an insightful essay some years ago, made a general study of manumission patterns in the Roman Empire in the first centuries of the common era.[44] His careful analysis showed that the system by which a slave could gain his or her freedom was directly related to the survival of slavery as a whole. In essence, it was customary for a slave upon gaining his freedom to pay a sum roughly equal to his value to his master as an act of piety and respect. That money in turn would be used to reinvest in new slaves, ones who were undoubtedly younger and healthier. Former *servi*, in other words, provided the means by which their new patrons purchased more slaves. While Hopkins limited his study to a specific area and time, the general mechanism could have quite possibly applied to the larger *oikumene* and over some period of time.

The procedures for freeing slaves in late antiquity are not nearly as well documented as during other periods. It seems that the customary payment for freedom became of lesser importance as testamentary manumissions gained greater significance. Indeed, it was apparently not uncommon for a loyal slave not only to receive his freedom when his master died, but a significant portion of his estate (*legata*).[45] The customs – if not laws – of manumission, then, changed markedly in the latter period. Whether this was a result of Christian influence is difficult to say, but we know from much later formularies and charters of manumission in the Byzantine world that much of the impetus for freeing slaves came from a personal – although not ideological – belief that slavery was contrary to the true nature of man.[46]

Such sentiment, however, was still far off in the future. What was of importance was not so much the practice of manumission, but rather the parallel effects of the classical system of freeing slaves and the manner in which Christianity insinuated itself into their treatment. In the same manner by which *servi* achieving freedom supported the institution of slavery, so, too, did the Church's role as mediator accomplish similar results. When the councils of Orange and Orleans had permitted churches to be used as places as *refugium*, it is interesting to note the circumstances under which a slave could claim sanctuary.[47] They could not claim permanent safety unless they were under imminent threat of life by intractable masters. Whatever wrongs they had done would still have to be answered. Nor could they even receive protection if they had committed a serious crime. What the Church offered instead was protection from the retributive punishment of a momentarily bloodthirsty *dominus*. The slave-owner, for his part, had to swear that he would not harm his property and was furthermore prevented from taking emphyteutic slaves owned by the local parish.

The Church thus adopted the role of peacemaker. In fact, a cleric by law was required to formally contact a master in order let him know of his runaways.[48] Actual surviving accounts where the Church had to act as a facilitator, however, are almost non-existent. We know of a slave of Stilicho, who made a small fortune in selling false appointments while hiding out in Milan's central basilica. When discovered, the general permitted Ambrose to punish the criminal as he saw fit.[49] We have also mentioned the assault of a priest at the end of the sixth century in the city of Naples.[50] The reaction of the clergy to the event well represented the broader policy of the Church. So contentious was the incident that it forced Pope Gregory's involvement. He noted in closing the case that it had been customary for slaves fleeing their masters to take refuge at the monastery of St Severinus at Lucullanum. The Roman bishop therefore ordered that all masters forgive under oath slaves who had committed 'venial sins', and ordered both parties to be taken to the episcopal court in the city when addressing more serious complaints. Similar compromises were likely brokered in an age where civil authority still existed.

The significance of such mediation was twofold. First, it had the pragmatic result of restoring the domestic peace. By playing a neutral role, officially at least, the Church could bring together disputing sides in a situation that avoided unnecessary violence. More significantly, however, such action had the unintended effect of inherently supporting the institution of slavery itself. True, there was no comprehensive ideology until the eighteenth century which questioned the essential moral and ethical problems tied in with subjugating a class of people – not even by slaves themselves. Stoics had addressed the way in which slavery was conducted, but not its existence. The Church categorically refused, as a corporate body, on the other hand, to aid slaves in their escapes. The clergy was also forbidden to ordain *servi* (and *coloni*) without a master's permission precisely because it might provide a means of escape from their servitude.[51] Instead, they eased the tensions and problems that kept the master–slave relationship from working. By smoothing over difficulties and disagreements, they not only solved specific problems, but also generally discouraged slaves from running away permanently.[52] The alternative could be much worse: we hear of slaves, for example, becoming dangerous criminals (or soldiers), running off to join groups such as the *circumcelliones*.[53] So slavery was never questioned, in part because the Church had, perhaps unintentionally, made it a more palatable position. It is hardly surprising to learn the Church itself controlled enormous numbers of slaves, *liberti* and *coloni*.

Legal changes

Comparatively speaking, the government was even less innovative than the Church had been. Imperial constitutions for the most part merely recapitulated long-held policies regarding *servi*. They had almost no standing to act in any legal capacity. Valentinian III, for example, had legitimized some last-minute wills that had no witnesses, citing an example of a person only being in the presence of slaves when he expired![54] Only in the case of crimes committed in their presence could they testify, and then only under the inducement of violence. Judicial torture of slaves had, moreover, never been abolished: one novel notes that slaves involved in tomb violation were to be tortured immediately.[55] Theodosius moreover stipulated that household slaves could be tortured by the *paterfamilias* in cases of adultery, providing they were allegedly in attendance of the crime.[56] And of course, slaves were not able to accuse or testify against their masters except in cases of treason (*maiestas*).[57]

Moreover, slaves could only be freed by their master's actions or will. Their status as slaves in any other circumstance did not change. Even if they attempted to join the military as much-needed soldiers, they nevertheless remained in servitude: Honorius gave a *dominus* the right to recover his property in any circumstance (and apparently over any period of time) provided he attended to the proper procedure.[58] Slaves were even forbidden the right to become monks.[59] The permanence of the state of slavery thus remained until a master declared otherwise. Roman law never altered this principle.

Slaves did seem to gain the right to marriage, however, if only indirectly. A novel of Majorian's, which concerned decurions, ordered that if their daughters wedded slaves, they would have to be restored to their homes once their parents died.[60] The implication seems to be that the union was considered legitimate to a certain point. It is possible, too, that this meant slaves wedding persons of a rank lower than decurion could do so legally. A law of Anthemius perhaps puts the problem into focus. In its preamble, the emperor explained that the lack of marriageable men due to barbarian wars made women turn to slave husbands.[61] The novel then went on to address the case of Julia, a woman of relatively high rank, who had married one of her former slaves in contravention to laws forbidding the union of a freedman to his patroness.[62] It is, moreover, clear that Julia had freed him specifically for the purpose of marriage and the emperor's answer to this case was somewhat unusual. He declared that it was still illegal for high-ranking women to enter into unions with their slaves but that all such *matrimoniae* made before the time of the law's passage would be considered valid and any children borne out of such marriages were legitimate.[63] We read of no restrictions placed on *humiliores* marrying slaves, but Anthemius' novel showed in certain circumstances the government's willingness to accept such unions as well.

In sum, *servi* remained almost completely under the power of their masters. Other than Constantine's constitution about purposely killing slaves, few limits were ever placed upon masters in the fourth and fifth centuries by the government. Theodosius II ordered that pimps (*lenones*) be flogged and banished if they attempted to prostitute their own or another man's slaves[64] and there were some restrictions placed on Jews owning *servi*.[65] But taken as a whole, a slave's lot had improved only slightly. Christianity had clarified the distinction between the position of the *servus* on earth and in heaven. Roman law had not addressed that issue – it did not have to – but a slave's role in the *familia* had expanded. He could freely enter into permanent, legally recognized affective relationships with *conservi* and with freedmen and, in certain cases, even with free citizens. Christians had brought such unions to light from the time of Tertullian. Jerome may have disapproved of the actual ceremony, but he never disapproved of the institution of slave marriage.

Slaves in the *domus*

Slaves as victims

The continued existence of slavery inevitably led, despite what Christian authors had advocated, to sexual and physical abuse. Such activities were bound up in a more basic problem, however: a slave, even one employed solely in the *domus*, was generally held in very low regard. It is true that certain servants were deemed invaluable and merited both manumission and financial recompense. But more often they were reviled and always suspect. An extended soliloquy by a grumpy slave, Pantomalus (or All-bad), in the fifth-century play, *Querolus*, is particularly instructive.[66] While his humorous tirade ostensibly criticizes his ever-complaining master, it is in fact a catalogue of the many shortcomings of slaves. Among other things, they were commonly believed to steal from the family, whether it be gold coin or silver cutlery. They drank morning, noon, and night, usually at the expense of their master's larder. They were clumsy: they broke, burned and scratched personal property. They were always trying to avoid work. Moreover, they were always sleeping, which Pantomalus reasonably explained was due to their all-night orgies. Most disturbing of all and revealing the paranoid psychology which Roman society must have felt, all the *servi* and *ancillae* of the world were in league with one another, carefully watching the movements of their masters. These charges might have been nothing more than generic complaints which could be traced back to the plays of Aristophanes and certainly the archetypal clever but lazy slave was a standard feature of ancient drama. But both indicate the generally poor opinion of slaves and the silent fear that pervaded every master's mind.

Like the anonymous author of the *Querolus*, many Romans dealt with these issues by a sort of abusive humor. Ausonius wrote a clever and cruel poem about a runaway slave who was branded for his troubles.[67] Another describes a homosexual eunuch who was forced to perform oral sex on his wife.[68] Actors and mimes (*histriones* and *mimi*), who were also considered among the disreputable (*infames*), typically lampooned buffoonish slaves in the theaters of late antiquity.[69] Claudian's poem, *In Eutropium*, was one long pun on the literal shortcomings of Arcadius' grand chamberlain. Not even Christian authors were immune from such cruel merriment. Jerome had sarcastically complained of domestic servants: '*Querulum servulorum genus est et, quantumcumque dederis, semper eis minus est.*'[70]

The low regard in which they were held manifested itself in far less pleasant ways than cutting humor. Physical violence was a common feature of every slave's existence. The fear of violence from the earliest days of the Republic was seen as the best way to control one's slave. Indeed, Propertius perhaps foreshadowed Machiavelli when he claimed it was a good idea to be feared, since it incurred loyalty.[71] The Christian rationale was not much better. The suggestion of Ambrose to *patresfamilias* that they should govern their slaves by the rule of slave law rather than by fear was a model that seems to have been largely ignored in everyday life.[72] The legal rule of thumb was of little help: the only guide for excessive violence was the vague watchword *immoderate*.[73] For example, even Sidonius Apollinaris, a bishop known for his eloquence and his station (he was the son-in-law of the emperor, Avitus), was so furious at one slave that he would not see him for days lest he do him serious bodily injury.[74] He managed to control himself, but the intensity of his anger was such that he well could have seriously hurt his *hermam stolidissimum*.[75] Clearly, the messenger thought he was going to be severely punished, too, when he was brought before his master: Sidonius almost bragged that he was *trepidus* and *sternax* and *prae reatu balbutiret ore*.[76]

Some masters lacked the bishop's Herculean self-control. Augustine's grandmother had his father beat some of his house slaves for circulating stories that had estranged her from her daughter-in-law.[77] The old woman later warned the rest of the domestic staff that the same thing awaited them if they, too, tried to stir up trouble. After that, there were no more problems. The *pueri* and *ancillae* of the house, however, were so afraid that no one '*mali aliquid loqueretur nulla iam audente*'.[78] The language, incidentally, is interesting: Augustine wrote that Patricius had them whipped rather than administering the punishment himself. No doubt at times a *dominus* found it easier to have a professional *lictor* or perhaps another slave to enforce correction.

It is true that in this case, the rationale could arguably have been valid in the Church's eyes, but there were other cases more arbitrary. Ammianus Marcellinus mentioned that in the houses of some of the great senators of Rome, slaves would receive 300 lashes of the whip if they were too slow in bringing hot water.[79] Whether or not this was sour hyperbole on the historian's part – Ammianus had been rather deflated at his own lukewarm reception in Rome – it nevertheless illustrates the capricious nature of many masters and their predilection to impetuous violence when they did not get their way. Nor should eunuchs be overlooked. While castration was expressly forbidden within the bounds of the Empire, there nevertheless remained a large market for *castrati*, especially among the wealthy.[80] Their value was high in part because they were so difficult to produce.[81] One late source states that only one in thirty survived the procedure.[82] True, this violence carried out against slaves was not perpetrated by Romans (at least as far as we know), but the demand for them assured the continuation of castration.

Finally, while it was illegal to kill one's slaves intentionally, it was relatively easy to get away with doing so.[83] Nor did the Church's strictures against doing so necessarily stop domestic homicide.[84] Ammianus had mentioned in the same passage that by a simple defense of claiming he was trying to beat some sense into his *male . . . famosus*, a master could literally get away with murder.[85] Sometimes, the act was overtly intentional. In Germany, for example, the Emperor Valentinian I had a group of slaves put to death because he feared they might escape and inform the Alemanni that he was attacking.[86] In sum, the relative worthlessness of a slave's life, at least to the wealthy and powerful, made the unfree an expendable if not inexpensive commodity.

Of course, these problems also underscored a deep sense of distrusting slaves, not just for potential violence, but for potential sin. The realities of family life made slaves, male and female, targets for sexual exploitation. Sexual power over another was simply another means of asserting a master's *potestas*.[87] More than one illegitimate bastard had been born in the houses of the wealthy, as Paulinus of Pella and others could personally attest.[88] Indeed, Lactantius noted with some disdain that to many, fidelity meant keeping only to the women within one's own house.[89] The problem for pre-Christian moralists, such as Musonius Rufus, was not, as Michel Foucault put it, to 'assert an explicit prohibition, but rather [to present] a concern with preserving the conjugal bond with all that it may entail in the way of individual relationship, attachment, affection, and personal respect between marriage partners'.[90] For the Church, this was nonsense. True, often its officers preached forgiveness for sexual transgressions. But they not only saw such peccadilloes as adultery and therefore a sin, but also considered it a threat to the stability of the *familia*. That is why the boundaries of continence were firmly set around the marriage bed. We have already discussed the necessity Christians placed on respecting the bonds of matrimony. Clearly, though, the clergy saw the greatest threat from those who were most readily available. What better place to start than in one's own household?

And some did. Augustine's father seems to have transgressed in this manner, since the bishop described Patricius' infidelities in the same breath as he discussed the scurrilous rumors passed along by the household's slaves.[91] So, too, did Fabiola's unnamed first husband, who apparently had an insatiable sexual appetite.[92] It was clearly expected by Christians and pagans alike that young men would sow their wild oats. Once married, however, such activities were supposed to cease. But the availability and pervasiveness of slaves of both sexes made them a particularly inviting temptation. Adultery was accordingly a real danger and therefore guarded against. That no doubt explains the hen-pecking tone of some of Augustine's surviving sermons.[93]

To be sure, probably only a minority of a household's slaves were so used, but the literature of the classical and the late antique ages suggests that most were also quite young. We have already mentioned Fabiola's husband, who did not simply like *ancillae*, but rather *ancillulae*.[94] Such behavior was precisely what the Church had wanted to avoid. Even so, Christians, too, seemed to have enjoyed the company of their slaves. Paulinus of Pella admitted that in his youth he was *'contentus domus inlecebris famulantibus'*.[95] Prudentius, called the Christian Vergil, admitted to much the same thing in his debauched youth.[96] Augustine, moreover, affirmed that it was common for both husbands and wives to be discovered in bed with slaves, although he cursed the moral double-standard by noting that it was only women who were brought up on criminal charges.[97] And he noted that most husbands customarily slept with the women of their house.[98] The Church, despite its protestations, seemed unable to change the predominating behavior of a society largely unfettered by practical deterrents.

To be sure, we have been focusing on the negatives. It is undoubtedly true that many slaves were treated well, sometimes to the extent that they were honored in the family. Sextus Petronius Probus, for example, made it a point to treat his slaves well and defend them from any attacks, legal or otherwise, with every means at his disposal.[99] But these are distinctions between individuals and a system of behavior. Certain masters and mistresses might have been extraordinarily kind, but the institution of slavery was predisposed to domination and violence. It is hardly surprising, then, in such an environment there was at times considerable friction between master and servant.

Slave anger

Under these circumstances, many slaves, particularly domestic slaves, hardly wanted to continue in their servitude. Some sought to escape by any means possible. We know that slaves disappeared into the countryside or headed to lands on the periphery of the Roman world. Severinus, the apostle of Noricum, for example, was apparently such a slave.[100] Others sought protection by attempting to hide their identities rather than their persons. According to one novel of the Emperor Severus, *famuli* had been secretly enrolling in public guilds to ensure freedom for their children.[101] Others had tried to enroll in the army, which was forbidden to *liberti* and *coloni* as well.[102] Still others tried to join the regular clergy or enroll in a monastery, which incited both the government and some who were high in the Church hierarchy.[103] The Church in particular was concerned about the possibility of unintentionally harboring escaped slaves: Pachomius in his rule ordered that any man who wished to enter the monastery had to prove he was not a runaway slave or guilty of some crime.[104] Occasionally, some went to further extremes. We have one case in the mid-sixth century of a slave, admittedly not a domestic servant, who impersonated a *curialis* in order to hide his status.[105]

On occasion, slaves went further. The violence inflicted on them as a group would periodically be turned back on the master. We have several examples of domestic slaves, either singly or in groups, attacking their own *domini* or even other free persons of the community.[106] While these incidents survive only in Egyptian papyri, they could not have been unusual for the society as a whole. We even mentioned the example of slaves attacking free men in Italy at the end of the sixth century. Servants of Clementina, a local Neopolitan noble, had apparently assaulted a priest and had sought escape by taking refuge in the monastery of Saint Severinus.[107] The cause of the incident is unclear, but it seems to have been a spur-of-the-moment assault, which no doubt was common in such events. It is impossible even to approximately suggest the preponderance of behavior in such circumstances, but the existence of such material certainly says something about the variety of responses.

More frightening still were slaves who actually joined large, violent insurrections. We have already mentioned the *circumcelliones* in fourth-century North Africa, where angered slaves joined with *coloni* and disenfranchised Donatists to attack people and property.[108] Gaul, where slavery was almost exclusively within the household (*famularum*), seems to have also been rife with revolt. The so-called Bacaudae were active from the third to the fifth centuries and appear to have been made up of mostly free peasant revolts against heavy-handed Roman authority.[109] But it is clear, too, that many slaves joined these periodic insurrections or at least ones like them. Rutilius Namantianus, for example, mentioned how the Prefect of Gaul, Exuperantius, had put down a large insurrection of household slaves in Armorica in 417.[110] Some years later we hear of another outbreak of the violence where '*omnia paene Galliarum servitia in Bacaudam conspiravere*'.[111] And Paulinus of Pella noted that a local slave revolt had erupted in Vasatis while he was taking refuge there from the advancing Visigoths, suggesting that the slave population was taking advantage of the civil unrest to alter their status.[112]

We have no reports of such revolts in Italy, but they must have occurred, if only sporadically.[113] These attempts to avoid servitude or to actually rebel against it, however, share a common thread: almost all involve the *servi* of the house. No doubt agricultural and mining slaves attempted or succeeded in running away, but there is no corroborating literary evidence to support that supposition. The existence and variety of these passages, however, exemplify the regard in which slaves, even slaves of the *familia*, were held. It also implies something about their relatively poor treatment. It is true that children and, as we have seen, wives were frequently the target of physical violence as well. But for them, the glimmer of hope lay in their free status and the promise of wealth and independence in the future. For a slave, on the other hand, such hope was largely non-existent.

In sum, behavior, attitude and custom did not greatly change in regards to the treatment of domestic servants. Although some may have been treated well, many were also routinely brutalized physically and sexually. Their persons and their status were easily and commonly violated. On the other hand, late antiquity is perhaps distinguished in that many from that age seemed to have a keener awareness that slaves were human beings. They felt joy and pain, had their virtues and vices, and most importantly, had eternal souls. Masters, possibly because of the moral imperative to treat their slaves well, were also concerned with the potential retribution that their servants could wreak. As one master from the *Querolus* retorts to a threatening slave: 'by Hercules, to the contrary: I hope that what you have desired for me will happen to your own flesh and bones!'[114] Like the Christian ideology of reciprocal responsibilities between family members, the reciprocity of violence became ingrained in the public dialogue as well.

Freedmen and freedwomen

The place of *liberti* ought also to be briefly mentioned, although there is less on this member of the *familia* than on any other. The freedman of late antiquity, like those several hundred years before, was truly in a state of betweenness. His life did not change noticeably at manumission and he was likely to continue in his work for his former master, now *patronus*. And like his predecessor, unless freed by will or by act (*vindicta*[115]), a *libertus* or *liberta* in the later Roman Empire would have the status of a Junian Latin. *Liberti* thus held an inferior legal state to many, even to their fellow freedmen. It was not until the 530s that the emperor finally did away with the concept of *latinitas* and granted all freed individuals the full status of Roman citizen.[116] In either case, freedpersons were *humiliores* and so subject to all the attendant restrictions of that state. Valentinian III, for example, had preserved Diocletian's law that prevented *liberti* from becoming town councilors (*curiales*).[117] Even with Roman citizenship, there could be, in theory at least, little social advancement.

The expectations between a freedperson and his or her patron had, moreover, changed little throughout the course of imperial history. The relationship seems optimally to have been based on a traditional form of obligations to one another. A freedman would likely perform the same duties for the household's head as he would have before manumission. No doubt, too, he would carry out pretty much any duty that was requested, as is perhaps visible in the numerous epitaphs set up by freedpersons to their former masters.[118] In return for various services rendered, a *patronus* used whatever authority and influence he had to protect his clients from legal and other forms of trouble. Ammianus Marcellinus, for example, noted that the Praetorian Prefect, Sextus Petronius Probus, not only made it a personal policy not to order any of his clients (and slaves) to do anything illegal, but defended them in any way possible had they committed a crime.[119]

Freedmen and freedwomen, however, do not appear to have been greatly referred to in any of the sources, although the few legal references we possess seemed to have been oriented towards keeping them mindful of their *obligationes* to the *paterfamilias*. True, a Church canon from the early fourth century had excused a Christian *libertus* from his responsibilities if his patron was heathen, but subsequent Roman constitutions suggest that this view was not shared by the imperial government nor, was it likely, by many pagan slave-owners.[120] Even Jewish masters and patrons were given some measure of support by the government.[121] Constantine had early permitted rescinding the freedom of *liberti* who behaved haughtily towards their masters,[122] and Honorius extended that ruling by permitting the heirs of patrons the right of re-enslavement under similar circumstances.[123] Only those who had been freed as Roman citizens were given some protection against losing their free status, although they, too, had to defend their actions before a magistrate.[124]

Moreover, other restrictions and indignities could be visited upon a former *servus*. Valentinian II, for example, had made it a crime for freedmen to bring charges that carried capital punishment against their patrons.[125] Honorius went further and proscribed an unspecified punishment for a *libertus* who accused his patron of *any* crime.[126]

Nor should we ignore the fact that *liberti*, too, were ill used. While we have no accounts of freedmen being subject to corporal punishment, there were tales of sexual play. Jerome's disgust at old widows who took young freedmen in as ostensible godsons only to turn them into *concubini* has been mentioned.[127] But rumors also flew about women and the usually freed managers of their estates. The Empress Honoria, sister of Valentinian III, was said to have had an affair with her *procurator*, Eugenius, and had become pregnant by him.[128] And many women had tried in the mid-fifth century to actually marry freedmen, not, as our source contends, because of a lack of eligible free men, but more likely to retain a certain financial autonomy.[129] A free woman's status and power over her freed husband's standing were clearly unquestioned.

This is not to say that freedmen had neither rights nor power, especially when compared to the state of slavery. They could own their own property outright and could leave it to whomever they wished. Valentinian III, for example, stated categorically that *liberti* could will their property in accordance with the laws of free persons, and thus not subject to meddling from their former *domini*.[130] This extended even to circumstances where they had died intestate. Furthermore, with certain provisos, *liberti* could join various guilds and so improve their status in a limited, but tangible way.[131]

Most important was the fact that children born subsequent to their manumission would be free citizens. Nor, despite the restrictions placed on their social mobility, were all freedmen inconsequential. Imperial freedmen, in particular, had some place in the world and the powerful chamberlains (*cubicularii*) were made up almost entirely of freed eunuchs.[132]

Admittedly, however, these rights and privileges were few and like the institution of slavery, Christians accepted the institution without much comment. Like their unfree brethren, *libertinitas* was a second-class citizenship, but one which offered a glimmer of hope for future generations.[133] In that sense, a freedman or freedwoman's status differed little from the mass of 'free' Roman citizens.

Conclusions

In spite of the impression that may have been given, no one should doubt that emotional ties between many masters and slaves existed in late antiquity did exist and could be warm and cordial. *Servi* felt as acutely as free men and women and occasionally joined with their *domini* or *patroni* in relationships equal in stature to any *iustum matrimonium*. Augustine, whose concubine was probably a freedwoman, was emotionally committed to her and felt incredibly guilty when he sent her back to Africa. Some might even be adopted as children, as perhaps in the case of Belisaurius' godson, Theodosius.[134] But despite their essential humanity, which both the Church and most of Roman society believed slaves possessed, they remained dispensable. Children, no matter how sorely treated, represented one's future. The death of a slave may have been regrettable and a master could not simply kill one with impunity. But if a slave died, even one loved and honored, it did not represent the end of the world, because it did not mean the end of the *familia*.

Perhaps Geoffrey de Ste Croix's words about slavery in late antique Christianity are worth quoting

> It was precisely the exclusive concentration of the early christians upon personal relations between ... man and God and their complete indifference, as christians, to the institutions of the world in which they lived, that prevented christianity from ever having much effect for good upon the relations between man and man.[135]

No Christian in antiquity – nor pagan, for that matter – could practically conceive of a world without slavery. As Christians, slaves and masters were equal in the sight of the divine. What did it really matter that their positions were different in this world?

9

FINAL THOUGHTS

Consuetudo oculis nil sinit esse novum.[1]

This survey of the family in the later Roman Empire has attempted to accomplish two things. First, it has sought to present an overview of how men and women of late antiquity conceived of the family and its role in relation to the larger social forces that affected it. It has, moreover, tried to give some indication of how people actually seem to have behaved in the period roughly covering the fourth to sixth centuries CE. Second, this study has tried to show that the success of Christianity in actually altering behavior was remarkably limited. In such a synthesis, some things will inevitably be anachronistic: the motivations for a canon to be issued at Arles in 314 would be quite different from one produced at Agde in 506. Nevertheless, if one can speak of late antiquity as a roughly singular era, then one can certainly offer some generalizations for the period.

Moreover, in a broader context, there has also been some discussion of the behavioral and intellectual evolutions of these subjects. From the perspective of Roman history, the family remained a unit essentially unchanged in its composition, in its habitation patterns and in the dynamics of interfamilial relationships. From the perspective of Christian history, early formulations about the family flowered fully in the period of this study. While there was at times a significant difference of opinion, as a general rule the Church and its fathers attempted to remain true to the spirit of Paul and other early Christians. The confluence of the two traditions resulted in a fusion of concepts probably to the Church's liking, but failed to manifest itself into a behavior consistent with those concepts.

What this study has not directly addressed is the question of why. Those who had espoused a stricter personal code of behavior themselves often failed to follow it. Why, in short, did Christianity not make a greater impact on late ancient family life? Did its shortcoming imply something inherently unworkable about its essential beliefs? These questions would be topics worthy of study in and of themselves, but I want to end this study with three general observations.

First, deep-rooted social, legal, financial and even biological pressures all conspired to make change in the late antique family extremely difficult. The instinct of humans beings to produce offspring of any sort, combined with an unalterable societal emphasis placed on having children within affective relationships, mostly overpowered Christian calls for virginity, chastity and celibacy. But more than working against the strength of deeply entrenched Roman customs, Christianity faced the imposing foe of the basic desire of reproduction. The confines of marriage may have channeled that desire, but should that institution fail to produce offspring, remarriage and other, less respectable means were still viable options. Augustine knew from personal experience that a total abstinence of humankind was highly unlikely.[2]

Moreover, laws of inheritance simply had not changed that radically in the entire history of the Empire. If anything, they became more flexible in late antiquity, legalizing for women a variety of heirship options comparable to their male relatives and allowing greater latitude generally in disposing of a patrimony. Yet, for all that, the essential dominance of the agnatic line over the cognatic, the guidelines for dividing an inheritance should an individual die intestate, and the rules for challenging a will as *inofficiosus* remained basically the same. Nor did these features disappear in Western Europe after the late antique age. Furthermore, an inheritance given to the under-aged would usually be controlled by the *paterfamilias* or, should he be dead, the *materfamilias* through a variety of means.[3] As a result, the essential patriarchal character of the law did not change and the ability for parents to control their progeny's purse strings kept the latter beholden until they themselves became adults or *sui iuris*.[4]

Finally, the strength of the male prerogative was never actively challenged. Christianity had not extended its notions of husband–wife equality past the realm of fidelity. The broad powers a father might have over all the members of his *familia*, in law as well as by custom, guaranteed that many heads of households did not respect even the few admonitions of the Church on connubial loyalty. True, marriage patterns and mortality rates suggested that a majority of children would be fatherless at adulthood, but fathers continued to fulfill the traditional functions and traditional behavior that society expected and permitted. To paraphrase Shakespeare's Cassius, the fault was not in the message, but in ourselves.[5]

Second, a large part of Christianity's negligible effect lay in its inability to enunciate a mode of behavior sufficiently distinct from earlier Roman practices. As we saw in the preceding chapters, much of what Christian writers had taught was not completely exclusive of the Roman experience. Emphasis on male dominance, the virtues of *univira*, the *pietas* of children to parents and the *obsequium* of slaves to masters are only a few of the ideals both espoused. This was not entirely the due to a 'Romanness' of the early apologists nor of the Church: Christianity had been a religion borne out of a

Mediterranean culture and so shared some basic tenets with Graeco-Roman civilization. As such, there were considerable similarities which transcended the area of pure belief. Nevertheless, while its essential roots were Judaic, Christianity's growth and formation, in the East and the West, were also heavily influenced by social issues and ills unique to the Roman Empire. The most obvious expression of this fact was the proliferation of numerous unorthodox positions that were highly dependent on local circumstances. The Donatists in North Africa are a case in point.

Christianity's acceptance and favor in the fourth century muddied matters even further. As a religion to a certain extent of *refuseniks* in its early years, it was able to take stances, both politically and socially, which were extreme. Martyrs and the desert hermits were able to radicalize Christian belief and so make it more visible in its distinctiveness. But once it became, as it were, mainstream, the Church's hierarchy became more intent on the unity of practice and belief. Such a thing, of course, was never fully realized, but many synods and councils, both local and ecumenical, attempted to regulate and standardize Christian life. When personal comportment was the issue, the Church was almost always inherently conservative. It had, despite the protestations of some of its most eloquent spokesmen, become sensitive to the society in which it operated. And this had a distinct advantage in that it made the religion more palatable to a greater number of people. As Rome became more Christian, Christianity became more Roman.

Finally, part of Christianity's shortcomings also lay in the Church's inability to present a unified front on many of these issues. Unity may have been an ideal in a truly catholic religion, but it was (and is) difficult both to conceptualize and to practice. In the attempt to produce a synthesis of ideas on beliefs on family matters, we have necessarily muted some of the more dissonant voices in the Christian quire. But as should be evident even from this overview there was a disparity in a number of areas.

On the most basic level, there was often a gap between Church canon and Roman law. The imperial government was often sympathetic to Christian ideals and at times actively tried to promote them, but it is difficult to discern a pattern of legislative response to specific Church movements, let alone to their formal requests. A canon from the eleventh synod at Carthage, to take one example, requested a law be passed by the imperial government, ordering that all couples divorced because of adultery remain permanently separated or be reconciled.[6] While Honorius subsequently enacted a sweeping divorce law, it was issued some fourteen years later and had nothing in common with the Carthaginian canon.[7] Moreover, at times, as Evans Grubbs has demonstrated, imperial law in fact conflicted with contemporary Christian thought.[8] In practice, Christian emperors did not always find it politically expedient to back up Church law.

There were also conflicts between some of the canons themselves. The relatively harsh moral pronouncements of the council at Elvira, for example, were qualified by or were even contradicted by later canons. To be sure, opinions changed over time and many synods were convened to face strictly local issues. But taken as a whole, official Church policy could vacillate as much as that of the government. Like the imperial government, the body of Christ was often forced to clarify its own positions. And over certain issues, it did so on multiple occasions.

The musings and assertions of various religious thinkers, moreover, were not always in accordance with one another nor with official Church policy. We have referred, at times indirectly, to the doctrinaire acerbity of Jerome, the ponderous fence-sitting of Augustine and the intangible pragmatism of Ambrose.[9] The ambiguity of Augustine's opinions on remarriage, for example, would be rejected out-of-hand by Jerome. Other authors, mostly from the East, also offered a variety of opinions on proper behavior in regards to the *familia*. The many letters that the rich and powerful wrote to these men about divorce, marriage and remarriage, and children have sometimes been interpreted as a general ignorance on the part of the lay public. It seems more likely, however, that these highly educated men and women were more victims of conflicting thought than they were of a basic naïveté.

Moreover, the teachings of such religious revolutionaries as Jovinian and Pelagius offered quite different ideas on the relationship of Christian theology to private life. Not only did their convictions incite frantic consternation among orthodox believers, but also seem to have attracted a fair number of followers for extended periods of time. Some Priscillianists, for example, apparently attracted a considerable following by damning marriage entirely, to say nothing of the procreation of children.[10] Pelagius shocked and inspired thousands in the East and West with his belief of true free will not dependent on divine grace. While occasionally these sects would be successfully suppressed, such as Jovinian's followers, there were always a plethora of heretics and along with them, a host of shocking and potentially popular beliefs.

For the educated elite, this disagreement stood in sharp contrast to a respected body of secular literature which still provided a blueprint – admittedly fraying badly at the ends – for Graeco-Roman civilization. In a society where education was still highly standardized, the bibles of Homer and Vergil offered a compass by which all gentlefolk found their way in late antiquity. Macrobius and Martianus Capella may seem staid and derivative to modern sensibilities and certainly they did not offer deep spiritual truths, but they appealed to a culture which placed great value on reiterated themes and *topoi*. Indeed, it was a trait that survived long into the history of Byzantium and it is unsurprising that that civilization successfully intellectually and spiritually melded piety and *paideia*.[11]

Nevertheless, despite the failure of Christianity to more fully affect late antique society in the arena of family life, it cannot be considered a categorical failure in the larger scope of Western civilization. The grains of Christian thought were only sown in late antiquity; they had not yet blossomed. Like the parable of the seeds, some ideas – such as the ideals of marriage and divorce – took root and grew strong in Europe. In the Byzantine world, for example, the sanctity and permanence of the wedded state became a fact in law and life with the publication of the *Ecloga* in the mid-eighth century.[12] Even before then, in the sixth century, there were strong, Christian-motivated restrictions on divorce and remarriage in both East and West. Other ideas – such as the order of widows to match the order of virgins – withered and died, although the success of female chastity and asceticism in monastic institutions was a powerful and pervasive movement in all of Europe for a millennium. Indeed, it often subsumed widowhood into it by actively promoting the cloistered life as a means of ensuring post-marital celibacy.[13]

Thus, as classical literature had been a model for the classical *oikumene*, the patristic authors of late antiquity had busily built a new foundation for the extended *domus* of Christendom. Medieval historians such as Caroline Bynum have shown that that foundation was not limited to the public sphere, but also provided the building blocks for issues surrounding personal comportment, male–female relationships and familial imagery.[14] The elision of the last, familial imagery, with biblical archetypes became a particularly powerful and influential tool for directing behavior, shaping custom and of course producing law. True, it did take time for the Christian belief to wash over all of Europe's people. But once it had firmly taken root, Western civilization has never fully operated without its influence.

There still remains a great deal of confusion as to what specifically motivated families and its constituent members to behave in the manner they did. It is difficult to link beliefs to actions when so much of the material remains scattered, both temporally and spatially. There are enormous gaps in our basic knowledge of family life quite apart from the critical issue of placing it in its social, cultural and religious context. To be sure, there are certain areas in our record which are much better attested than others, such as the relatively large amount of information on married life. But taken as a whole, much still remains speculative.

I want, in the end, to return to that funeral Jerome described in the winter of 384.[15] Jerome's criticism and Christian sense of moral superiority are, in respect, completely out of place. The hindsight and historicism of the modern age did not weigh heavily on that poor old widower in his sorrow. His wife had died and his grief was expressed as it had been for many centuries, by all Romans of his rank. It was the weight of the past and not of the future that dictated his actions.

APPENDIX

Attested and possible divorces, 268 CE–527 CE

These divorces are drawn from the *Prosopography of the Later Roman Empire*, volumes one and two, and thus do not take into consideration divorce from the curial classes and lower. They come only from the western part of the Roman Empire, although there are very few additional records of divorce for the east. They have been arranged alphabetically, with the husband's name first.

Key

D: divorce definite
P: divorce probable
*: indicates the divorce took place within the imperial household.

U: divorce uncertain
H: divorce unlikely, but possible

An *italicized name* indicates the party who initiated, or likely initiated, the divorce.

1 *Flavius Aetius*/Anonyma * U – Greg. Tuor., *HF* ii:8.
2 Albinus/Anonyma H – *CIL* v:1976.
3 Anonymous/Anonyma P – Jer., *Ep.* 123:10. Both husband and wife supposedly had over twenty spouses each.
4 *Anonymous*/Aetheria D – Cass., *Var.* iv:12.
5 Anonymous/*Fabiola* D – Jer., Ep. 77:3.
6 Anonymous/*Paulina* U – CJ v:4:10.
7 Bonifatius/Anonyma U – Aug., *Ep.* 220:4.
8 Basilius/*Agapita* D – Cass., Var. ii:10–11; iv:40. Note they were reunited.
9 *Constantine*/Minervina * P – Aur. Vict., *Epit.* 40:12. This assumes that Minervina was the emperor's wife rather than concubine. *Cf. Pan. Lat.* vi:4:1.
10 *Constantius I*/Helena * U – Anon. Val. i:1, ii:2. This also assumes that Helena was a wife rather than a concubine.
11 *Constantius II*/Anonyma * U – Eus., *V. Const.* iv:49. This was the first of Constantius' three wives.

12 *Diocletian*/Eleutheria * H – *Lib. Pont.* lxi:6.
13 Nichomachus Flavianus/Anonyma U – Symm., *Ep.* ii:22.
14. Afranius Hannibalianus/*Eutropia* * P – *Pan. Lat.* ii:11:4.
15 *Honorius*/Thermantia * D – Zos. v:35:3, 37:5.
16 Huneric/*Eudocia* * U – Nic. Call., *HE* xiv:12, states Eudocia left him to go to Jerusalem. But see Theoph. AM 5946, who claims she stayed in Africa until her death.
17 Marcellus/*Anonyma* P – Aus., *Prof.* xix.
18 *Galerius Maximianus*/Anonyma * D – Jer., *Chron.* s.a. 292.
19 Rusticius/Artemia H – Jer., *Ep.* 122.
20 *Valentinian I*/Marina Severa * D – *Chron. Pasch.* p. 559.
21 *Galla Placidia* threatened Constantius III with divorce * – Olymp., *fr.* 38.

NOTES

1 INTRODUCTION

1 Jer., *Ep.* 123:10.
2 For the modern period, see, for example, Stone (1979).
3 The greatest bulk of our knowledge of the structure and behavior of the family unit comes from the legal codes of late antiquity, as well as a number of partially surviving and complete legal works. The two great surviving legal documents, Theodosius II's *Codex* (published in 438) and Justinian's *Corpus Iuris Civilis* (published in 530), are massive compilations of several centuries of legal jurisprudence and thus provide both a comprehensive legal definition of the family as well as a redacted look at how that definition changed over time. Studies of family Roman life in the nineteenth and early twentieth centuries thus unsurprisingly understood the family in a largely legal sense. Rivier (1891), one of the earliest works on the Roman family, focuses exclusively on the law. Lacombe (1889) barely looks beyond the codes to examine the social setting in which the law was understood and functioned. Corbett (1930) has similar limitations, although it was the standard text on the subject for thirty years. It was not really until the 1960s that scholars tried to look at the family from a different perspective. Balsdon (1969), for example, synthesized contributions in sociology, anthropology and psychology into a general social history. Hareven (1971) was one of the best musings concerning the value of breaking away from law in the historiography. The value of Roman law to family history makes it invaluable even today. Treggiari (1991), for example, considers law focal in her recent study. In this large volume, the law is central to structuring a significant portion of her argument.
4 The two recent wide-ranging studies are Goody (1983) and Herlihy (1985). See also Boswell (1994).
5 Lane Fox's (1986:344) words on marriage echo the words of classical Roman jurists and moralists, despite his study concentrating on the post-classical age: 'Marriage, finally, was only one social form of cohabitation and it was valued [by Christians] because it legitimized children and eased the transmission of property.' Compare to *G* i:55 for children from an *iustum matrimonium* and *D* v:2:2–4 for legitimate children as *sui heredes*.
6 See Brown (1988); Rouselle (1988); and Veyne (1987).
7 For topics directly dealing with the family: Evans Grubbs (1994), Arjava (1988,

1996, and 1998), and Gaudemet (1947, 1953, 1958, 1978 and 1980). For related topics, see Arjava (1996), Cooper (1996).

8 For example, Gaudemet (1947, 1951, 1953, 1955a, 1955b, 1958, 1960, 1962, 1976, 1978 and 1980), Biondi (1952), Sargenti (1938, 1975), Arjava (1996, 1998). Cooper (1996) is a notable exception.

9 Gardner (1986a:2–3).

10 See Kertzer and Saller (1991), for the possibilities and the limitations of using Roman law over long periods of time.

11 Most of these exceptions cover the papyrological evidence from Egypt; see Bagnall (1993:182–207). *Cf.* Barker (1985). Apart from those, see Hopkins (1965) and (1978); and Campbell (1978).

12 See, for example, Bradley (1986). For other works on the lower classes, see Rawson (1966), Kajanto (1969) and Gardner (1997).

13 As Beryl Rawson has noted, there are some 23,000 inscriptions in Rome alone that refer to non-elite persons (that is, those who were neither of the senatorial or equestrian orders); Rawson (1986:44, n. 4).

14 As Gardner and Wiedemann (1991:63), note:

> We can only speculate on the extent to which the family ideals of the citizen community were shared by others. They were certainly shared by those freedmen whose views have been preserved on inscriptions – but they were by definition those who integrated successfully.

15 For example, see Wightman (1978); even within Italy itself, there could be considerable differences; Garnsey (1979). For cultural differences, see MacMullen (1990:56–66).

16 MacMullen (1990:65–6).

17 For a good overview with an impressive bibliography, see Momigliano (1989). The effects of colonization in Italy by Roman and Latin citizens aided in the syncretization of Italian culture; see Salmon (1970:13–19, 112–27). The structure of social life in central Italy was so similar to that of Rome that the foundation of Italian colonies also helped to create a similar model on the Italian peninsula: Garnsey (1979) synthesizes enough of the archeological evidence to talk of an 'Etrurian' model of habitation (it should be noted in opposition to this idea, however, that Garnsey is at pains to prove there was some difference between northern and southern Italian life).

18 In Rawson (1991), not one of the nine essays go much beyond the mid-second century CE, and most concentrate on the first centuries BCE and CE. In the latest general study of the Roman family, Dixon (1992:241–2), presents a chronological guide to Roman history that ends, significantly, with the Edict of Caracalla in 212.

19 The degree to which the Empire was Christianized at the time of Constantine's Edict of Milan in 313 has been much argued, but almost all scholars agree that it was a minority religion, even in the cities. On the subtleties of the situation, see Chadwick (1978).

20 See Brown (1981).

21 See Momigliano (1963) *passim*.

22 For a recent general history of the Goths and their settlement in the Roman

Empire, see Wolfram (1988); for the Visigoths in particular, see 117–71. For an alternative view, see Heather (1991).

23 Concerning the economic survival of the cities, see Jones (1964:712–66). See also Wickham (1981: 21–7), and Dyson (1992: 215–44). For the endurance of games in late antiquity, see Alan Cameron (1976). While it centers on the east, and on the politics of the circus factions, it does discuss the games' longevity elsewhere (*passim*). For a synthesis of the historical and archeological evidence, see Humphrey (1986:579–638). For the survival of local education and educators, see Riché (1976:3–60).

24 Procopius mentions that at the end of the siege of Rome by the Ostrogoths in the 540s, no more than a few citizens remained in the entire city; vii:17:23–5.

25 See, for example, *Eps.* iii:56, ix:58, and xi:77.

26 Again, for example, *Eps.* i:18, i:44, vi:37, or ix:6. For a recent study on Gregory's role in Italy and in the Church, see Richards (1980).

27 For a detailed account concerning the effect of these struggles on individuals, see Brown (1984). His approach is prosopographical and so stresses the fortunes of various families.

28 Goody (1983) and Herlihy (1985).

29 Kertzer and Saller (1991). The first article in the medieval section of the book, J. Bestor's 'Ideas about procreation and their influence on ancient and medieval views of kinship,' 150–67, seems to separate the two ages with the writings of Isidore of Seville (c. 560–636).

30 For practical purposes, I use these terms synonymously.

31 One of the earliest attempts to define the *familia* beyond a legal context was Henrion (1940).

32 See most recently, Saller (1994:1–86). See also Bradley (1991:91–2); Rawson in Rawson (1986:1–57); Dixon (1992:1–36); and Saller (1987b).

33 Although, that, too, presents a number of problems; see Saller (1994: 83–6), for four different definitions.

34 Engels (1884).

35 Le Play (1871).

36 For recent criticisms of such terminology, in particular the 'nuclear family', see Martin (1996).

37 But see Laslett (1970–1) and Hareven (1971) for more anthropological definitions, which emphasize co-residency over kinship.

38 Most now have rejected the notion of the role of the father in the family as being absolute in any practical sense; see most recently Saller (1997:7–34). For a thorough study on the distinction between family and *familia*, see Gardner (1998).

39 See Saller (1994:80–95). *Cf.* Saller (1984b).

40 Much of what is stated here is based on Bender (1967).

41 Bradley (1991: 164–5).

42 Normally the husband.

43 Bradley (1991:171); *cf.* Bauman (1984–85).

44 On this particular point, see Lightman and Zeisel (1977).

45 Tac., *Ann.* xiv:42–5, for example, relates a story of how strong these connections could be. L. Pedanius Secundus, the city prefect in 61, was murdered by one of his slaves in a dispute about the sexual affections of another (male) slave.

46 Trying to establish the 'truth' about an event or series of events in this context is not directly relevant. The depiction of an affair is the central concern; for regardless of historical accuracy, the image the author is seeking to evoke in his reader is as much material culture as 'true' stories.

47 Some of the methodological concerns here are addressed in Kertzer and Saller (1991:1–22). Additionally, see Rawson (1986:243–57) and Gardner and Wiedemann (1991:196–202) for lists of different issues of concern to the study of the classical Roman family.

48 Moxnes (1997a).

49 The rhetorical as well as the moral value of each was understood even in antiquity: Aug., *de civ. Dei, passim*; but see, for example, i:23–4; ii:8–9, 14, 21.

50 The only document really comparable to it is Marcus Aurelius' *Meditations*, which, after the rather traditional first book, offers a collection of reflections and free associations on the human condition and the often existential impressions of rulership. But his maxims are hardly organized and offer no general conclusions. See Misch (1950) for a fuller treatment on the subject.

51 For example, Ammianus' famous digression on Rome, xiv:6, or his opinions of various nobles in Constantius' court, xvi:8.

2 TWO TRADITIONS

1 See, for example, Cic., *de off.* i:53–5.

2 See Treggiari's statement, (1990:503–4).

3 *D.* xii:4:8 and xxiii:2:4.

4 For the age of marriage, see Hopkins (1964–5). For the age differences in the upper and lower classes, see Shaw and Saller (1984a).

5 *G.* i:11, 59. Most of book one is concerned with the subtleties of citizenship and the different ways it is attained or denied. Clearly, though, in its purest form, citizenship was granted to those who had, in a sense, inherited it.

6 Suet., *Caes.*, lii:3; Val. Max., vii:7:2; and Livy, *Epitome*, 59.

7 If we look at freedmen, for example, we know that they owed considerable allegiance to the former masters who had now become their patrons, and in fact could be prosecuted for being poor or undutiful *clientes*: *D.* xxiv:2:11 and xlvii:10.7.2. There were some limits to the degree of control patrons had over their previous slaves; for example, *D.* xxxviii:1.38 *pr.* See also Petronius' hyperbolic description of Trimalchio's *gauche* freedman behavior in book 5 of the *Satyricon*.

8 Again, looking at freedmen, see Cicero's comments on their state; *ad Quintum fratrem* i:1:13.

9 See Plutarch's *Quaest. Rom.* 1–2, 7, 29–31, and 86–7 for a fuller description of the traditional marriage event.

10 *D.* xxiv:1.

11 There is evidence, however, of it surviving in the late Republic. See the *Laudatio Turiae* below and Cic., *pro Flac.* 84.

12 *G.* i:110–11 states that it was abolished as well as simply falling out of use. Tacitus reports that during Tiberius' reign, marriage with *manus* became an issue because of sacral duty; and so only allowed *manus* to be in force when it applied to the religious duties of a husband; *Ann.* iv:16.

13 See Flory (1984) and Orlin (1996) *passim*.
14 *CIL* vi:9499. For more on slave marriages, particularly in the epigraphic evidence, see Treggiari (1981b).
15 Val. Max., ii:1:6.
16 Tac., *Ann.* iii:34: '*consortia rerum secundarum adversumque*'.
17 Tac., *Agr.* vi:1: '*vixerumque mira concordia, per mutuam caritatem et in vicem se anteponendo*'.
18 Musonius Rufus 13b:13–14.
19 *D.* xxiii:2:1
20 Paul., *Sent.* v:15.
21 Dixon (1991):108.
22 *D.* xxiii:2:1.
23 Aul. Gel., *Att. Noct.* i:17:4–6 (Bücheler, fr. 83): '*Vitium . . . uxoris aut tollendum aut ferendum est. Qui tollit vitium, uxorem commodiorem praestat; qui fert, sese meliorem facit.*' From Varro's now lost *Satura Menippea*.
24 Pliny, *Ep.* viii:11; *cf.* viii:10: '*fuit nulla sua culpa, sed aetatis aliqua*'.
25 Pliny, *Ep.* i:16.
26 Pliny, *Ep.* i:14.
27 *CIL* vi:11602 (*ILS* 8402): 'a spinner, devoted, virtuous, thrifty, chaste, and a stay-at-home'.
28 *CIL* vi:35536.
29 *CIL* iii:3572 (Aquincum); also dedicated by a family of local notables (the woman's husband was a centurion).
30 Griffin (1976); Lightman and Zeisel (1977).
31 For a detailed discussion on this issue, see Horsfall (1983).
32 *Laud. Tur.* (*ILS* 8393), col. i, ll. 30–3:

> Why should I note your domestic qualities of chastity, obedience, kindness, an easy manner, constancy in your spinning, religious without being superstitious, well-groomed without being ostentatious and yet modestly refined? Why should I speak of the love for your parents and the piety for your family, since you tended my own mother in the same way as your own, and provided the same peace for her as you did for your own parents?

33 *Laud. Tur.* col. i, ll. 25–6: 'Because of your constancy, they stopped and no longer pursued the matter any longer. By this, you successfully prosecuted this legal affair all alone, displaying a reverence for your father, piety for your sister and loyalty to your husband.'
34 Pliny, *Ep.* iv:19: 'She [Calpurnia] is the height of sharpness, the height of thriftiness.'
35 M. Fronto, ii:8 (*Ambr.* 107): 'Nor is my Gratia [Fronto's wife] a big eater, as lawyers' wives are thought to be.'
36 Pliny, *Ep.* iv:19.
37 Plut., *Brut.*, 13.
38 Plut., *Brut.* 53.
39 One of the ongoing debates in the study of Roman family history is the issue of love as a marital ideal between partners and between parents and children. Until

recently, most have generally accepted the notion that before Christianization, marriages were largely depicted as dutiful rather than loving; see Hallett (1984), for example. Others have stated that the romantic ideal was absent in the late Republic (Veyne 1978) and only appeared later in the Empire. More recently, some have argued that the sentimental element was evident even in the Republic: Dixon (1991).

40 Tac., *Agr.* vi:1.

41 *D.* xxiv:1:32. See Suet., *Tib.* xi for an example of a father-in-law sending a *repudium* in the husband's name!

42 *D.* xxiv:2:9 states that seven people had to witness the divorce. See also *D.* xxiv:1.35 and xlviii:5:44.

43 Treggiari (1990:450–1); Treggiari (1991:37); and Yaron (1963).

44 Such evidently was the case for Turia, whose husband insisted on remaining married despite her apparent infertility; *Laud. Tur.* ii:41–53.

45 Although husbands were fully within their rights to kill unfaithful wives (or even those who seemed unfaithful: see below), there are no attested cases in the late Republic. Plutarch notes that Cato the Younger simply divorced his first wife, Atilia, because of her sexual indiscretions. And he notes that Cato's sister, Servilia, was also divorced by Lucullus for the same offense: Plut. *Cat. min.* xxiv.

46 Suet., *Aug.*, 62.

47 Val. Max., vi:3:10.

48 Val. Max., vi:3:11.

49 In this case, adultery is the actual crime. Dio Cassius implies that Augustus attempted to first pass such measures in 18 BCE; liv:16. Furthermore, Propertius makes an oblique reference to a *lex sublata* perhaps introduced in 28 BCE; ii:7. On the problems associated with the introduction of these marriage laws, see Badian (1985).

50 Aul. Gel., *Att. Noct.* x:23.

51 Ulp., *Reg.* vi:13.

52 Tac., *Ann.* iv:21.

53 Pet., *Sat.* lxxiv.

54 Plaut., *Men.* ll. 830–50.

55 For example, Val. Max. vi:3:9.

56 Pub. Syr., *Max.* 260 and 498.

57 Ulp., *Reg.* vii:1.

58 Several are presented in Hunt and Edgar (1932–4). See also Bagnall (1987) and (1993:191–5).

59 Cic., *pro Marc.* 23.

60 An ideal espoused even by the imperial poets; see Prop. iv:11:36 and Hor., *Odes* iii:14:1–5.

61 Treggiari (1991):45–6. For the prevalence of divorce, see Raepsaet-Charlier (1981–2).

62 Ulp., *Reg.* xiv:16. See also Suet., *Aug.* 34.

63 *D.* xxxiii:1:21:2 and xxxiii:2:32:2.

64 Val. Max. ii:1:3 and Plut., *Quaest. Rom.* 105.

65 Paul., *Sent.* i:21:13. See also its extension to one year; *CJ* v:9:2 (534).

66 Tac., *Ann.* iv:39; Dio lviii:10–11.

67 Although Pliny notes that they frequently did so; *Ep.* ix:13.

68 Suet., *Vesp.* 3.

69 *SHA, Marc. Aur.* 29.

70 For a good discussion of the stepmother and her portrayal in Roman literature, see Noy (1991).

71 Treggiari (1981a).

72 Treggiari (1981b: 59).

73 There is a notable lack of children mentioned in the surviving epitaphs; Treggiari (1981a:68–9). But see also Nielson (1997).

74 Saller (1987a).

75 Corbier (1982) . See also Raepsaet-Charlier (1981–2).

76 Kajanto (1969).

77 Humbert (1972) *passim.*

78 Hopkins (1978:164–5), presents several examples of slave families being torn apart.

79 It also referred to a formal companionship for soldiers, an area upon which I shall only touch upon briefly. See Watson (1969:133–42).

80 See Gardner (1997:50–3). Gardner notes, too, that with the introduction of the *Constitutio Antoniniana* in 212 CE, many of these legal fictions disappear.

81 The question of transmitting patrimony has occupied a considerable portion of modern interest in the ancient family. We have mentioned already Saller in Kertzer and Saller (1991:26–47). Saller also discussed its transmission *vis-à-vis* the mother's estate in (1984). See also Saller (1994:155–80). A more specific study is Wallace-Hadrill (1981).

82 Pub. Syr., *Max.* 108.

83 Dixon (1988:168–232), describes the degree to which mothers could control their children.

84 Suet., *Claud.*, xxvii.

85 See Mus., *fr.* 15 and Plut., *de Am. Prol.* 497E.

86 Justin Martyr notes with distaste the frequency of such acts, which frequently resulted slavery, prostitution and especially incest: Just.Mart., *Apol.* xxvii:29. Pseudo-Quintilian, however, states that very few exposed children were claimed; Ps.-Quin., *Decl.* ccxxxviii. *Cf.* Boswell (1989).

87 Suet., *Vesp.*, iii. See also Suet., *de gramm.* xxi, where a slave, Gaius Melissus, actually refused to accept his former status, despite his mother's assertions. A child could even claim his or her patrimony, since a father's *potestas* did not end with exposure: see Lanfranchi (1964).

88 Women, technically under permanent guardianship, were not eligible for *adrogatio*, since it was an act carried out by the *comitia curiata* or its representatives until the reign of Diocletian. *Adoptio*, in contrast, was a private transaction.

89 There were also cases of *contra tabulas testamenti* and *secundum tabulas testamenti*; see Ulp., *Reg.* xxviii:2–6.

90 See Crook (1967:119).

91 The second book of Soranus' *Gynaikeia*, for example, deals exclusively with child care in the first years of life. Galen in *de Hyg.* also discusses these issues in detail.

92 Ariès (1962) argued that the high rate of infant mortality meant that adults in general did not invest emotional support in a child until he or she had reached

a certain age. The reactions to Ariès, at least in the ancient field, have been fairly unified in rejecting much of what he argued. See Néraudau (1979) and (1984); DeMause (1979:1–73); and Veyne (1978). For a different view of the place of children, see Wiedemann (1989).

93 Shaw and Saller (1984b) and Saller (1987a) have completed the arduous task of summarizing the funerary evidence for children under ten years. Also more recently, see Shaw (1992).

94 Saller (1987a).

95 *CIL* vi:20158: '*optimo reverentissimo obsequentissimo*'; 'To the best, most pious and obedient son.'

96 *CIL* vi:8517 (*ILS* 1660).

97 *CIL* xiv:4899 (suppl.).

98 If, however, a son was sold three times, he was afterwards free; *G.* i:132.

99 For a list, see Bradley (1991:107).

100 *D.* xlviii:9:5.

101 Pliny, *Ep.* vii:19.

102 The existence of burial societies for those often too poor to afford a burial and monument is well known. What is frequently less known is that often they were organized along kinship lines; see Flory (1978). Also see Hopkins (1983:311–17).

103 Ovid, *Met.*, viii:631–6.

104 Valerius Maximus suggests that this was done both to honor one's ancestors and to inspire his descendants to emulate their deeds and behavior: v:8:3. See Wallace-Hadrill (1994:38–61) for a complete discussion.

105 The definitive work detailing these political alliances is still Syme (1939). See also Bradley (1991:156–76).

106 *D.* xxiii:3:2. Paul, *Sent.*, v:6:15, however, seems to suggest that there were limits to this in the case of sons. See also Apul., *Apol.* 77.

107 *D.* xxiii:2:21.

108 Aul. Gel. *Att. Noct.*, ii:7:19: 'if the father orders it, he ought to be obeyed'.

109 The *Senatusconsulta Tertullianum* and *Orfitianum* in the second century CE recognized the legitimacy of the mother–child relationship and thus stipulated a mother's child as her natural heir.

110 Involvement in industry, for example, could be grounds for the censors disqualifying someone from the rolls of the Senate; *e.g.*, Cic., *de leg.*, iii:7.

111 Sen., *de ben.* iv:27:5.

112 For a fully documented explanation of such an attitude, see Eyben (1991) and (1993) *passim*.

113 Sen., *de clem.* i:15–16.1.

114 But see *de clem.* i:15–16.1 on the inclusion of Augustus in such council meetings. It also might have included friends: Cicero, in *pro Clu.* 176 mentions friends (*amici* and *hospites*). In cases of manumission, it was assumed that family friends had to witness the event; Cic., *Att.* vii:2.

115 For example, see Plut., *Cato* xxi.

116 *D.* xlviii:8:2 only states that public *consilia* be called in certain cases.

117 Suet., *Aug.* 65:1–2.

118 Lacey (1986).

119 See, for example, *Tab. Herc.* v where a L. Vennidius Ennychus acknowledged

that he fathered his wife's child. Presumably there was some question of paternity.

120 Such children were not *in potestate* of their fathers and thus they had no claim over them; *G* i:64 and Ulp., *Reg.* v:7.

121 *D*. l:16:195:4.

122 Ulp., *Reg.* xxvi:7–8.

123 Plut., *Cato min. passim.*

124 Bradley (1991:130–9).

125 Rawson (1986:196).

126 Some are called *filiaster*: *CIL* vi:19412 and 28519.

127 Two rare citations are *D*. xxxii:38:2 and xxxiv:2:15. See Rawson (1986:190, 200).

128 Rawson (1986:182–3).

129 *G*. i:19: note they are referred to here as *collactei*.

130 *D*. xxxi:88:6.

131 For example, *CIL* vi:15983.

132 Juv., *Sat.* vi:307; D lx:2:13. More rarely there is an occasional reference to *collacteae*; *D*. xxxiv:4:30:1.

133 Sen., *Ep. Mor.* xii:3.

134 *AE* 1983, # 253 (in Calabria).

135   He was not a simple house slave nor a product of the money-grubbing slave-market, but a boy deserving of his master's affections. Although he could not appreciate his patron's gift at his age, Glaucia was Melior's freedmen already. He had been given grace and beauty: who was more sweet? Was anything more winning than that smile like Apollo's? Life is too short to be greatly blessed, and old age is rare. Whatever it is you cherish, hope that it does not please too much!
        See also Mar. *Epi.* vi:28.

136 Rawson (1986):177 (*CIL* vi:9499).

137 *D*. l:16:195:4.

138 Agnatic *tutela* was automatic unless otherwise specified in a will: *G*. i:155–7. The rules of *bonorum possessio*, which stipulated the order of heirship, named close agnates after direct descendants: *G*. iii:9–16; *cf.* Ulp., *Reg.* xxviii:7.

139 *CIL* vi:1478: 'the most beloved grandmother, the dearest foster-mother.'

140 Tac., *Agr.* iii: 'This work will either be praised . . . or excused for its profession of loyal devotion.'

141 Pliny, *Ep.* vi:30.

142 Cic., *Att.* v:17.

143 Cic., *Att.* x:6:2.

144 *D*. xlviii:8:2.

145 Suetonius does note, however, that Augustus left much to unnamed relatives (and friends) as heirs of the third degree; Suet., *Aug.*, 101.

146 Bettini (1991:14–112). But see Saller (1997) in response.

147 For a good overview on land use, see Garnsey and Saller (1987:64–82).

148 Hopkins (1978:99–132) offers a valuable study on the system of manumission as a pillar of the institution of slavery.

149 Plut., *Sulla* 1.

150 A number between 15 and 20 seems to be repeated in the sources; *e.g.* Apul., *Apol.* 47. See also Plut., *Cat. min.* 9:4 and Pet., *Sat.* 57. The epigraphy seems to concur: Musconius Scurranus, a freedmen, received a dedication from his sixteen slaves; *ILS* 1514.

151 *D.* l:16:195:2–3.

152 *D.* i:5:4.

153 *D.* i:5:4:1 calls slavery a control '*contra naturam*'.

154 See *AE* 1971, #88 for an example in Puetoli; see also *D.* xlviii:19:28.11. For an example of such behavior, see Tac., *Ann.* xiv:43:4. Slaves could also be crucified and consigned to the wild beasts of the amphitheater.

155 Sen., *Ep. Mor.*, xlvii:19: 'only dumb animals need be whipped'.

156 Nepos, *Att.* xiii. But compare this to Cato the Elder, who believed in working his slaves into the ground, as well as selling off old or unhealthy ones; Cato, *de Ag.* i–ii.

157 Bradley (1991:35–6) offers fifty-eight references to such monuments; Rawson (1986:201–29). Pliny, *Ep.* vi:3, mentions an estate he presented to his former nurse.

158 *CIL* x:26 (*ILS* 8434): 'Alimma who in her life served with the greatest discipline, . . . a most pious and well-deserving woman.'

159 George (1997:316–17), has recently described the difficulties in trying to identify archeologically any differences in their respective statuses within the house.

160 *D.* xxxvii:14:2.

161 Except in the case of a Senator and a freedwoman; *D.* xxiii:2:4 pr.

162 Augustan legislation stipulated that a patron could otherwise claim half of the estate against any other heirs; the *lex Aelia Sentia* offers some complicated explanations.

163 *D.* xxxviii:1:31. There were limits against excessive services or payments: *D.* xxxviii:2:1 pr.

164 *D.* xxxviii:1:38 pr, for example, notes that prostitution was considered as part of this category. See also *D.* xxxviii:1:16.

165 *D.* xl:6:1.

166 Quint., *Inst.* i:3:13.

167 Cic., *de repub.* iii:37: '*propter oboediendi facilitatem*' as opposed to '*{servum} coercet et frangit*'.

168 Saller (1991b:144–65).

169 Ps.-Cato, *Disticha* iv:52.

170 Sen. Maior, *Cont.* ix:5:7.

171 Sen., *de cons. sap.* xi:12.

172 Ps.-Plut., *de lib. educ.* xvi:12CD.

173 Aug., *Conf.* i:14.

174 Pub. Syr., *Max.* 569.

175 For example, Sen., *de ira* ii:21:1–6.

176 Cic., *pro Cael.* xxviii: '*ludus aetati*'.

177 See Augustine, *Conf.* ii:4, iii:3 and v:12.

178 Sen., *de clem.* i:15:1.

179 Pub. Syr., *Max.* 108.

180 *CJ* iv:29:6 (294).

181 See for example, Tac., *Ann.* iv:60.

182 As opposed to a father's disciplinary attitude: *de prov.* ii:5.
183 Terentia, for example, forced the decision for Tullia's third marriage; Cic., *Att.* v:4:1 and vi:6:1.
184 Cic., *pro Clu.* 176–94.
185 Plut., *Caes.* 7 and 9.
186 Gardner (1995) discusses some of the subtleties a woman's relationship in these contexts.
187 See Dixon (1988), Ch. 7.
188 *D.* xviii:1:42.
189 As in the case of Sassia; Cic., *pro Clu.* 175–8.
190 *G.* i:13.
191 Sen., *Ep. Mor.* xlvii:3.
192 Tac., *Ger.* 25.
193 *G.* i:13–15.
194 For example, Plut., *Cato* 21. Sometimes torture would precede an execution; Suet., *Caes.* 74.
195 *D.* xxix:5:*passim.*
196 Sen., *Ep. Mor.* xlvii:5.
197 Pub. Syr., *Max.* 124. See also 363.
198 See Sen., *Ep. Mor.* xlvii.
199 Livy, iii:16:3: 'Everyone has an enemy in his own home.'
200 See Bradley (1991:13–36) for the affective ties between nurse and nursling.
201 Neyrey (1995:156–7).
202 Brown (1988:64).
203 I Cor. 7:29, 32, 34. All biblical quotes, unless otherwise noted, are NRSV.
204 Most famously recounted in Min. Fel. *Oct.*, ix. See von Geisau (1968:coll. 952–1002; 1365–78), with bibliography.
205 See, for example, Arav (1989), Killbrew and Fine (1991), and Hirschfeld (1995) *passim.*
206 Barclay (1997:68–72).
207 See Deut. 21:14; *cf.* Exod. 21:7–8.
208 Deut. 24:1–4; for polygamy, Gen. 16. The multiple references in the Dead Sea Scrolls texts criticizing polygamy perhaps suggest its survival into the Hellenistic era; see Martínez (1994) *passim.*
209 Martínez (1994:36); *CD* cols. iv:20–v:6.
210 *Bab. Tal.: Yebamoth* 63b; trans. Slotki (1936:426).
211 Cross and Livingstone (1997):1054.
212 *Cf.* Matt. 19:4–6; Mark 10:6–9.
213 Matt. 19:6 (Mark 10:9).
214 Martínez (1994:233): 1QapGenn, col. xx:12–18.
215 Matt. 19:9. The matter is complicated by several issues. First, this exception seems to be in contradiction to several other statements made by Jesus which suggest that there were no exceptions. Second, it is not clear whether 'being released' from one's spouse – *apoluein* (in the passive) – is necessarily a divorce; in a legal sense, it generally meant to be acquitted. Certainly, divorce seems to be Paul's understanding, but see below. Finally, if it does not mean divorce in the technical sense, it raises further complications about the permanence of the marriage bond, even in the case of adultery.

216 I consider only those epistles that can be definitively attributed to Paul. For the best discussion, see Bornkamm (1971) *passim*.

217 Martin (1997:201). *Cf.* Martin (1995) *passim*.

218 I Cor. 7:1.

219 I Cor. 7:7.

220 Jos., *Bel. Jud.* ii:155–62. This, according to Josephus, was to insure that sexual desire never became the purpose of intercourse. *Cf.* Sor., *Gyn.* i:10:39, for an analogous notion.

221 I Cor. 7:8–9.

222 I Cor. 7:10–16. And perhaps the one divorced as well, but it is by no means clear. This could of course cause problems for Roman citizens, and this was addressed by fourth-century emperors; see below concerning Constantine's restrictions on divorce; *cf.* Evans Grubbs (1995:225–60).

223 Eph. 5:31.

224 See Schürer (1973–84:2:485–6). Deut. 24:1–4.

225 Eph. 5:31.

226 I Cor. 11:7.

227 Eph. 5:22: 'Wives should be subordinate to their husbands, just as to the Lord.' I use the *vetus* Latin instead of the original *koine* Greek when available.

228 Eph. 5:25–33.

229 *Bab. Tal.: Yebamoth* 62b; trans. Slotki (1936:419).

230 *The Rule of the Community*, 1Qs, col. 4:6–8; Martínez (1994:6–7).

231 I Cor. 7:5.

232 I Tim. 2:11–15.

233 Eph. 6:1–2, referring to Exod. 20:12.

234 Eph. 6:4.

235 Jesus saw fathers as the primary care-givers and nurturers, rather than mothers; Mark 5:21–43; 9:17–27. *Cf.* Luke 11:11–13.

236 Gal. 3:28.

237 Eph. 6:9. Paul also states that Christian masters would have to answer in heaven for their actions.

238 Eph. 5–8.

239 Phil., *passim*; *cf.* Col. 4:9. See also Harrill (1995:68–128).

240 Bartchy (forthcoming). A special thanks to Scott Bartchy who permitted me to see an advanced copy of the manuscript.

241 Matt. 10:37–8; *cf.* Luke 14:26–7: 'He who loves his mother or father more than me is not worthy of me; and he who loves his son or daughter more than me is not worthy of me.'

242 Lassen (1997:103).

243 There is some question as to whether Hermas is representative of Western Christianity. Since he was apparently a Greek writing to a Greek-reading audience, and there are surviving Eastern manuscripts, this work could arguably be unrepresentative of second-century Rome. On the other hand, all early Christian authors, East or West, wrote in Greek. Moreover, there is a second-century tradition which makes Hermas out to be the brother of the Roman bishop, Pius (*c.* 142–*c.* 155). Pius was apparently an Italian from Aquileia (*Lib. Pont.* i:73). The matter is not clear, but it is likely that Hermas' visions are at least consistent with contemporary Western thought and interests. See

Muratorian Fragment ii:74–7. Moreover, Tertullian's vehement reaction to the work implies that it was well known and popular (*de Mod.* x). Finally, we do have several early Latin translations of his work.

244 Herm. *Shep.* i:2:2–3.

245 Matt. 19:9.

246 Herm. *Shep.* ii:4:1.

247 Bradley (1991:37–75) has seen the role of fathers in child care mostly focused on insuring material success for their offspring. For the role of servants in moral teaching, see Bradley (1991):13–36, 125–55. For the role of the mother, see Dixon (1988) *passim*.

248 It is perhaps significant that Hermas is visited by the personification of the Church in his visions, an elderly Roman matron.

249 *Att.* x:4:6. It is more likely that in the context of a personal letter, rather than a legal speech, Cicero was giving an honestly believed opinion.

250 *Didascalia Apostolorum*, iv:11:5–6.

251 He was Carthaginian by birth, but apparently practiced law in Rome; Eus., *HE* ii:2:25. He returned to Africa sometime after his conversion in the 180s or 190s. See Barnes (1971).

252 Most recently and exhaustively, see Rankin (1995).

253 Tert., *Ad Ux.* i:3.

254 *Ad. Ux.* i:5.

255 *Ad. Ux.* i:5. Tertullian is quoting Luke xxi:23: 'But woe to those who are with child and breast feeding!'

256 *Ad Ux.* i:2; *de Mon.* xvi; *Ex. ad cast.* 5–6.

257 See Raepsaet-Charlier (1982) for the best discussion on the issue of inequality in marriage.

258 *Ex. ad cast.* 9.

259 *Ad Ux.* i:8. Only Ignatius of Antioch in the longer version of his letter to the Philadelphians, offers some detailed discussion of widows, mostly to say they should be of a serious mind; *Ep. ad Phil.* 5.

260 *Ex ad. cast.* 9.

261 *Ad Ux.* ii:3 and 6.

262 *Ad Ux.* ii:7.

263 *De Pud.* 5.

264 *De Mon.* xiii–xvii.

265 *De Pallio* 5 and 6.

266 *Ex. ad cast.* 1.

267 *Ad Ux.* i:7.

268 *Ad Ux.* i:6. Tertullian's reference to male priests is interesting. Before this statement, he had been talking about women taking vows of chastity or virginity. His dismay at men doing so may have made him acutely aware of men's roles in the marriage. But he offers no further comment.

269 Tertullian calls his wife 'beloved fellow-servant in the Lord'; *ad Ux.* i:1; ii:1.

270 *De Virg. Velan.* 17.

271 Comm., *Inst.* 51.

272 Min. Fel., *Oct.* ii:6.

273 *Oct.* ii:1:

Octavius had rushed to Rome on business and to visit me, having left his home, his wife and his children: and children who could, because of their young years, only speak half-formed words, a language so sweet for its imperfection of stumbling speech.

274 On the innocence of children in early Christian thought, see Brown (1988:70–1).

275 Comm., *Inst.* 73. He continues in 74 with a general criticism of funeral pomp.

276 There was some question during Caracalla's reign among the Roman Church, for example, as to whether Paul's epistle to the Hebrews was authentic: Eus., *HE* vi:20. There is not even a mention in Eusebius of a serious heresy in the West until Novatus arose in the 250s: vi:43, 45–6; vii:7–9.

277 Moxnes (1997b:36–8).

278 He says nothing about upper-class men. It is, however, an early suggestion of a wife's importance in the process of Christianization within the family. Callixtus may have taken this idea from Tertullian, who argued that such unions would be considered valid: *ad Ux.* ii:8:4.

279 A proviso for which Hippolytus thoroughly castigated the bishop: *Ref. Haer.* ix:7. See Gaudemet (1955).

280 Chastagnol (1979). These were admittedly cases of women marrying freeborn men, however. *Cf.* Eck (1971) and Evans Grubbs (1994).

281 See Attwater (1983:216).

282 Eus., *Mart. Pal.*, ii:4:10. Eusebius was bishop of Caesarea at the time and thus is likely to be generally reliable. For the alternative traditions, see Delehaye (1962:126–40).

283 *Vitae Patrum: Mac.*, ii:

When I had left my boyish years, my father strongly against my desires, betrothed me to a wife, and set a wedding day. While the bridal chamber was adorned and when the invited guests were there in aplenty, my father became even more high-spirited, inviting the rest to the table to enjoy the feast.

284 The *topos* of fleeing an unwanted marriage, in fact, was a common literary feature found in early *vitae*; see Elliot (1987:85–92 and 206–7).

285 For her father, *Pass., Ss. Perp. et Fel.* iii:1–2 and vi:2; for her mother, iii:8 and v:6. Of possibly greater interest, the two are never seen together, perhaps implying some sort of separation.

286 Sadly, the *passio* offers little more about marriage than mentioned above, since Perpetua's husband is not mentioned. He might have repudiated her upon learning she was a Christian or he might have been dead. Her father, who was not Christian, presumably arranged the marriage. It would not be hard to assume that the chosen husband was also a polytheist.

287 Just. Mar., *Sec. Apol.* i–ii.

288 Just. Mar., *Sec. Apol.* ii, refers to the notice of divorce as a '*repoudion*', the Greek transliteration of the Latin, *repudium*. Additionally, as the wife was able to successfully appeal to the emperor with a *libellos*, there can be no doubt the couple held Roman citizenship.

289 Although clearly drunkenness could imply a whole host of other sins, Egnatius Maecenius supposedly beat his wife to death for being publicly drunk, justifying his actions on the grounds that her lack of self-control would lead to other vices. *Val. Max.* vi:3:9.

290 Ter., *ad Ux.* ii:7.

291 See especially Clem. Al., *Paed.* 1:5 for an extensive passage about children and their nature. It delves more into the issue of the metaphorical children of the Father, but Clement must in the process address the nature of childhood as well.

292 *Pass., Ss. Perp. et Fel.*, i:6

293 *Pass., Ss. Perp. et Fel.*, vi:5: 'such that I felt sorry for his miserable old age.'

294 *Pass., Ss. Perp. et Fel.*, ix:3: 'I felt sorry for his unhappy old age.'

295 *Pass., Ss. Perp. et Fel.*, v:6: 'I was sorry for my father's sake, because he alone among my family would not be joyous over my suffering.'

296 *Pass., Ss. Perp. et Fel.*, iii:3.

297 It is, of course, unclear as to whether Perpetua or Felicitas were connected to a spouse, although the fact that they were not virgins is not in dispute.

298 *Pass., Ss. Perp. et Fel.*, vi:8.

299 See Müller (1992).

300 *Oct.* ii:1. Herm, *Shep.* ii:2.

301 Herm, *Shep.* i:1:1.

302 Most of this account comes from the Hippolytus; *Ref. Haer.*, ix:7.

303 Ign., *Ad Polycarp* iv:3. For a full exegesis, see Harrill (1995):158–92.

304 Harrill (1995):158–67.

305 See Bartchy (1992) and (forthcoming) for interpreting the missive.

306 Brown (1988):54.

307 MacMullen (1984):33–5.

3 CONSTANTINE AND THE CONFLUENCE OF TWO TRADITIONS

1 I am heavily indebted to Professor Judith Evans Grubbs for much of this chapter. Her work on Constantine's social legislation has been pioneering and I have drawn a considerable amount of my source material from her various works. Her private correspondence with me has also proved extremely helpful.

2 Amm. Mar., xxi:10:8: 'Then [Julian] damned the memory of Constantine as an innovator and overturner of ancient laws and customs taken of old.'

3 See Dio lxxvii:9–10. Fergus Millar (1964) argues for a date of 214.

4 From *FIRA*, vol. 1, no. 88. *Cf. D.* i:5:17.

5 Hadrian had ruled that *honestiores* were free from capital punishment except in the case of murdering one's father: *D.* xlviii:19:15. There were also rulings made by Antoninus Pius and Marcus Aurelius: *D.* lxviii:18:10:1 and *CJ* ix:14:11:pr. And there is a reference in Pliny suggesting that these distinctions had existed early in the second century; *Ep.* ix:5.

6 *D.* xlviii:19:15.

7 And later to veterans of the legions: *CTh* vii:20:2 (320). See Dobson (1974).

8 See *D.* xxxviii:17. The *sc. Orfitianum* also extended those rules; *D.* xxxviii:17: *passim* and *CJ* vi:57:*passim*.

9 For example, *CJ* ii:21:2 (240), 22:2 (238), 23:2 (287), 24:2 (287), and 37:2 (238).

10 *D.* xxxvii:14:7.
11 *D.* xxxvii:14:8.
12 *D.* xxviii:1:28.
13 Evans Grubbs (1987, 1989, 1993a, and 1995). For the more traditional view, see Basanoff (1936). *Cf.* Dupont (1937).
14 Conveniently listed by Evans Grubbs (1995), Appendix 1.
15 Although, as Evans Grubbs points out, (1995:217–18), the death penalty for adultery had been decreed in the third century CE: *e.g. CJ* ix:9:9 (224) and 27 (294).
16 Nor did imperial innovations appear to be well enforced, save perhaps sporadically. For example, as Jones (1964:407), states:

> Emperors are not usually so frank in revealing their impotence [in the case of Gratian], but the fantastic penalties with which they often threaten governors and their *officia* who may connive at breaches of their commands are almost as revealing of their helplessness in face of the interested inertia of their agents, whether such inertia was due to personal sympathies, to their desire to conciliate local opinion and in particular to win the favor of local magnates, or to bribery.

No doubt this ineffectiveness trickled down to all levels of society.

17 A point noted by J. Gaudemet (1947), but frequently under-emphasized by Basanoff (1936) and Evans Grubbs (1993a, 1995).
18 The year 320 seems to have been a particularly active year, suggesting that there were indeed certain principles and rules that Constantine wanted in place.
19 Evans Grubbs (1995:342).
20 *CTh* i:22:1 (316).
21 *CJ* ii:12:21 (290–304?). It is addressed to the *consilium* of the province of Africa.
22 *CTh* ix:1:3 (322).
23 It was issued in Constantinople and the official to whom it was addressed, Agricolanus, is otherwise unknown; see Martindale, *et al.* (1970:31). Moreover, some of the *novellae* of fifth-century emperors suggest that general laws came out of specific petitions; for example, *N. Val.* xxi:1 (446) and 2 (446).
24 And it is clear that particularly in the case of a free woman and a slave or former slave, the situation would be heavily criticized: *e.g.* Cic., *pro Cael.* 23 or Juv., *Sat.* vi:279 and 331–2.
25 *D.* xxiii:2:42.
26 *D.* xxxviii:5:43. Or alternatively, a patron's wife.
27 Of course, one may argue that the women's status was diminished (she became the *liberta* of her spouse's master) and that her children would be slaves. Previously, under the laws of *ius gentium*, the children would take their mother's status. But the fact that the children took their father's status implies that this sort of *contubernium* was recognized in law. See Rawson (1974). And, of course, the military *contubernium* always had a legal, if somewhat inferior, status.
28 *CTh* iv:12.
29 Biondi (1952). Evans Grubbs (1987) cites Biondi:144. *Cf.* Rougé (1983), for problems with this argument.
30 Pharr (1952) has taken it to read, 'But if any woman should be so unmindful of her own honorable status'. Evans Grubbs (1987) has accepted this translation

and thus assumes that it refers to all freeborn. But it can easily be interpreted to refer more directly to well-born women. So much is clear in the following constitutions, which call other free women either '*ingenuae*' (free-born) or '*libertae*'. Cf. *CTh* iv:12:4–5 (331, 362).

31 *D.* xxiii:2:13.

32 *CTh* iv:12:3 (326).

33 *CTh* iv:12:2 (317).

34 *CTh* iv:12:4 (362).

35 *CTh* iv:12:7 (398).

36 *CJ* ix:14:1 (319).

37 See Evans Grubbs (1993b:144–7).

38 Although the use of imperial rescripts declined by the end of the third century in favor of more general edicts; see Millar (1977:ch. 5, §4). We do, however, have several surviving *subscriptiones* ruling on specific cases from Constantine's reign; *Frag. Vat.*, *passim*.

39 Constantine made provisions for informers to be despised and punished: *CTh* x:10:1–3 (313, 319, 335). No doubt these constitutions were extremely popular.

40 Evans Grubbs (1993a:147).

41 Children and their statuses are mentioned in the second and fifth subsections of the law.

42 'And for those who come back together secretly after being properly separated by the law, renewing their forbidden congress . . . shall undergo a similar punishment.' Of course, the express thought here is that the couple has come back together secretly because they had already first been discovered.

43 In particular, it would prove valuable to the upper-class ascetics of late antiquity; Evans Grubbs (1995:119–39).

44 *CJ* v:26:1 (320).

45 With obvious Christian implications, such as suggested by Niziolek (1980: ch. 1).

46 See *CJ* v:3:*passim* and *D.* xxiii:*passim*.

47 See, for example, Tert., *de Virg. Vel.* 11. Evans Grubbs (1995:177–80) also points to the canons of the council of Elvira (particularly canon 54), which was held *c.* 306. Ossius, bishop of Cordova and an advisor of Constantine at Nicaea, attended the council.

48 *CTh* iii:5:2:1–2 (319, 319).

49 Evans Grubbs (1995:165).

50 *CJ* v:17:7 (337) issued shortly after Constantine's death.

51 Volterra (1959). *Cf.* Volterra (1958).

52 Correctly questioned by Evans Grubbs (1995:258).

53 While the government might not require a wife to divorce her husband if he were a convicted criminal, it was encouraged: *D.* xxiv:3:31.

54 Sargenti (1975:279–81).

55 Admittedly she does state that the law is 'enigmatic' and accepts it until a better explanation comes along; Evans Grubbs (1987:80). She does not address the question directly in (1995: 228–32)

56 Although against the prevalence of divorce, see the appendix.

57 *Sirm. Cons.* i refers to Ablabius' '*probae religionis*'. It is only made manifest that

this refers specifically to Christianity from the nature of the law itself, which confirms the judicial decisions of episcopal courts. The second reference, in Athanasius *Festal Epistle* iv, mentions that Ablabius *'deum timet'*.

58 It is also brings into question one of Evans Grubbs' conclusions. Her argument that Ablabius had a Christianizing influence in the latter years of Constantine's reign becomes more open to debate: (1995:258–60).

59 See Chapter 5.

60 Bagnall (1993:193–199). *Cf.* more fully Bagnall (1987). This evidence comes primarily from the late fourth century and of course from the East, so its value could be limited. Nevertheless, it does give some indication of the prevalence of the Church in these matters.

61 For example, *CTh* xv:8:2 (428). This early fifth-century law makes no secret of the opprobrium that befell a *husband* who prostituted his own daughters and female slaves.

62 To be sure, astrology was special and not technically magic. It did not possess the same fear attached to it that magic or certain religious rituals had. But there was a general suspicion of the practice held by the emperors, particularly when it was employed by the upper classes. See Liebeschuetz (1979:119–39). *Cf.* Xella (1976) *passim*.

63 *CTh* ix:16:1–3 (all from 319).

64 *CTh* ix:16:4 (357). Nevertheless, astrology remained immensely popular. Firmicus Maternus published a popular book on the subject and Augustine was extremely interested in its charms in his early adulthood: *Conf.* iv:3.

65 *Honestiores* would only be exiled, unless the murder was also *maiestas*. For those offenses which carried a death sentence, see *D.* xlviii:18:10.

66 While it is not clear that concealment, too, was a capital crime, it is implied in *D.* xlviii:8:3:4. *Cf. D.* xlviii:19:*passim*.

67 *D.* xlvii:12:8.

68 *D.* xlvii:12:1.

69 *D.* xlvii:12:11 lays out the circumstances in which such a crime was punishable by death.

70 See, surprisingly, Tert., *de Test. Ani.* 4.

71 Evans Grubbs (1995, Appendix I) helpfully lists these pieces of legislation, along with the rest of his edicts concerning the family.

72 Musonius Rufus was incensed that wealthy parents chose to expose their children so as to avoid diminishing their patrimonies to too great an extent: *fr.* 15. ('ΕΙ ΠΑΝΤΑ ΤΑ ΓΙΝΟΜΕΝΑ ΤΕΚΝΑ ΘΡΕΠΤΟΝ'). No doubt there was extensive local variation in what constituted a legitimate reason for exposure.

73 Aug, *Ep.* 10*.

74 Aug, *Ep.* 10*:2: *'Nam vix pauci reperiuntur a parentibus venditi quos tament non, ut leges Romanae sinunt, {ad} operas viginti quinque annorum emunt isti, sed prorsus sic emunt ut servos et vendunt trans mare ut servos.'* 'For hardly a few in number were found who had been sold by their parents, and those [slavers] had not bought them to do work for a period of twenty-five years, as Roman laws permit, but instead they bought them as slaves and sold them across the sea as slaves.'

The only surviving law that this might refer to is *CTh* iii:3:1 (391), which allowed parents to sell their free children for a relatively short and unspecified period of time. The service was only to pay off debts. Afterwards, *'non minimi* *temporis spatium*', the child's freedom had to be restored. The confusion is made worse in a second letter, *Ep.* 24*, wherein Augustine wrote to a friend, the jurist Eustochius, asking legal questions about the status of children in such circumstances. The bishop inquired on a number of difficult topics; among other things, whether the enslaved became free if his father died while he was still in captivity.

75 *N.Val.* 33:pr (451).

76 Eus., *V. Cons.*, iv:28.

77 Theod., *HE* iv:4.

78 See Boswell (1988).

79 Just. Mart, *Apol.*, 27–9. Justin's great fear, however, was the danger of incest. Authors of Constantine's day also railed against exposure; see Lactantius, *Div. Inst.*, vi:20. Lactantius' passage is part of a larger attack on publicly permitted forms of homicide, such as the gladiatorial games.

80 Aug., *Ep.* 10*:7.

81 There were, however, rules governing the process of adopting an abandoned child. But these did not come in until the mid-fifth century; see Chapter 6.

82 The first, sent to Ablavius or Ablabius, has some problems with the dating. While the consular date is 315, Barnes and Evans Grubbs prefer to place its publication somewhere around 329: Barnes (1982:78); Evans Grubbs (1987:180). That would correspond with Ablabius' possible visit to Italy with Constantine. This is highly speculative, but the events surrounding the law's introduction suggest the earlier date. Italy had recently seen the end of a civil war in 312–13 between Constantine and Maxentius. It had been a short, but hard-fought battle. Maxentius had gathered troops from all over Italy and Sicily, as well as from Sardinia and Corsica (Zosimus referred to the 'Tyrrhenians': ii:15.), which undoubtedly put great strain on the peninsula. Moreover, shortly thereafter, in 314, Constantine and Licinius fought the first of their wars not far from Italy. Assuming, then, that these pressures on Italian manpower and material were severe and *CTh* xi:27:1 was in reaction to specific circumstances, then it is likely that the law's consular date is accurate.

83 Martindale, *et al.* (1970:595–6), speculates that Menander was *comes* of Africa.

84 Pliny, *Pan.* i:26:5–6. Admittedly, though, the *alimenta* grew out of private philanthropy, such as referred to in Pliny, *Ep.* vii:18 or *ILS* 977. These private donations were made in deference of a patron to his clients; *cf.* Hands (1968:108–15).

85 Zos., ii:38:3.

86 Zosimus notes, however, that Constantine was too free with imperial funds, which he characterizes as the mark of a poor emperor; ii:38:1.

87 *CTh* ix:15:1 (319).

88 Constantine also offered a law, *CTh* ix:18:1 (315), for enforcement in Africa, that dealt harshly with those who kidnapped children. It was not apparently a law that Augustine was familiar with. The fact that he mentions the fact of kidnapping slave-traders implies that the stricture was largely ignored or at least hard to enforce.

89 *D.* xx:3:5 and xl:4:29; Paul., *Sent.* ii:24:10 and v:1:1. See Evans Grubbs (1987), Appendix III.

90 *CTh* v:9:1 It is not clear whether a woman could claim an exposed child or not.

91 Although Justin Martyr states categorically that enslaved prostitution was the fate of exposed children; *Apol.*, xxvii–xxix.
92 For example, see *CJ* vii:51:1 (294–305?).
93 *CTh* v:10:1 (329). It is likely that the law applied to all of Italy as Evans Grubbs (1987:197) suggests: *CJ* iv:43:2 (329) seems to make the same provisions and seems to come from the same law, but is directed to all provincials. The distinction, parenthetically, is an interesting separation: it implies that the dichotomy between Italy and the rest of the Empire still survived, at least in the legal rhetoric.
94 This follows a *subscriptio* of Constantine, written *c.* 315 to a private individual, which sets out much of the same reasoning; *Frag. Vat.* 34 in *FIRA*², ii:468–9.
95 Future laws governing exposure required the officiation of a bishop to legitimize the transfer of the abandoned child to its rescuer, *CTh* v:9:2 (412). No doubt the government hoped that a child would be raised as an adoptee rather than as a slave.
96 *CTh* ix:14:1 (374).
97 For examples of enforcing public services: *CTh* xi:16:4 (374) and xv:2:1 (330). For hereditary occupations: *CTh* vii:22:1 (319), xiii:5:1 (314) and 2 (315).
98 *CTh* iii:30.
99 *CTh* iii:30:2 (316), 4 (331) and 5 (333), respectively. For gifts, *CTh* viii:12:1:pr (316).
100 *CTh* iii:32:2 (326?). There are problems with interpreting this law, however, as it is fragmentary.
101 We should also note that *tutores* were responsible for protecting the virginity of their female wards as well. *CTh* ix:8:1 (326) prevents a girl from marrying a suitor until her virginity is proven. If the tutor is, moreover, found to have violated the girl himself, his property was taken and he was exiled to an island. This undoubtedly provided considerable comfort for the *pupilla*.
102 *CTh* ii:24:1 (321). In the case of grandchildren, however, the *testator* had to be the paternal grandfather. Constantine was preserving the concept of the agnatic line's dominance.
103 *CJ* vi:21:15 (334).
104 *CTh* viii:18:1–3 (319, 319, 334). *CTh* viii:18:2, however, decreed that a father who emancipates his child after his mother's death was entitled to one third of the mother's estate.
105 *CTh* ii:2:1.This law have only been in effect in the East: the subscription notes that it was received in Corinth.
106 *CTh* ii:16:2 (315).
107 *CTh* ii:17:1 (321). The age for such actions – *firmata aetas* – was 20 for men and 18 for women.
108 See *D.* l:16:195. Ulpian gives several definitions of *familia*, including kin, extended relations, slaves and property: '*nam et in res et in personas deducitur*'; 'for it relates to things and to persons'.
109 Hor., *Sat.* i:6:104–10.
110 *CTh* ix:12:1–2 (319, 326 or 329).
111 *CTh* ix:12:2: '*suis . . . vernulis*'.
112 As Keith Bradley put it, 'The loophole for the master is obvious': Bradley (1984:126, n. 79).

113 There are several examples of urban populations becoming incensed at the purposeful or involuntary killing of a slave or slaves: *e.g.* Tac., *Ann.* xiv:43:4 and 45:1; or Sen., *de clem.* i:15:1. Horace also noted that a master who murders his slaves was mad: *Sat.* i:3:80–2 and ii:3:128–30.

114 *CTh* iv:10:1 (332). It was addressed to the council of Byzacium.

115 *CJ* vii:14.

116 *CTh* iv:8:7 (331) refers to the lost law. This provision apparently extended to children of *colonae* mothers as well.

117 Jones (1964:682–3) for the army; (1964:51–2) for the *officia*. These numbers refer to the first half of the fourth century, after Diocletian's reforms.

118 *CTh* ii:25:1 (325). The date is uncertain. It could also be 334 CE.

119 *CTh* ii:25:1:pr. (334): 'For in truth who could allow children to be torn from their parents, sisters from their brothers, [and] wives from their husbands?'

120 *CTh* ii:25:1:pr. (334): 'In the case of . . . our estates in Sardinia which were recently divided up among various landowners [*domini*].'

121 See, however, Hopkins (1983:52–3) for evidence in Egypt. He notes that there are no records of husbands and wives or husbands with wives and children being sold as a group.

122 *CTh* ii:25:1:2 (334): 'And be on guard that in the future in your province there are no more complaints concerning the separation of those dear to slave families.'

4 MARRIAGE

1 For the Jews, these included prohibitions on building new temples: *CTh* xvi:8:22 (415), 25 (423), and 27 (423); no 'provocative' rites: *N. Just.* cxlvi (533); and expulsion from the army and the *officia*: *CTh* xvi:8:24 (418); cf. *N. Th.* iii:1 , 5–6 (438) and *CJ* i:9:18 (no date).

2 As occasioned in the brutal murder of the Neoplatonist philosopher, Hypatia, by Christians at the instigation of the Alexandrian bishop, Cyril; Soc., *HE* vii:15. Ambrose, to cite a Jewish example, protected the bishop and people of Callincum from the emperor's justice after they burnt a local synagogue; Amb., *Ep.* 11 and 12.

3 *De civ. Dei* xviii:51: 'Moreover, in order that love be shown even to her enemies, [heretics] exercise [the Church's] benevolence and even beneficence, whether this takes the form of persuasive teaching or stern discipline.' *Cf.* xviii:51–4:*passim.*

4 Augustine, in a letter to Marcellinus, however, mentions that floggings were common in episcopal courts; *Ep.* 133:2. But it is not clear whether these courts had the legal authority to carry out such punishments, particularly among the *honestiores*; cf. Aug., *Ep.* 9*.

5 A third work, *De incompetentibus nuptiis*, or *On adulterous marriages*, is also frequently included. It was not a direct response to Jovinian, since it was written much later in 419 or 420, but clearly many of the same issues were being addressed. The work was not originally meant to be published as a treatise, or at least not in its surviving form. It was circulated and published by Pollentius, to whom it had been addressed, as a letter answering various errors he had concerning divorce and remarriage; *de incomp. nupt.* ii:1.

6 Aug., *de civ. Dei* xv:16:3; *cf. de bono coniug.* i:1.

7 *Ep. ad cast.* v–vi. The author is commenting on I Cor. 7:6–9.

8 For the most recent discussion of Jovinian's ministry, see Hunter (1987), where Hunter argues that Jovinian was combating what he perceived as Manichaean tendencies among Christian ascetics.

9 Jer., *Adv. Jov.* i:13–15.

10 Carthage (398), canon 13. This incidentally illustrates how much marriage was still a legal contract, even among Christians. The Church ceremony remained optional until well into the medieval period. The development of an impressive and powerful ceremony, however, had been developed in the third and fourth centuries; Gaudemet (1958:515–39).

11 Aug., *de bono coniug.* vii. Augustine actually uses the word '*sacramentum*'.

12 Aug., *de bono coniug.* i: 'It is therefore so that the first natural tie of human society is the bond of husband and wife.' Brent Shaw has noted the Stoic influence in this passage, referring back to Cic., *de off.* i:17:54; Shaw (1987a:11, n. 16).

13 See his *de incomp. nupt.* ii:4, where Augustine attacks the possibility of remarriage, even in cases of divorce because of adultery.

14 Aug., *de bono coniug.* iii: 'a natural affinity between the sexes'.

15 Aug., *de bono coniug.* iii. Cf. Brown (1988:402–4).

16 Jer., *Adv. Jov.* i:29.

17 Aug., *de civ. Dei* xiii:23. Cf. Aug., *de Gen. ad litt.* 3.

18 Aug., *Serm.* 51:15.

19 See Aug., *de sanct. virg.* xlv; *cf.* Aug., *Enarr. in psalmos* cxx:13 and cxxxvii:3.

20 Jerome's sharp tongue, however, was nothing if not entertaining. He perhaps summed up his views of marriage best in a letter on widowhood to the noble lady, Furia: *Ep.* 54:4:

> *Quid angustiarum habeant nuptiae, didicisti in ipsis nuptiis et quasi coturnicum carnibus usque ad nauseam saturata es. Amarissimam choleram tuae sensere fauces, egessisti acescentes et morbidos cibos, relevasti aestuantem stomachum.* You have learned what anguish being married was in your own marriage and how you were filled almost to nausea with the flesh of quails [Num. xi:31–4]. For your mouth has tasted that most bitter bile, you have vomited up that sour and sickening food, and you have relieved your seething stomach.

21 Aug., *Ep.* 6*:3 and 5.

22 Aug., *de bono coniug.* iii: marriages forces a 'mother and father to be more moderate'.

23 Amm. Mar., xxxi:8:8.

24 Lux., *In mulierum pulchram castitati studentum*: 'Wouldn't it be wonderful to be the wife of someone similar to you?'

25 *CIL* vi:1779: 'preferring her husband to herself, and Rome to her husband, chaste, faithful, pure in mind and body, kind to others, and useful to the household gods'. Paulina died some time in the late fourth century.

26 '{Se}d lumen omne vel decus nomen viri.' There is some confusion concerning this extensive inscription. The front of the base seems to be commemorating the death of Paulina by Praetextatus, but the rear seems to be honoring the memory

of the latter by his wife. This may represent the words of both partners. Since the front of the base does not survive complete, it is likely that it was inscribed when Paulina died, sometime after Praetextatus' death.

27 For example, *CIL* ix:5300 in Picenum. See Shaw and Saller (1984a).

28 *CIL* ix:5566, which uses almost identical language to the polytheist inscription, ix:5300. Catervius died sometime in the 380s.

29 See Arjava (1996:52–62).

30 Elvira, canon 54 (306); *CTh* iii:5:*passim*.

31 For more on Claudian, see Cameron, (1970); and Schanz *et al.* (1920:iv:2, 3–32). The poet also wrote *Fescennia de nuptiis Honori Augusti*.

32 Cameron (1970:98–101) for the date.

33 Honorius was, moreover, Maria's adoptive uncle, although no violations of sanguinity apparently existed. They were cousins of the fifth degree and thus did not violate *CTh* iii:12:3 (396). But it does show the prevalence of marrying relatives, at least in the imperial circles. Both Gallus Caesar and Julian married cousins once removed as well.

34 Holum (1982:49).

35 On Maria's death and Honorius' remarriage, see Zos. v:28:1. On Thermantia's repudiation, Zos. v:35:3 and v:37:5. Thermantia died in 415, possibly still married to Honorius, *Chron. Pasch.*, s.a. 415.

36 Claud., *Epith. de nup. Hon. Aug.* ll. 20–1.

37 *Epith.* ll. 10–13. A necklace supposedly worn by Livia and other empresses is the prized gift.

38 *Epith.* l. 28: 'I have not violently ravished a woman joined in marriage to another.'

39 *Epith.* ll. 31–2: 'A suppliant, I have rejected my station and have acted the noble suitor.'

40 *Epith.* ll. 32–3.

41 *Epith.* ll. 37–8: 'Pay back to me the interest due my father, and return to the palace its own.' The implication, of course, is that Maria is worth even more than Serena because she was the daughter of both Serena *and* Stilicho.

42 *Epith.* ll. 300–5.

43 *Epith.* l. 44: 'Why not give a child born to you to your foster-son?' Gaius seems to imply that this was a relatively common event; *G.* i:60.

44 *Epith.* ll. 229–32: 'She [Maria], however, being secure from thoughts of the wedding bed and not being aware of her impending nuptials, delighted in the lessons of her holy mother and took drink of her motherly morals and stories so as to learn old-fashioned chastity.'

45 *Epith.* ll. 256–7: 'live the common life of a private citizen'.

46 *Epith.* l. 260.

47 *Epith.* l. 340–1.

48 *Epith.* ll. 282–94. Nothing apparently came of it.

49 *Epith.* ll. 295–341.

50 See *CTh* iii:5:1–3 (319, 319 and 330), 6 (335), 8 (363), 10 (380), 13 (428), 13:3–4 (422, 428); viii:13:5 (393), 15:6 (380); and ix:42:1 (321).

51 One Jewish marriage contract, dated at 417, seems to recapitulate all this, although it is clearly much more affected by Greek law than Roman; see Sirat *et al.* (1986). A second divorce contract, this one from Egypt and so also more

subject to Greek influence, describes a case where the groom promised an orphaned girl various gifts with the agreement of her legal guardian. The man was not able to provide the gifts immediately, so gave her a promissory note! See Bagnall (1993:192–3). While these examples are Eastern, they do substantiate a general behavior pattern for Mediterranean peoples. The evidence for this applying to Western regions must remain legal, but these surviving papyri do add circumstantial evidence. Finally, we know that so-called nuptial donations were made by husbands before marriage as a surety for prospective wives. While also Eastern in origin, its popularity allowed it to spread westward in the fifth and sixth centuries; see Katzoff (1985).

52 Amb., *Ep.* 83:3: '*Illam paternae electionis praerogativa attolis atque erigit*'; 'The prerogative of a father in choosing [his daughter-in-law] ennobles and elevates her.'

53 *CTh* iii:5:12 (422).

54 Aug., *Conf.* vi:13:23. See also Chapter 6.

55 She had also chosen to remain unmarried and had at least two other children, Navigius and an unnamed daughter.

56 *Cento nuptialis*, ll. 33–45.

57 *Epith.* ll. 232–3: 'to unroll the scrolls of Latin and Greek authors'.

58 For an example of the physical freedom of women in the Greek world, see Patterson (1991).

59 As cited by Veyne (1987):19. See Bonner (1977:27–8, 135–6).

60 Although Jerome and other Christians had sung their praises and tried to recreate wool-making as a wifely virtue; for example, Jer., *Ep.* 107:10.

61 Gaud., *Serm.* 9. Admittedly, Gaudentius made this argument to encourage *permanent* virginity among many girls.

62 Jer., *Ep.* 107. See Chapter 6.

63 Symm., *Ep.* vi:1–81. Some of these letters are addressed to his daughter as well. Ironically, and perhaps indicating the relative worth of women, Symmachus never addresses her by name.

64 *CIL* vi:1782 (*ILS* 2947).

65 Symm., *Ep.* iv:4; cf. ix:93, 106–7.

66 See Martindale (1980:1042–3; 1046–7).

67 Symm., *Eps.* vi:3, vii:120; ix:7, 43, 49.

68 Discussed in detail in the anonymous *Carmen adv. Flavianum*. At one point, the author accused Nicomachus of trying to bribe Christians to return to the old religion; *Car. adv. Flav.* ll. 79–80.

69 For Nicomachus' support, see Ruf., *HE* ii:33; cf. Soz., *HE* vii:22. He subsequently committed suicide at Theodosius' victory. See also McLynn (1994:343–4, 361–2).

70 Symm., *Ep.* iv:14: 'joining together our children out of need'.

71 Amb., *de virg.* i:11:65–6.

72 See Brown (1988:343–5).

73 Aug., *Ep.* 3*.

74 Plut., *Quaest. Rom.* 1–2, 7, 29–31, and 86–7 offer descriptions of traditional Roman marriage ceremonies.

75 For a good summary of the *Iuris Civilis*' codification, see Honoré (1986). *Cf.* Harries and Wood (1993:19–67).

76 *CJ* i:17:2 :1 (533).

77 *CJ* i:17:2:*passim.*

78 Lib., *Or.* i:145, which is an autobiography of sorts. Libanius expressed in the same passage his happiness in Valens for copying his Western colleague by enacting a similar law.

79 See, for example, *CTh* ii:25:1 (334) on slave families.

80 *CTh* ii:1:7 (392).

81 *CTh* xvi:2:10 (probably issued in 353). It refers to a no longer extant law of Constantine, probably issued in 320. The exemption also applied to a cleric's children and slaves. Constantine himself had in 333 exempted physicians and professors, along with their families from municipal obligations; *CTh* xiii:3:3 (333); *cf. CTh* xiii:3:16 (414) and *CJ* x:53:6 (321).

82 See Arjava (1996:76–101). See also Chapter 6.

83 *CTh* viii:13:4 (355).

84 *CTh* viii:19:1 (426).

85 *CTh* iv:13:6 (366). Despite its place of issuance, however, the law may have been in effect only in the East: it was addressed to the *praetorio praefectus orientis,* Saturninus Secundus Salustius.

86 *CTh* x:20:5 (371), addressed to Philematus, who was *comes sacrarum largitionum* for the West. Presumably he was charged with overseeing that group of imperial servants.

87 For example, *CTh* x:20:10 (330), *CJ* viii:16:8 (422), xi:59:13 (414).

88 For the importance of legal *formulae* and the formulary system, see Nicholas (1962:19–28). Spoken *formulae* had disappeared in late antiquity, replaced by the *cognitio extraordinaria,* but the importance of the written contract endured.

89 *CTh* iii:16:1 (321).

90 *CJ* v:3:16 (336).

91 The amount of legislation on these issues which came out of the Eastern Empire is significant. *CTh* iii:13:4 (428), for example, states plainly that dowries would be considered legal, even if the formula was not correct. Another law, *CTh* iii:5:13 (428), infers that gifts of less than 200 *solidi* were permissible, since they could be recovered even if they were not publicly recorded. The reasons for the issuance of these constitutions in the East rather than the West or both halves of the Empire is not clear. Certainly, they were theoretically valid for the whole Roman world after 438 (the publication date of the *Codex Theodosianus*), but that begs the question. The matter remains unresolved.

92 *CTh* viii:15:6 (380).

93 *CTh* iii:5:8 (363).

94 *CTh* iii:13:3 (422).

95 *CJ* v:4:22 (428).

96 Carthage (398), canon 13. The canon also instructed the newly married couple to refrain from consummating the marriage on their wedding night out of respect for that blessing. But it was not until the tenth century that such blessings were required under law.

97 Paul. Mil., *V. Amb.* 27:5.

98 On privileges, see, for example, *CTh* xvi:2:10 (353); on judicial powers, see *Sirm. Cons.* i–iii. A comprehensive law on episcopal courts was published in 452: *N. Val.* xxxv:1.

99 Four such examples can be found in *CTh* ix:38:5–8 (all published 381), forgiving various crimes because of Easter. There were, however, several exceptions to these amnesties, which typically included murder, the rape of virgins, and adultery.

100 *N. Val.* xvii:1.

101 See Shaw and Saller (1984b) for a good discussion on the complexities involved with incest's definition and practice.

102 Suet., *Claud.* xxvi:3; Tac., *Ann.* xii:2. This third degree marriage was only permitted to a *patruus*; the *avunculus, amita*, and *matertera* could not. It was in any circumstance an uncommon occurrence; see Treggiari (1991:38–9).

103 See Humbert (1972) *passim*.

104 See Saller (1994:43–69). Goody earlier took an opposing view, arguing for endogamous practices: Goody (1990:397).

105 Jer., *Ep.* 22:20.

106 Cooper (1992). For a somewhat different view, see Yarbrough (1976).

107 She drew upon Martindale *et al.* (1970 and 1980).

108 Salzman (1989). This in part refutes Peter Brown's argument that women as wives and mothers had a more influential role: Brown (1961).

109 Schürer (1979, ii:578 and iii:410–11). It is important to note, however, that Schürer believed that the sect at Qumran were Essenes.

110 The fictive kin group, as anthropologists call it, is made up of individuals who are not related by marriage or blood and yet treat those in their group as family members. In the case of early Christianity, it can be seen in their language. They tended to refer to each other as *adelphhos* and *adelphe* (or *frater* in Latin). For more on fictive kin groups in early Christianity, see Malina (1986:100–6) and Moxnes (1997a). Cf. Bartchy (1991).

111 A notable exception is canon 12 from the regional council held at Hippo Regius in October 398. Under the presidency of archbishop Aurelius of Carthage, the council decreed that sons of the clergy could not marry polytheists, heretics or schismatics.

112 See for example, Amm. Mar. xxxi:7:11 or Oros., *Hist. adv. pag.* i:16:4.

113 Elvira (306), canon 11. That this rule appeared in the canons before the one proscribing such a marriage outright implies that Christian families also placed great responsibilities on the father and mother in the matter of contracting unions.

114 Aug., *Conf.* ix:9.

115 Aug., *Conf.* i:11.

116 Amb., *Ep.* 4:2.

117 Elvira (306), canons 16 and 17, respectively. Apparently, men were not forbidden to marry Jewish or pagan wives.

118 Elvira (306), canon 67. The terms seem to refer to effeminate or homosexual men, although Hefele argues that it refers to actors and men in the circus: Hefele (1893 i:165–6). Again, there appears to be no proscription against a man marrying a *tribas*.

119 Elvira, canon 78.

120 *CTh* iii:7:2 (388). Cf. *CJ* i:9:6 (388).

121 *CTh* xv:8:1 (383). Again, this, too, was issued in the East. A third law, addressed to the Western *magister equitum*, Theodorus, also prohibited marriage

between Roman citizens and barbarians; *CTh* iii:14:1 (370 or 373). But it was addressed to a military official who was actively campaigning against the Alemanni at the time of its issuance, and there were many prisoners who were captured and taken to farm the Po river valley; Amm. Mar. xxviii:5:15. *CTh* iii:14:1 therefore was likely a law discouraging Roman soldiers from taking captured barbarians as wives.

122 Amb., *Ep*. 40 gives the details. *Cf*. Paul. Mil., *V. Amb*. xxii–xxiii. For a recent interpretation of these events, see McLynn (1994:298–300).

123 For Hypatia, see Soc., *HE* vii:15.

124 See for example Basil, *Ep*. 160.

125 Min. Fel., *Oct*. 31. Cf. Theo., *ad Auto*. iii:4.

126 For example, Ps.-Clem., *Recogn*. ix:20.

127 Aug., *de civ. Dei* xxii:22. Of the sexual crimes, the list includes, '*fornicationes, adulteria, incesta et contra natura utriusque sexus tot stupra atque immunditiae, quas turpe est etiam dicere*' 'fornications, adultery, incest, and so many vile and foul vices against nature in both sexes, which are too dirty even too mention.'

128 *CTh* iii:12:1 (342). While, as we mentioned above, there were only a few examples of such marriages, and mostly around the time of the law's actual passage in the first century CE, this law seems to be concerned with stopping the practice in the province of Phoenicia, rather than halting the practice among Romans. See in comparison Lee (1988). It is perhaps ironic that Constantius' first wife was his first cousin.

129 Amb., *Ep*. 60. Among the moral arguments against it, Ambrose actually mentions *CTh* iii:12:1. Paternus had been under the impression that the law had been relaxed, perhaps suggesting that such unions were not as uncommon as we assume.

130 Elvira (306), canon 66.

131 Agde (506), canon 61. It included a brother's widow, a dead wife's sister, stepmothers, stepdaughters, an uncle's widow, nieces and nephews, and grand-nieces and nephews. *Cf*. Epaon (517), canon 30.

132 Rome (401), canon 61.

133 Orleans (511), canon 9.

134 *CTh* iii:12:2 (355).

135 There is some problem dating this constitution. The subscription reads that in addition to Constantius, it was issued by Constans and Julian (as Caesar). Clearly this is impossible, since Constans died in 350 and Julian did not receive the title of Caesar until November of 355 (some five months after the constitution's supposed publication).

136 'Even though it were deemed lawful by the ancients'.

137 Lee (1988) offers an important exception, although he discusses behavior that at best can be assigned to easternmost reaches of the Empire. Egyptian brother–sister marriages had officially ended in the third century, although probably it endured in more remote spots; see Hopkins (1980).

138 E.g., *CTh* xvi:2:8 (343), 10 (353), 14–15 (357, 360). While many of these benefits were enacted first for the Eastern clergy, they were extended to the West in 356; Jones (1964:118–19). Elliott (1978), however, has questioned whether these were actual tax privileges or simply attempts to close loopholes in a much-abused system.

139 For prohibitions on sacrifices, *CTh* xvi:10:2 (341) and 5 (353). For closure of temples, *CTh* xvi:10:4 (346). *CTh* xvi:10:3 (346) implies that it was permitted to destroy temples situated within city walls, unless they were associated with common amusements such as the circus.

140 Lib., *Or.* lxii:8.

141 See Michaels-Mudd (1979), where he argues that the emperor's Arianism was deeply felt, and thus repressive towards orthodox Christians and others. But see also Leedom (1978), where the author argues that Constantius' semi-Arianism was simply a political stance to encourage religious unity.

142 Perhaps a useful comparison is the Donatist schism in Africa and Augustine's approach to the problem. In Aug., *Ep.* 220, we learn that he attempted to deal with the controversy as a doctrinal issue, despite the practical issues associated with the division. In *Ep.* 235, written in 417 and sometimes called *de Correctione Donatistarum*, the bishop emphasized the heretical and criminal (*viz.* the *Circumcelliones*) aspects of Donatism, rather than the apparently real differences in attitudes towards familial and social relations: *Ep.* 235:47. Even in cases where disagreements on such things existed, the clergy *had* to emphasize doctrinal issues to establish their positions as orthodox. If therefore there were a variation of opinion between Athanasianism and Arianism about these issues, it is unlikely they would be emphasized. For an opposite opinion to this interpretation, see Harnack (1903). Harnack argues that there were visible differences of opinion in matters of marriage and virginity, at least in regards to the clergy, within Arian and Athanasian circles.

143 *CTh* iii:12:1 (342).

144 *CTh* iii:12:3:pr.

145 Since Constantius' first wife was a cousin, it is likely that the law was published some time after his death in 361.

146 It is difficult to tell from the language, '*hoc est ignium et proscriptionis*', but it was clearly not fatal. Based on the nature of the crime, it might have been branding instead of burning, since the latter was usually reserved for arson or treachery; see Crook (1967:273). *Cf. N. Val.* xxiii:4 (447), which proscribes branding in the case of violating tombs.

147 Agde (506), canon 61.

148 Bas., *Ep.* 160.

149 I suggest the date of 363 at the earliest based on the assumption that the Emperor Julian would not have passed a law which rejected Roman tradition and certainly not one with such a harsh sentence. I pick the year 395, since that was the year that Arcadius, the titular author of the law, became Augustus in his own right. Finally, I offer the possibility of a pre-379 date based on the admittedly arguable assumption that Arcadius would not overturn a law passed by his father, Theodosius, who acceded to the purple in that year.

150 See Clark (1984:1–13) for a good accounting of the multiple manuscripts and their relation to each other. Clark hypothesizes that the original *vita* was written in Greek and that a Latin version was written shortly thereafter. These lives do not include multiple mentions of her in Palladius *Lausiac History* and in the letters of Augustine, Jerome and Paulinus of Nola.

151 Symeon Logothetes, the tenth-century Byzantine scholar, offers the earliest complete Greek *vita*.

152 Elm (1994:100).

153 See Cox (1983), for a detailed discussion on the content and form of late antique *vitae*.

154 Jer., *Chron.* s.a. 377: not to be confused with the *Praefectus urbis*.

155 For the possible identity, see Martindale *et al.* (1970:753–4).

156 Although Melania the Elder outlived her son by 25 years.

157 *V. Mel.* 1.

158 *V. Mel.* 15. The Latin version says that Melania's properties brought in this income, apart from Pinian's. The modern-day value would be approximately $10.5 million (£7 million). They also owned an estate in Rome so valuable that not even the empress could afford to buy it: *V. Mel.* 14.

159 Olymp., *fr.* 44. There were 72 *solidi* to the pound. *Cf.* Clark (1984:95–6).

160 It is her parents who sent Melania to the baths, *V. Mel.* 2; and it is in her own private chapel that she prayed for deliverance from married life, *V. Mel.* 5.

161 *V. Mel.* 4.

162 *V. Mel.* 49.

163 *V. Mel.* 1.

164 *V. Mel.* 1: 'If and when by the ordinance of God we have two children to inherit our possessions, then both of us together shall renounce this world' (Elizabeth Clark translation).

165 Aug., *Ep.* 262. It is not clear when Augustine wrote to Ecdicia, although it was admittedly likely to have been some years after Pinian and Melania had resolved their differences. Augustine is quite forceful in condemning Ecdicia's behavior, and insists she be an ornament to her husband and to her religion by acting as a wife ought: *Ep.* 262:9.

166 *V. Mel.* 12. Greed, of course, is described as the family's motivating factor, yet slave unrest on the couple's property in the suburbs of Rome suggest that there was a desire in the family to keep their estates intact: *V. Mel.* 10. For a summary of alternative suggestions, Clark (1984:105–9).

167 They needed special dispensation to do so: *CTh* ii:17:1 (321 or 324). *Cf. CJ* ii:44:1–2. The *praefectus urbanus* had to approve any decisions to sell property owned by minors of Senatorial standing: *CTh* ii:17:1 (321).

168 This assumes that Melania was born in 385 and was indeed married at 14. Palladius says that Melania was 13; Pall., *Hist. Laus.* 54, 58, and 61. *Cf.* Aug., *Eps.* 124, 126, 202. For Melania's birthdate, see Clark (1984:196, n. 18).

169 Greg. Tuor., *Hist. Franc.* i:47.

170 For Celsus' death, Paul. Nol., *carmen* xxi, ll. 601–20. After that, he and his wife took up a religious life and moreover sold off their wealth to donate to charity; *carmen* xxi, ll. 421–7. *Cf.* Amb., *Ep.* 81 and Aus., *Ep.* 27:115–16 (who was greatly displeased by Paulinus' actions).

171 Aug., *de bono coniug.* vi.

172 Aug., *Ep.* 127.

173 As Paulinus of Nola had: *Ep.* 18:5.

174 For extended family households in rural areas, see Shaw (1984).

175 Symm., *Ep.* vii:1 referred to their separate residences. It was dated in 399, two years before the younger Symmachus' marriage. Moreover, we learn that his father was looking for a rhetoric tutor for the young man in 401, implying that his schooling may not have been complete and thus some years before his majority: *Ep.* vi:34.

176 John Chrysostum, *Contra eos qui subintroductus habent virgines* 4. For other examples of this behavior, see Sid. Ap., *Ep.* vi:2 and Paul. Nol., *Ep.* 44:4.

177 On Monnica's pursuit, see *Conf.* v:8; on her living with him at Milan, vi:1 and ix:4; and on her ill-fated trip with Augustine back to Africa, ix:8.

178 *V. Mel.* 4.

179 *V. Mel.* 10–11.

180 *V. Mel.* 6.

181 Aug., *de Gen. ad litt.* 9:5.

182 Jer., *Ep.* 22:20.

183 *V. Mel.* 49.

184 Aug., *de bono coniug.* vii. The term *sacramentum* in this instance may have a more general meaning of a divinely approved act.

185 Aug., *de bono coniug.* xiv.

186 Jer., *Adv. Helv.* xx.

187 Aug., *de incomp. nupt.* ii:12.

188 Jer., *Ep.* 22:13. See also Caes. Arles, *Serm.* 44:2.

189 Joh. Chrys., *de virginitate*, xix:1.

190 Aug., *Serm.* 51:15.

191 Aug., *de bono coniug.* xviii.

192 Aug., *de bono coniug.* xi.

193 Aug., *de bono coniug.* xvii.

194 Aug., *Serm.* 9:12 stated a clear equality between the sexes in this regard. The tone of much of this particular sermon is withering: Augustine seemed to be purposely antagonizing his male parishioners on the matter of conjugal fidelity: cf. 9:3–4.

195 Aug., *de incomp. nupt.* ii:7.

196 Hor., *Odes* iii:6.

197 But see *CTh* ix:40:2 (315), which implies definitively that a man could be criminally charged.

198 Aus., *Epi.* iii: *In Eumpinam adulteriam.*

199 Lux., *de oe qui uxorem suam prostare faciebat pro filiis habendis.* Proconius may have been a pseudonym, deriving perhaps from *procus.*

200 Paul. Pella, *Euch.*, ll. 159–68.

201 Paul. Pella, *Euch.* l. 167: 'touch of crime'.

202 Aug., *Conf.* ii:3.

203 Although see Klegeman (1957), for a Freudian interpretation of this incident.

204 Aug., *Serm.* 224:3.

205 *D.* xlviii:5:24:2.

206 There is a story in Palladius' *Historia Monachorum in Aegypto* in which a simple shepherd, Paul, found his wife in bed with a lover. But the husband chose the desert instead of murder, preferring to 'herd scorpions rather than live with an adulteress'. *Cf. Laus. Hist.* 22 and Soz., *HE* i:13. It was not until 1981, incidentally, that a partial defense of *ius occendi* in such cases was finally stricken from the books in the Italian parliament; see Cantarella (1991).

207 Only the senator Eumenius' fate is unclear; Amm. Mar., xxviii:1:48–9.

208 Eumenius, the fifth man, may have been executed as well.

209 *CTh* ix:40:10 (366); Matthews (1989:210). These punishments were subject to the approval of the emperor. Matthews suggests that the 367 law marked the starting point for these trials.

210 A law of Constantine, *CJ* ix:9:29:4 (326) orders that both husbands and wives were subject to the death penalty if found guilty of adultery, but it appears to have been appended at a much later date. Its survival in *CTh* ix:7:1 (326) makes no provisions for such punishments.

211 *CTh* ix:7:1 (326).

212 Brown (1970). *Cf.* Barb (1963), where he argues that magic represented the last breath of ancient religion.

213 Amm. Mar., xxviii:1:50–6.

214 Amm. Mar., xxviii:1:17–19.

215 Amm. Mar., xxviii:1:34–5, 48–50, 56. This never really made clear in Ammianus' account.

216 Amm. Mar., xxviii:1:28.

217 Although see Matthews (1989:216–17).

218 In the case of Aginatius, Ammianus clearly stated that the charges were brought by a political enemy; xxviii:1:30.

219 Aug., *Conf.* ix:13.

220 Aug., *Conf.* ix:9.

221 'For [Monnica] looked to [God] to show [Patricius] mercy, hoping that continence would appear with belief.'

222 Jer., *Ep.* 77:3: 'he had such terrible vice that not even a prostitute or a slave could handle it'.

223 *N. Maj.* ix:1 (459). This law made clear what punishments should befall individuals in cases of *'pudoris extincti'*. Majorian rebuked the *consularis*, Rogatianus, for allowing Ambrosius to live after his crime, but then orders those guilty of sleeping with another man's wife to forfeit their property and suffer permanent exile.

224 Jer., *Ep.* 1. The accused wife was also tortured, but did not confess and Jerome ebulliently described her hideously long execution. One suspects Jerome of hyperbole at several points.

225 At one point, for example, Augustine notes that his entire household was Christian except for his father; *Conf.* i:11. Despite his own polytheism, however, Patricius had no objections to having Augustine – and at least two of his siblings – raised Christian. He was also admired by all for the sacrifices he made to insure his gifted son's complete education: *Conf.* ii:3.

226 Aug., *Conf.* ix:9.

227 Toledo (400), canon 17 and Rome (402), canon 9.

228 Caes., *Serm.* 42:5.

229 Cass., *Var.* iv:12 and 46. See Chapter 5.

230 *N. Maj.* ix:1:pr (459): 'Ambrosius confessed to the nefarious crime.' *Cf.* Jer., *Ep.* 1:3 for the torture of an accused lover.

231 Aug., *Ep.* 78:6.

232 Salv., *de gub. Dei* iv:9.

233 Kirshner (1991).

234 For example, Aug., *Serm.* 224:2.

235 An analogous situation may be found in the area of 'mixed' marriages; see Cooper (1992).

236 Caes., *Serm.* 42.

237 Caes., *Serms.* 42:3 and 43:7.

238 For example, Aug., *Serm. 9,passim.*

239 Aug., *Serm.* 82:11. The complaints were brought anonymously in the *secretarium. Cf. Serm.* 9:4, where Augustine states categorically that the women were *not* complaining about their husbands. But it seems as if he may have been protecting them from possible repercussions. It is difficult to imagine who else would be protesting at such behavior.

240 Jer., *Ep.* 117.

241 Amm. Mar., xxi:16:6.

242 Fox (1986:353–4).

243 Sextus, *Sent.* 236.

244 Aug., *Conf.* ix:9.

245 See Tac., *Agr.* vi:1.

246 Brown in Veyne (1987:263).

247 Aug., *de serm. Dom. in mon.* i:43–5. He actually stated that any serious sin – murder, adultery, abuse or the like – was grounds for separation.

248 For example, see Epi., *adv. Haer.* lix:4, wherein he states that second marriages were permissible in cases of adultery or other serious transgressions in first marriages.

249 Aug., *de bono coniug.*, iii: 'A natural affinity between the sexes'.

250 Eph. 5:25 and Col. 3:19. Repeated in Aug., *de civ. Dei* xiv:23.

251 Aug., *Conf.* ix:9:

> Many women, whose faces were blackened by blows from men who were far more pleasant than her own, used to gossip among their friends and complain of the life with their husbands . . . And they were amazed, knowing how hot-tempered a husband with which my mother had to cope. And they remarked how surprising it was that they had never heard or seen any marks to show that Patricius had beaten his wife, or that even for one single day there had been any domestic disagreement between them.

252 Salv., *Ep.* 4. The matter is complicated by the passage's fragmented character.

253 Toledo (398), canon 7 permitted such punishments in certain circumstances.

254 *CJ* v:17:8 (449).

255 *N. Jus.* 22:15.

256 See, for example, Beaucamp (1976). It is important to mention that Beaucamp characterizes this language as something pre-Christian. See also Clark (1993:56–62).

257 Aug., *de civ. Dei* xix:16. Cf. Ps-Aug., *Serm.* 117:12.

258 Aug., *Serm.* 196:2.

259 Brown (1995:3–23).

260 See Salzman (1990:193–231).

261 See, however, Dixon (1992:83–90) for a discussion of their importance during the late Republic and early Empire.

5 ALTERNATIVES TO MARRIAGE

1 Two synods, one at Rome and one at Milan, both held in 390, condemned Jovinian's teachings on the equality of virgins, wives and widows. He also denied the virginity of Mary once Jesus was born.

2 Arles (314), canon 24.

3 Arles, canon 10.

4 Elvira (306), canon 8. *Cf.* canon 9, which states even if a woman leaves an adulterous husband she could not marry another. If she did, however, she could receive communion only in sickness or in death. *Cf.* canon 11 for even more specialized circumstances.

5 Vennes (465), canon 2.

6 Angers (453), canon 6. Presumably this referred to the divorced rather than cases of bigamy.

7 See Nathan (1993) for a brief summary.

8 Elvira (306), canon 69.

9 Elvira (306), canon 47. The rule goes on to state that he would be permanently excommunicated if he recovered and failed to change his behavior.

10 Carthage (407), canon 8. Paul's statement: I Cor. 7:10–11.

11 Although, see Honorius and Constantius III's reformulation of Constantine's divorce law (*CTh* iii:16:1), *CJ* ix:9:34 (421).

12 Elvira (306), canon 70. This ruling was similar to Augustus' law on adultery, which charged men with procuring for their wives if they knowingly allowed them to engage in these activities.

13 Arles, canon 22. This council was held either in 443 or 452. It is not immediately clear due to the corruption of the dating. Given the disorder in Gaul with the invasion of the Huns, not to mention the presence of other warring Germanic tribes, I prefer the earlier date.

14 Ambr., *Quaest. vet. et nov. Testam.* cxv:12.

15 They only required that a duly witnessed *repudium* be sent.

16 *CTh* iii:16:2 (421).

17 *CTh* iii:16:2:pr. (421).

18 *CTh* iii:16:2:pr. The constitution does not in fact specifically state what charge a husband could bring, but it is logical to assume it would have been one of adultery.

19 *CTh* iii:16:2:1.

20 His wife could also remarry after a year. Presumably the delay, like that of widowhood, was to resolve all questions of children born during that time.

21 *CTh* iii:16:2:2–3.

22 Arjava (1988); Arjava (1996:177–92).

23 Olymp., *fr.* 34.

24 See Oost (1968:165–7). *Cf.* Holum (1982:127–8).

25 Olymp., *fr.* 34.

26 Olymp., *fr.* 39. Many of his ministers were upset by his behavior as well and it apparently caused some financial burden on the Western court after his death.

27 Olymp., *fr.* 38.

28 Theophanes claimed he was murdered; Theo., *Chron.*, AM 5913.

29 *N. Jus.* cxvii:8–9, 12 (542). See Clark (1993:25–7) for a summary of those changes.

30 *N. Jus.* cxl (566).

31 A novel of Theodosius II, *N. Th.* xii:1 (439), implies there may have been.

32 *CJ* v:17:8 (450).

33 *N. Th.* xii:1 (439). It specifically rescinded all penalties for unilateral divorce, providing an official *repudium* had been sent by one of the parties.

34 *N. Val.* xxvi:1 (448).

35 *N. Val.* xxvi:1: 'so in the same way . . . they [both parts of the Empire] will also be governed by the same laws'.

36 See also *N. Jus.* xxii:15 (535).

37 For a full treatment on the subject, see Ville (1960). It is important to note, however, that there had been early in Rome's history opposition to women from respectable families attending the games, especially unattended: Val. Max., vi:3:11.

38 Carthage (398), canon 86, for example, instructed the newly baptized to avoid the theater and feasts for a period of time. Another, Arles (443 or 452), canon 20, condemns *agitores* and *actores* to excommunication until they quit their professions.

39 *CTh* ix:7:9 (383) required a trial had to be held in such cases, even if the accused had a military commitment.

40 *CTh* ix:2:5 (409). Immediate trials were required for homicide and rape as well.

41 *N. Maj.* ix:1 (459).

42 'The injury of another man's sorrow'; 'in a case of the disgrace of destroyed chastity and that highest crime'; 'the chastity of the marriage bed'.

43 For example, Greg. Tuor., *Hist. Franc.* i:47 or *V. Mel.* (Latin version), 6, where Melania's husband, Pinian, swears *castitas* if his wife recovers from a life-threatening illness.

44 *CJ* v:17:8 (449).

45 Ambr., *Quaest. vet. et nov. Testam.* cxv:12. The author was admittedly talking about the consequences of Julian's law on divorce, but it seems, too, that he thought imperial law in general was too lenient in this area.

46 See Corbier (1982). Cf. Treggiari (1991:473–82).

47 Raepsaet-Charlier (1981–2). Of these 27, 24 took place in the Julio-Claudian period and 15 within the imperial family. *Cf.* Treggiari (1991), Appendix 6, for a slight revision.

48 Kajanto (1969). One significant drawback to his study is that it is based on the surviving epigraphy. The commemoration of divorce on stone was not likely to be common. *Cf.* Dorken and Treggiari (1981).

49 Salzmann (1993:450–79).

50 See the appendix for the complete breakdown. There are of course some basic methodological problems with such a survey. The entries do not necessarily represent an accurate sampling of the society as a whole. They only deal with the most powerful portion of the population, something on the order of 1/10 of 1 percent of the whole. Indeed, we do not even know whether the surviving material is representative of these upper classes. Moreover, they may have been subject to forces that were not found in other classes of society and, by extension, there may have been forces to which they were not subject. Finally, our knowledge of these individuals varies greatly: it is possible that many more of these known individuals were separated. Nevertheless, we can say something

about the variety of reasons cited in divorce and gain some indication of the circumstances that facilitated a separation.

51 Jer., *Ep.* 77:3. Jerome teases his reader by almost describing the specific event that caused Fabiola to divorce her husband, but then demurs with '*paene dixi*'; 'I almost said it.'

52 Cass., *Var.* ii:10–11; iv: 40.

53 Even Jerome pointed out that this was technically wrong in his praise of the woman; Jer., *Ep*, 127:3: '*facile culpam fatebor*'. There may have been a second divorce, although it does not seem likely, between Rusticius and Artemia, over breaking a vow of continence: Jer., *Ep.* 122. But if so, Artemia wanted to be reconciled.

54 Olymp., *fr.* 38.

55 Arjava (1988). His paper takes into account both Eastern and Western marriage patterns. Although there are some problems with applying his assumptions to the West, Arjava has drawn a clear connection between the law and broader practices and beliefs.

56 Jer., *Chron.* s.a. 292. *Cf. CIL* xiv:2825 and 2826 (*ILS* 666 and 667), which attest to the first wife's offspring.

57 Raepsaet-Charlier (1981–2). She also notes that twenty-four of the divorces took place during the reign of the Julio-Claudians.

58 See Treggiari (1991:473–7). Treggiari also demonstrates, however, that often politics and marriage were kept separate: (1991:478–80).

59 *Chron. Pasch.*: 559.

60 Zos. v:35:5, 37:5.

61 Aug., *de civ. Dei* xv:16.

62 Schürer (1979:ii:240–2). Some Jews may have looked upon divorce and remarriage as polygamous; see Yadin (1972).

63 See Clark (1993:61). Cloke (1995:89–91) makes no mention of the order of widows in the patristic age surviving in any formal sense. *Cf.* Torjesen (1993:146–9). The order of widows seems to have died out in the East sometime in the fifth century; Herrin and Kazhdan (1991c).

64 Aug., *de sanct. vir.* 21.

65 Not until the eighth century did Byzantine jurists outlaw multiple marriages, summarized in the *Ecloga*. See Patlagean in Veyne (1987:597–604).

66 Lux., *Ana. in med.*

67 Jer., *Ep.* 123:10.

68 Livy, x:23. There were actually two cults, Pudicitia Patricia and Pudicitia Plebeia, with the implied memberships, but their rules for membership both insisted that a woman have had only one husband. See Nathan (forthcoming).

69 Jer., *Ep.* 54:2.

70 Brown (1988:148).

71 A law of Valentinian II, issued in 390, stated that deaconesses had to be at least 60 years old, have a certain number of children, had to make sure that all those children had tutors, and promise not to leave any of their monies to the Church or to any cleric. On the other hand, canon 26 of synod at Orange (441), completely forbade women to be so ordained. Chalcedon's (451) canon 15 did not go that far, but insisted that she must be at least 40 and cannot have been married.

72 Carthage (398), canon 101.

73 Jer., *Hom. in Psalm.* lv:14.

74 Lightman and Zeisel (1977).

75 Ter., *de Mon.* 17:3–5.

76 Jer., *Ep.* 77:4.

77 Amb., *de virg.* 10.

78 For an early example (first century BCE), Pub. Syr., *Max.* 260.

79 Amb., *de vid.* 88.

80 Chalcedon (451), canon 15, set the minimum age of deaconesses at 40. *N. Maj.* 6 (458) required women who had been widowed under that age to be remarried.

81 *CJ* vi:58:2 (532). For women's fertility rates, see Amunsden and Diers (1970).

82 *CTh* iii:17:4 (390). The widow herself, however, had to be an adult.

83 Dixon (1988). Chapter 7 on the mother–son relationship is particularly instructive: (1988:168–209).

84 Clark (1993:95–118) offers a useful synthesis on the issues of late Roman domesticity.

85 Jer., *Ep.* 7:6. He compares her to Anna, who recognized the baby Jesus as the Christ; Luke ii:36–9. On Anna and her importance to the role of widowhood, *cf.* Aug., *Serm.* 196:2 and 262:4; and Jer., *Ep.* 127:2.

86 Jer., *Ep.* 54:1. She theoretically was descended from Furius Camillus, the savior of Rome against the Gauls in 387 BCE. Jerome also relates her to the mother of the Gracchi, referring to '*Cornelia vestra*': *Ep.* 54:4.

87 Jer., *Ep.* 54:13.

88 Marcella in particular was extolled for her devotion to her own mother: Jer., *Ep.* 127:4.

89 Amb., *de vid.* 7, where Ambrose states that this is a widow's first responsibility.

90 Amb., *de vid.* 44: 'A widow rules the people; a widow leads armies; a widow chooses generals; and a widow decides victories and orders triumphs.'

91 Jer., *Ep.* 54:15: 'A mother does not set a stepfather over her children, but an enemy; not a parent, but a tyrant.'

92 See, for example, Amb. *de virg.* 3–5 and Aug., *Serm.* 239:3. Taken from I Kings 17:8–24.

93 Amb., *de vid.* 75–81.

94 While there were constant cries for marital fidelity, there seems to have been little pressure placed on men to remain celibate after the death of a spouse. Only the Novationists systematically discouraged remarriage for men; see Gregory (1975).

95 See Shaw (1987b). Working partially from epigraphical records for the entire imperial era, Shaw notes the endurance of the age difference. *Cf.* Hopkins (1964–65); Saller (1987b); and Shaw and Saller (1984a).

96 Aug., *Conf.* vi:13:23. He had, incidentally, sent away his concubine of thirteen years in preparation for the marriage.

97 See Lightman and Zeisel (1977:19–32).

98 See Kötting (1973).

99 Carthage (398), canon 101. See Lane Fox (1986):310 for evidence of support in the African town of Cirta in the early fourth century.

100 Eus., *HE* vi:43:11.

101 Sardica (343 or 344), canon 7. Sardica was meant to be an ecumenical council,

but the Eastern bishops demurred over the legitimacy of Athanasius. The Western bishops under the presidency of Ossius met, however, and so the canons were meant to apply to the whole West.

102 Carthage (398), canon 17.

103 Peter Brown (1988:148) notes some of the difficulties the early Church had with orders of widows.

104 Orange (441), canon 27. The council at Orange was held in November of 441. *Cf.* Aug., *Ep.* 3* for an actual case of a woman dedicating her widowhood to Christ.

105 Carthage (398), canon 104.

106 Elvira (306), canon 72. Should she marry again after that, however, she would be permanently excommunicated and her third husband would have to perform ten years of penance.

107 Arles (443 or 452), canon 21. The threat of excommunication extended to the widows who married while doing penance.

108 Agde (506), canon 13. *Cf.* Toledo (400), canon 18.

109 Toledo (400), canon 4. *Cf.* Toledo, canon 3.

110 Rome (386), canon 5. The matters before this synod were a number of issues raised by African clergymen, and so its decisions might have affected only the provinces of North Africa.

111 Aug., *Conf.* iii:4.

112 Aus., *Epita.* 35. This work was supposedly commemorating those who fought in the Trojan war, but the last several epitaphs are to Romans. She apparently died through complications of childbirth, but it is possible that Anicia was a fictional character as well.

113 Aug., *de fide et oper.* 35.

114 For example, *CJ* v:9:9 (529).

115 Typically one year in the event of death, but in the case of justified divorce, five years; *CTh* iii:16:2 (421).

116 See *CTh* viii:18:10 (426) and *N. Th.* xiv:1:6 (439); *cf. CTh* ii:16:3 (414), v:1:8 (426), viii:18:2 (319), and *CJ* vi:60:3 (426). See also laws published in the East: *CTh* ii:21:1 (358), iv:3:1 (393) and ix:42:10 (383).

117 Cass., *Var.* iv:12.

118 Cass., *Var.* iv:46. Theodoric ordered that the case go into arbitration.

119 Sid. Ap., *Ep.* vii:14:3.

120 Jer., *Ep.* 54:15.

121 As visible in Apuleius' depiction of the baker's wife; *Met.* ix:*passim*, but see especially ix:23–7.

122 *CJ* v:17:8 (449).

123 Soc., *HE* iv:34. She was also distrusted by Gratian for her Arian leanings; on the assassination, *Chron. Pasch.* p.562. *Cf.* Jones (1964:140, 158–9).

124 *ILS* 1264 (cf. *CIL* vi:31902, which contains the inscription in part): 'Your loving wife weeps tears for you day and night along with your small children – to have had lost your comforts, sadly being thrust onto the bed of widowhood.' Ceionius Iulianus died in September of 385 at the age of 42.

125 Sid. Ap., *Ep.* ii:8.

126 Aug., *Ep.* 104.

127 Salv., *Ep.* 1.

128 Amb., *de vid.* 28. One could scarcely imagine Jerome making such a rebuke.

129 Sid. Ap., *Ep.* vi:2.

130 Lux., *Ana. in med.*

131 See Martindale *et al.* (1970:226 and 300–1).

132 Aug., *Ep.* 3*:1.

133 *V. Mel.* 7.

134 Aus., *Epi.* xxiv:2: 'a chaste girl is an old woman'.

135 Jer., *Ep.* 54:18.

136 Marcella also had the advantage of not having to worry about pressure from her father, who had died about the same time as her husband.

137 He chose 'not to put a stepmother over his children'; *SHA Marcus* 29:10.

138 Amm. Mar. xxi:6:4. He finally did have a daughter, Constantia, although she was born posthumously.

139 Amb., *de vid.* 86.

140 Jer., *Ep.* 54:2.

141 Leo, *Ep.* 167:13.

142 Sid. Ap., *Ep.* ix:6:1. Sidonius calls it *'facilitate iuvenali'*. His slave-concubine was called a *contubernalis*.

143 Toledo (400), canon 17. *Cf.* Rome (402), canon 9. Of course, there were those, such as Constantine who did apparently have both; see Martindale *et al.* (1970:223).

144 Lux., *In eum, qui, cum senior dici nollet, multas sibi concubas faciebat.*

145 *Epitome novellae*, xxxiv:5 (ed. Hänel [1873]). Iulianus, the author, probably produced it in Constantinople, but its survival in the West implies that it was in part produced for Western provinces.

146 Jer., *Ep.* 125:6: 'I also know that some widows now in advanced age are pleased by young freedmen on many occasions; and calling them their spiritual sons, they little by little give vent to the license of marriage, overcoming decency and the fiction of the name of mother.'

147 Rapp (1994).

148 Procopius, *Anecdota* i:15–ii:25.

149 Prosp. Tiro, *Chron.* s.a. 423; *cf.* Olymp., *fr.* 40. The stories may have also been aggravated by Placidia's widowhood.

150 On the divorce, see *Chron. Pasch.* p. 559 (369); on marriage to Iustina, see Soc., *HE* iv:34. Socrates' account, not repeated elsewhere, states that Valentinian had issued a scandalous edict which permitted a man to have two wives and so wed Iustina while still married to Severa.

151 Agde (506), canon 25.

152 See Herrin and Kazhdan (1991b). *Cf.* Laiou (1985).

153 Jer., *adv. Jov.* i:15. The treatise was so criticized that it was actually removed from circulation; Jer., *Ep.* 49:2.

154 Aug., *Enarr. in psalmos* 25:ii:18.

155 Symm., *Ep.* ii:22.

156 See Holum (1982:30–44).

157 See Cameron (1985).

158 Sid. Ap., *Ep.* iv:21:1.

159 Aug., *Ep.* 3.

160 Aus., *Ep.* xii::2:32–4. Note that both Petronius and his wife, Anicia Faltonia

Proba, were only married once, but the example still holds. Four of their five children took the Anician name. Only three took Probus as well.

161 Symm., *Ep.* ii:22.

162 Both Aur. Vic., *Epit.* 39:2 and Anon. Val. i:2 use the term *filia* to describe her, even though she was actually fathered by Afranius Hannibalianus. See Martindale *et al.* (1970:407–8, 895 and 1128).

163 Mentioned in Symm., *Ep.* i:25.

164 *CTh* ix:25:1 (354). The subscription does not state where its issued, but since it was addressed to the city prefect, Memmius Orfitus, we can assume Rome. See also Evans Grubbs (1989).

165 For example, *N. Maj.* vi:1 (458).

166 *CTh* xiii:10:4 (368). It also extended to children who were not yet 20 or were not yet married.

167 *CTh* xvi:2:20 (370). The law is even more unusual in that is addressed to Damasus, the bishop of Rome. That he should be the addressee is intriguing: it implies that the bishop was considered at least an honorary official of the emperor. It also ties more closely imperial legislation to the Church hierarchy.

168 *CTh* iii:17:4 (390).

169 *N. Maj.* vi:1 (458). That it was a matter of manpower is related in the preamble: '*ut rem publicam armis et religione fundarent*'. 'that [our ancestors] should found the republic by arms and religion'.

170 See *CTh* iii:16:2.

171 *CTh* iii:16:2:1 (421).

172 *CTh* iii:8:2 (382). It was promulgated in the West 449; *N. Th* xiv:1 (439). Cf. *N. Maj.* vi:1 (458) and *N. Sev.* i:1 (463). This law modified the *senatusconsultum Tertullianum* of the second century CE.

173 *CTh* iii:8:3 (412). This was at variance with an Eastern constitution issued by Arcadius in 398, which stated that the usufruct went to her children should she remarry.

174 *CJ* v:9:2 (381).

175 Inn., *Ep.* 4:6.

176 See Treggiari (1981a:59).

177 Paul. Pella, *Euch.* ll. 155–78. He also had at least one illegitimate child from his affairs.

178 Aug., *Conf.* iv:2.

179 Aug., *Conf.* vi:15. In Roman divorces, the children always went with their father.

180 Augustine describes his son crying for Monnica at her death: *Conf.* ix:11.

181 Aug., *Conf.* vi:15.

182 Aug., *de bono coniug.* v.

183 Aug., *Serm.*, 392:2.

184 Toledo (400), canon 17. But it also provides that a man who has a concubine *and* a wife would be refused communion.

185 Rome (402), canons 9 and 11.

186 Elvira (306), canons 14 and 31.

187 Rome (402), canon 1; Arles (443 or 452), canon 52.

188 Jer., *Ep.* 54:2: 'And I wish solely that these men would imitate the public example of their women and that their shriveled old age would give them that which youth offers freely.'

189 Elvira (306), canons 9 and 72.
190 Carthage (398), canon 104.
191 Arles (443 or 452), canon 21.
192 Aus., *Epi.* 89:7–9: 'For should she not possess these qualities [Ausonius had earlier listed a number of lewd and vitriolic qualities], but rather acts chastely, modestly, and with a sense of shame, she will – I tremble to say – be my wife!'
193 See Aug., *Ep.* 20* for the case of Antoninus and Theod., *HE* xiii:16 for his own experience.
194 As noted by Boswell (1984:11–19).
195 For Judaism, see Schürer (1979:ii:240–1 and iii:175). For Rome, see Cameron and Kurht (1983) *passim.*
196 *CTh* ix:25:1 (354).
197 *CTh* ii:1:3 (357).
198 For example, *CTh* ix:25:2 (363).
199 Carthage (418), canon 18. This was the sixteenth synod of Carthage.
200 Chalcedon (451), canon 27. Those committing *raptus* or helping someone who had would be excommunicated. Clerics would lose their office.
201 *CTh* ix:25:3 (420).
202 *N. Maj.* vi:1 (458).
203 Orange (441), canon 29. See also Angers (453), canon 5 and Vennes (465), canon 4.
204 Chalcedon (41), canon 16.
205 Elvira (306), canon 13.
206 Rome (402), canon 2. *Cf.* canon 1, which also offers fallen virgins some hope of grace.
207 Elvira, canon 14.
208 Arles (443 or 452), canon 52.
209 Amb., *de excessu fratris Satyri* 30.

6 CHILDREN

1 Arjava (1996) *passim.*
2 For example, *CTh* xiii:10:4 (328), vi:4:2 (327), xiv:3:5 (364). A law of Constantine's, ii:17:1 (331), permitted males the age of 20 and females the age of 18 to petition for adult status.
3 The one exception, of course, is legislation regarding inheritance, but that mostly applied to all heirs, minor or adult. See Gaudemet (1960) and Saller (1991d).
4 Lyman (1974). But Arjava (1996:29) disagrees, save in the case of legal source material.
5 Wiedemann (1989).
6 Saller (1991c).
7 Among other contradictory opinions, see Hopkins, (1983:ch. 4); Dixon (1991); and Bradley (1991:13–75). There is some archeological evidence, too: more recently, Soren and Soren (1995) and Rose (1997).
8 Aug., *Conf.* i:10; Paul. Pella, *Euch.* ll. 117–41.
9 See Vigilius Tridentinus' account in his report of martyred Christians in the area; Vig. Tri., *Ep.* 1 and 2 (*PL* xiii, coll. 549–58). See also Lizzi (1990:169–72).

The missionaries had exacerbated the situation badly by disrupting an old lustration rite. See also Nathan (1998a).

10 See Elliott (1987:19), for the hagiographical *topos* of 'baptism by blood'.

11 Eus., *V. Cons*. iv:61:1–2.

12 Although Augustine, later in life and under pressure from the Pelagian position, argued for infant baptism; see especially his discussion in *de quant. anim*. xxxvi:80. *Cf. Serm*.131; *de nat. et gratia* lii:60–liv:64.

13 Aug., *de cat. rud*. 5–6. Chapters 29–40 actually gave a brief synopsis of biblical history, and chapter 46 is in part an exhortation to follow the Nicene creed.

14 Amb., *de myster*. iv:20.

15 Aug., *Ep*. 2*, for example, rebukes a nobleman, Firmus, for failing to take the final step while his wife had been baptized. See also the example of Victorinus in Milan; Aug., *Conf*. viii:2. *Cf. Ep*. 151:14.

16 Aug., *Conf*. i:11:1–4.

17 Arles (314), canon 10, noted that baptisms done even by heretics or schismatics might be legitimate as long as it was done in the name of the Trinity. It was a significant point, although there was never any ecumenical decision on this thorny issue.

18 Carthage (398), canon 37.

19 Carthage (401), canon 7.

20 Rome (447), discussed in Leo, *Ep*. 16 *passim*.

21 Most came out of the African synods of the late fourth and early fifth century. See, for example, Hippo Regius (398), canons 11, 13 and 31; and Carthage (401), canon 1. See also Toledo (400), canon 19.

22 Elvira (306), canon. 12. The canon refers to '*lenocinium*' of parents, suggesting that they equated such sales with pandering and consigning their children to prostitution.

23 *CTh* v:9:2 (412).

24 Vaison (442), canons 9 and 10.

25 Arles (443 or 452), canon 51; and Agde (506), canon 24. Indeed, in the fifth and sixth centuries, the Church, the imperial government and even private individuals all set up houses especially to provide for women who were former prostitutes.

26 Although the Church certainly welcomed former prostitutes: Elvira (306), canon 44. See, however, Arles (314), canons 4 and 5, which excommunicate Christian charioteers and theater employees respectively if they continue in their work.

27 *CTh* xv:8:2 (428).

28 *CJ* viii:47:10 (530) finally outlawed a father's right to choose whether to raise a child. But it was concern over the possible polytheistic roots of *ius vitae necisque* that inspired its passage, not the act in itself.

29 *CTh* iii:3:1 (391), which referred to '*parentum miseranda fortuna*'. Constantine had mentioned this as well, but instead offered material assistance: *CTh* xi:27:2 (322). One could see why: parental need could and probably was broadly interpreted.

30 *N. Val*. xxxiii:1 (451).

31 Most prominently in Aug., *Ep*. 10*:2.

32 Gaud., *Tract*. 8.

33 Aug., *Ep.* 20* for the whole story; *cf. Ep.* 209. While Antoninus' mother still lived, she was incapable of supporting him and permitted her son to live with other boys – '*consortes*' – in the monastery; *Ep.* 20*:2. The mother eventually became senile in a hospice set up for the widowed.

34 See above, Chapter 3.

35 Jones (1964:794–5).

36 Greg. Mag., *Ep.* ix:104. Gregory also ordered strong restrictions on Jews who dealt in Christian slaves in this letter, which perhaps implied another long-established tradition.

37 Aug., *Serm.* 124:3 and 344:11.

38 Theod., *Ep.* 70. Eudaemon was perhaps a provincial governor: Theoderet calls him 'most magnificent' (*megaloprepestatos*). The bishop in his letter was trying to secure a passage for the girl from bishop Eustathius of Aegae.

39 *CJ* vi:1:4 (317).

40 *FIRA*² iii:135.

41 For example, *N. Jus.* vii:8 (529).

42 Acacius of Amida in the 420s secured the release of 7,000 Persian soldiers, destined for slavery; Soc., *HE* vii:21.

43 Aug., *Ep.* 10*; *cf. Ep.* 24*.

44 *Ep.* 10*:3.

45 Aug., *Enarr. in psalmos* cxxvii:11.

46 Aug., *Ep.* 10*:6. Augustine called the 20-year-old man '*calculator notarius*'.

47 Amb., *de off.*, ii:70 and 136.

48 Self-imposed indentured servitude was apparently more common in the late Empire with a lack of skilled slaves: for example, *Oxy. Pap.* viii:1122 from Egypt. See Bagnall (1993:208–14, 216).

49 Soren and Soren (1995). Significantly, the find included numerous polytheist symbols of protection for the dead, although it is not clear whether this was a Christian burial site or not. Polytheist Romans in theory did not commemorate a child before the *dies lustricus*, when he or she was given a name. See Chapter 2.

50 Lib., *Or.* xxvii:6:14.

51 *N. Val.* xxxiii:1 (451). Valentinian even called it a '*genus pietatis*'!

52 Aug., *Ep.* 10*:3.

53 Aug, *de civ. Dei* xxi:13.

54 See Aug., *Ep.* 133.

55 Aug., *Serm.* 297:2. His tenuous distinction between the two, a fear of a master's torture and a fear of a father's love, rings rather hollow.

56 Prud., *praef.* ll. 7–8: 'My early years cried under the cracking of the whip.'

57 See Jer., *Ep.* 107:9.

58 Lux., *epitaphion de filia Oageis infantula*.

59 Marrou (1948); *cf.* Marrou (1937): *passim*. For a discussion of the educational system in late antiquity, see Roberts (1989) and Riché (1976:17–51). For the education of girls, something not addressed in Marrou, see Kaster (1983).

60 See, for example, Caes., *Serm.* 99, which is perhaps the most thorough condemnation in late antiquity. While there had always been criticisms of Graeco-Roman science and philosophy from the earliest Christian authors, they were not complete denunciations of classical learning and culture.

61 Brown (1992:35–70).

62 Aug., *Ep.* 118:1.
63 Paul. Pella, *Euch.* ll. 66–7.
64 For example, Jer., *Ep.* 107:9 and 12.
65 As the author himself modestly notes: Av. Vienn., *Ep.* 38.
66 Enn., *Ep.* v:14.
67 Joh. Cass., *Conl.* xvii:16.
68 Euch., *de laud. her.* 42–3.
69 *Reg. Mag.,* 50. *Cf.* Ben., *Reg.,* 55.
70 Paul. Pella, *Euch.* ll. 68–71.
71 Aus., *Ep.* 22:10–11: 'For boyish eagerness fails, unless fun is mixed in with serious studies and holidays with workdays.'
72 Paul. Pella, *Euch.* ll. 63–5; Jer., *Ep.* 107:4. For Laeta and her daughter Paula, see below.
73 For the dating and general information about this 'will', see Champlin (1987). Jerome mentions this particular work's popularity; *Commentarium in Isaiam, praef.*
74 Jer., *Ep.* 54:4: 'Or do you fear that the Furian line might die out and that your father will not have a little boy of yours, who will crawl upon his chest and ring his neck with shit?'
75 Jer., *Ep.* 107, written to Laeta *c.* 400. Sometimes titled *de institutione filiae.*
76 Aug., *de civ. Dei* xxi:13: 'But who would not shudder and decide to die, should he be forced to endure death or a return to infancy?'
77 Aug., *Conf.* i:7.
78 Aug., *Conf.* i:8.
79 Sid. Ap., *Ep.* v:16:5
80 *N. Jus.* cliii (541). This of course says nothing as to its continued practice; Boswell (1989): *passim.*
81 See, for example, Cass., *Var.* ii:14.
82 Caes., *ad virg.* 5.
83 *ILS* 1286, referring to Junius Bassus, praetorian prefect, who 'went to God as a neophyte' – that is, unbaptized.
84 Arjava (1996:41–52) and (1998). Arjava notes a key shift of parental authority once a child, especially a male, reached adulthood. But see below.
85 *CTh* viii:13:2 (349); and *CJ* x:48:2 (367). Additionally, a law of Valentinian III permitted a father to recover a gift given at emancipation in extreme cases: *CTh* viii:13:6 (426).
86 Aug., *de civ. Dei* xiv:18–24 provides an ingenious, if somewhat perverse distinction.
87 Aug., *de civ. Dei* x:1:12.
88 Amb., *Ep.* 73:4.
89 *Quer.,* act i, scene 1. On the date of the *Querolus,* see Duckworth (1942), vol. 2, 893–5.
90 Aug., *Serm.* 216:8. Augustine extends the list all the way to old age.
91 Paul. Pella, *Euch.* ll. 125–41. Admittedly, his parents were concerned about Paulinus' health and wanted to make him happy.
92 Aug., *Conf.* ii:3. Patricius got his wish, although he died not too long thereafter.
93 Aug., *Conf.* iv:2.
94 For the classical period, see Hallett's (1984) problematic study.

95 Although her behavior in the baths was a notable exception; *V. Mel.* 2.
96 Syro-Roman lawbook, L1. See Arjava (1996:65–7).
97 Brown (1988:259–65).
98 *V. Mel.* 3; Aug., *Conf.* vi:15.
99 Parkin (1992:120–5).
100 Sid. Ap., *Ep.* vii:2.
101 Lact., *Div. Inst.* vii:18.
102 Jer., *Hom. in Psalm.* 83:3 (trans. M.L. Ewald).
103 See Amb., *Ep.* 83:5–8, for example, Prodigal son: Luke 15:11–32.
104 As in Caes., *Serm.* 121:1, comparing fathers and sons to Isaac and Jacob.
105 See Herlihy (1985:127–30).
106 Quint., *Inst.* i:3:13.
107 For example, Sen., *de cons. sap.* xi:12, where Seneca compares children to dumb beasts.
108 As demonstrated by Saller (1991b:144–65). See the example of Galen, v:17–8 (Kühn).
109 Aug., *Conf.* ii:4. Later, in Carthage, he associated with a group of rich thugs called the 'Destroyers', whose major goal was causing trouble: iii:3.
110 Aug., *Conf.* i:9.
111 Aug., *Ep.* 133:2.
112 Aug., *Ep.* 9*. The man, as a member of the local *curiales*, was an *honestus* and complained (correctly) that such action was illegal.
113 See especially, *Serm.* 13:9 and 15A:3.
114 Aug., *Serm.* 9:20–1, given in 420 CE.
115 Paul. Pella, *Euch.* 187–94.
116 Aus., *Ep. in patrem* l. 18: '*non auxi, non minui rem*'.
117 Paul. Pella, *Euch.* ll. 210–13.
118 Aug., *Serm.* 13:9. *Cf.* Aug., *Ep.* 133.
119 Sid. Ap., *Ep.* iii:3:2: 'ball and dice, hawk and hound, horse and bow'.
120 Cass., *Var.* iii:46. The affair took place sometime between 507–512 CE.
121 Sid. Ap., *Ep.* ii:12.
122 Paul. Pella, *Euch.* l. 134: '[so that] from these activities I might regain my good health'.
123 Aug., *Serm.* 9:4.
124 See Shaw (1987a:23–7). Shaw fails to mention, however, the possibility of a suit claiming an *inofficiosus* testament, a common tactic of an unsatisfied heir.
125 Paul. Pella, *Euch.* ll.229–31.
126 Sid. Ap., *Ep.* iii:13.
127 Symm., *Ep.* iv:20 mentions that he started to relearn Greek with his son. *Eps.* vi:51 and 61, and viii:38 also mentions his involvement in the younger Symmachus' education.
128 Jerome makes one reference to a husband's responsibility for religious activity in *Ep.* 66 (*cf.* more extensively Paul. Nol., *Ep.* 13), but it is addressed to a man who had recently lost his wife and had no children. Pammachius, the addressee in both letters, was known for his charitable works. *Cf.* Pall., *Laus. Hist.* 62.
129 A child hitting a parent, accordingly, was a great perversion consistent with heresy. Augustine described with rhetorical relish a Donatist who regularly beat his mother: *Ep.* 34.

130 Paul. Pella, *Euch*. ll. 219–44.

131 *CJ* iii:28:28 (321) and *CTh* v:1:2 (369).

132 Aug., *Conf*. ix:9, in part describes the initial tension between Monnica and her mother-in-law when the elder first came to live in their house. *V. Mel*. 25 and 49 describe how Albina traveled with her daughter and son-in-law after her husband's death. Paul. Pella, *Euch*. ll. 457–60, mentions that both his mother *and* his mother-in-law were living in his house.

133 Av. Cameron (1989b:190).

134 Jer., *Ep*. 22:41.

135 Aug., *Serm*. 195:1–3.

136 Jer., *Ep*. 22:18: 'Let married women have their own time and title: to me virginity is dedicated in Mary and in Christ.'

137 Jer., *Ep*. 22:19: 'be fruitful and multiply'.

138 On the importance of wet-nurses in the classical world, see Bradley (1991:13–36).

139 See *CTh* ix:24:1 (320) for evidence of their influence over girls.

140 Pub. Syr., *Max*., 659.

141 Aug., *frag*., in Bede, *Comm. in I Thess*. ii.

142 Amb., *Ep*. 63:108: '*Matres, ablactate filios, diligite eos.*'

143 Plut., *Mor*. 496A.

144 See Sor., *Gyn*. i:19–21, where Soranus argues both the scientific *and* the moral reasons for this phenomenon.

145 *ICR* i:943 and 1093, dated 509 and 558, respectively. See also Greg. Mag., *Dial*. ii:1 for a description of Benedict's dour nurse in the late fifth century. Part of this change may have also been in terms of usage: in many medieval saints' lives, the term *nutrix* and the masculine *nutritor* refer to foster mother and father, respectively; Herlihy (1985:42).

146 See, for example, *ILS* 1066, 1202, 3235, 3542, 6486, 7446, 8203, 8365, 8379[a], 8531, 8532, 8536, 8537, 8538, and 8539. Many of these inscriptions are undated, but seem to range from the first century BCE to the early fourth century CE. See also Bradley (1991:35–6) for a list of *CIL* and *AE* references.

147 Prud., *lib. cath*. vii (*hymnus ieiunantium*), ll. 57–8: '*oblita lactis iam vieto in pectore matris tetendit serus infans ubera*'.

148 Aug., *Serm*., 10:4.

149 Amb., *Ep*. 63:108: 'not in the world, but upon it'.

150 Paul. Pella, *Euch*. ll. 63–7.

151 Aug., *de cur. pro mort. ger*. 7.

152 Jer., *Ep*. 107.

153 For example, Tac., *Ann*. iv:60. On a mother's control, see Dixon (1988:168–232).

154 Although Jerome admits it was difficult to get such individuals to teach small children: *Ep*. 107:4.

155 All references from Jer., *Ep*. 107:4; except her handmaid: 107:9 and godparents: 107:5.

156 *Ep*. 107:9.

157 *Ep*. 107:12.

158 If we are to believe Ammianus, however, the weddings of the wealthy could be as equally effusive: Amm. Mar. xiv:6:24.

159 Evils of the world, 107:6; attending church, 107:7; night vigils, 107:9; public

baths and slaves' weddings, 107:11; boys, 107:4; *cincinatti*, 107:9; eating habits, 107:8; and leaving the city, 107:11.

160 Clothes, 107:5 and 10; spindle and distaff, 107:10; make-up and jewelry, 107:5; and the ascetic life, 107:10.

161 Paul. Pella, *Euch*. ll. 27–32.

162 Theod., *Ep.* 70.

163 Don., *Comm. Terenti*, 594–5.

164 Elvira (306), canon 12, 68; Carthage (398), canon 13.

165 Aug., *Conf.* i:11.

166 Aug., *Conf.* ii:3 and 11–12.

167 Aug., *Conf.* v:8.

168 Aug., *Conf.* vi:1 and 13.

169 Aug., *Conf.* ix:10.

170 Pall., *Laus. Hist.* 54:3. *Cf.* Paul. Nol., *Ep.* 29:8–9 and Aug., *Ep.* 94.

171 Paul. Pella, *Euch*. ll. 59–64.

172 Aug., *Ep.* 150:1. She had apparently been about to marry when she decided on the virgin's veil, indicating there was some friction about the situation: Jer., *Ep.* 130:5–7.

173 Aug., *Ep.* 188.

174 Aug., *Ep.* 3*. The letter also parenthetically mentions another case of similar importance. Augustine wanted to know if the child of the recently deceased Innocentia was baptized before his mother died. Again, it suggests the centrality of the mother in the religious upbringing of her offspring.

175 Av. Cameron (1989b:195).

176 On explaining the complicated transformation of ascetic house to ascetic institution, see Elm (1994):88–102.

177 Cass., *Var.* iii:6:6.

178 Cass., *Var.* xi:1:5–8.

179 Jer., *Ep.* 125:7: 'See your mother often.'

180 Aug., *Enarr. in psalmos* 124:7.

181 See Shaw (1987a:8) for the example of the decurial home of Patricius, whom Augustine describes as '*municeps Thagastensis admodum tenuis*': *Conf.* ii:3:5. Possidius calls him '*de numero curialem*': *V. Aug.* 1:1.

182 See Bradley (1991:13–36) who argues that the reasons for wet-nursing a child were as varied as other modes of parental behavior.

183 Aug., *Conf.* ix:8.

184 Sid. Ap., *Ep.* v:19:1. Sidonius was particularly annoyed at the other master.

185 Indeed, the continued use of torture to elicit information from slaves regarding crimes of their *domini* inherently assumes this basic fact.

186 *V. Mel.* 2.

187 Aug., *Conf.* ix:8: 'She diligently carried out her duties of her masters' daughters, correcting them at the appropriate time with a holy severity and teaching them to lead wise and sober lives.'

188 See Saller (1987b).

189 Arjava (1996:48–52) and (1998) consider the legal evidence for such a conclusion.

190 Symm, Eps. iv:14; ix:93, 106–7; vii:1, 6, 132, 137; *CIL* vi:1782 (*ILS* 2947); Olymp., *fr.* 44.

191 *V. Mel.* 3. *Cf.* note 3 above.

192 *Cons. Phil.* ii:3:8. Admittedly, they were still minors, but the principle remained the same.
193 Suidas, A 3803.
194 Paul. Pella, *Euch.* 229–44.
195 *CTh* iii:17:4 (390). *Cf. CJ* ii:12:28 and v:35:2 and *Lex Burgundionum* 59, 85.
196 Aug., *Conf.* iii:4. She never did so.
197 Nathan (1997).
198 Jer., *Chron.* s.a. 377.
199 Greg. of Nyssa, *V. Mac. passim.*
200 See, for example, Egeria, *Peregrinatio*, a surviving account of an aristocratic woman's travels. Jerome is particularly critical of such women: *Ep.* 54.
201 Aur. Vict., *Epit.* xli:12; Zos. ii:29:2; *Cf.* Suidas, s.v. *Krispos.*
202 See Holum (1982) *passim* for some fifth-century examples.
203 Aug., *Conf.* ix:9.
204 *Laud. Tur.* ii:35.
205 Cass., *Var.* ii:14.
206 Plut., *Cato* 20, where the Censor not only taught his son literature and the law, but also athletics and combat.

7 THE EXTENDED FAMILY

1 For example, Rawson (1986), (1991), and Rawson and Weaver (1997); Dixon (1992), Kertzer and Saller (1991), Arjava (1996) and Saller (1994).
2 Shaw (1984).
3 *CTh* ix:13:1 (365). Of course, should a crime be too heinous, the seniors were to bring the youth before a judge.
4 See Arjava (1996:41–52).
5 Arjava (1998:33, n. 91).
6 *CTh* ix:40:18 (399).
7 *CJ* vi:30:15 (349); cf. *CJ* vi:14:3 (349).
8 *CTh* v:1:8 (426).
9 *CTh* viii:18:4 (339), but apparently not valid in the West until 438.
10 *D.* xlviii:9. The list included parents, grandparents, siblings, first cousins, aunts and uncles, spouse, parents- and siblings-in-law, step parents and children, and patrons (*D.* xlviii:9:1).
11 Amb., *Ep.* 20.
12 Carthage (398), canon 83. The poor were also included in this admonishment.
13 Although apparently this son died in infancy: *Par.* x.
14 Aus., *Par.* vi:1–5 (fragmentary) and xxiii:11–12.
15 Bettini (1991:1–112), esp. 106–12.
16 See Saller (1997), however, for a thoughtful criticism of Bettini.
17 Aus., *Par. praef.*:5–18.
18 Fowler (1899:309); Ovid, *Fasti* ii:533–616.
19 Aug., *Ep.*, 22:3. Augustine also admitted that Christians seemed to have indulged in this practice as well. *Cf.* Amb., *de helia et ieiunio* 17:62.
20 The November 2nd celebration of the Christian rite was established in the tenth century; no official religious holidays exist in the Roman *fasti* from that time. Prior to that period, however, All Soul's Day's commemoration was uncertain

and thus it is possible that it was celebrated at the same time as the pagan festival.

21 Aus., *Par. praef.*:11–12: 'those whose ashes were interred are joyful at the utterance of their names: just as their graves with epitaphs so decree.'

22 Green (1991:298–9).

23 Aus., *Par.* xxix. Admittedly, Melania had died when she was still a child.

24 See Guastella (1980), however, who argues that the importance placed on uncles is an echo of earlier Celtic custom.

25 Aus., *Par.* xxii:9: 'I was not known to you nor were you joined to me by blood.'

26 Ausonius mentions in passing a certain Arborius who was apparently an Aeduan of some renown, perhaps one of the *vergobreti* (the Celtic equivalent of *duumvir*) who ruled the ancient Aedui: *Par.* iv:1–6. Ausonius also mentioned that his great-great-grandfather and his son had been exiled by Victorinus and the Tetrici in the late 260s or 270s: iv:8–10. But these were passing references rather than formal eulogies.

27 See Étienne (1964).

28 See Chadwick, (1981:9–10, 40–1), for something of his career. *Cf.* Martindale (1980:454–6).

29 For a list of letters, see Martindale (1980:456).

30 Enn., *Ep.* i:14: '*alter parens*'. I am leery of calling this a patron–client relationship, since we are not clear on the extent to which Faustus helped the younger bishop. I am also reluctant to call it a formal friendship that existed between social equals (*amicitia*), since we know that they travelled in different social circles and Ennodius was moreover of a much lower station. Suffice it to say that Ennodius used the connection and based his use on the fact that Faustus was kin.

31 For Parthenius, *Dictio* x:*pr*, for Lupicinus, *Eps.* iii:15 and iii:28.

32 Enn., *Ep.* v:19.

33 Enn., *Eps.* v:9–12. This group included the former consul and prefect of the city, Anicius Acilius Aginantius Faustus Iunior.

34 Enn., *Eps.* vii:30 and 31.

35 Enn., *Ep.* ix:9.

36 It is unclear whether it was ever publicly delivered. A forum for such public addresses had largely disappeared.

37 She was a widow with little means of support: *Ep.* ix:29.

38 Enn., *Ep.* ii:23.

39 Enn., *Ep.* v:4.

40 Enn., *Ep.* vii:14

41 The son had retired to a monastery: *Ep.* vi:24.

42 Cass., *Var.* iv:12.

43 Enn., *Ep.* vii:14.

44 Cass., *Var.* iv:46.

45 Shaw (1984). There is, however, some regional variation. In Latium, for example, the rate is the highest, at almost 15 percent. In Christian, Rome, with the exception of the aristocracy, the rate is much lower at a few percent.

46 Hopkins (1983) *passim* and Shaw and Saller (1984a).

47 Aug., *Serm.* 356:3.

48 Greg. Tuor., *Hist. Franc.* iv:15.

49 Amb., *Ep.* 20, *de virginitate*; Caes, *Ep.* 21.

50 Klingshirn (1994:77).
51 Cass., *Div. Inst*. Xxiii:1.
52 Paul. Pella, *Euch*. ll. 325–7.
53 See Saller (1994:80–95). *Cf*. Saller (1984b).
54 Paulinus Festus, in Lindsay (1930:iv:94): 'It is named the Aemilian clan, which was composed of many families.'

8 HOUSEHOLD SLAVES

1 Aug., *Serm*. 356:6.
2 Sulp. Sev., *V. S. Mar*. 2.
3 See most recently, however, Grieser (1997). An earlier and more problematic study is Köpstein (1966). *Cf*. MacMullen (1987).
4 Garnsey and Saller (1987:71–3).
5 Col., *de Re Rust*. i:7:1–4.
6 Most emphatically by Carandini (1981).
7 *V. Mel*., 18.
8 *V. Mel*., 10–11.
9 Oros., *Hist. adv. Pag*., vii:37:16. *Cf*. Amb., *de off*. ii:15 in the case of Valens' army being captured at Adrianople in 378.
10 Although admittedly, Palladius does make one reference to slaves, i:6:18, but it seems to have been directed to free tenants; see Rogers (1970) *passim*.
11 *CTh* vii:13:13 (367) and 14 (397).
12 Symm., *Ep*. vi:58, 62 and 64. The resistance voiced by Symmachus undoubtedly represented the recalcitrance of most of the senatorial order. It is perhaps why there is no surviving decree ordering a slave enlistment.
13 Jones (1958).
14 *CTh* xi:1:26 (399).
15 Aug., *Ep*. 20*:17–20.
16 *CTh* viii:2:5 (401).
17 On some of the issues inherent in the problem, see Av. Cameron (1993:85–8).
18 MacMullen (1987). In the cities, he estimates the figure to be around 25 percent of the population.
19 See Korsunski (1978).
20 Amb., *Ep*. 37. The passage in question was I Cor. vii:23.
Aug., *de civ. Dei* xix:15. This was an idea shared by many eastern theologians, including Gregory Nanzianzos: *Or*. 5.
e canon survives in a collection of all canons, the *codex Canonem Ecclesiae* ae, but it cannot be assigned to any known synod or council. The canon also ed *infames*, actors, heretics, polytheists and Jews.
e (401), canon 16. Their request was odd, since Constantine eighty years mitted such actions provided that they were officiated by priests: *CTh* . Even Sozomen was aware of its passage when he mentions it in a enefits and rights Constantine bestowed upon the Church and i:9.
ion 7.
46.
16.

27 See Sen., *Ep. Mor.* xlviii:19.

28 Elvira (306), canon 41.

29 Arles (443 or 452), canon 53.

30 Lact., *Div. Inst.*, iii:18; Aug., *de civ. Dei* i:17–23. *Cf.* Grisé (1982).

31 Agde (506), canon 11.

32 See Veyne (1987:66–7) about this distinction: 'The alleged humanization of slavery was in reality a moralization, resulting not from some "natural" tendency of civilized humanity but from a particular historical development.'

33 Elvira (306), canon 5.

34 *CTh* ix:12:1 (319).

35 Gel., *fr.* 28. Actually, Gelasius ordered the *peculium* divested to his sons, as opposed to other individuals, since his patrimony was technically Church property. Nevertheless, the principle holds.

36 Jerome had warned Laeta to keep her daughter, Paula, away from slave weddings: *Ep.* 107:11. Whether Jerome considered them polytheistic or ribald or both, it is impossible to say. He may have thought them '*perstrepentes*'. The Byzantine government, by contrast, did not accept the validity of slave marriages until the eleventh century; Zepos and Zepos (1931:vol. i:343–6).

37 Orange (441), canon 5.

38 Orleans (511), canon 2. *Cf.* canon 1, which applied to murderers, adulterers, and thieves.

39 Orange (441), canon 6; and Orleans (511), canon 3.

40 By the same token, criminals were not given permanent protection, but simply guarded against the summary judgment of outraged individuals. They still had to answer any charges brought against them.

41 *CTh* ix:45:5 (432). It was not in effect in the west until 438.

42 Soc., *HE* vi:5.

43 Greg. Mag., *Ep.* iii:1, viii:22, and ix:19 testifies to its popularity.

44 Hopkins (1978: 99–132). *Cf.* his essay on slave inscriptions at Delphi, 133–71.

45 Kazhdan *et al.* (1991:1202).

46 For the formularies, see Sathas (1972:6:617–19).

47 Orange (441), canon 6; Orleans (511), canon 3.

48 *CTh* ix:45:5 (432): '*a clericis quorum interest nuntietur*'.

49 Paul. Mil., *V. Amb.* 43. Ambrose used his supernatural powers to punish the slave.

50 Recounted by Pope Gregory, *Ep.* iii:1.

51 *CTh* 9:45:3 (398) and *N. Val.* xxxv:1:3 (452) both forbade ordination altogether. Later, Justinian permitted it with a master's permission; *N. Jus.* cxxiii:1:17 (542). Cf. Gel., *Ep.* 20–3, for specific instances of trying to enforce these rules.

52 Such behavior was apparently more common in the later days of the Empire or at least it is better attested by the number of slave-collars from the third and fourth centuries. See *ILS* 8726–8733: of the eight examples, only two can be approximately dated. Both are from late antiquity. *Cf.* Veyne (1987:58), for a fourth-century example. *Cf.* Sotgiu (1973–4).

53 Aug., *Eps.* 108:18 and 185:15 both mention slaves running away to join the *circumcelliones* as well as threatening their masters directly. The group preferred to be called *Agonistici*, or the Soldiers, implying that they saw their actions as

more of a religious and social struggle than strictly criminal behavior; Opt., *contra Par. Don.* iii:1–5. For an argument for its essential religious origin and function, see Beaver (1935).

54 *N. Val.* xxi:2:1 (446).

55 *N. Val.* xxiii:1 (447).

56 *CTh* ix:7:4 (385).

57 *CTh* ix:6:2 (376).

58 *CTh* vii:18:9 (396).

59 *N. Val.* xxxv:1:3 (452). There was in this situation, however, a 30-year statute of limitations: xxxv:1:6.

60 *N. Maj.* vii:1 (458).

61 *N. Anth.* i:1 (468).

62 *CTh* ix:9:1 (326).

63 By using the term *matrimonia*, the law implies that these were full marriages, as opposed to *contubernia*.

64 *N. Th.* xviii:1 (439).

65 *CTh* xvi:9:1 (336), 2 (339), and 3 (415). *Cf. Sirm. Cons.* iv (336).

66 *Quer.*, Act II, scene 4. See also Nathan (1998b).

67 Aus., *Epi.* xxxvi. The slave, Pergamus, was described as a '*segnis scriptor*'. *Cf. Epi.* xxxvii.

68 Aus., *Epi.* lxxviii, entitled '*De castore fellatore qui suam lingebat uxorem*', 'Concerning the castrated cocksucker who licked his wife.'

69 See Dunn (1989:65–71). *Cf.* Puchner (1983). For its survival in the west, see *CJ* xi:41:5 (409), which prohibited city officials from deporting actors and charioteers from their municipalities.

70 Jer., *Ep.* 117:8: 'This kind of puny servant is argumentative and, no matter how much you give them, it is always not enough.'

71 Prop., iii:6:6: '*oderint dum metuant*'.

72 Amb., *Ep.* 2:31.

73 *CTh* ix:12:1 (319). *Cf.* ix:12:2 (326), where a further distinction is made between *voluntate occidendi* and *simpliciter facta castigatio*!

74 Sid. Ap., *Ep.* iv:12:3: '*mihi bilem nuntii huiusce contrarietas excitavit*'; 'this messenger excited in me such a hostile anger.'

75 'That man thick as a post.'

76 Sid. Ap., *Ep.* iv:12:4: 'frightened, trembling and stammering from guilt'.

77 Aug., *Conf.* ix:9.

78 'No one now dared say anything evil.'

79 Amm. Mar., xxviii:4:16. Presumably this was bath water.

80 See Hopkins (1978:172–5).

81 For their prices, see *CJ* vii:7:1 (530). An unskilled man or woman's price was arbitrarily set at 20 *solidi*. An untrained eunuch was worth 50.

82 *N. Jus.* clxii (558).

83 *CTh* ix:12:1–2 (319, 326).

84 See Elvira (306), canon 5.

85 Amm. Mar., xxviii:4:16.

86 Amm. Mar., xxix:9:4.

87 As outlined in Cantarella (1992: 217).

88 Paul. Pella, *Euch.* ll. 166–75.

89 Lact., *Div. Inst.* vi:23.

90 Foucault (1986:173). See Mus. Ruf., *fr.* 12.
91 Aug., *Conf.* ix:9.
92 Jer., *Ep.* 77:3.
93 See in particular *Serm.* 9.
94 Jer., *Ep.* 77:3.
95 Paul. Pella, *Euch.* l. 166: 'happy to have sexual encounters with the household slaves of my own house'.
96 Prud., *praef.* ll. 10–12.
97 Aug., *Serm.* 9:4.
98 Aug., *Serm.* 21:5. Augustine actually uses the word *consuetudo*.
99 Amm. Mar., xxvii:11:4.
100 Eug., *V. S. Sev.* 2.
101 *N. Sev.* 2:1.
102 *CTh* vii:13:8 (380) and 11 (382), and 18:9 (396) all forbade slaves from enlisting and provided the means for reclaiming them with no statute of limitations. For freedmen, see *CTh* iv:10:3 (426).
103 For laws, see *CTh* ix:45:3 (398), *N. Val.* xxxv:1 (452) and *CJ* i:3:36 (no date). Pope Leo was particularly critical of their ordination: *Ep.* 4:1.
104 Pach., *Praec.* 49. That this had applicability in the west is unknown, but Jerome did translate the *Praecepta* into Latin.
105 Pope Pelagius, *Ep.* 64. He was caught and returned to his *massa*.
106 The accounts are from Egypt and summarized in Bagnall (1993:210–12).
107 The monastery, situated on the great estate of *Lucullanum*, had a special status in the area since it had been founded by the last western emperor, Romulus Augustulus. See Nathan (1992).
108 Aug., *Ep.* 108:18 and 185:15; Opt., *contra Par. Don.* iii:1–5. See Frend (1969).
109 The classic article on this is still Thompson (1952), but see also Drinkwater (1984), where Drinkwater argues the opposite: the Bacaudae arose because of the third-century's political vacuum. See Van Dam (1985: 17–20, 30–3).
110 Rut. Nam., *de red. suo* ll. 213–18.
111 *Chron, Min.* 1, 600 for the year 435 CE: 'almost all of the slaves of Gaul conspired with the Bacaudae [in revolt]'.
112 Paul. Pella, *Euch.* ll. 328–36. Paulinus added enigmatically that the slaves were supported by a small faction of youths and were trying in particular to assassinate him.
113 We do know, however, that Melania's slaves inhabiting her estates in Latium were less than pleased by her intention to sell them: *V. Mel.* 10–11.
114 *Quer.*, act iv, scene 1: '*Immo tibi hercle, pellibus ossibusque vestris eveniat quidquid optasti mihi!*'
115 The *vindicta* was technically a rod which was used in the formal manumission ceremony.
116 *CJ* vii:6:1 (531).
117 *CTh* iv:10:3 (426).
118 See Shaw (1984) for the figures in Rome, Latium and Italy. It is significant that while there is a sizeable number of freedperson commemorations of patrons, few slave to master epitaphs survive in the late Roman world. The disparity is curious, but perhaps underscores the generally low condition and treatment of the enslaved.
119 Amm. Mar., xxvii:11:4. Petronius' defense of his clients, however, was not

exemplary: according to Ammianus, he '*sine respectu boni honestique defendebat*'; 'he would defend them without any respect for what was good or virtuous.'

120 Elvira (306), canon 80.
121 *CTh* xvi:9:3 (415) assured that support as long as they allowed their slaves and freedmen to practice their religion freely. See, however, *CJ* i:10:1 (336) and *CTh* xvi:9:2 (339) for restrictions placed on Jews.
122 *CJ* vi:7:2 (320).
123 *CTh* iv:10:2 (423).
124 *N. Val.* xxv:1:1 (447).
125 *CTh* ix:6:1 (376).
126 *CTh* ix:6:4 (423). Arcadius made an exception in the case of *maiestas*: *CTh* ix:6:3 (397).
127 Jer., *Ep.* 125:6.
128 Marc. comes, s.a. 434 and John of Antioch, *fr.* 199. It is true that often great landowners employed free men as *procuratores* and *conductores*, but that tended to be in the eastern Empire. The accusation made the affair all the more scandalous if Eugenius had been *libertini*.
129 *N. Anth.* 1:1 (468). Frequently they were slaves manumitted specifically for marriage. That the defendant in the case, Julia, was acting in her own name, implies that she was legally independent from any male kin or husband.
130 *N. Val.* xxv:1 (447).
131 For example, *CTh* xiv:3:9 (368) and 10 (365).
132 These freedmen, however, had a 'one-generation status'; see de Ste Croix (1981:174–9). For the role of eunuchs, see Hopkins (1978: 172–96).
133 The term '*libertinitas*' was used *passim* in the *Digesta*; *cf.*, Amb., *Comm. in Iac.* i:3:12.
134 Proc., *Anec.* i:15:1–2. Theodosius was described as a member of Belisaurius' '*oikia*', and while that does not definitively decide his status, since he was unrelated by kin, it is highly possible that he was a slave. The subsequent story of Theodosius' affair with his adopted mother, Antonina, would thus take on an added sordidness to it.
135 De Ste Croix, (1975:36).

9 FINAL THOUGHTS

1 Anon. (edited with the works of Ausonius; *cf.* Teubner, vol. 22): 'Custom allows nothing to seem strange to the eyes.'
2 Aug., *Serm.* 51:15.
3 For example, *CTh* v:1:1 (321), viii:18:5 (349), and 18:9 (426).
4 With the changes to *potestas* outlined by Arjava (1998).
5 *Julius Caesar*, Act 1, scene 2, l. 140.
6 Carthage (407), canon 8.
7 *CTh* iii:16:2 (421).
8 Evans Grubbs (1989).
9 In the case of Ambrose, see McLynn (1994:x–xvii).
10 As well as being accused of some less wholesome practices; Sulp. Sev., *Chron.* ii:46–51.
11 See Mango (1980:125–48, 233–55) for an overview.

12 *Ecloga* ii:9:1–3. See Delpini (1979:112–22). *Cf.* Herrin and Kazhdan (1991a).
13 Elm (1994) *passim.*
14 Bynum (1982).
15 Jer., *Ep.* 123:10.

BIBLIOGRAPHY

Amunsden, D.W. and Diers, C.J. (1970) 'The age of menopause in classical Greece and Rome', *Human Biology* 42, 79–86.

Anné, L. (1935) 'La conclusion du mariage dans la tradition et le droit de l'Église latine jusqu'au viᵉ siècle,' *Ephemerides Theologicae Lovaniensis* 12, 513–50.

—— (1941) *Les Rites de fiançailles et la donation pour cause de mariage sous le Bas-Empire* (Louvain).

Arav, R. (1989) 'Hellenistic Palestine settlement patterns and city planning 337–37 BCE', *BAR International Series*, 485 (Oxford).

Ariès, P. (1962) *Centuries of Childhood: A Social History of Family Life*, trans. R. Baldick (New York).

Ariès, P. and Duby, G. (eds) (1987–91) *A History of Private Life*, 4 vols (Cambridge).

Arjava, A. (1988) 'Divorce in later Roman law', *Arctos* 22, 5–21.

—— (1996) *Women and Law in Late Antiquity* (Oxford).

—— (1998) 'Paternal power in late antiquity', *Journal of Roman Studies* 88, 147–65.

Arnheim, M.T.W. (1972) *The Senatorial Aristocracy in the Later Roman Empire* (Oxford).

Attwater, D. (1983) *Dictionary of Saints*, 2nd edition (London).

Auerbach, E. (1953) *Mimesis*, trans. L. Trask (New York).

Badian, E. (1985) 'A phantom marriage law', *Philologus* 29, 82–98.

Bagnall, R. (1987) 'Church, state and divorce in late Roman Egypt', in R.E. Somerville and K.-L. Selig (eds) *Florilegium Columbianum: Essays in Honor of Paul Oskar Kristeller* (New York).

—— (1993) *Egypt in Late Antiquity* (Princeton).

Balsdon, J.P.V.D. (1969) *Life and Leisure in Ancient Rome* (London).

Barb, A.A. (1963) 'The survival of magic arts', in A. Momigliano (ed.) *The Conflict Between Christianity and Paganism in the Fourth Century* (Oxford), 100–25.

Barclay, J.M.G. (1997), 'The family as the bearer of religion in Judaism and early Christianity', in H. Moxnes (ed.) *Constructing Early Christian Families* (London).

Barker, D. (1985) 'Some findings from the census returns of Roman Egypt', *Ancient Society: Resources for Teachers* 15, 138–47.

Barnes, T.D. (1970) 'The lost Kaisergeschichte and the Latin historical tradition', *Bonner Historia-Augusta Colloquium* 1968/9, 13–27.

—— (1971) *Tertullian: A Historical and Literary Study* (Oxford).

—— (1981) *Constantine and Eusebius* (Cambridge).

—— (1982) *The New Empire of Diocletian and Constantine* (Cambridge, MA).

Bartchy, S. (1991) 'Community of goods in Acts: idealization or social reality?' in B.A. Pearson *et al.* (eds) *The Future of Early Christianity: Essays in Honor of Helmut Koester, 309–18.*

—— *(1992)* 'Philemon, Epistle to', in D.N. Freedman (ed.) *The Anchor Bible Dictionary*, vol. 5, (New York), 305–10.

—— (forthcoming) *Undermining Ancient Patriarchy: Paul of Tarsus on Gender Roles, Slave-Ownership, and Elite Privilege* (Peabody, Massachusetts).

Basanoff, V. (1936) 'Les sources chrétiennes de la loi de Constantine sur le repudium et le champ d'application de cette loi', *Studi in onore di S. Riccobono*, iii, 177–99.

Bauman, R. (1984–85) 'Family law and Roman politics', *Scritti in onore di Antonio Guarino* 3, 1283–330.

Beaucamp, J. (1976) 'Le vocabulaire de la faiblesse féminine dans les textes juridiques romains du iiie au vi^e siècle', *Revue historique de droit français et étranger* 54, 485–508.

Beaver, R.P. (1935) 'The Donatist circumcellions', *Church History* 4, 123–33.

Bender, D. (1967) 'A refinement of the concept of household: families, co-residence, and domestic functions', *American Anthropologist* 69, 493–504.

Benko, S. (1984) *Pagan Rome and the Early Christians* (Bloomington and Indianapolis).

Berrouard, M.F.O. (1972) 'Saint Augustin et l'indissolubilité du mariage: l'évolution de sa penseé', *Studia Patristica* 11, 291–306.

Bettini, M. (1991) *Anthropology and Roman Culture*, trans. J. Van Sickle (Baltimore).

Biondi, B. (1952) 'Vicendi postclassiche del SC. Claudiano', *Iura* 3, 142–54.

Boak, A.E.R. (1955) *Manpower Shortage and the Fall of the Roman Empire in the West* (Ann Arbor).

Bonner, S. (1977) *Education in Ancient Rome* (Berkeley).

Bornkamm, G. (1971) *Paul*, trans. by D.M.G. Stalker (New York).

Boswell, J. (1980) *Christianity, Social Tolerance and Homosexuality: Gay People in Western Europe from the Beginning of the Christian Era to the Fourteenth Century* (Chicago).

—— (1984) *'Expositio* and *oblatio*: the abandonment of children and the ancient and medieval family', *American Historical Review* 89, 10–33.

—— (1988) *The Kindness of Strangers* (New York).

—— (1994) *Same-Sex Unions in Pre-Modern Europe* (New York).

Boyarin, D. (1989) 'Language inscribed by history on the body of living beings: Midrash and martyrdom', *Representations* 25, 139–51.

Bradley, K. (1984) *Slaves and Masters in the Roman Empire* (Oxford).

—— (1986) 'Wet-nursing at Rome – a study in social relations', in B. Rawson (ed.) *The Family in Ancient Rome* (Ithaca), 201–29.

—— (1991) *Discovering the Roman Family* (Oxford).

Brown, P.R.L., (1961) 'Aspects of the Christianization of the Roman aristocracy', *Journal of Roman Studies* 51, 1–11.

—— (1967) *Augustine of Hippo* (Berkeley).

—— (1970) 'Sorcery, demons, and the rise of Christianity', originally published in M. Douglas (ed.) *Witchcraft, Confessions and Accusations*, 17–45. Reprinted in Brown's (1972) *Religion and Society in the Age of St. Augustine* (London), 119–46.

—— (1971) *The World of Late Antiquity* (London).

—— (1981) *The Cult of the Saints* (Chicago).

—— (1983) 'Sexuality and society in the fifth century AD: Augustine and Julian of

Eclanum', in E. Gabba (ed.) *Tria Corda. Studi in onore di Arnaldo Momigliano* (Como), 49–70.

—— (1988) *The Body and Society* (New York).

—— (1992) *Power and Persuasion in Late Antiquity* (Madison, Wisconsin).

—— (1995) *Authority and the Sacred* (Cambridge).

—— (1996) *Western Christendom* (Oxford).

Brown, T. (1984) *Gentleman and Officers: Imperial Administration and Aristocratic Power in Byzantine Italy, A.D. 554–800* (Rome).

Brunt, P.A. (1971) *Italian Manpower*, revised 1987 (Oxford).

Büchler, F. (1922) *Petronii Saturae et Liber Praeporum*, ed. W. Heraeus (Berlin).

Burnish, R.F.G. (1982) 'The role of godfather in the East in the fourth century', *Studia Patristica* 17, 558–64.

Bynum, C. (1984) *Jesus as Mother: Studies in the Spirituality of the High Middle Ages* (Berkeley).

Cameron, Alan (1970) *Claudian: Poetry and Propaganda at the Court of Honorius* (Oxford).

—— (1976) *Circus Factions* (Oxford).

—— (1985) 'Polyonomy in the late Roman aristocracy: the case of Petronius Probus', *Journal of Roman Studies* 75, 164–82.

—— (1988) 'Flavius: a nicety of protocol', *Latomus* 47, 26–33.

Cameron, Averil (ed.) (1989a) *History as Text: The Writing of Ancient History* (Chapel Hill).

—— (1989b) 'Virginity as metaphor: women and the rhetoric of early Christianity', in A. Cameron (ed.) *History as Text* (Chapel Hill), 181–205.

—— (1993) *The Mediterranean World in Late Antiquity AD 395–600* (London).

Cameron, Averil and Kurht, A. (eds) (1983) *Images of Women in Antiquity* (London).

—— (1986) 'Redrawing the map: Christian territory after Foucault', *Journal of Roman Studies* 76, 266–71.

Campbell, J.B. (1978) 'The marriage of soldiers under the Empire', *Journal of Roman Studies* 68, 153–66.

Cantarella, E., (1991) 'Homicides of honor: the development of Italian adultery law over two millennia', in D. Kertzer and R. Saller (eds) *The Family in Italy* (New Haven), 229–44.

—— (1992) *Bisexuality in the Ancient World* (New Haven).

Carandini, A. (1981) 'Sviluppo e crisi delle manifatture rurali e urbane', in A. Giardina and A. Schiavone (eds) *Società romana e prudozione schiavistica*, vol. 2 (Bari), 249–60.

Cardascia, G. (1953) 'La distinction entre *Honestiores* et *Humiliores* et le droit matrimonial', *Studi in memoriale di Emilio Albertario* 2 (Milan), 655–67.

Castelli, E. (1992) 'I will make Mary male: pieties of the body and gender transformation of Christian women in late antiquity', in J. Epstein and K. Straub (eds) *The Cultural Politics of Gender Ambiguity* (New York).

Castello, C. (1983a) 'Assenza d'ispirazione cristiana in *CTh* 3,16,1', in *Religion, société et politique: Mélanges en hommage à Jacques Éllul* (Paris), 203–12.

—— (1983b) 'Norme conciliari ed autonomia legislativa degli imperatori cristiani in tema di divorzio', in *Atti V Convegno Internazionale dell'Accademia Romanistica Constantiniana* (Perugia), 263–73.

Chadwick, H. (1976) *Priscillian of Avila* (Oxford).

—— (1978) 'Conversion in Constantine the Great', in D. Baker (ed.) *Religious Motivation: Biographical and Sociological Problems for the Church Historian* (New York), 1–13.

—— (1981) *Boethius: The Consolations of Music, Logic, Theology, and Philosophy* (Oxford).

Champlin, E. (1987) 'The testament of the piglet', *Phoenix* 41, 174–83.

Chastagnol, A. (1966) *Le Sénat romain sous le règne d'Odoacre: recherches sur l'épigraphie du Colisée au Ve siècle* (Bonn).

—— (1979) 'Les femmes dans l'ordre sénatoriel', *Revue Historique* 262, 3–28.

Clark, A. (1986), '"Adam's only companion": Augustine and the early Church on Christian marriage', *Recherches Augustiniennes* 21, 139–62.

Clark, E. (1983) *Women in the Early Church* (Wilmington).

—— (1984) *The Life of Melania the Younger* (New York and Toronto).

—— (1986) *Ascetic Piety and Women's Faith: Studies in Women and Religion* (Lewiston, NY).

—— (1991) 'Sex, shame and rhetoric: engendering early Christian ethics', *Journal of the American Academy of Religion* 59, 221–45.

Clark, G. (1993) *Women in Late Antiquity* (Oxford).

Cloke, G. (1995) *'This Female Man of God.' Women and Spiritual Power in the Patristic Age, AD 350–450* (London and New York).

Clover, F.M. (1978) 'The family and early career of Anicius Olybrius', *Historia* 27, 169–96.

Cohen, H. (1880) *Description historique des monnais frappées sous l'Empire romain communement appelées médailles imperialles* (Paris).

Cooper, K. (1992) 'Insinuations of womanly influence: an aspect of Christianization of the Roman aristocracy', *Journal of Roman Studies* 82, 150–64.

—— (1996) *The Virgin and the Bride: Idealized Womanhood in Late Antiquity* (Cambridge).

Corbett, P.A. (1930) *The Roman Law of Marriage* (Oxford).

Corbier, M. (1982) 'Les Familles clarissimes d'Afrique proconsulaire (I^e-IIIe siècles)', *Epigrafia e ordine senatorio I, Tituli* 5, 685–754.

—— (1987) 'Les Comportements familiaux de l'aristocratie romaine (IIe siècle avant J.-C.-IIIe siècle après J.-C.)', *Annales: économies, sociétés, civilisations* 42, 1267–85.

—— (1991a) 'Divorce and adoption as Roman familial strategies (Le Divorce et l'adoption "en plus")', in B. Rawson (ed.) *Marriage, Divorce and Children in Ancient Rome* (Oxford), 47–78.

—— (1991b) 'Constructing kinship in Rome', in D. Kertzer and R. Saller (eds) *The Family in Italy* (New Haven), 127–44.

Corrington, G.P. (1989) 'The milk of salvation: redemption by the mother in late antiquity and early Christianity', *Harvard Theological Review* 82, 474–5.

Costa, E. (1910) 'La vendita e l'esposizione della prole nella legislazione di Costantino', *Atti della Reale Accademia delle Scienze dell'Istituto di Bologna* 4, 117–23.

Cox, P. (1983) *Biography in Late Antiquity: A Quest for the Holy Man* (Berkeley).

Crook, J.A. (1967) *Law and Life of Rome, 90 B.C.–212A.D.* (Ithaca).

Cross. F.L. and Livingstone, D.A. (eds) (1997) *The Oxford Dictionary of the Christian Church* (Oxford).

Crouzel, H. (1971) *L'Église primitive face au divorce* (Paris).

D'Arms, J. (1970) *Romans on the Bay of Naples: A Social and Cultural Study of the Villas and their Owners from 150 B.C. to A.D. 400* (Cambridge).

Daube, D. (1967) 'The marriage of Justinian and Theodora: legal and theological reflections', *Catholic University Law Review* 16, 380–99.

DeGrassi, A. (1963) 'Dati epigrafici in iscrizione cristiane di Roma', *Rendiconti dell'Accadenia Nazionale dei Lincei*, ser. 8, vol. 18, 20–8.

Delehaye, H. (1962) *The Legend of the Saints* (New York).

Delpini, F. (1979) *Indissolubilità matrimoniale e divorzio dal I al XII secolo* (Milan).

DeMause, L. (ed.) (1979) *The History of Childhood: The Evolution of Parent–Child Relationships as a Factor in History* (New York).

De Mendieta, D. and Moons, M.C. (1953) 'Une curieuse homélie grecque inédite sur la virginité adressée aux pères de famille', *Revue Bénédictine* 63, 18–69, 211–38.

Dessau, H. (1889) 'Über Zeit und Persönlichkeit der S.H.A.', *Hermes* 24, 337–57.

De Ste Croix, G. (1975) 'Early Christian attitudes to property and slavery', *Studies in Church History* 12, 1–38.

—— (1981) *The Class Struggle in the Ancient Greek World* (Ithaca).

Dixon, S. (1988) *The Roman Mother* (London).

—— (1991) 'The sentimental ideal of the Roman family,' in B. Rawson (ed.) *Marriage, Divorce and Children in Ancient Rome* (Oxford), 99–113.

—— (1992) *The Roman Family* (Baltimore).

Dobson, B. (1974) 'The centuriate and social mobility during the Principate', in C. Nicolet (ed.) *Recherches sur les structures sociales dans l'antiquité classique* (Paris), 99–115.

Dorken, S. and Treggiari, S. (1981) 'Women with two living husbands in *CIL 6*', *Liverpool Classical Monthly* 6/10, 269–72.

Drijvers, J. (1987) 'Virginity and asceticism in late Roman Western elites', in J. Blok and P. Mason (eds) *Sexual Asymmetry* (Amsterdam).

Drinkwater, J. (1984) 'Peasants and bagaudae in Roman Gaul', *Classical Views* 3, 349–71.

Duckworth, G. (1942) *The Complete Roman Drama*, 2 vols (New York).

Duncan-Jones, R.P. (1977) 'Age-rounding, illiteracy and social differentiation in the Roman Empire', *Chiron* 7, 333–53.

—— (1982) *Economy of the Roman Empire*, revised edn (Cambridge).

Dunn, E.C. (1989) *The Gallican Saint's Life and the Late Roman Dramatic Tradition* (New Haven).

Dupont, C. (1937) *Les constitutions de Constantin et le droit privé au début du iv* siècle: les Personnes* (Lille).

—— (1964) 'Les successions dans les constitutions de Constantin', *Iura* 15, 57–116.

Dyson, S. (1992) *Community and Society in Roman Italy* (Baltimore).

Eck, W. (1971) 'Das Eindringen des Christentums in den Senatorenstand bis zu Konstantin d. Gr.', *Chiron* 1, 381–406.

Elliot, A. (1987) *Roads to Paradise* (New York).

Elliott, T.G. (1978) 'The tax exemptions granted to clerics by Constantine and Constantius II', *Phoenix* 32, 326–36.

—— (1987) 'Constantine's conversion: do we really need it?' *Phoenix* 41, 420–38.

Elm, S. (1994) *Virgins of God: The Making of Asceticism in Late Antiquity* (Oxford).

Emmett, B. (1983) 'The digressions in the lost books of Ammianus Marcellinus', in

B. Croke and A. Emmett (eds) *History and Historians in Late Antiquity* (Sydney), 42–53.

Engels, F. (1884) *The Origins of Family, Private Property and the State* (London).

Étienne, R. (1964), 'La démographie de la famille d'Ausone', in *Études et Chroniques de démographie historique* (Paris), 15–25.

—— (1978) 'La démographie des familles impériales et sénatoriales au IVe siècle après J.C.', in *Transformations et conflits au IVe siècle après J.C.* (Bonn), 133–67.

Evans Grubbs, J. (1987) '"Munitia coniugia": *the emperor Constantine's legislation on marriage and the family*' (diss., Stanford: UMI).

—— (1989) 'Abduction marriage in antiquity: a law of Constantine (*CTh* ix:24:1) and its social context', *Journal of Roman Studies* 79, 59–83.

—— (1993a) 'Constantine and imperial legislation on the family', in J. Harries and I. Wood (eds) *The Theeodosian Code* (London).

—— (1993b) '"Marriage more shameful than adultery": slave–mistress relationships, "mixed marriages", and late Roman law', *Phoenix* 47, 125–54.

—— (1994) '"Pagan" and "Christian" marriage: the state of the question', *Journal of Early Christian Studies* 2, 406–12.

—— (1995) *Law and Family in Late Antiquity: The Emperor Constantine's Marriage Legislation* (Oxford).

Eyben, E. (1991) 'Fathers and sons', in B. Rawson (ed.) *Marriage, Divorce and Children in Ancient Rome* (Oxford), 114–43.

—— (1993) *Restless Youth in Ancient Rome* (London).

Fantham, E. (1995) 'Aemillia Pudentilla: or the wealthy widow's choice', in R. Hawley and B. Levick (eds) *Women in Antiquity*, London, 220–32.

Flandrin, J.-F. (1979) *Families in Former Times: Kinship, Household and Sexuality*, trans. R. Southern (Cambridge).

Flory, M. (1978) 'Family and *familia*: kinship and community in slavery', *American Journal of History* 3, 78–95.

—— (1984) '*Sic exempla paruntur*: Livia's shrine to Concordia and the *Porticus Liviae*', *Historia* 33, 309–30.

Foucault, M. (1978, 1984a, 1984b) *L'Histoire de la sexualité*, vols 1–3 (Paris).

—— (1986) *History of Sexuality: The Care of the Self*, trans. R. Hurley (New York).

Fowler, W.W. (1899) *The Roman Festivals of the Period of the Republic*, reprinted 1969 (Port Washington, NY).

Fox, R.L. (1986) *Pagans and Christians* (New York).

Frend, W.H.C. (1969) 'Circumcellions and monks', *Journal of Theological Studies* 20, 542–9.

Gardner, J. (1986a) *Women in Roman Law and Society* (London/Sydney).

—— (1986b) 'Proofs of status in the Roman world', *Bulletin of the Institute of Classical Studies* 33, 1–14.

—— (1995) 'Gender-role assumptions in Roman law', *Classical Views* 39, 377–83.

—— (1997) 'Legal stumbling blocks for lower-class families in Rome', in B. Rawson and P. Weaver (eds) *The Roman Family in Italy* (Oxford), 35–53.

—— (1998) *Family and Familia in Roman Law and Life* (Oxford).

Gardner, J. and Wiedemann, T. (1991) *The Roman Household: A Sourcebook* (London).

Garnsey, P. (1968) 'Trajan's alimenta: some problems', *Historia* 17, 367–81.

—— (1975) 'Descendants of freedmen in local politics: some criteria', in B. Levick (ed.) *The Ancient Historian and His Materials* 167–180.

—— (1979) 'Where did Italian peasants live?' *Proceedings of the Cambridge Philological Society* 29, 1–25.

—— (1991) 'Childrearing in ancient Italy', in D. Kertzer and R. Saller (eds) *The Family in Italy* (New Haven), 48–65.

Garnsey, P. and Saller, R. (1987) *The Roman Empire* (Berkeley).

Gartner, M. (1985) *Die Familienziehung in der alten Kirche'* (diss., Munich).

Gaudemet, J. (1947) La législation religieuse de Constantin', *Revue de l'Histoire de l'Église de France* 33, 25–61.

—— (1951) 'Constantin et les curies municipales', *Iura* 2, 44–75.

—— (1953) 'Droit romain et principes canoniques en matière de mariage au Bas-Empire,' reprinted in J. Gaudemet *Sociétés et mariage* (Strasbourg).

—— (1955a) 'La décision de Callixte en matière de mariage', in *Studi in onore di Ugo E. Paoli*, 333–44, reprinted in J. Gaudemet *Sociétés et mariage* (Strasbourg).

—— (1955b) 'L'Originalité des fiançailles romaines', in J. Gaudemet *Sociétés et mariage* (Strasbourg).

—— (1958) *L'Église dans l'Empire Romain (ive-ve siècles)*, Histoire du Droit et des Institutions de l'Église en Occident, vol. 3 (Paris).

—— (1960) 'La Transmission des constitutions relatives au droit succesoral au Bas-Empire et dans les royaumes barbares', *Revue Internationale des Droits de l'Antiquité* 7, 399–435.

—— (1962) 'Les transformations de la vie familiale au Bas-Empire et l'influence du Christianisme', *Romanitas* 5, 58–85.

—— (1976) 'Lactance et le droit romain', in *Atti II Convegno dell'Accademia Romanistica Constantiniana* (Perugia), 83–101.

—— (1978) 'Tendances nouvelles de la législation familiale au ive siècle', *Transformations et Conflits au ive siècle apres J-C, Antiquitas* 29, 187–207.

—— (1979) *La Formation du droit séculier et du droit de l'Église aux ive et ve siècles* (Paris).

—— (1980) *Sociétés et mariage* (Strasbourg).

—— (1983) 'Les constitutions constantiniennes du Code Théodosien', in *Atti V Convegno Internazionale dell'Accademia Romanistica Constantiniana*, (Perugia), 135–56.

Geisau, H. von. (1968) *Real-Encyclopädie der klassischen Alterumwissenschaft supplementum*, 11 (Berlin).

Gelzer, M. (1969) *The Roman Nobility*, trans. P. Needham (Oxford).

George, M. (1997) 'Repopulating the Roman house', in B. Rawson and P. Weaver (eds) *The Roman Family in Italy* (Oxford), 299–319.

Gilliam, J.F. (1972) 'Ammianus and the Historia Augusta: the lost books and the period 117–284', *Bonner Historia-Augusta Colloquium* 1970, 125–47.

Glare, P.G.W. (ed.) (1968) *Oxford Latin Dictionary* (Oxford).

Goody, J. (1983) *The Development of Family and Marriage in Europe* (Cambridge).

—— (1990) *The Oriental, the Ancient and the Primitive* (Cambridge).

Gouma-Peterson, T. (ed.) (1994) *Bibliography on Women in Byzantium* (Wooster).

Green, R.P.H. (1991) *The Works of Ausonius* (Oxford).

Gregory, T. (1975) 'Novationism: a rigorist sect in the Christian Roman Empire', *Byzantine Studies/Études Byzantine* 2, 1–18.

Grieser, H. (1997) *Sklaverei im spätantiken und frühmittelalterlichen Gallien (5. – 7. Jh.). Das Zeugnis der christlichen Quellen* (Stuttgart).

Griffin, J. (1976) 'Augustan poetry and the life of luxury', *Journal of Roman Studies* 66, 87–105.

Grisé, Y. (1982) *La Suicide dans Rome antique* (Paris).

Guastella, G. (1980) 'I *Parentalia* come testo antropoligico: l'avunculato nel mondo celtico e nella famiglia di Ausonio', *Materiali e discussioni per l'analisi dei testi classici* 4, 97–124.

Guthrie, C. (1966) 'The execution of Crispus', *Phoenix* 20, 325–31.

Hallett, J. (1984) *Fathers and Daughters in Roman Society: Women and the Elite Family* (Princeton).

Hands, A.R. (1968) *Charities and Social Aid in Greece and Rome* (London).

Hareven, T.K. (1971) 'The history of the family as an interdisciplinary field', *Journal of Interdisciplinary History* 2, 399–414.

Harnack, A. (1903) 'Der pseudocyprianische Traktat *"de singularitate clericorum"'* *Texte und Untersuchungen* N.F. 9:3.

Harries, J. (1994) *Sidonius Apollinaris and the Fall of Rome* (Oxford).

Harries, J. and Wood, I. (eds) (1993) *The Theodosian Code* (London).

Harrill, J.A. (1995) *The Manumission of Slaves in Early Christianity* (Tübingen).

Hawley, R. and Levick, B. (eds) (1995) *Women in Antiquity: New Assessments* (London).

Head, C. (1982) 'Women in the life and writings of the Emperor Julian', *Byzantina* 11, 9–20.

Heather, P. (1991) *Goths and Romans, 332–489* (Oxford).

Hefele, K.J. (1893) *A History of the Councils of the Church*, vols. 1–5, second edition, trans. W. R. Clark (Edinburgh).

Hellems, F.B.R. (1899) 'The Pupus Torquatianus inscription: paleographical notes', *American Journal of Archeology* 3, 202–11.

Henrion, R. (1940) 'Des origines du mot *familia*', *L'Antiquité classique* 9, 37–9.

Herlihy, D. (1985) *Medieval Households* (Cambridge).

Herrin, J. and Kazhdan, K. (1991a) 'Divorce', in A. Kazhdan *et al. The Oxford Dictionary of Byzantium* (Oxford), vol. 1, 640–1.

—— (1991b) 'Remarriage', in A. Kazhdan *et al. The Oxford Dictionary of Byzantium* (Oxford), vol. 3, 1783.

—— (1991c) 'Widows', in A. Kazhdan *et al. The Oxford Dictionary of Byzantium* (Oxford), vol. 3., 2195–6.

Hirschfeld, Y. (1995) *The Palestinian Dwelling in the Roman-Byzantine Period* (Jerusalem).

Holum, K. (1982) *Theodosian Empresses* (Berkeley).

Honoré, T. (1986) 'The making of the Theodosian Code', *Zeitschrift der Savigny-Stiftung für Rechtgeschichte* 104, 133–222.

Hopkins, K. (1964–65) 'The age of Roman girls at marriage', *Population Studies* 18, 309–27.

—— (1965) 'Contraception in the Roman Empire', *Comparative Studies in Society and History* 8, 124–51.

—— (1966) 'On the probable age-structure of the Roman population', *Population Studies* 20, 245–64.

—— (1978) *Conquerors and Slaves* (Cambridge).

—— (1980) 'Brother-sister marriage in Roman Egypt', *Comparative Studies in Society and History* 22, 303–54.

—— (1983) *Death and Renewal: Sociological Studies in Roman History* (Cambridge).

Horsfall, N. (1983) 'Some problems in the "Laudatio Turiae"', *Bulletin of the Institute of Classical Studies* 30, 85–98.

Huchthausen, L. (1976) 'Zu kaiserlichen Reskripten an weibliche Adressaten aus der Zeit Diokletians (284–305 u.Z.)', *Klio* 58, 55–85.

Humbert, M. (1972) *Le Remariage à Rome: étude d'histoire juridique et sociale* (Paris).

Humphrey, J. (1986) *Roman Circuses* (Berkeley).

Hunt, A.S. and Edgar, C.C. (eds) (1932–4) *Selected Papyri* (Cambridge).

Hunter, D.G. (1987) 'Resistance to the virginal ideal in late-fourth-century Rome: the case of Jovinian', *Theological Studies* 48, 45–64.

—— (1989) '*On the Sin of Adam and Eve*. A little known defense of marriage and childbearing by Ambrosiaster', *Harvard Theological Review* 82, 283–99.

Jones, A.H.M. (1958) 'The Roman colonate', *Past and Present* 13, 1–13.

—— (1964) *The Later Roman Empire 284–602* (Baltimore).

Joshel, S. (1992) *Work, Identity and Legal Status at Rome: A Study of the Occupational Inscriptions* (Norman, Oklahoma).

Kajanto, I. (1969) 'On divorce among the common people in Rome', *Revue des Études Latines: Mélanges Marcel Durry* 47 bis, 99–113.

Kaster, R.A. (1983) 'Notes on primary and secondary schools in late antiquity', *Transactions of the American Philological Association* 113, 323–46.

Katzoff, R. (1985) '*Donatio ante nuptias* and Jewish dowry additions', *Yale Classical Studies* 28, 232–44.

Kazhdan, A. *et al.* (eds) (1991) *The Oxford Dictionary of Byzantium* (Oxford).

Kennel, S.H. (1991) 'Women's hair and the law: two case studies from late antiquity', *Klio* 73, 526–36.

Kertzer, D. and Saller, R. (eds) (1991) *The Family in Italy: From Antiquity to the Present* (New Haven).

Killbrew, A. and Fine, S. (1991) 'Qatzrin: reconstructing village life in Talmudic times', *Biblical Archeological Review* 16, 3: 45–56.

Kirshner, J. (1991) 'Introduction to Part Two [medieval Italy]', in D. Kertzer and R. Saller (eds) *The Family in Italy* (New Haven), 148–9.

Klegeman, C. (1957) 'A psychoanalytic study of the confessions of St. Augustine', *Journal of the American Psychoanalytic Association* 5, 469–84.

Kleiner, D.E.E. (1977) *Roman Group Portraiture: The Funerary Reliefs of the Late Republic and the Early Empire* (New York).

Klingshirn, W. (1994) *Caesarius of Arles: Life, Testament, Letters* (Liverpool).

Köpstein, H. (1966) *Zur Sklaverei im ausgehenden Byzanz* (Berlin).

Korsunski, A.R. (1978) 'The Church and slavery problem in the 4th century', in *Miscellanea Historiae Ecclesiasticae, VI: Congrès de Varsovie; Section I: Les Transformations dans la société Chrétienne au IV siècle*, 95–110.

Kötting, B. (1973) 'Univira in Inschriften', in W. van den Boer *et al.* (eds) *Romanitas et Christianitas. Studia I.H. Wasznik oblata*, 195–206.

Lacey, W.K. (1986) '*Patria potestas*', in B. Rawson (ed.) *The Family in Ancient Rome* (Ithaca), 121–44.

Lacombe, P. (1889) *La Famille dans la société romaine: étude de moralité comparée* (Paris).

LaFontaine, J. (1970) 'La femme dans la poésie de Prudence', *Revue des études latines* 47 bis: Mélanges M. Durry, 55–83.

Laiou, A. (1985) 'Consensus facit nuptias – et non', *Rechtshistorisches Journal* 4, 189–201.

Lanfranchi, F. (1964) *Ricerche sulle azioni di stato nella filiazione in diritto Romano. II. La c.d. presunzione di paternità* (Rome).

Laslett, P. (1970–1) 'The comparative history of household and family', *Journal of Social History* 4, 75–87.

Lassen, E.M. (1997) 'The Roman family: ideal and metaphor', in H. Moxnes (ed.) *Constructing Early Christian Families* (London).

Lee, A.D. (1988) 'Close-kin marriage in late antique Mesopotamia', *Greek, Roman, and Byzantine Studies* 29, 403–13.

Leedom, J. (1978) 'Constantius II: three revisions', *Byzantion* 48, 132–45.

Le Play, P.G.F. (1871) *L'Organization de la Famille* (Paris).

Leuchli, S. (1972) *Power and Sexuality: The Emergence of Canon Law at the Synod of Elvira* (Philadelphia).

Liebeschuetz, J.H.W.G. (1979) *Continuity and Change in Roman Religion* (Oxford).

Lightman, M. and Zeisel, W. (1977) '*Univira*: an example of continuity and change in Roman society', *Church History* 46, 19–32.

Linderski, J. (1986) 'Religious aspects of the conflict of the orders: the case of *confarreatio*', in K. Raaflaub (ed.) *Social Struggles in Archaic Rome* (Berkeley), 244–61.

Lindsay, W.M. (ed.) (1930) *Glossaria Latina*, 4 vols (Paris).

Lipold, A. (1965) 'Ursinus and Damasus', *Historia* 14, 105–28.

Lizzi, R. (1990) 'Ambrose's contemporaries and the Christianization of northern Italy', *Journal of Roman Studies* 80, 156–73.

Lyman, R. (1974) 'Barbarism and religion: late roman and early medieval childhood', in L. Demause *The History of Childhood* (New York), 75–100.

Lynch, J. (1986) *Godparents and Kinship in Early Medieval Europe* (Princeton).

McLynn, N. (1994) *Ambrose of Milan* (Berkeley).

MacMullen, R. (1984) *Christianizing the Roman Empire A.D. 100–400* (New Haven).

—— (1987) 'Late Roman slavery', *Historia* 36, 359–82.

—— (1990) *Changes in the Roman Empire: Essays in the Ordinary* (Princeton).

Malina, B.J. (1986) *Christian Origins and Cultural Anthropology* (New York).

Mandouze, A. (1982) *Prosopographie chrétienne du Bas-Empire I: Afrique, 303–533*, Éditions du Centre national de la recherche scientifique (Paris).

Mango, C. (1980) *Byzantium: The Empire of New Rome* (New York).

Marrou, H.-I. (1937) *Saint Augustin et le fin de la culture antique* (Paris).

—— (1948) *Histoire de l'education dans l'Antiquité* (Paris).

Martin, D.B. (1995) *The Corinthian Body* (New Haven).

—— (1996) 'The construction of the ancient family: methodological considerations', *JRS* 86, 40–60.

—— (1997) 'Paul without passion: on Paul's rejection of desire in sex and marriage', in H. Moxnes (ed.) *Constructing Early Christian Families* (London).

Martindale, A., *et al.* (1970, 1980 and 1992) *The Prosopography of the Later Roman Empire*, 3 vols (Cambridge).

Martínez, F. G. (1994) *The Dead Sea Scrolls Translated. The Qumran Texts in English*, 2nd edn, (ed.) W.G.E. Watson, (1992) trans. from 1st edn (Leiden).

Matthews, J. (1967) 'Continuity in a Roman family: the Rufii festi of Volsinii', *Historia* 16, 484–509.

—— (1975) *Western Aristocracies and Imperial Court AD 364–425* (Oxford).

—— (1989) *The Roman Empire of Ammianus* (Baltimore).

Matthisen, R. (1993) *Roman Aristocrats in Barbarian Gaul* (Austin).

Michaels-Mudd, M. (1979) 'The Arian policy of Constantius II and its impact on Church–state relations in the fourth-century Roman Empire', *Byzantine Studies/Études Byzantines* 6, 95–111.

Millar, F. (1964) *A Study in Cassius Dio* (Oxford).
—— (1977) *The Emperor in the Roman World (31 BC–AD 337)* (Ithaca).
Misch, G. (1950) *The Autobiography in Antiquity* (New York).
Momigliano, A. (1956) 'Gli Anicii e la storiografia latina del vi sec. d.C.', in *Secondo contributo alla storia degli studi classici* (Rome), 231–54.
—— (ed.) (1963) *The Conflict between Paganism and Christianity in the Fourth Century* (Oxford).
—— (ed.) (1989) *The Cambridge Ancient History*, vol. 1 (Cambridge).
Montevecchi, O. (1979) 'Endogamia e cittadinanza romana in Egitto', *Aegyptus* 59, 137–44.
Moxnes, H. (ed.) (1997a) *Constructing Early Christian Families: Family as Social Reality and Metaphor* (London).
—— (1997b) 'What is family? Problems in constructing early Christian families', in H. Moxnes (ed.) *Constructing Early Christian Families* (London), 13–41.
Müller, P. (1992) *In der Mitte der Gemeinde: Kinder im Neuen Testament* (Neukirchen-Vluyn).
Münzer, F. (1920) *Römische Adelsparteien und Adelsfamilien* (Berlin).
Nathan, G. (1992) 'The last emperor: the fate of Romulus Augustulus', *Classica et Mediaevalia* 43, 261–71.
—— (1993) 'Medicine and sexual practices in late antiquity', *Epoche* 18, 20–32.
—— (1997) 'Anicia Juliana, the *Vienna Dioscurides'* portrait, and the idealized patron', unpublished paper given at the annual meeting of the American Philological Association, December 1997.
—— (1998a) 'The rogation ceremonies of late antique Gaul: creation, transmission and the role of the bishop', *Classica et Mediaevalia* 49, 275–303.
—— (1998b) *'Querolus* and the domestic slave', unpublished paper given at the annual meeting of the Byzantine Studies Conference, November 1998.
—— (forthcoming) '"Pudicitia plebeia": womanly echoes of the struggle of the orders'.
Néraudau, J.-P. (1979) *La jeunesse dans la littérature de la Rome républicaine* (Paris).
—— (1984) *Être enfant à Rome* (Paris).
Neyrey, J. (1995) 'Loss of wealth, loss of family and loss of honor', in P.F. Esler (ed.) *Modelling Early Christianity: Social-Scientific Studies of the New Testament in its Context* (London), 139–58.
Nicholas, B. (1962) *An Introduction to Roman Law* (Oxford).
Nielson, H.S. (1997) 'Interpreting epithets in Roman epitaphs', in B. Rawson and P. Weaver (eds) *The Roman Family in Italy* (Oxford), 169–204.
Niziolek, M. (1980) *Legal Effects of Concubinage in Reference to Concubine's Offspring in the Light of Imperial Legislation of the Period of the Dominate, Series: Zeszty naukowe Uniwersytetu Jagiellonshiego, zesz.* 84 (Warsaw-Krakow).
Noy, D. (1991) 'Wicked stepmothers in Roman society and imagination', *Journal of Family History* 16, 345–61.
Oost, S. (1968) *Galla Placidia Augusta: A Biographical Essay* (Chicago).
Orlin, E. (1996) *Temples, Religion and Politics in the Roman Republic* (Leiden).
O'Roark, D. (1994) 'Urban family structure in late antiquity as evidenced by John Chrysostom' (diss., Ohio State University; UMI).
Parkin, T. (1992) *Demography and Roman Society* (Baltimore).
—— (1997) 'Out of sight, out of mind: elderly members of the Roman family',

in B. Rawson and P. Weaver (eds) *The Roman Family in Italy* (Oxford), 123–48.

Patlagean, E. (1969) 'Birth control in the early Byzantine Empire', *Annales E.S.C.* 24, 1353–69 (reprinted in 1975 in R. Forster and O. Ranum, (eds) *Biology of Man in History*, (Baltimore), 1–22).

—— (1976) 'L'Histoire de la femme déguisée en moine et l'évolution de la sainteté et pauvreté à Byzance', reprinted in *Studi Medievali* 17, 597–623.

—— (1978) 'Familles chrétiennes d'Asie Mineure et histoire démographique du ive siècle', *Transformations et conflits au ive siècle après J.-C., Antiquitas* 29 (Bonn), 169–86.

Patterson, C. (1991) 'Marriage and the married woman in Athenian law', in S. Pomeroy (ed.) *Women's History and Ancient History* (Chapel Hill, North Carolina), 48–72.

Pauley, A., Wissowa, G. *et al.* (eds) (1893–) *Real-Encyclopädie der klassischen Alterumwissenschaft* (Berlin).

Pharr, C. (1952) *The Theodosian Code and Novels and the Sirmondian Constitutions: A Translation with Commentary, Glossary, and Bibliography* (Princeton).

Puchner, W. (1983) 'Byzantinischer Mimos, Pantomimos und Mummenschanz im Spiegel der griechischen Patristik und ekklesiastischer Synodalverordnungen', *Maske und Kothurn* 29, 311–17.

Raaflaub, K. (ed.) (1986) *Social Struggles in Archaic Rome: New Perspectives on the Conflict of the Orders* (Berkeley).

Raepsaet-Charlier, M.-T. (1981–2) 'Ordre Sénatoriel et divorce sous l'Haut-Empire: un chapitre des mentalités', *Acta Classica Univ. Scient. de Brecen* 17–18, 161–73.

—— (1982) 'Tertullian et la législation des mariages inégaux', *Revue Internationale des droits de l'Antiquité* ser. 3, #29, 253–63.

Rankin, D. (1995) *Tertullian and the Church* (Cambridge).

Rapp, C. (1994) 'A different kind of parenthood: baptismal sponsorship in late antiquity', unpublished paper delivered at the 126th Annual Meeting of the American Philological Association, (Atlanta) December.

Rawson, B. (1966) 'Family life among the lower classes at Rome in the first two centuries of the Empire', *Classical Philology* 61, 71–83.

—— (1974) 'Roman concubinage and other de facto marriages', *Transactions of the American Philological Association* 104, 27–305.

—— (ed.) (1986) *The Family in Ancient Rome* (Ithaca).

—— (ed.) (1991) *Marriage, Divorce and Children in Ancient Rome* (Oxford).

Rawson, B. and Weaver, P. (eds) (1997) *The Roman Family in Italy: Status, Sentiment and Space* (Oxford).

Rich, J. (ed.) (1992) *The City in Late Antiquity* (London).

Richards, J. (1980) *Consul of God* (London).

Riché, P. (1976) *Education and Culture in the Barbarian West*, trans. J. Contreni (Chapel Hill, North Carolina).

Riddle, J.M., Estes, J.W., and Russell, J.C. (1994) 'Birth control in the ancient world', *Archeology* 47, 29–33.

Rivier, A. (1891) *Précis du droit famille romain, contenant un choix des textes* (Paris).

Roberts, M. (1989) *The Jewelled Style: Poetry and Poetics in Late Antiquity* (Ithaca).

Rodgers, R. H. (1975), *An Introduction to Palladius* (London).

Rose, M. (1997) 'Ashkelon's Dead Babies', *Archeology* 50, 2, 12–3.

Rosenblum, M. (1961) *Luxorius: A Latin Poet Among the Vandals* (New York).

Rossi, M.-A. (1984) 'The passion of Perpetua, everywoman in late antiquity', in R. Smith and J. Lounibos (eds) *Pagan and Christian Anxiety: A Response to E.R. Dodds* (Lanham, Maryland), 53–86.

Rossiter, J. (1991) '*Convivium* and villa in late antiquity', in J. Slater (ed.) *Dining in a Classical Context* (Ann Arbor), 119–214.

Rostovtzeff, M. (1925) *Gesellschaft und Wirtschaft im römischen Kaiserreich* (Leipzig).

Rougé, J. (1983) 'Questions d'Époque Constantinienne', in E. Frézouls (ed.) *Crise et redressement dans les provinces européennes de l'Émpire. Actes du colloque de Strasbourg (1981)* (Strasbourg), 113–25.

Rouselle, A. (1988) *Porneia: On Desire and the Body in Antiquity*, trans. F. Pheasant (Oxford).

—— (1991) 'La Politique des corps', in G. Duby and M. Perrot (eds) *Histoire des femmes, i: L'Antiquité* (Paris), 319–59.

Rudikoff, S. (1989) 'How they thought about sexuality in late antiquity', review of Brown (1988), *Hudson Review* 42, 307–13.

Ruether, R. (1979) 'Mothers of the Church', in R. Ruether and E. McLaughlin (eds) *Women of Spirit: Female Leadership in Jewish and Christian Traditions* (New York), 72–98.

Ruggini, L. (1988) 'Gli anicii a Roma e in Provincia', *Mélanges de l'École Française de Rome: Moyen âge, temps modernes* 100, 69–85.

Russell, J.C. (1958) *Late Ancient and Medieval Population* (Philadelphia).

—— (1985) *The Control of Late Ancient and Medieval Population* (Philadelphia).

Saller, R. (1984a) 'Roman dowry and the devolution of property in the Principate', *Classical Quarterly* 34, 195–205.

—— (1984b) '*Familia, domus,* and the Roman conception of the family', *Phoenix* 38, 336–55.

—— (1987a) 'Slavery and the Roman family', *Slavery and Abolition* 8, 65–87.

—— (1987b) 'Men's age at marriage and its consequences in the Roman family', *Classical Philology* 82, 21–34.

—— (1991a) 'European family history and Roman law', *Continuity and Change* 6, 335–46.

—— (1991b) 'Corporal punishment, authority, and obedience in the Roman household', in B. Rawson (ed.) *Marriage, Divorce and Children in Ancient Rome* (Oxford), 144–65.

—— (1991c) 'Childhood in imperial Rome', *Journal of Roman Archaeology* 4, 240–2.

—— (1991d) 'Roman heirship strategies in principle and in practice', in Kertzer and Saller R. (eds) *The Family in Italy* (New Haven), 26–47.

—— (1994) *Patriarchy, Property and Death in the Roman Family* (Cambridge).

—— (1997) 'Roman kinship: structure and sentiment', in B. Rawson and P. Weaver (eds) *The Roman Family in Italy* (Oxford), 7–34.

Salmon, E.T. (1970) *Roman Colonization under the Republic* (Ithaca).

Salzman, M. (1989) 'Aristocratic women: conductors of Christianity in the fourth century', *Helios* 16, 207–20.

—— (1990) *On Roman Time: The Codex-Calendar of 354 and the Rhythms of Urban Life in Late Antiquity* (Berkeley).

—— (1993) 'How the West was won: the Christianization of the Roman aristocracy in the West in the years after Constantine', *Latomus* 52, 450–79.

Sargenti, M. (1938) *Il diritto privato nella legislazione di Costantino. Persone e famiglia* (Milan).

—— (1975) 'Il diritto privato nella legislazione di Constantino', in *Atti I Convegno dell'Accademia Romanistica Constantiniana* (Florence), 229–332.

Sathas, K.N. (1972) *Mesaionike Bibliotheke*, 7 vols, originally published 1872–94 (Athens, Venice and Paris).

Schanz, M., Hosius, C. and Krueger, G. (1920) *Geschichte der römischen Literatur des 5. und 6. Jahrhunderts*, 4 vols, reprinted 1959 (Munich).

Schürer, E., (1973–84) *The History of the Jewish People in the Age of Jesus Christ (175 BC–AD 135)*, revised and translated by G. Vermes, F. Millar, and M. Black (Edinburgh).

Shaw, B. (1984) 'Latin funerary epigraphy and family life in the Later Roman Empire', *Historia* 33, 457–97.

—— (1987a) 'The family in late antiquity: the experience of Augustine', *Past and Present* 115, 3–51.

—— (1987b) 'The age of Roman girls at marriage: some reconsiderations', *Journal of Roman Studies* 77, 30–46.

—— (1991) 'The cultural meaning of death', in D. Kertzer and R. Saller (eds) *The Family in Italy* (New Haven), 66–90.

—— (1994) 'Women and the early Church', *History Today* 44, 21–8.

Shaw, B. and Saller, R.P. (1984a) 'Tombstones and Roman family relations in the Principate: civilians, soldiers and slaves', *Journal of Roman Studies* 74, 124–56.

—— (1984b) 'Close kin-marriage in Roman society', *Man* n.s. 19, 431–44.

Sherwin-White, A.N. (1980) *The Roman Citizenship*, 2nd edn (Oxford).

Sirat, C. *et al.* (1986) *La Ketouba de Cologne: Un contrat de mariage juif à Antinoopolis* (Opladen).

Sirks, B. (1993) 'Reconsidering the Roman colonate', *Zeitschrift der Savigny-Stiftung* 123, 331–69.

Slotki, W. (trans.) (1936) *Yebamoth*, in I. Epstein (ed.) *Babylonian Talmud*, (London).

Soren, D. and Soren, N. (1995) 'What killed the babies of Lugnano?' *Archeology* 48:5, 43–8.

Sotgiu, G. (1973–4) 'Un collare di schiava rinvenuto in Sardegna', *Archeologia Classica* 25–6, 688–90.

Souter, A. (1949) *A Glossary of Later Latin* (Oxford).

Stone, L. (1979) *The Family, Sex and Marriage in England 1500–1800* (Harmondsworth).

Straub, J. (1967) 'Constantine as ΚΟΙΝΟΣ ΕΠΙΣΚΟΠΟΣ', *Dumbarton Oaks Papers* 21, 37–55.

Syme, R. (1939) *The Roman Revolution* (Oxford).

—— (1972) 'The composition of the Historia Augusta', *Journal of Roman Studies* 42 (reprinted 1983), 12–29.

Talbert, R.J.A. (1984) *The Senate of Imperial Rome* (Princeton).

Thomas, J.A.C. (1976) 'Delictal and criminal liability of the young in Roman law', *Recueils de la Société Jean Bodin* 38, 9–31.

Thompson, E.A. (1952) 'Peasant revolts of late Roman Gaul and Spain', *Past and Present* 2, 11–23 (reprinted in M. Finley (ed.) [1974] *Studies in Ancient Society* (London), Ch. 14).

Torjesen, K.J. (1993) *When Women Were Priests* (San Francisco).

Treggiari, S. (1981a) 'Concubinae', *Papers of the British School at Rome* 49, 59–81.

—— (1981b) 'Contubernales in CIL 6', *Phoenix* 35, 42–69.

—— (1990) *Roman Marriage* (Oxford).

—— (1991) 'Divorce Roman style: how easy and how frequent was it?' in B. Rawson (ed.) *Marriage, Divorce and Children in Ancient Rome* (Oxford), 31–46.

Trombley, F. (1993–4) *Hellenic Religion and Christianization, c. 370–529* (Leiden).

Tsirplanis, C. (1985) 'Saint Gregory the theologian on marriage and the family', *Patristic and Byzantine Review* 1, 33–8.

Van Dam, R. (1985) *Leadership and Community in Late Antique Gaul* (Berkeley).

Veyne, P. (1978) 'La Famille et l'amour sous le haut-empire Romain', *Annales: économies, sociétés, civilisations* 33, 35–63.

—— (ed.) (1987) *A History of Private Life, vol. I: From Pagan Rome to Byzantium*, G. Duby and P. Ariès, gen. eds (Cambridge).

Ville, G. (1960) 'Les Jeux de gladiateurs dans l'Empire chrétien', *Mélanges d'archéologie et d'histoire de l'École Française de Rome* 72, 273–335.

Vogt, J. (1945) 'Zur Frage des christlichen Einflusses auf die Gesetzgebung Konstantins des Grossen', in *Festschrift für Leopold Wagner*, vol. 2 (Munich), 118–48.

Volterra, E. (1958) 'Intorno ad alcune costituzioni di Costantino', *Rendiconti dell'Accademia Nazionale dei Lincei* series 8, vol. 13, 61–89.

—— (1959) 'Quelque remarques sur le style des constitutions de Constantin', *Mélanges Lévy-Bruhl*, 325–334.

Wallace-Hadrill, A. (1981) 'Family and inheritance in the Augustan marriage laws', *Proceedings of the Cambridge Philological Society* 2, 58–80.

—— (1991) 'Houses and households: sampling Pompeii and Herculaneum', in B. Rawson (ed.) *Marriage, Divorce and Children in Ancient Rome* (Oxford), 191–228.

—— (1994) *Houses and Society in Pompeii and Herculaneum* (Princeton).

Watson, G.R. (1969) *The Roman Soldier* (Ithaca, NY).

Weaver, P.R.C. (1986) 'The status of children in mixed marriages', in B. Rawson (ed.) *The Family in Ancient Rome* (Ithaca), 145–69.

—— (1991) 'Children of freedmen (and freedwoman)', in B. Rawson (ed.) *Marriage, Divorce and Children in Ancient Rome* (Oxford), 166–90.

Whittaker, C.R. (1987) 'Circe's pigs: from slavery to serfdom in the later Roman world', *Slavery and Abolition* 8, 88–123.

Wieacker, F. (1971) 'Le droit romain de la mort d'Alexandre Sévère à l'avènement de Diocletien', *Revue de l'Histoire du Droit* 49, 221–3.

Wiedemann, T. (1989) *Adults and Children in the Roman Empire* (New Haven).

Wickham, C. (1981) *Early Medieval Italy* (Ann Arbor).

Wightman, E.M. (1978) 'Potentates and peasants: an investigation of social structure and land tenure in Roman Gaul', *American Journal of Ancient History* 3, 97–128.

Wolff, H.J. (1945) 'The background of the post-classical legislation on illegitimacy', *Seminar* 3, 21–45.

—— (1950) 'Doctrinal trends in post-classical Roman marriage law', *Zeitschrift der Savigny-Stiftung für Rechtsgeschichte. Romanistische Abteilung* 67, 261–319.

Wolfram, H. (1988) *History of the Goths*, trans. T. Dunlap (Berkeley).

Xella, P. (ed.) (1976) *Magia: Studi in memorie di Raffaela Garosi* (Rome).

Yadin, Y. (1972) 'L'Attitude essénienne envers la polygamie et le divorce,' *Revue Biblique* 79, 92–104.

Yarbrough, A. (1976) 'Christianization in the fourth century: the example of Roman women', *Church History* 45, 149–65.

Yaron, R. (1963) 'Divortium inter absentes', *Tijdschrift voor Rechtsgeschiedenis* 31, 54–68.

Zepos, J. and Zepos, P. (eds) (1931) *Ius graecoromanum* 8 vols. (Athens repr. Aalen [1962]).

Zhishman, J. (1864) *Das Eherecht der orientalischen Kirche* (Vienna).

INDEX

Ablabius 63, 208-209n.57, 210n.82
Abraham and Sarah 40
Acacius of Amida 138, 233n.42
Aconia Faltonia Paulina 77
adelphos 43, 93, 217n.110
Adeodatus (Augustine's son) 129, 230n.180
adoption 25, 210n.81, 211n.95; *adoptio* 25, 198 n. 88; *adrogatio* 25, 198 n. 88
aduescens/adulescentia see children
adultery 40, 45, 46, 55, 63, 97–103, 108, 109, 112–113, 114–115, 148, 180, 207n.15, 213n.13, 217n.99, 221n.206, 222n.210, 223nn.239 and 248, 224nn.4 and 18, 241n.38; *adulterare* 108; *stuprum* 20–21, 46, 102, 109, 148; young men and 100, 101; women 108
Adrianople, Battle of 240n.9
Aedui 239n.26
Aelius Seianus, L. 22
Aemilia Melania 163, 239n.23
Aemilii 168
Aemilius Florus Paternus 89
Aetheria 101, 121, 165, 190
Aetius, Fl. 190
Afranius Hannibalianus 191, 230n.162
Agapita 114–115, 190
Agde, council of 89, 125, 185
Aginatius 99, 222n.218
Agonistici 241–242n.53
Agricola, Cn. Iulius 30
Agricolanus 207n.23
Agrippina (the Younger) 86

akolastainein 50
Albina (mother of Melania) 92, 236n.132
Albinus 190
Alemanni 179, 218n.121
Alfenius Ceionius Iulianus 122
alimenta 67, 137, 210n.84
All Soul's Day 163, 238–239n.20
alumnus/a 29–30; definition of 29
Amalasuintha 154
Ambrose 13, 82, 86, 88, 89, 123, 129, 132, 138, 149, 155, 167, 171, 175, 178, 188, 212n.2, 241n.49; as *consularis* 100; and marriage 86, 161, 218n.129; on motherhood 150, 151, 155
Ambrosiaster 113, 115
Ambrosius 100, 101, 112, 222n.223
amita 217n.102
Ammianus Marcellinus 14, 102, 177–178, 179, 183; adultery trials in 98–100
Ampliatus 173
Anastasius 125, 157
ancilla see slaves
Anepsia 99
Anicia 120, 228n.112
Anicia Faltonia Proba 153–154, 156, 229–230n.160
Anicia Iuliana 153–154
Anicia Juliana 157
Anicii 126, 168, 230n.160
Anicius Acilius Aginantius Faustus Iunior 239n.33

262

Anicius Faustus Iunior Niger, Fl. 164
Anna 227n.85
Annius, L. 27
Anthemius 176
Antonina 124, 244n.134
Antoninus (bishop) 231n.193, 233n.33
Antoninus Pius 206n.5
Antony, St. 77
Arborius 239n.26
Arcadius 108, 155, 178, 219n.149,
    230n.173, 244n.126
Archotamia 121, 165
Ardabur 156
Ariadne 125
Arianism 90, 219nn.141 and 142,
    228n.123
Aristophanes 177
Arles, council of 108, 130, 185
Artemia 191, 226n.53
Aspar 156
Athanasius, Athanasianism 90, 152,
    219n.142, 227–228n.101
Atilia 197n.45
Atticus, T. Pomponius 31
Augustine 13, 33, 65, 66, 74, 75–7,
    78, 87, 94, 95, 98, 99–100, 101,
    102, 103, 105, 119, 120, 125, 129,
    130, 134, 145, 146, 147, 148,
    156–157, 158, 159, 162, 166, 178,
    179, 184, 186, 188, 209n.64,
    219nn.142 and 150, 220n.165,
    222n.225, 237n.174, 238n.19; and
    adultery 98, 100, 101–102, 179,
    180, 221n.194, 223n.239; children
    in 125, 136, 143, 148, 149, 151,
    153, 155, 232n.12; and education
    140, 141, 142, 147; and incest 116,
    198n.86; and remarriage 120; on
    slaves and slave-traders 136, 138,
    139, 140, 154, 169, 171, 180,
    210n.88; theories on good marriage
    76–77, 96, 213n.11; and violence
    against non-believers 74; and
    violence in the *familia* 103–104,
    105, 172, 233n.55
Augustus 21, 22, 60, 63, 72, 98–99,
    115, 127, 197n.49, 200n.145,
    201n.162; use of the *consilium*

27–28, 199 n. 114; *lex Julia de
    adulteriis* 21, 36, 60, 98, 224n.12
Aulus Egrilius 25
Aurelia (Julius Caesar's mother) 34
Aurelia L.l. Philematio (freedwoman)
    17
Aurelius (archbishop of Carthage) 135,
    217n.111
Aurelius L.l. Hermia, L. (freedman) 17
Ausonius 13, 81, 97, 120, 126, 130,
    142, 148, 162–164, 166, 177–178
Ausonius Iunior (grandson) 142
Avienus 99
Avitus 178
Avitus of Vienne 141
avunculus 217n.102

Bacaudae 181, 243n.109
Baucis 26
Basil of Caesarea 90
Basilius 114–115, 190
Belisaurius 124, 184, 244n.134
Benedict, St. 236n.145
Boethius 156, 167
Bonifatius 190
bonorum possessio see inheritance
Brutus, M. Junius (cos. 509 BCE) 31
Brutus, M. Junius (Caesar's assassin) 20
Byzacium, council of 212n.114

Caesaria the Younger 167
Caesarius of Arles 101, 102, 167
Calendar of 354 105
Caligula 115
Callixtus 48, 52, 205n.278
Calpurnia 18, 19–20
Camilla 165, 239n.37
Caracalla 55, 56, 205n.276
Carthage, fourth synod of 117, 119,
    161–162; sixth synod of 135, 172;
    eleventh synod of 187, sixteenth
    synod of 231n.199; unknown synod
    of 172
Carpophorus 52
Cassiodorus 101, 140, 154, 167
Casssius 186
castitatis 112, 123, 204n.268, 225n.43
castration 179

Catervius, Fl. Iulius 77, 214n.28
Cato *see* Porcius Cato
Ceionius Iulianus 228n.124
celibacy 12, 13, 45, 46, 47, 54, 107,
   108, 117, 120, 123, 132; Paul's
   admonitions against 40; *see also*
   marriage
Celsus 94, 220n.170
Chalcedon, council of 131
children *passim*, ch. 6 *passim*;
   aduescens/adulescentia 25, 124, 130,
   148, 161; adult chidren 50–51,
   155–158, 231n.2; baptism of
   135–136; breastfeeding and weaning
   51, 150, 198n.91; commemoration
   of 25, 47, 198n.73; disciplining and
   violence 33–34, 143, 147, 182, 184,
   202n.182, 233n.55, 235n.107;
   education of 135, 140–142, 144,
   148–149, 151, 152, 164–165,
   220n.175, 235n.127, 236n.154;
   exposure 24–25, 65, 66–68, 136,
   198n.86, 209n.72, 210n.90,
   211nn.91 and 95; *iuvens* 79, 97, 133,
   143; mortality 24, 25, 134,
   139–140, 198–199n.92, 238n.13;
   natural outcome of marriage 24, 39,
   42, 96, 133; orphans 52, 67, 119,
   137; Prodigal son 235n.103; *proles*
   96, 125; sale of 26, 65, 67–68,
   136–138, 149, 199n.98,
   209–210n.74, 210n.88, 232n.22;
   similarities to slaves 29–30, 33–34,
   136–137, 139, 182; *spurii* 28, 30,
   36, 128–129, 148, 169, 230n.177;
   violence by 235n.129
Christians, Christianity *passim*
Chromatius 118
Cicero, M. Tullius 11, 22, 31, 33, 44,
   140
Cicero, Q. Tullius Iunior (nephew) 31
circumcelliones 175, 181, 219n.142,
   241n.53
Claudian 77–81, 178
Claudius 24, 86, 89
Clemens Contemtus 164
Clementina 181
clinical baptisms 134–135

Codex Iustinianus 83
Codex Theodosianus, publication of 83,
   192n.3
coemptio 39
collatio lustralis 67
coloni 138, 170–171, 175, 180, 181,
   212n.116, 240n.10
Commodianus 47
Commodus 28
concordia 10, 18, 20, 93, 103, 104;
   definition of, 17; in Christianity 42
concubine/concubinage 23, 36, 61,
   101, 109, 113, 123, 128–130, 183,
   184, 227n.96, 229n.142, 230n.184;
   concubini/concubitores 124, 183;
   synonymous with prostitution 128
consilium 27; *see also* Augustus
consocer 122, 163, 164
Constans 218n.135
Constantia 229n.138
Constantine I 3, 11, ch. 3 *passim*, 78,
   83, 84, 85, 98–99, 101, 104, 110,
   157, 173, 177, 183, 190, 193n.19,
   203n.222, 206nn.1 and 2, 207n.18,
   208nn.38, 39, 47 and 50, 209n.58,
   210nn.79, 82, 86, and 88, 211nn.94
   and 102, 216n.81, 222n.210,
   224n.11, 229n.143, 231nn.2 and 29,
   240n.23
Constantine II 101
Constantius I 190
Constantius II 64, 88, 89, 90, 102,
   109, 122, 123, 131, 161, 190,
   195n.51, 218nn.128 and 135,
   129nn.141 and 145
Constantius III 109, 110–111, 115,
   127, 191, 224n.11
constitutio Antonina 55, 193n.19,
   198n.80
contubernium/contubernalis 17, 23, 24,
   59–60, 85, 207n.27, 229n.142,
   242n.63; for soldiers 198n.79,
   207n.27
conubium 86
copulatio 75
Cornelia 227n.86
Cornelii 168
Cornelius Sulla, L. 29, 31–32, 115

Corpus Iuris Civilis, publication of 83, 192n.3, 215n.75
Crispus 121
Cynegia 164
Cynegius 89
Cyprian 152
Cyril 212n.2

Damasus 230n.167
daughters *see* children
Decii 154, 168
Demetrias 153–154
Deuterius 165
dies lustricus 233n.49
Digesta passim; composition of 83
Diocletian 4, 57, 67, 73, 115, 182, 191, 198n.88, 212n.117
discipline 33–5, 40
divorce 20–22, 28, 36, 40, 53, 62, 83, 84, 101, 107–116, 120, 124–125, 127, 129, 190–191; 197n.42, 203n.222, 208n.53, 213n.13, 223n.247, 224n.4, 225–226n.50, 228n.115, 230n.179; *apoluein* 202n.215; commonality of 23–24, 113–116; Jewish 40, 41, 226n.62; contracts 213–214n.26; *CTh* iii:16:1 62–65, 109, 110; *divortium* 113; Jewish laws concerning 39, 41; *repudium* 20, 64, 103, 115, 197n.41, 205n.288, 224n.15, 225n.33
domus passim; definitions of 8, 168; *domus Caesaris* and *Augusti* 59, 70, 115, 125; *domus ecclesiae* 141; symbolic purity of 17, 172–173
Donatists 181, 187, 219n.142, 235n.129
dowries 16, 17, 21, 62, 109–110, 146, 216n.91; *pactio dotalia* 16, 21, 61;
Drusus Julius Caesar 22
Duchess of Marlborough 130

Ecdicia 93, 220n.165
Ecloga 189, 226n.65
Edict of Milan 193n.19
Elagabulus 52
Eleutheria 191
Elijah 118

Elvira, council of 87, 88, 89, 108, 129, 130, 131, 187, 208n.47
Ennodius, Magnus Felix 141, 162, 164–167, 239n.30
Epaon, council of 89
Epitynchanus 25
Essenes 40, 87, 207n.109
Eucherius 80
Eudaemon 138, 233n.38
Eudocia 191
Eugenius 183, 244n.128
Eumenius 221nn.207 and 208
Eumpina 97
eunuchs 118, 178, 179, 184, 242nn.68 and 81, 244n.132
eusebeia 144
Eusebius of Caesarea 48, 49, 66, 119, 205n.282
Eusebius (correspondent of Jerome) 118
Eustathius of Aegae 233n.38
Eustochius 210n.74
Eutropia 191
Eutropius 178
exposure *see* children
extended family 30–31, 122, ch. 7 *passim*, 220n.174, 238n.10; *stirpes* 126
Exuperantius 181

Fabiola 190; *see also* Jerome
familia passim; definitions of 8, 194n.31, 211n.108; virginity as a denial of 130
famuli 180, 181
fathers *see* paterfamilias
Fausta 121, 157
Fausti 168
Faustina 123
Faustus 239n.30
Felicitas 50–52, 206n.297
Felix 82–83, 122–123
Festus 168
fideicommissum 22
filiafamilia/filiusfamilia see children
filiaster 200n.126
Firmicus Maternus 209n.64
Firmus 232n.15
Flavia Domitilla 24

frater 50, 88–89, 217n.110
freedmen 32–33, 52, 59, 70, 124, 171, 172, 175, 176, 180, 182–184, 195n.7, 201nn.150 and 161, 207n.27, 208n.30, 243nn.102 and 118, 244n.128; imperial freedmen 59, 85 (*murileguli*), 184, 216n.86
Fronto, M. 11, 19
Furia 118, 120, 142, 213n.20
Furii 168, 234n.74
Furius Camillus 227n.86

Galerius Maximianus 115, 191
Galla (*nepticula* of Symmachus) 82, 126
Galla Placidia 110, 115, 122, 125, 191, 229n.149
Gallus Caesar 214n.33
Gaudentius 215n.61
Gelasius 173, 241n.35
gens 31
Gerulus 71
Geta 55
Gibbon, Edward 1
gifts *see* marriage
Gildo 170
Gnaea Servilia 29
Gracchi 168, 227n.86
Gratian 109, 121, 207n.16, 228n.123
Gregory (pope) 6, 137–138, 140, 175
Gregory of Tours 166–167

Hadrian 26, 206n.5
hagiography 92, 220n.153, 232n.10
Helena 157, 190
Helisaea 165
heres see inheritance
Hermas 43–44, 203n.243, 204n.248
Hilary 152
Hippo Regius, council at 217n.111
Homer 188
homicide (including murder) 63, 64, 173, 210n.79, 217n.99, 223n.247, 225n.40, 241n.38; *parricidium* 67, 161, 166
homonoia 18
homosexuality 29, 96, 178, 217n.118
honestiores 55, 56, 206n.5, 209n.65, 235n.112

Honoria 183
Honorius 78–82, 85, 91, 108, 109, 110, 111, 112, 115, 122, 125, 127, 136, 151, 161, 170, 176, 183, 187, 191, 224n.11; marriage of 78–82, 214nn.33 and 35
Horace 97, 212n.113
humiliores 55, 99, 176
Huneric 191
Huns 224n.13
Hymetius, Julius Festus 99
Hypatia 88, 212n.2, 218n.123
Hypatius 104

Ignatius 52
infamia 64, 127, 128
inheritance *passim*; *bonorum possessio* 24, 161, 200n.138; *heres* 17, 23, 32, 33, 36, 121, 146, 161, 192n.5; protection of minors' 121–122; shares of deceased children 148; tutors, tutorships/curators, curatorships 17, 68–69, 118, 127, 133, 200n.138, 211n.101, 214–215n.51,
Iniuriosus 93–94
Innocent 128
Innocentia 237n.174
Inportunus, Fl. 155
Institutiones 83
Irenaus of Lyon 38
Isaac 235n.104
Isidore of Seville 194n.29
Iulianus 229n.145
ius gentium 71, 169, 207n.27
ius naturale 169
Iustina 121, 125, 229n.150
iustum matrimonium see marriage
ius vitae necisque 24, 67, 232n.28
iuvens see children

Jacob 235n.104
Jerome 1, 13, 76, 81, 86, 87, 96, 100, 102, 120, 121, 124, 125, 142, 146–147, 149, 154, 155, 177, 178, 183, 188, 189, 215n.60, 219n.150, 243n.104; and Fabiola 100, 101, 114, 116, 117, 120, 129, 179–180, 226n.51, 229n.128 (*see also* Fabiola);

and Laeta 142, 151–152, 234n.75, 241n.36 (see also Laeta); marriage as a tool of conversion 86–87, 95; on motherhood 150; and stepfathers 121
Jesus 40, 51, 147, 150, 202n.215, 203n.235, 224n.1, 227n.85
John Cassian 141
John Chrysostom 94, 96
Joseph 147
Jovinian 75, 76, 108, 188, 212n.5, 213n.8, 224n.1
Julia (daughter of Augustus) 27–8
Julia (criminal defendant) 176, 244n.129
Julian 61, 85, 109, 110, 111, 115, 206n.2, 214n.33, 218n.135, 219n.149, 225n.45
Julianus Censor 164
Julius Caesar, G. 34
Julius Lysippus, P. 25
Julius Toxotius 151
Junian rights 29, 182
Junius Bassus 234n.83
Justin II 111
Justin Martyr 49–50, 66, 210n.79
Justinian 5, 27, 83, 104, 111, 117, 143, 161, 192n.3, 241n.51

Lactantius 179, 210n.79
Laeta 81, 142, 234n.72; see also Jerome
lares and penates 153
latifundia 170
Laudatio Turiae see Turia
Leo 123, 135–136
lex Aelia Sentia 201n.162
lex Julia de adulteriis see Augustus
lex Julia de vi publica 64
lex Pompeia 161
Libanius (orator) 84, 90, 139, 155, 216n.78
Libanius (mystic) 110
Liberius 165
libertus/a see freedmen
Licerius Firminus Lupicinus, Fl. 164
Licinius 210n.82
Livia (Augustus' wife) 214n.37

Livia Drusa (mother of Cato the Younger) 28–9
Livilla (wife of Drusus) 22
Livius Drusus, M. 28
Livy 35
Lombards 5
Lucia of Syracuse 49
Lucretia 31
Lucullanum 175, 243n.107
Lucullus, L. Licinius 197n.45
Lupicinus 239n.31
Luxorius 77, 97, 116, 122, 123

Macarius, St. 49
Machiavelli 178
Macrina 157
Macrobius 188
maiestas 99, 109, 176, 209n.65, 244n.126
Majorian 100, 102, 112, 117, 127, 131, 176, 222n.223
Manichaeism 213n.8
manumission 32–33, 52, 172, 174, 184, 199n.114, 243n.115, 244nn.129 and 132; Christian role in 53, 137–138, 172, 174; recension of 33, 183; testamentary 174, 182
manus see marriage
Marcella 120, 123, 227n.88, 229n.136
Marcellinus 212n.4
Marcellus 191
Marcus Antonius 29
Marcus Aurelius 23, 123, 195n.50, 206n.5
Maria (Honorius' first wife) 78–82, 91, 151, 214nn.33, 34 and 41
Maria (kidnapped girl) 138, 152
Marina Severa 125, 191, 229n.229
Marius, G. 168
marriage passim; Adam and Eve 45, 76; celibacy in 42, 92–94, 112, 226n.53; and the Fall 76–77, 95, 96, 103; gifts 21, 58, 61–62; iustum matrimonium 16, 24, 48, 58, 78, 83, 85, 86, 106, 114, 161, 176, 184, 192n.5, 242n.63; Jewish 39, 40, 214–215n.51; manus marriages 21, 28, 30, 195n.12; 'mixed'

pagan/Christian marriages 45–46, 50, 86–87, 217n.117, 222n.235; pre-nuptial preparations 77–83, 109, 195n.9, 205n.283, 205n.286, 215n.51, 217n.113; priest's blessing of 85–86, 213n.10, 216n.96; prohibitions 59, 86, 87–91, 161, 217n.118, 217–218 n.121, 218nn.129 and 137, 226n.65; remarriage 9, 22–24, 107, 108–109, 116, 119, 121, 122, 124–128, 129, 213n.13, 223n.248, 224nn.4 and 20, 228n.106, 230n.173; violence in 21, 50, 103–105, 182, 197n.45

Martianus Capella 78, 188

Martin, St. 169

Mary 81, 150, 224n.1

massa 170, 243n.105

materfamilias (including wives and mothers) 24, 34, 56, 80, 82, 84, 118, 129, 149, 150–154, 156–157, 159, 186, 198n.87, 203n.235, 204n.248 215n.60, 236n.153; Christian archetypes of 150; *muliebris* 98; rights and duties similar to a *paterfamilias* 84, 118, 119, 146, 154, 199n.109

matertera 163, 217n.102

Maxentius 210n.82

Melania the Elder 92, 153, 154, 157, 220n.156

Melania the Younger 91–96, 123, 130, 133, 145, 146, 155, 156, 170, 220nn.157, 160, 165 and 168, 225n.44, 235n.95, 243n.113

Melissus, G. 198n.87

Memmius Orfitus 230n.164

Menander 210n.83

meretrix see prostitute

Milan, synod at 224n.1

Minervina 61, 190

Minucius Acilianus 18

Minucius Felix 53

Modestinus 18

Monnica 79–80, 87, 98, 99–100, 104, 135, 151, 153–154, 155, 156–157, 221n.177, 230n.180, 236n.132; *see also* Augustine

Montanism 37, 44

mos maiorum 142

mothers *see materfamilias*

murder *see* homicide

Musconius Scurranus 201n.150

Musonius Rufus 18, 42, 179, 209n.72

Navigius 215n.55

Neoplatonism 212n.2

Nicaea, council of 208n.47

Nichomachus Flavianus, Virius 82, 215nn.68 and 69

Nichomachus Flavianus Iunior 82, 191

Novatus, Novationism 205n.276, 227n.94

noverca see stepmothers

nurus 80

nutrix see wetnurse

oboedientia 42

obsequium 26, 31, 42, 54, 144, 147, 149, 166, 167, 186; definition of 26

oikia 43

Olybrius 157

Olympiodorus 92

Onesimus 43, 52

Oppicianus 29

Orange, council of 172, 173, 174

Origen 38

Original Sin 76, 89, 143, 144–145, 150, 169, 171

Orleans, council of 89, 173, 174

Oscia Modesta 30

Ossius 208n.47, 228n.101

Ostrogoths 5, 165, 194n.23

Ovid 26, 72, 163

Pachomius 181

pactio dotalia see dowries

pactio nuptialis 16, 61, 80

paideia 140

paelex 23, 96, 121, 129

Palladius (monastic historian) 219n.150, 220n.168

Palladius (court official) 110

Palladius, Rutillius (poet) 170

Pammachius 235n.128

Pantomalus 177

parentalia 163
Parthenius 164–165, 239n.31
paterfamilias (including husbands and
    fathers) 7, 15, 16, 24, 26–27, 32,
    33, 35, 36, 54, 67, 80, 84, 119,
    126, 140, 143–149, 156, 157, 159,
    172, 175, 178, 186, 203n.235,
    204n.247; Christian archetypes of
    146–147; good and bad 27–8,
    235n.128
Paternus 218n.129
Patricius (Augustine's father) 100, 120,
    145, 157, 178, 179, 222n.225,
    234n.92, 237n.181; *see also Augustine*
Patricius (Augustine's nephew) 166
patruus 217n.102
Paul (hermit) 221n.206
Paul of Tarsus 37–8, 39–43, 45–46,
    47, 50, 53, 54, 103, 108, 185,
    202n.215
Paula (lampooned Afcrican widow) 116
Paula (Jerome's correspondent) 120
Paula (Laeta's daughter) 151–152,
    234n.72, 241n.36
Paulina (divorcee?) 190
Paulina (wife of Praetextatus)
    213–214n.26
Paulinus of Nola 94, 219n.150,
    220n.170
Paulinus of Pella 13, 97, 98, 101, 129,
    134, 141, 142, 145, 148–149, 151,
    152, 156, 158, 162, 167, 179, 180,
    181, 234n.91, 243n.112
Paulus 18
peculium 149, 173, 241n.35
Pedanius Secundus, L. 194n.45
pederasty 29–30, 180
Pelagius, Pelagianism 75–76, 154, 188,
    232n.12
Pergamus 242n.67
Perpetua, Vibia 49, 50–52, 54,
    206n.297
Petronius (satirist) 21
Petronius Probus, S. 126, 156, 180,
    183, 229–230n.160, 243–244n.119
Philematus 216n.86
Philemon (in Ovid, *Met.*) 26
Philemon (correspondent of Paul) 52

pietas 26, 29, 32, 123, 143, 144, 147,
    149, 158, 166, 167, 186; definition
    of 26
Pinian 91–96, 123, 130, 133, 156,
    170, 220nn.158 and 165, 225n.43
Pius 203n.243
Plautius Silvanus 21
Plautus 21
Pliny (the Younger) 11, 18, 31
Plutarch 35, 150, 159
Pollentius 212n.5
Polycarp 52
Pompeius Magnus, G. (Pompey) 22
Pomponia Urbica 163
Porcia 20
Porcius Cato, M. (the Elder) 21, 159,
    173, 201n.156, 238n.206
Porcius Cato, M. (the Younger) 29,
    197n.45
Porcius Cato Solanianus, M. 28–29
porneia 40, 46, 203n.220
postliminium 109
potestas/patria potestas 24, 25, 28, 47,
    57, 58, 67, 84, 142, 156, 179,
    198n.87, 200n.120; definition of 16;
    meaning in late antiquity 144, 156,
    244n.4
Praetextatus, Vettius Agorius 77,
    213–214n.26
Priscillianism 188
Proba 167
Proconius 97, 221n.199
Procopius (historian) 124
Procopius, St. 49
proles see children
pronuba 79
Propertius 178
prostitute, prostitution 49, 66, 97,
    113, 117, 125, 128, 130, 136, 177,
    198n.26, 201n.164, 209n.61,
    222n.222, 232nn.22, 25 and 26;
    meretrix 130, 136
Prudentius 101, 139–140, 180
Pseudo-Plutarch 34
Publicola 92, 153, 157
Publius Syrus 34
pudor/pudicitia 77, 81, 105; Pudicitia
    Patricia and Plebeia 226n.68

Quieta 104
Quintilian 33, 34, 147
Qumran 39, 40, 87, 217n.109

Radagasius 170
raptus 126, 131, 173, 231n.200
refugium 173–174, 175
remarriage *see* marriage
repudium see divorce
Rogatianus 112, 222n.223
Rome *passim*; church of 119; synods
  held at 89, 129, 224n.1
Romulus (criminal defendant) 158
Romulus Augustulus 243n.107
Rufinus 103
Rusticus 124, 154, 191, 226n.53
Rutilius Namantianus 181

Salvian 102, 104
Sassia 34
Saturninus Secundus Sallustius 216n.85
Satyrus 132
Scribonia 21
Sempronius Sophus, G. 21
senatrix 113
senatusconsultum Claudianum 59
senatusconsultum Orfitianum 199n.109,
  206n.8
senatusconsultum Tertullianum 56,
  199n.109, 230n.172
Seneca 32, 33–34, 35, 42, 172
Seppius Proculus 29
Septimia Severina 77
Septimius Severus 55
Serena 79–81, 93, 214n.41
Servilia and Servililia 28, 197n.45
Servilius Caepio, Cn. 28
Servilius Caepio Iunior, Cn. (son) 28
servus see slaves
Severinus, St. 175, 180, 181
Severus (emperor) 180
Severus (Pinian's brother) 93, 95
Sextus 103
Shakespeare 186
Sidonius Apollinaris 121, 123, 141,
  146, 149, 155, 178
Simplicianus 171
slaves, slavery *passim*, ch. 8 *passim*;

ancilla 150–151, 173, 177, 178,
  180, 236n.155; and the clergy
  172–173, 175, 176; commonality of
  31–32, 169; enslavement 136–138,
  177, 209n.61, 209–210n.74,
  233n.48; and the Fall 169, 171; and
  Jews 177, 183, 233n.36, 244n.121;
  legal rights and protections 56, 70,
  174–175, 176, 241n.36, 244n.121;
  servitus 144; as sexual objects 23, 96,
  97, 100, 113, 124, 169, 177–179,
  211n.91; slave families 32, 51, 71–2,
  152, 176, 198n.78, 212 nn.119, 121
  and 122, 237n.159, 241n.36; slave
  trade 136–140, 172, 209n.74,
  242n.81, 243n.113; violence against
  32, 33, 35, 70, 139, 157, 169, 172,
  173, 174, 175, 177–179, 184,
  201n.154, 201n.156, 202n.194,
  212n.113, 233n.55, 237n.185;
  violence by 180–182, 194n.45,
  220n.166, 243n.112
Solomon 151
sons *see* children
soror 88–89
Sozomon 240n.23
spurii see children
stepmothers 23, 121, 126, 218n.131;
  -fathers 28, 121, 126
Stilicho, Fl. 78–80, 170, 175, 214n.41
stirpes see extended family
Stoics, Stoicism 35, 42, 171, 172, 173,
  213n.12
stuprum see adultery
suicide 172
Sulla *see* Cornelius Sulla
Sulpicius Gallus, G. 21
Sulpicius Severus 169
Symeon Logothetes 219n.151
Symmachus (pope) 165
Symmachus, Q. Aurelius 82, 94, 126,
  149, 156, 173–174, 215n.63,
  220n.175, 240n.12
Symmachus, Q. Fabius (son) 94,
  220n.175, 235n.127
synagogue 52, 88, 149, 156

Tacitus,, P. Cornelius 17, 30–31, 35

Talmud 39
Tertullian 37, 38–9, 44–47, 50, 53, 54, 117, 177, 204n.268
Testamentum Porcelli 142
Tetrici 239n.26
Theodoret 138
Theodoric 148, 158, 164, 165, 228n.118
Theodorus 217–218n.121
Theodosius (Belisaurius' godson) 124, 184, 244n.134
Theodosius I 79, 80, 109, 176, 215n.69, 219n.149
Theodosius II 85, 104, 111, 121, 173, 177, 192n.3
Therasia 94
Thermantia 78, 80, 115, 191, 214n.35
thlibemenoi 119
Tiberius 21, 99, 195n.12
Teridius 167
Toledo, council of 129
Tribonian 83
Tricho 34
Trimalchio 21, 195n.7
Trojan War 228n.112
Turia 19, 158, 195n.44
Twelve Tables 83

Ulpian (jurist) 64
univira 10, 22, 35, 45, 47, 99–100, 105, 107, 117, 118–119, 186
usufruct 21–22, 69, 230n.173
usus see usufruct

Vaison, council of 136
Valens 127, 216n.78, 240n.9
Valentinian I 109, 115, 125, 126–127, 179, 191, 229n.150
Valentinian II 84, 88, 121, 127, 136–137, 155, 183, 226n.71
Valentinian III 65–66, 84, 85, 86, 110, 111, 136, 137, 155, 161, 176, 182, 183, 233n.51, 234n.85
Valeria 115
Valerius Messalinus 17
Valerius Maximus 35
Vandals 135

Varro, M. 17
Venidius Ennychus, L. 199–200n.119
Vennes, council of 108
Venus 79, 81
Vergil 180, 188
Veria Liceria 163
vernus/a 29, 30
Vespasian 24
Vesta 153
Vettius Agorius Praetextatus *see* Praetextatus, Vettius Agorius
Victor 52
Victorinus (rhetor) 232n.15
Victorinus (Gallic emperor) 239n.26
vidua/viduitas see widows
virgins, virginity 12, 13, 47, 74–75, 82, 103, 105, 108, 116–117, 124, 126–127, 129, 130–132, 148, 150, 152, 153–154, 204n.268, 206n.297, 211n.101, 215n.66, 217n.99, 224n.1, 231n.206, 237n.172; *comitata virgineis* 150; in Jewish culture 130–131; regulation of 131; *virginitas* in classical culture 77, 107, 130–131
Visigoths 5, 167, 181, 194n.23

wetnurses 32, 36, 150–151, 152, 155, 201n.157, 202n.200, 236nn.138 and 145, 237n.182; *nutritor* 236n.145
widows, widowers, widowhood 22–23, 36, 40, 45, 46, 47, 63, 74, 77, 82–83, 84, 105, 107, 108, 116–128, 129, 137, 149, 154, 158, 183, 204n.259, 213n.20, 218n.131, 224n.1, 227nn.80, 85 and 89, 228nn.104 and 110, 233n.33, 239n.37; freedom of 117–118, 156–157; nature of 116–117; order of 119, 226n.63

Yahweh 147

Zarephath 118
Zeno 125
Zosimus 67